The Foreign Trade of China

Gene T. Hsiao

The Foreign Trade
of China: Policy, Law,
and Practice

University of California Press

Berkeley • Los Angeles • London

University of California Press
Berkeley and Los Angeles, California
University of California Press, Ltd.
London, England
Copyright © 1977 by
The Regents of the University of California
ISBN 0-520-03257-8
Library of Congress Catalog Card Number: 76-14304
Printed in the United States of America

To My Parents and Family

Contents

List of Tables and Charts

Tables

Charts

Foreword

SINCE the spring of 1971, when ping-pong diplomacy captured the world's imagination, trade has proved to be perhaps the most consistently satisfactory vehicle of Sino-American communication.

Politically, after the dramatic and hopeful events of 1971-73 which initiated the long overdue process of "normalization" of relations between the United States and the People's Republic of China, there has been a lull in the relationship. First Watergate, then the collapse of America's anti-Communist allies in Indochina, and then the 1976 presidential election prevented Washington from moving forward to complete normalization by establishing formal diplomatic relations at the ambassadorial level in accordance with the Shanghai Communiqué of February, 1972. Sino-American political contacts have cooled and may actually deteriorate unless carefully nurtured.

As the Marco Polo-itis that marked the American rediscovery of China in the early 1970s has receded, we have also become aware of the limits of cultural exchange with the PRC. Because of its failure to establish full diplomatic relations with Peking, the United States has undoubtedly been more handicapped than other major nations that have maintained cultural exchanges with China. Yet virtually every nation has become aware of the very restricted nature of many, although not all, forms of intellectual, educational, and artistic contact with the Chinese. In most fields, prospects are not bright for more than superficial exchanges between the open and pluralistic societies of the West and the closed and controlled society of the People's Republic.

Even tourism has proved a disappointment, compared with the Western experience in the Soviet Union and Eastern Europe. Strictly speaking, there is very little tourism in China, at least for Americans. The relatively small number of ordinary citizens who are permitted to travel there, whether in groups or as individuals, are generally admitted because their visit is thought to serve the political purpose of fostering Sino-American relations. Normalization will improve opportunities for a larger number of Americans to visit China, but the experience of countries that maintain ambassadors in Peking suggests that the improvement will be a modest one. Moreover, vast areas of China, including many of immense touristic interest, are likely to remain closed to foreigners.

Similarly, after the first flush of euphoria faded, the visits to China of American print and broadcast journalists became rather infrequent. The media in the United States have had to rely largely on foreigners for coverage from the People's Republic. No American wire service, newspaper, or television network has been permitted to open up a Peking office. If as a result of normalization this situation should improve, American journalists will then encounter the same obstacles to free reporting that have long frustrated foreign reporters stationed in China.

Trade, of course, has not been exempt from either bilateral diplomatic vicissitudes or the many distinctive aspects of contemporary Chinese life. Trade too has been affected by the failure of Sino-American political relations to develop as rapidly as was anticipated at Shanghai in 1972. After surprising many observers by sharply rising from virtually nothing at the beginning of this decade to almost $1 billion (U.S.) in 1974, bilateral trade just as quickly dropped to roughly half that sum the following year and promises to remain at that level in 1976. Although such factors as China's shortage of foreign exchange and reduced need for American agricultural products help to account for this marked decline, it also appears attributable to a new Chinese policy of providing Washington with a fresh incentive for normalization by generally treating the United States as a mere residual supplier—a source of commodities and products that cannot be readily obtained elsewhere—until full diplomatic relations are established.

American traders have also met their share of frustrations in coping with the challenge of doing business with China. The uniqueness of Chinese negotiating style, the frequent refusal to allow foreign sellers to deal with the end-users of the products in question, the unwillingness to adapt to capitalist marketing techniques or to enter into long-term contracts, the absence of a conventional legal system for the conduct of trade, the incantation by Chinese officials of the slogan "equality and mutual benefit" even while acting in ways that accord unequal treatment to the foreign enterprise, and the extreme reluctance to resort to arbitration and adjudication as means of settling disputes are only a few of the novel features that have occasionally perplexed and sometimes disillusioned American businessmen.

Nevertheless, despite the exotica, the Chinese experiences of American traders have usually proved quite satisfying. This is testified to not merely by the fact that thousands of our businessmen have visited China—after all, it would be difficult to resist one visit on sightseeing grounds alone—but also by the fact that many have returned for second, third, and subsequent trips. Some specialists have been there more than even Secretary of State Henry Kissinger and have forged regular lines of communication with Chinese counterparts. Certain major transactions, such as the sale of Boeing aircraft in 1972, have required months of negotiation in China, with the same parties meeting day after day to question, explain, assure, haggle, and finally conclude a contract, often taking further months of interaction, including Chinese visits to the United States, to implement the contract. Other important deals, such as the sale of ammonia plants by the M. W. Kellogg Company, have led American technicians and their spouses to live in remote parts of China for considerable periods of time, working with local counterparts to secure smooth installation and operation of the imported equipment.

Businessmen who go to China seem often to have better opportunities to become acquainted with life there than do other visitors. Diplomats are highly restricted in their movements and inhibited by their status in mingling with ordinary people. Guests of the state are clucked over and cared for to such an extent that they have little chance for casual, continuous meetings with the Chinese people. Nor do other visitors, who generally travel in groups and pursue relentless itineraries, joyously conquering one monument after another but seldom enjoying sustained exchanges with other people than their sanitized escorts. The businessman who lives in Canton, Shanghai, or Peking for several weeks or months at a time and returns there periodically, as some do, is in a different category, as is the technician who resides in a less accessible area. For most, of course, the linguistic barrier is as great as any of those specifically erected by the People's Republic to limit contacts with its people. Yet, even for those who do not speak Chinese, some things rub off, with or without an interpreter. For those who do speak the language, the possibilities of meaningful contact are plainly greater.

This was brought home to me personally in the spring of 1973 when I spent two weeks at the Kwangchow (Canton) Fair as a consultant to an American importer. I had visited China twice during the previous year, once as a guest of the state for a month and once for a fortnight as, in effect, a tourist. In terms of gaining access to the Chinese people the status of "businessman" proved preferable to the others. The leisurely pace of negotiations at the fair afforded many chances for talks with personnel of the China Council for the Promotion of International Trade, the Ministry of Foreign Trade, and the PRC's export-import corporations. There was also ample time to explore the city and to strike up what often turned out to be lengthy conversations in parks, restaurants, and shops. The identifying badge worn by participants in the fair seemed to assure the masses that it was safe to talk with the foreigner, at least during that relaxed era.

Thus, whatever intrinsic economic significance trade may eventually assume following the normalization of diplomatic relations, trade already constitutes a very important means of Sino-American communication, and, unless we misplay our cards, this non-economic significance is likely to grow.

It is vital, therefore, that we learn as much as possible about China's foreign commerce in order to make the most of this opportunity for restoring ties between two countries that have been too long estranged.

Gene T. Hsiao's comprehensive study *The Foreign Trade of China: Policy, Law, and Practice* takes us a giant step in the right direction. It is a fine introduction to the institutional and transactional aspects of trade under the People's Republic since its founding in 1949. Hsiao, whose earlier essays marked him as a leading scholar in the field, describes contemporary China's foreign trade objectives and their relation to broader policy goals, the PRC's network of relevant organizations, its treaties and other international agreements relating to trade, the various types of contracts concluded by Peking's state trading corporations, and the ways of settling disputes that arise under those contracts. All of this information and the accompanying analysis should prove to be helpful not only to businessmen and their lawyers but also to diplomats, journalists, scholars, and others who scrutinize the supposedly inscrutable. Of particular interest, so long as relations between Washington and Peking remain in their present abnormal state, is a chapter which details the Japanese experience trading with China in the decades prior to the normalization of ties between Tokyo and Peking in 1972.

In clear, detached, and readable style Professor Hsiao, who received his academic training in law and political science in both China and the United States, places his study of trade in the context of the PRC's domestic and international politics and thereby avoids what might in other hands have become a tedious recitation. Moreover, by heeding the admonition of Chairman Mao Tse-tung to link theory with practice, Hsiao has produced a scholarly book that is sure to be useful beyond the academic world.

Jerome Alan Cohen
Cambridge, Massachusetts
August 15, 1976

Preface

FOR their generous support of this study in various periods of time, I am indebted to the Social Science Research Council and the American Council of Learned Societies; the Rockefeller Foundation; the Center for Chinese Studies, the Project on Comparative Study of Communist Societies, the Institute of International Studies, and the School of Law at the University of California, Berkeley; the School of Social Sciences, the Graduate School, and the Asian Studies Program at Southern Illinois University, Edwardsville.

For their permission to let me use my previous articles for the present study, I wish to extend my thanks to *California Law Review* 53:1029 (1965); *China Quarterly,* nos. 57 and 60 (1974), pp. 101 and 720 respectively; *U.S.-China Business Review,* no. 3 (1974), p. 9; *Vanderbilt Law Review,* 20:303 (1967), 21:626 (1968), 22:503 (1969); Jerome Alan Cohen, ed., *The Dynamics of China's Foreign Relations* (Cambridge, Mass.: Harvard University Press, 1970), p. 41; Jerome Alan Cohen, ed., *China's Practice of International Law* (Cambridge, Mass.: Harvard University Press, 1972), p. 129; Howard M. Holtzmann, ed., *Legal Aspects of Doing Business with China* (New York: Practising Law Institute, 1976), p. 135. Sincere thanks are also due to RCA Global Communications, Inc. for its permission to let me reproduce as an appendix in this volume its contract (January 22, 1972) and agreement (May 23, 1972) with the China National Machinery Import and Export Corporation for the sale of an earth station for satellite communications from Shanghai and the installation in Peking of an "Intelsat" earth station respectively.

For their personal support of my undertaking, I am grateful to Earl S. Beard, Richard M. Buxbaum, Chih-ping Chen, George Fong, George Ginsburgs, Choh-Ming Li, Nicholas H. Ludlow, George Mace, Josephine Pearson, the late John S. Rendleman, Ralph W. Ruffner, Robert A. Scalapino, Eugene A. Theroux, Anthony J. Van Patten, and other colleagues and friends. In particular, I am grateful to Jerome Alan Cohen for his constant support of my project and his contribution of a Foreword to this volume; to Gregory Grossman, John N. Hazard, Chalmers A. Johnson, Allan J. McCurry, and H. Franz Schurmann for their kind encouragement and moral help in difficult times of my research and writing; to John S. Service for his patient reading and editing of the manuscript; and to Philip E. Lilienthal and his colleagues for their friendly assistance and cooperation in the publication of this volume. It goes without saying that I alone am responsible for all errors and opinions in my work.

The primary materials used in this study fall into four groups. The first group consists of trade treaties and agreements, laws and decrees published by the Chinese government in Peking; and textbooks, yearbooks, collections of essays and comments, newspaper reports and magazine articles published by various concerns in China. This is supplemented by newspaper reports, periodicals, specialized monographs and yearbooks published by Peking-controlled and independent firms in Hong Kong. These sources are valuable because China ceased publishing treaties, agreements, laws, decrees, regulations, yearbooks and the like in 1966 when the Cultural Revolution began. The most valuable legal and economic studies, such as *Cheng-fa yen-chiu* and *Ching-chi yen-chiu,* as well as textbooks and specialized magazines have also been discontinued since that time. For example, *China's Foreign Trade,* published in both Chinese and English, resumed publication only in 1974, after an interruption of nearly ten years. *China Trade Report,* published in Hong Kong, not only helped fill the gap but also provided useful information from other countries.

The second group comprises documentary information and materials from areas and countries other than Hong Kong. For example, the trade agreements with Australia, Japan, and the Philippines were made available to me by the governments of these countries concerned. Eventually, of course, China or her foreign treaty partners will file these documents with the United Nations. But it may take several years before they are made accessible to the public. In addition, business executives in various parts of the world furnished me with about one hundred sample and executed contracts with China. Without these documents, it would not have been possible for me to undertake the present study.

The third group is information in the form of specialized books, magazines, periodical and newspaper reports originating mostly from the United States and some from other countries. For example, the publications of the East Asian Legal Studies Program of the Harvard Law School are very helpful reference works, and those of the United States government and the National Council for United States-China Trade are informative both legally and economically.

The final group is interviews with officials, scholars, business executives, and journalists knowledgeable about China's foreign trade. Due to the nature of such information, documentation cannot be made on every occasion. A selected bibliography based on the source materials cited in this work appears at the end of this volume.

Romanization of individual Chinese names is based on the Wade-Giles system, but apostrophes and diaereses are omitted to conform to usage in

China, except for the names of those individual Chinese abroad who choose to use such marks or other romanization systems. The principal titles of all documents, books, periodicals, and newspapers published in Chinese are romanized in accordance with the Wade-Giles system. Their English translations (except those for the periodicals and newspapers) are available in the bibliography. The individual titles of Chinese laws, regulations, treaties, agreements, essays, articles, and the equivalent in both the footnotes and bibliography are not romanized, but translated into English by me in order to provide the non-Chinese-speaking reader with some idea about the nature of the source materials involved. The names of Chinese institutional authors, editors, and compilers are also translated into English in accordance with official Chinese standards (whenever available); however, those of Chinese publishers are romanized. All romanized Chinese first names follow their romanized surnames, unless the individual Chinese persons choose to arrange their names in accordance with the American style. In the case of Japanese individuals, however, their romanized surnames follow their romanized first names to conform to common usage in most English publications in Japan. All other non-English names are printed exactly in the same manner as they appear in the source materials cited.

As the development of Chinese trade institutions will follow the expansion of Chinese external political and economic relations, there is no doubt that more information will become available to scholars and practitioners in the field, who then will be able to offer more profound and better informed interpretations of Chinese foreign trade to the interested public. With this in mind, and in a traditional Chinese manner of speaking, I am merely "casting a brick to attract a gem!"

Gene T. Hsiao
Edwardsville, Illinois
June 3, 1976

Abbreviations

I have tried to use abbreviations only when necessary. Shortened titles and standard abbreviations are not included in this list.

CAAC—Civil Aviation Administration of China
CAL—China Airlines
CCP—Chinese Communist Party
CCPIT—China Council for the Promotion of International Trade
FKHP—Chung-hua jen-min kung-ho-kuo fa-kuei hui-pien
FLHP—Chung-yang jen-min cheng-fu fa-ling hui-pien
FTAC—Foreign Trade Arbitration Commission
FYP—Five-Year Plan
JAA—Japan Asia Airways
JAL—Japan Airlines
LDP—Liberal Democratic Party (Japan)
L-T Memorandum—Liao Cheng-chih and Tatsunosuke Takasaki Memorandum
MAC—Maritime Arbitration Commission
MFT—Ministry of Foreign Trade
NPC—National People's Congress
PRC—People's Republic of China
TWKH—Chung-hua jen-min kung-ho-kuo tui-wai kuang-hsi wen-chien chi
TYC—Chung-hua jen-min kung-ho-kuo t'iao-yüeh chi

1   Introduction

THE roots of China's foreign trade lie in the ancient tribute system. For Confucian China, the universe was essentially an extension of Chinese society, and the world a hierarchy in which the Celestial Empire was destined to play a patriarchal role on the strength of its cultural superiority and material wealth. From this, there developed the complex diplomatic institution known as the tribute system, which required all foreign states desiring formal relations with China to observe an elaborate procedure of rituals *(li)* in order to define their respective statuses as superordinate and subordinates.[1] Acceptance of this relationship constituted mutual diplomatic recognition which was to be followed by formal cultural, political, and economic exchanges.

Culturally, the tribute system functioned as a means to Sinify the "barbarians," as the Chinese viewed all other peoples in the dynastic period; politically, it served to ensure China's security by maintaining a degree of influence over the tribute states; economically, it inaugurated the interflow of goods and services between China and other nations—known as "tribute trade"—and thus provided a source of revenue for the imperial treasury through the collection of duties and taxes. The tribute system was the only legal means of access to the Chinese market, for it was an established practice of the Celestial Rulers that all major tribute trade transactions be conducted at designated localities and ports in China, rarely abroad. The earliest institutions to administer trade regulations were established by the T'ang dynasty (618-907), and known as *hu-shih chien,* or Superintendency of the Trade Market, and *shih-po szu,* or Department for the Supervision of Merchant Vessels—the latter being a prototype maritime customs office that continued to exist until the early Ch'ing period (1644-1911) when it was replaced by the Kwangchow (Canton) trade system.[2] A more detailed customs regulation was promulgated by the Yüan dynasty (1280-1368),[3] but commercial treaties regulating mutual relationships on the basis of equal status and rights were unknown to the imperial court until 1727: such arrangements were simply

---

1. See Shang-wu yin-shu kuan, ed., *Chung-kuo-kuo-chi mao-i shih,* pp. 1-17. The forms of these rituals varied. For a collection of essays discussing the tribute system and its relevance to trade, see John K. Fairbank, ed., *The Chinese World Order.*

2. For reference to the T'ang regulations and institutions, see *T'ang liu tien;* also see Shang-wu yin-shu kuan, ed., *op. cit.,* p. 20.

3. *Ibid.,* pp. 25-29.

contrary to the nature of the tribute system. And even the 1727 commercial agreement with Russia—the first of the kind with a Western power—was made to conform to Chinese tradition: the Russians, for example, were allowed to send a trade delegation of no more than two hundred persons to Peking once every three years, and tribute presentation formed part of the intercourse.[4]

Although dynastic policies restricted the conduct of foreign trade within China to the tribute system, individual Chinese were generally not prohibited from going abroad for reasons of commerce. In 1374 the Ming Emperor Tai-tsu banned all foreign travel without permits and suspended the operation of the three most important Departments for the Supervision of Merchant Vessels, at Chuanchou, Ningpo, and Kwangchow, because foreign pirates and their Chinese collaborators threatened the security of the coastal provinces. But the lifting of the ban in 1403 and the subsequent naval expeditions to South and Southeast Asia by Imperial Eunuch Cheng Ho revived Chinese emigration and overseas commerce.

When the Ch'ing (Manchus) came to power, two factors arose affecting China's policy towards foreign trade. One was the attempt of the Ming loyalists, mostly based on Taiwan but allied with overseas Chinese elsewhere in Asia, to overthrow the Ch'ing and restore the previous Ming dynasty. This immediately resulted in the complete prohibition of all mainland Chinese communication with the outside world, including trade. Death penalties were imposed on those who left China without permits or remained abroad for a prolonged period of time without legitimate reason. After the capitulation of the Ming loyalists and other rebels, the Ch'ing court changed its emigration and foreign trade policies several times, but as late as 1805 a revised edition of the Ch'ing code still contained the following clause:

Whoever in a similar manner passes, without submitting himself to examination, any of the barriers or posts of government at the frontiers, shall be punished with 100 blows, and banished for three years. If such individual proceeds afterwards so far as to have communication with the foreign nations beyond the boundaries, he shall suffer death by being strangled, after the customary period of confinement.[5]

The second factor confronting the Manchus was European colonial expansion in Asia, which had worried those responsible for China's security even before the Ch'ing. The Emperor K'ang-hsi (1662-1722) summed it up: "There is cause for apprehension lest, in the centuries or millenniums to come, China may be endangered by collisions with the various nations of the

---

4. For the text of the agreement, see Wang Tieh-yai, ed., *Chung wai chiu yüeh-chang hui-pien*, Set I (1689-1901), vol. 1, pp. 7-14.
5. In *Ta Tsing Leu Lee*, trans. by George Thomas Staunton, p. 232.

West who come hither from beyond the seas.''[6] While the founding emperors of the Ch'ing had followed traditional practice toward foreign traders in China, the Emperor Yung-cheng (1723-1735) reduced the four principal trading ports to one at Kwangchow to avoid the dangerous "collisons" inherent in expanded cultural, economic, and religious contacts with Europeans. And although the Emperor Ch'ien-lung (1736-1795) was well aware of the actual value of foreign trade to the Chinese economy, he answered King George III's request for a commercial treaty in 1792 saying, "I set no value on objects strange and ingenious, and have no use for your country's manufactures.''[7] Behind his arrogance lay the fear of foreign economic and political penetration, soon to be all too evident in the increasing introduction of opium into China.

A major crop of British India, opium was brought into China by the East India Company to offset the flow of silver, largely British, which paid for the Chinese tea, silk, and porcelain Europe demanded. Until opium, China had sought little in the way of Western imports, but once begun, the opium trade grew exponentially, and soon reversed the silver flow. This threat, plus the obvious peril of the drug to the nation's health, as well as growing demands that the official corruption which allowed the trade to flourish be curtailed, led the Emperor Tao-kuang in 1839 to attempt the suppression of the opium trade. This resulted in two "opium wars" in 1839-1842 and 1856-1860 respectively. As a price for her defeat, China was forced to accept a "treaty system" as a substitute for the tribute system, on which traditional Chinese foreign trade had been based.[8]

The new system was built on three-hundred-odd principal treaties, supplemental agreements, rules, and contracts with eighteen powers, written over a period of almost sixty years (1842-1901). They may be divided into three groups: the first group of treaties were mainly signed with Britain, the United States, and France in the aftermath of the first opium war; the second group with the same three powers and Russia as a result of the second opium war; and the third group with Japan and ten other powers in consequence of the Sino-Japanese war (1894-1895) and the Boxer Uprising (1900).[9] Each

6. Quoted in Herbert H. Gowen and Josef Washington Hall, *An Outline History of China*, p. 209.

7. In Harley Farnsworth MacNair, *Modern Chinese History: Selected Readings*, p. 4.

8. For reference to the wars and their settlement, see Immanuel C. Y. Hsü, *The Rise of Modern China*, pp. 183-241, 253-269; Arthur Waley, *The Opium War Through Chinese Eyes*. For a discussion of the treaty system and its relevance to the tribute system, see John K. Fairbank, "The Early Treaty System in the Chinese World Order," in Fairbank, ed., *The Chinese World Order*, pp. 257-275.

9. The principal treaties are those with Britain, August 29, 1842, in Wang Tieh-yai, ed., *Chung wai chiu yüeh-chang hui-pien*, Set I, vol. 1, p. 30; with the United States of America, July

succeeding group complemented what the powers had not been able to accomplish in the preceding group.

The foreign powers' general purpose in establishing the treaty system consisted of two interrelated goals: to achieve maximum protection for their citizens and property interests in China; and to make optimum use, for their own benefit, of China's human and material resources. Towards these ends, they took two legal steps. Their first step was the immediate restriction of Chinese national sovereignty by numerous treaty provisions under which the opium trade was legalized and the treaty powers could control Chinese tariffs; exercise extraterritorial and consular jurisdictions; establish foreign spheres of influence, and concessions in the treaty ports; establish foreign courts and station foreign police and troops in certain localities; navigate in inland waterways and conduct coastal trade; and appoint foreign personnel to key Chinese customs and post office positions. A distinctive feature of this treaty system lay in its unilateral nature: although provisions were made in some treaties implicitly or explicitly according citizens of both contracting parties equal treatment, concessions granted to foreign powers by the Ch'ing court were never reciprocated by these powers in their relationships to China and in their treatment of Chinese citizens under their jurisdiction.[10] Further, every concession that the Ch'ing made to a foreign power was automatically extended to all other treaty powers (totalling nineteen after 1905) in accordance with the "most-favored-nation" clause.[11] The lack of reciprocity led Chinese of all political beliefs to denounce these arrangements as "unequal treaties."[12]

The foreign powers' second step involved the revision and creation of Chinese domestic legislation, including the establishment of a new legal system in conformity with Western interests, norms and values. They realized

---

3, 1844, *ibid.*, p. 51; with France, October 24, 1844, *ibid.*, p. 57; with Russia, May 28, 1858, and June 13, 1858, *ibid.*, pp. 85, 86; with the United States of America, June 18, 1858, *ibid.*, p. 89; with Britain, June 26, 1858, *ibid.*, p. 96; with France, June 27, 1858, *ibid.*, p. 104; with Japan, April 17, 1895, *ibid.*, vol. 2, p. 614; with Germany, Austria, Belgium, Japan, the United States of America, France, Britain, Italy, Russia, Spain, and Holland, September 7, 1901, *ibid.*, vol. 3, p. 1002. The English translations of these treaties can be found in the following two sources: William Frederick Mayers, ed., *Treaties Between the Empire of China and Foreign Powers;* John V. A. MacMurray, ed., *Treaties and Agreements With and Concerning China 1894-1919,* vol. 1 (1894-1911). For an American interpretation of these treaties, see John K. Fairbank, *Trade and Diplomacy on the China Coast;* for a recent Chinese interpretation, see Ku Yun, *Chung-kuo chin-tai shih shang ti pu-p'ing-teng t'iao-yüeh.*

10. Restrictions on Chinese emigration were removed in 1860 due to pressure of the British government. See Supplemental Treaty with Great Britain, October 24, 1860, art. 5, in Wang, ed., *op. cit.,* Set I, vol. 1, p. 145.

11. In addition to the eleven powers which were parties to the September 7, 1901, treaty settling the Boxer Uprising, the other eight powers were Norway, Switzerland, Sweden, Denmark, Portugal, Peru, Brazil, and Mexico.

12. For a history of these treaties, see Liu Yen, *Chung-kuo wai-ch'iao shih.*

that the implementation of the treaty provisions restricting Chinese national sovereignty was based on force, not on domestic legislation or the support of local and national Chinese courts. Conflict with Chinese authorities could easily arise from the enforcement of these provisions, and a major change in Chinese government or in the balance of forces among the foreign powers in China could conceivably jeopardize the treaty system. Thus, in accordance with the terms of three Chinese treaties with Britain (September 5, 1902), the United States (October 8, 1903), and Japan (October 8, 1903) which provided for the reform of the Chinese legal system as a condition for the relinquishment of extraterritorial rights,[13] the Washington Conference resolved on December 10, 1921, to set up a commission to investigate the matter.[14] The recommendations of the commission, signed by twelve treaty powers on September 16, 1926, called for, among other things, the establishment of an independent judiciary free from any unwarranted interference by other branches of the Chinese government; the adoption of a civil code, a commercial code (including negotiable instruments law, maritime law, and insurance law), a revised criminal code, a banking law, a bankruptcy law, a patent law, a land expropriation law, a notary law; and the rendering of judicial assistance.[15]

The task of creating such a new legal system was, of course, enormous. Charles Sumner Lobingier, who served as judge of the United States Court for China in 1914-1924 and member of the Law Faculty at the Comparative Law School of China in 1915-1923, observed:

It is no easy task to restate a legal system, already more than four thousand years old, so as to meet the needs of a nation of 400 million. In fact the danger lies rather in haste than in deliberation. Jurists from [Friedrich Karl von] Savigny down have pointed out the folly of imposing bodily upon any nation the laws of another. That folly becomes greatly aggravated when each represents a totally diverse type of civilization. Importation of foreign codes into China will not solve the problem.[16]

In spite of these difficulties, the Chinese Nationalist government promulgated five basic codes in a period of about five years: Civil Law (1929), Civil Procedure (1935), Criminal Law (1935), Criminal Procedure (1935), and Administrative Law (issued at various dates).[17] However, owing to their alien concepts and their highly technical vocabularies, borrowed mainly from German and Japanese, these codes were neither relevant to the realities of

13. In MacMurray, *op. cit.,* pp. 342, 351; 411, 414; 423, 431.
14. See Kuo Tzu-hsiung, and Hsueh Tien-tseng, ed., *Chung-kuo ts'an-chia chih kuo-chi kung-yüeh hui-pien,* pp. 317, 322-323.
15. *China Law Review,* 3.3:91-94 (1927).
16. Charles Sumner Lobingier, "An Introduction to Chinese Law," in *China Law Review,* 4.5:121,129 (1930).
17. See Chang Chih-pen, ed., *Tsui-hsin liu-fa ch'uan-shu;* for English translation, see *Laws of the Republic of China.*

Chinese life nor comprehensible to laymen. In consequence, they had little effect on Chinese society; for all practical purposes their only use was to persuade the foreign powers to abrogate their extraterritorial rights. This was finally realized in 1943, because of China's role as an Allied power during World War II.[18]

The founding of the People's Republic in 1949 opened a new era in Chinese history. Mindful of China's recent past, and conscious of its revolutionary task ahead, the People's Government abolished all Nationalist institutions and set out to build a new socio-political order based on the programs of the Chinese Communist Party (CCP) for the elimination of class distinctions, the transfer of private property to society, the establishment of a rationally planned economy, and the pursuit of an independent foreign policy.

After a period of twenty-five years of transformation, the 1975 Constitution formally proclaimed China "a socialist state of the dictatorship of the proletariat led by the working class and based on the alliance of workers and peasants" (article 1).[19] In conformity with this class structure of the Chinese state, the forms of ownership of means of production (productive property) were reduced from four to two: socialist ownership by the whole people (state ownership) and socialist public ownership by working people (article 5).[20] In the rural people's commune, the system of collective ownership, which is a component part of socialist public ownership, was further divided into three levels: the commune, the production brigade, and the production team (article 7). Operating on the basis of this property arrangement, the state share of industrial assets in the national economy now accounted for 97 percent and that of farmland and agricultural produce for 5

18. The United States was the first power to relinquish its extraterritorial rights in China; other powers followed suit. See Treaty Between the Republic of China and the United States of America for the Relinquishment of Extraterritorial Rights in China and the Regulation of Related Matters, January 11, 1943, in Ministry of Foreign Affairs, ed., *Treaties Between the Republic of China and Foreign States 1927-1957* p. 659. For a discussion, see Chien Tai, *Chung-kuo pu-p'ing-teng t'iao-yüeh chih yüan-ch'i chi ch'i fei-ch'u chih ching-kuo.*

19. For the text of the 1975 Constitution, see Appendix A.

20. Under the Common Program of the Chinese People's Political Consultative Conference, September 29, 1949, the Chinese state consisted of four social classes: the working class, the peasant class, the petty bourgeoisie, and the national bourgeoisie as well as several social strata, including "all patriotic democratic elements." The text of the Common Program is in *FLHP 1949-1950,* vol. 1 (1952), p. 16. The first Constitution of the People's Republic, September 20, 1954, which superceded the Common Program, retained almost the same class structure while emphasizing the leadership of the working class and its alliance with the peasant class (article 1). The English translation of the Constitution was published by the Foreign Languages Press in Peking in 1954. Corresponding to this class structure were four forms of ownership of means of production: state ownership, cooperative ownership or collective ownership by the working masses, ownership by individual working people, and capitalist ownership (article 5).

and 8 percent respectively. In addition, the state controlled about 93 percent of the total retail sales volume of domestic commerce.[21]

The role and operation of foreign trade, which is part and parcel of the national economy and Chinese diplomacy and is governed by a new system of organization and law within the context of this new socialist order, is the subject of the present study.

21. See Chang Chun-chiao, "On Exercising All-Round Dictatorship Over the Bourgeoisie," in *Hung-ch'i,* no. 4 (1975), p. 5.

2.   Foreign Trade Policy Objectives

THE development of modern economies is intimately related to foreign trade. Since the supply of and demand for natural resources, capital, management and labor are not equal among the peoples of the world, and consequently since the costs and prices of goods and services produced by them are not the same, a nation can obtain more and better goods and services, satisfy its needs and desires, and improve the living standards of its people only through trade with other nations.[1] According to Chinese economists, "foreign trade is an outcome of the development of the productive forces and division of labor in human society. Nations must exchange needed goods to make up for each other's deficiencies. Only in this way can they mutually satisfy the needs of production and the people's livelihood. Whether or not we want foreign trade is a question that cannot be determined by our subjective wishes."[2] Based on his many years of experience, Minister of Foreign Trade Li Chiang elaborated on China's view of trade:

Facts prove that foreign trade is necessary to the development of our national economy. At the same time, through foreign trade, China can increase mutual support and cooperation in the economic sphere with fraternal socialist countries and friendly countries of the Third World, thus benefiting each other's economic construction and reinforcing economic independence. Through foreign trade, we are able to increase economic and technical interchange with more and more countries and peoples on the basis of the Five Principles of Peaceful Co-existence so as to promote relationships between China and the other nations of the world and enhance the friendship between the Chinese people and the people of other countries.[3]

International trade, however, does not take place in a political vacuum. Historically, nations have used it as leverage to advance their diplomatic interests. Moreover, differences in national economic policies, trade and tariff

1. See Roland L. Kramer et al., *International Trade,* p. 2.
2. Lu Shih-kuang, *Shih-mo shih tui-wai mao-i* p. 28. In Marxist terminology, the "productive forces" consist of the instruments of production, the people who use them and their experience and skill. See R. N. Carew Hunt, *Marxism Past and Present* p. 50.
3. Li Chiang, "New Developments in China's Foreign Trade," *China's Foreign Trade,* no. 1 (1974), p. 4.

regulations, monetary systems, and domestic laws governing the freedom and rights of alien traders require mutual concessions of sovereign rights by the states involved. Hence, the nature of international trade is at once both economic and political. As a Chinese textbook relates, ''foreign trade is also a weapon of international political struggle. The ruling class of each nation always uses foreign trade to protect its own interests, with the result that the conduct of foreign trade expresses itself in various forms of political and economic struggles.''[4] Since the foundation of the People's Republic, Chinese officials have consistently maintained that while China is willing to trade with nations of different social systems, ''political sovereignty cannot be separated from economic independence.'' Recalling China's experience from 1842 to 1943, when foreign powers manipulated its external trade through their treaty privileges,[5] Vice-Minister of Foreign Trade Chou Hua-min noted in his policy speech to the Third United Nations Conference on Trade and Development in 1972 that, ''In the absence of political independence, economic independence is out of the question, and independence of any country is incomplete without economic independence.'' He then outlined China's general position on trade relations:

International trade should be based on equality and mutual benefit, and respect for each other's sovereignty and aspiration. It should conform to the requirements and possibilities of both sides and promote both sides' economic development. We firmly oppose the imperialists who, under the disguise of trade, control and plunder other countries, and seek by various selfish means to seize important resources, extort huge profits and obstruct the economic development of other countries. We resolutely support the reasonable demands of many developing countries to develop their national economy, gradually reshape their ''single-product economy,'' stabilize the prices of raw materials, remove the tariff and non-tariff barriers set up by the ''developed countries,'' participate in the reform of the international monetary system and develop national shipping, insurance and other enterprises so as to break the monopoly by a few countries. We support the proposal put forward by many Asian, African and Latin American countries for the active expansion of inter-trade. We consider that the expansion of inter-trade among the developing countries is not a mere exchange of goods, but is an important form of mutual support and mutual help in their struggle against imperialism and for complete independence. China wishes, within the scope of its requirements and capabilities, to continuously expand its trade with countries in Asia, Africa and Latin America for the exchange of needed goods and the promotion of each other's production and self-reliance. At the same time, China also wishes to further its trade with other countries of the world on the basis of the principles of equality and mutual benefit.[6]

4. Kuo Chung-yen, *Hsin Chung-kuo ti kung-yeh-p'in ch'u-k'ou mao-i*, p. 34.
5. For reference to China's trade before 1937, see Ho Ping-ying, *The Foreign Trade of China*, and Chi-ming Hou, *Foreign Investment and Economic Development in China 1840-1937*.
6. Chou Hua-min, ''China's Principled Stand on Relations of International Economy and Trade, April 20, 1972,'' *Peking Review*, no. 17 (1972), p. 11.

Thus, China's foreign trade policy consists of two basic objectives: development of the national economy and promotion of international relations. In some cases, economic considerations are predominant; in others politics take precedence. But in all cases, both elements are present: relative importance in their mutual relationship to China's overall foreign trade policy is determined by the state on the merits of each individual case.

Trade and Economic Development

Foreign trade has never played a major role in the development of the Chinese national economy: the annual volume of trade from 1950 to 1974 averaged no more than 4 percent of the gross national product. In specific areas of the economy and at various stages of its development, however, foreign trade has been a significant factor. During the period of economic rehabilitation (1950-1952), it helped restore domestic production, stabilize commodity prices, and enable China to acquire certain strategic goods that were essential to the national defense but were banned by the Western embargo.[7] As a result, the annual value of two-way trade surpassed the levels before the Sino-Japanese War (1937-1945). The direction of trade, however, departed radically from the prewar patterns because of China's new foreign relations. The Soviet Union, followed by Hong Kong and Malaya-Singapore, replaced the United States and the United Kingdom as China's top trading partners.

By the end of 1952, in spite of the damaging effects of the Korean War, China had basically rehabilitated its economy, paving the way for the First Five-Year Plan (1953-1957).[8] Under this plan, the government assigned foreign trade a critical role in industrialization through the importation of machinery, equipment, and materials. According to the late Minister of Foreign Trade, Yeh Chi-chuang, the guiding principle of foreign trade during that period, and since, has been the development of exports to exchange for imports, while trying to maintain a relatively even balance between the two.[9] Yeh summarized this policy in one sentence: "Export is for the sake of import, which, in turn, is for the socialist industrialization of our country."[10] Underlying this policy was the fact that although China received loans from

---

7. Chao Chi-chang, "The Great Change and Development of Our Country's Foreign Trade in the Past Seven Years," in MFT, ed., *Tui-wai mao-i lun-wen hsüan*, vol. 3 (1957), p. 10. See also Gunnar Adler-Karlsson, *Western Economic Warfare 1947-1967*.

8. For reference to the text of the Plan, see *FKHP 1955*, vol. 2 (1956), p. 131.

9. See Yeh Chi-chuang, "China's Foreign Trade in the Past Ten Years," *Jen-min shou-ts'e 1960*, p. 91.

10. Yeh Chi-chuang, "Speech to the Second Session of the First National People's Congress, July 1955," in MFT. ed., *Tui-wai mao-i lun-wen hsüan*, vol. 2 (1956), p. 130.

the Soviet Union and some Eastern European countries, they were insufficient to meet the needs of industrialization. Moreover, it was reasoned that heavy reliance upon foreign loans and investments would once again reduce China to a dependent state.[11] Thus, a nation-wide effort to expand the export trade followed,[12] with the result that for the first time in its recent history China in 1956 earned an export surplus ($150 million out of a total trade of $3,120 million). After that, China remained a creditor nation in its worldwide trade except in 1960, 1967, 1970, 1973, and 1974 when it incurred some trade deficits (see table 1). The total trade turnover for the entire First Five-Year Plan (FYP) amounted to $13,855 million (communist countries accounted for $9,560 million and non-communist countries for $4,295 million)—a successful fulfillment of the planned annual trade growth rate of more than 10 percent.

The first two years of the Second FYP (1958-1962), known as the Great Leap Forward, witnessed an unprecedented upsurge in China's trade with both communist and non-communist countries, amounting to $3,765 million in 1958 and $4,290 million in 1959—a peak that China did not reach again until 1970. The thrust behind this upsurge was an attempt of the Chinese government to realize its self-reliance policy through accelerated development of the economy. However, the annual turnover of trade with communist countries declined steadily, from a high of $2,980 million in 1959 to $2,620 million in 1960, $1,680 million in 1961, and $1,405 million in 1962. By contrast, the annual volume of trade with non-Communist countries remained only slightly below the 1958 peak of $1,385 million. In all, the total turnover of trade for the Great Leap Forward was $17,730 million, an increase of $3,875 million over the First FYP. The share of communist countries accounted for $11,065 million, an increase of $1,505 million over the previous period, and that of non-communist countries for $6,665 million, an increase of $2,370 million.

The slow increase in China's overall trade during the Second FYP period and the steady decrease in China's trade with communist countries in the last three years of that period reflected difficulties in the domestic economy caused by natural calamities and the withdrawal of Soviet assistance. Indeed, the combined effect of these internal and external crises on China's economy was so great that it called for a complete reorientation of the direction of trade to free China from Soviet economic influence and a readjustment of the composition of imports to meet China's urgent domestic needs.

---

11. Ma Nai-shu, ''Socialist Industrialization and the Task of Export,'' in MFT, ed., *Tui-wai mao-i lun-wen hsüan-chi* (1955), p. 139.
12. For reference to this nation-wide effort, see the six essays in *ibid.,* passim.

TABLE 1
CHINA: BALANCE OF TRADE, 1950-1974

Unit: one million U.S. dollars

Year	Total Trade				Communist Countries				Non-communist Countries			
	Total	Exports	Imports	Balance	Total	Exports	Imports	Balance	Total	Exports	Imports	Balance
1950	1,210	620	590	30	350	210	140	70	860	410	450	−40
1951	1,900	780	1,120	−340	980	465	515	−50	920	315	605	−290
1952	1,890	875	1,015	−140	1,315	605	710	−105	575	270	305	−35
1953	2,295	1,040	1,255	−215	1,555	670	885	−215	740	370	370	—
1954	2,350	1,060	1,290	−230	1,735	765	970	−205	615	295	320	−25
1955	3,035	1,375	1,660	−285	2,250	950	1,300	−350	785	425	360	65
1956	3,120	1,635	1,485	150	2,055	1,045	1,010	35	1,065	590	475	115
1957	3,055	1,615	1,440	175	1,965	1,085	880	205	1,090	530	560	−30
1958	3,765	1,940	1,825	115	2,380	1,280	1,100	180	1,385	660	725	−65
1959	4,290	2,230	2,060	170	2,980	1,615	1,365	250	1,310	615	695	−80
1960	3,990	1,960	2,030	−70	2,620	1,335	1,285	50	1,370	625	745	−120
1961	3,015	1,525	1,490	35	1,680	965	715	250	1,335	560	775	−215
1962	2,670	1,520	1,150	370	1,405	915	490	425	1,265	605	660	−55
1963	2,775	1,575	1,200	375	1,250	820	430	390	1,525	755	770	−15
1964	3,220	1,750	1,470	280	1,100	710	390	320	2,120	1,040	1,080	−40
1965	3,880	2,035	1,845	190	1,165	650	515	135	2,715	1,385	1,330	55
1966	4,245	2,210	2,035	175	1,090	585	505	80	3,155	1,625	1,530	95
1967	3,895	1,945	1,950	−5	830	485	345	140	3,065	1,460	1,605	−145
1968	3,765	1,945	1,820	125	840	500	340	160	2,925	1,445	1,480	−35
1969	3,860	2,030	1,830	200	785	490	295	195	3,075	1,540	1,535	5
1970	4,290	2,050	2,240	−190	860	480	380	100	3,430	1,570	1,860	−290
1971	4,720	2,415	2,305	110	1,085	585	500	85	3,635	1,830	1,805	25
1972	5,920	3,085	2,835	250	1,275	740	535	205	4,645	2,345	2,300	45
1973	10,090	4,960	5,130	−170	1,710	1,000	710	290	8,380	3,960	4,420	−460
1974	14,005	6,515	7,490	−975	2,300	1,345	955	390	11,705	5,170	6,535	−1,365

Source: U.S. Government, *People's Republic of China—International Trade Handbook (1975)*, reprinted in William F. Rope, "U.S.–China Trade: The Facts and Figures," in Howard M. Holtzmann, ed., *Legal Aspects of Doing Business with China*, p. 30.

The process of reorientation started in 1960 and continued through 1965 when, for the first time in fifteen years, Japan replaced the Soviet Union as China's principal trading partner. For the rest of the decade—the period of the Third FYP (1966-1970)—China basically returned to the trade patterns before 1937. In addition to Japan, Hong Kong, and Malaysia-Singapore, other major trading partners included Australia, Canada, France, West Germany, Italy, and the United Kingdom. The United States was the only noteworthy exception. During the same period, Sino-Soviet trade continued to shrink, from $318 million in 1966 to a mere $45 million in 1970. Overall, the trade for the period of economic readjustment (1963-1965) amounted to $9,875 million—$3,515 million for communist countries and $6,360 million for non-communist countries. The Third FYP generated a total trade of $20,055 million: the share of communist countries fell to $4,405 million, $6,660 million less than during the Second FYP; and that of non-communist countries more than doubled to $15,650 million, $8,985 million more than in the Second FYP. In the readjustment of commodity imports, the single most important change was in the grain trade. Between 1961 and 1965, China's annual payment for this single item averaged $350 million, about one-third of its total import purchases. Starting with a nominal trade volume in the 1950s which averaged about $16 million and $5 million a year respectively, Australia and Canada became China's leading grain suppliers in the 1960s, each netting an annual export surplus with China of over $100 million. By 1965, China's agricultural problems had eased, and the role of Chinese grain imports began to change. Instead of using it to relieve domestic food shortages, China began importing grain to fill its food reserves, to aid North Vietnam and other countries, and to use as a substitute for the more expensive rice in domestic consumption so that the latter can be exported in exchange for Cuban sugar, Ceylonese rubber, and other important import commodities.[13]

After entering the Fourth FYP (1971-1975), China's worldwide trade rose by leaps and bounds as a result of its economic growth and the expansion of foreign relations. The total turnover was $4,720 million in 1971, $5,920 million in 1972, $10,090 million in 1973, and about $14,005 million in 1974. The most remarkable development was in trade with the United States. Direct trade between the two countries was about $218 million in 1950, $47 million in 1951, $28 million in 1952, $10 million in 1953, and less than $1 million a year thereafter until 1971, when it rose to $5 million following the removal of certain restrictions by the United States government.[14] From this

13. See "Chou En-lai on the Chinese Economy," *China Trade Report*, no. 3 (1971), p. 7.
14. See "President Ends 21-Year Embargo on Peking Trade," *New York Times*, June 11, 1971, p. 1. For trade figures before 1970, see Robert F. Dernberger, "Prospects for Trade Between China and the United States," in Alexander Eckstein, ed., *China Trade Prospects and U.S. Policy*, p. 296.

modest level, the trade jumped to $111 million for 1972, $876 million for 1973, and $1,064 million for 1974, making the United States China's second largest trading partner, topped only by Japan, in both 1973 and 1974 (see table 2). The share of communist countries in China's total trade during the early 1970s fell from less than 25 percent in 1971 to less than 20 percent in 1974 (see tables 1 and 3).[15]

In recent years, the most important items in China's export trade were foodstuffs, crude materials, fuels, edible oils, textile yarn, and fabric; in its import trade, machinery, equipment, iron and steel, grains, and chemical fertilizer. Table 4 provides a general outline of the commodity composition of Chinese exports and imports from 1967 to 1974; Table 5 explains the commodity composition of China's trade by area from 1973 to 1974; Tables 6 and 7 illustrate the commodity composition of China's trade with the United States in 1973 and 1974.

On the whole, then, the role of foreign trade in the development of the Chinese national economy has been to facilitate and accelerate modernization, to acquire raw materials which are not available or insufficient in China, to purchase machinery and equipment which China cannot produce or does not produce in sufficient quantities, to borrow modern technology through the importation of foreign goods, and to compensate for serious shortfalls in domestic production.[16]

The future of China's foreign trade will be determined by a number of factors. First, the overall economic policy of the Chinese government will be decisive. The Fourth FYP was formulated on the basis of Chairman Mao Tse-tung's "strategic line" of "taking agriculture as the foundation [of the national economy] and industry as the leading factor." In substance, it means that the Chinese government will continue to view the development of heavy industry as the ultimate goal, laying the groundwork through rapid development of agriculture and light industry, and giving due consideration to the people's standard of living.[17]

In this context, Chinese exports will continue to help pay for imports for the development of industry and agriculture, such as the increased importation of complete plants, iron and steel, grains, and chemical fertilizer in the last few years. Japan and West European countries will remain the

15. See Nai-Ruenn Chen, "China's Foreign Trade 1950-1974," in Joint Economic Committee of the U.S. Congress (1975), China: A Reassessment of the Economy, pp. 631, 645-650.

16. In addition to the sources indicated above, for a recent study on the Chinese economy and foreign trade, see the other essays in Joint Economic Committee of the U.S. Congress (1975), op. cit.

17. See Peking Municipal Revolutionary Committee Writing Group, "The Path of China's Socialist Industrialization," Hung-ch'i, no. 10 (1969), p. 22; and Chou En-lai, "Report on the Work of the Government, January 13, 1975," ibid., no. 2 (1975), p. 20.

TABLE 2

CHINA'S MAJOR TRADING PARTNERS, 1973-1974

Unit: One Million U.S. Dollars

Country & Area	1973 Trade	1973 Rank	1974 Trade	1974 Rank
Japan	2,007	1	3,327	1
U.S.	876	2	1,064	2
Hong Kong	793	3	895	3
Malaysia-Singapore	495	4	595	5
West Germany	486	5	652	4
Canada	409	6	575	6
United Kingdom	340	7	328	9
Soviet Union	272	8	282	10
Romania	265	9	250	11
Australia	247	10	478	7
France	231	11	349	8
Italy	198	12	223	12

Source: U.S. Government, *People's Republic of China: International Trade Handbook (1975),* in William F. Rope, "U.S.–China Trade: The Facts and Figures," in Howard M. Holtzmann, ed., *Legal Aspects of Doing Business with China,* pp. 31-32.

principal sources of Chinese imports, and Hong Kong and Malaysia-Singapore the major markets for Chinese exports and therefore the principal sources of Chinese foreign exchange income. China will never again depend on a single partner for the supply of all important machinery and equipment, as it did with the Soviet Union in the 1950s.

Second, the size of trade will be determined by the pace of industrialization which, in turn, will be decided by the output of agriculture. In other words, since China's import capability is dependent upon its export capability, the growth rate of foreign trade is decided by that of the domestic economy. At present, the state of the Chinese economy is basically sound. From 1952 to 1974, the gross national product rose from $67 billion to $223 billion, the annual output of grain from 154 million to 255 million metric tons, crude steel from 1.35 million to 23.8 million metric tons, and crude oil from 0.44 million to 65 million metric tons (see table 8). According to some estimates, Chinese crude oil production may reach an annual output of 200

TABLE 3
CHINA: TRADE BY AREA AND COUNTRY, 1972-1974

Unit: One Million U.S. Dollars

Area and Country	1972				1973				1974			
	Turnovr.	Exports	Imports	Balance	Turnovr.	Exports	Imports	Balance	Turnovr.	Exports	Imports	Balance
Total, All Countries[1]	**5,920**	**3,085**	**2,835**	**250**	**10,090**	**4,960**	**5,130**	**-170**	**14,005**	**6,515**	**7,490**	**-975**
Non-communist Countries	**4,645**	**2,345**	**2,300**	**45**	**8,380**	**3,960**	**4,420**	**-460**	**11,705**	**5,170**	**6,535**	**-1,365**
Developed Countries	**2,740**	**1,070**	**1,670**	**-600**	**5,270**	**1,805**	**3,465**	**-1,660**	**7,690**	**2,400**	**5,290**	**-2,890**
East Asia and Pacific	1,220	530	690	-160	2,290	1,025	1,265	-240	3,870	1,395	2,475	-1,080
Of which:												
Australia	104	55	49	6	247	86	161	-75	478	121	357	-236
Japan	1,108	468	640	-172	2,007	918	1,089	-171	3,327	1,241	2,086	-845
Western Europe	1,065	460	605	-145	1,695	665	1,030	365	2,180	825	1,355	-530
Of which:												
France	158	91	67	24	231	128	103	25	349	160	189	-29
Italy	161	73	88	-15	198	111	87	24	223	102	121	-19
Netherlands	51	39	12	27	94	57	37	20	156	84	72	12
Sweden	66	18	48	-30	83	25	58	-33	103	34	69	-35
Switzerland	39	17	22	-5	73	25	48	-23	94	31	63	-32
United Kingdom	167	77	90	-13	340	102	238	-136	328	136	192	-56
West Germany	282	92	190	-98	486	130	356	-226	652	168	484	-316
North America	455	80	375	-295	1,285	115	1,170	-1,055	1,640	180	1,460	-1,280
Of which:												
Canada	345	49	296	-247	409	53	356	-303	575	62	513	-451
United States	111	32	79	-47	876	64	812	-748	1,064	115	949	-834
Less Developed Countries	**1,365**	**740**	**625**	**115**	**2,280**	**1,335**	**945**	**390**	**3,085**	**1,860**	**1,225**	**635**
Southeast Asia	420	330	90	240	835	665	170	495	1,010	805	205	600
Of which:												
Indonesia[2,3]	75	70	5	65	115	110	5	105	155	150	5	145
Malaysia & Singapore[2,4]	235	190	45	145	495	355	140	215	595	450	145	305
Near East & South Asia	350	180	170	10	605	300	305	-5	890	530	360	170
Of which:												
Egypt	71	26	45	-19	43	22	21	1	61	12	49	-37
Pakistan	35	20	15	5	60	46	14	32	64	52	12	40
Sri Lanka (Ceylon)	41	14	27	-13	70	31	39	-8	124	74	50	24

Latin America	230	20	210	−190	325	55	270	−215	510	60	450	−390
Of which:												
Argentina	3	Negl.	3	−3	18	Negl.	18	−18	105	Negl.	105	−105
Brazil	78	1	77	−76	74	2	72	−70	161	1	160	−159
Chile	82	3	79	−76	121	16	105	−89	99	14	85	−71
Peru	47	Negl.	47	−47	43	1	42	−41	77	Negl.	77	−77
Africa	350	195	155	40	485	295	190	105	635	440	195	245
Of which:												
Nigeria	30	25	5	20	41	33	8	25	50	40	10	30
Sudan	70	24	46	−22	93	27	66	−39	99	49	50	−1
Tanzania	86	65	21	44	106	91	15	76	94	80	14	66
Southern Europe[5]	15	15	Negl.	15	30	20	10	10	40	25	15	10
Hong Kong and Macao	540	535	5	530	830	820	10	810	930	910	20	890
Of which:												
Hong Kong[6]	513	509	4	505	793	784	9	775	895	876	19	857
Communist Countries	1,275	740	535	205	1,710	1,000	710	290	2,300	1,345	955	390
USSR	255	134	121	13	272	136	136	–	282	139	143	−4
Far East[7]	260	180	80	100	480	355	125	230	735	580	155	425
Eastern Europe	495	230	265	−35	605	305	300	5	640	320	320	–
Of Which:												
Czechoslovakia	57	28	29	−1	84	44	40	4	72	29	43	−14
East Germany	98	50	48	2	109	59	50	9	153	80	73	7
Hungary	53	20	33	−13	65	26	39	−13	60	30	30	–
Poland	62	34	28	6	67	34	33	1	88	44	44	–
Romania	218	96	122	−26	265	136	129	7	250	120	130	−10
Other Communist Countries[8]	265	196	69	127	355	205	150	55	640	305	335	−30

Source: U.S. Government, *People's Republic of China: International Trade Handbook (1975)*, in William F. Rope, "U.S.-China Trade: The Facts and Figures," in Howard M. Holtzmann, ed., *Legal Aspects of Doing Business with China*, pp. 31-32.

1. Data for individual countries, except where noted, are rounded to the nearest $1 million. All other data are rounded to the nearest $5 million.

2. Data are rounded to the nearest $5 million.

3. Official statistics from Indonesia are believed to include re-exports of Chinese goods from Hong Kong and Singapore.

4. In the past few years the proportion of Chinese goods re-exported to Malaysia through Singapore has declined. Chinese exports to Singapore have been reduced by 10% for 1972 and 3% for 1973 and 1974 to eliminate double counting of re-exports to Malaysia.

5. Includes Spain, Portugal, Greece, and Malta.

6. Net of entrepot trade with third countries.

7. Includes North Korea, North Vietnam, and Mongolia.

8. Includes Yugoslavia, Cuba, and Albania.

TABLE 4
CHINA: COMMODITY COMPOSITION OF TRADE, 1967-1974

Percent

	1967	1968	1969	1970	1971	1972	1973	1974
Total exports	100	100	100	100	100	100	100	100
Foodstuffs	26	28	30	31	31	31	31	32
Crude materials, fuels, and edible oils	23	21	22	21	20	19	18	21
Chemicals	4	4	4	5	5	5	5	6
Manufactures	44	44	40	42	44	43	45	40
Other	3	3	3	1	1	1	1	1
Total imports	100	100	100	100	100	100	100	100
Foodstuffs	19	23	19	16	13	16	19	21
Crude materials, fuels, and edible oils	16	16	17	17	17	19	21	20
Chemicals	15	17	17	15	14	13	9	8
Manufactures	48	43	46	52	56	51	50	51
Other	1	1	1	Negl.	Negl.	1	1	Negl.

Source: U.S. Government, *People's Republic of China: International Trade Handbook (1975)*, reprinted in William F. Rope, "U.S.–China Trade: The Facts and Figures," in Howard M. Holtzmann, ed., *Legal Aspects of Doing Business with China*, p. 33. Note: The inconsistencies in percentage figures are inherent in the original source because of rounding.

TABLE 5

CHINA: COMMODITY COMPOSITION OF TRADE BY AREA, 1973-1974

Unit: one million U.S. dollars

	1973					1974				
	Total	Developed	Less Developed	Hong Kong and Macao	Communist	Total	Developed	Less Developed	Hong Kong and Macao	Communist
Exports	**4,960**	**1,805**	**1,335**	**820**	**1,000**	**6,515**	**2,400**	**1,860**	**910**	**1,345**
Foodstuffs	**1,530**	**345**	**440**	**430**	**315**	**2,100**	**410**	**650**	**575**	**465**
Of which:										
Animals, meat, and fish	470	135	30	240	65	535	160	25	320	30
Grains	445	15	235	75	120	605	40	330	90	145
Fruits and vegtables	245	125	50	50	20	290	130	70	65	25
Crude materials, fuels, and edible oils	**880**	**650**	**70**	**30**	**130**	**1,365**	**930**	**120**	**70**	**245**
Of which:										
Oilseeds	110	85	15	5	5	135	105	15	5	10
Textile fibers	330	325	–	–	5	170	155	5	–	10
Crude animal materials	170	105	20	5	40	185	125	25	10	25
Petroleum and petroleum products	80	40	5	5	30	525	405	20	25	75
Chemicals	**255**	**105**	**75**	**35**	**40**	**395**	**190**	**105**	**40**	**60**
Manufactures	**2,260**	**690**	**745**	**325**	**500**	**2,610**	**860**	**985**	**225**	**540**
Of which:										
Textile yarn and fabric	855	315	280	110	150	780	365	265	25	125
Clothing	345	95	135	50	65	330	180	55	25	70
Iron and steel	120	–	65	20	35	170	5	120	25	20
Nonferrous metals	60	40	5	5	10	80	55	5	5	15
Machinery and equipment	215	5	95	20	95	255	10	115	25	105
Other	**35**	**15**	**5**	**–**	**15**	**45**	**10**	**–**	**–**	**35**
Imports	**5,130**	**3,465**	**945**	**10**	**710**	**7,490**	**5,290**	**1,225**	**20**	**955**
Foodstuffs	**1,000**	**840**	**95**	**–**	**65**	**1,555**	**1,095**	**305**	**–**	**155**
Of which:										
Grains	840	820	20	–	–	1,170	1,070	100	–	–
Sugar	115	15	40	–	60	340	15	180	–	145

TABLE 5 *(Continued)*

Unit: one million U.S. dollars

	1973					1974				
	Total	Developed	Less Developed	Hong Kong and Macao	Communist	Total	Developed	Less Developed	Hong Kong and Macao	Communist
Crude materials, fuels, and edible oils	**1,070**	**390**	**570**	**5**	**105**	**1,480**	**650**	**665**	**15**	**150**
Of which:										
Oilseeds	60	55	5	—	—	155	155	—	—	—
Rubber	170	5	165	—	—	160	10	150	—	—
Textile fibers	450	210	240	—	—	615	375	240	—	—
Chemicals	**485**	**390**	**55**	**—**	**40**	**595**	**510**	**25**	**—**	**60**
Of which:										
Fertilizer	220	160	35	—	25	230	155	20	—	55
Manufactures	**2,545**	**1,840**	**215**	**5**	**485**	**3,805**	**3,000**	**225**	**5**	**575**
Of which:										
Textile yarn and fabric	110	100	5	—	5	170	160	5	5	—
Iron and steel	930	885	5	—	40	1,190	1,130	10	—	50
Nonferrous metals	410	220	170	—	20	445	220	175	—	50
Machinery and equipment	860	510	10	—	340	1,610	1,235	5	—	370
Other	**30**	**5**	**10**	**—**	**15**	**55**	**35**	**5**	**—**	**15**

Source: U.S. Government, *People's Republic of China: International Trade Handbook 1975*, in William F. Rope, "U.S.–China Trade: The Facts and Figures," in Howard M. Holtzmann, ed., *Legal Aspects of Doing Business with China*, p. 34.

TABLE 6

COMMODITY COMPOSITION OF CHINA–U.S. TRADE, 1973

Chinese Imports

	US $ Millions	%
1. Wheat	277.7	40.3
2. Corn	132.4	19.2
3. Raw Cotton	100.5	14.6
4. Passenger aircraft	53.3	7.7
5. Soybeans	43.4	6.3
6. Iron and steel scrap	24.2	3.5
7. Soybean oil	17.9	2.6
8. Aircraft parts and accessories	5.4	0.8
9. Fertilizers	4.7	0.7
10. Telecommunications equipment	4.2	0.6
Total	**$663.7**	**96.3**
All Imports	**$689.1**	**100.0**

Chinese Exports

	US $Millions	%
1. Tin and tin alloys	7.8	12.2
2. Animal products (bristles)	7.1	11.2
3. Cotton fabrics	6.1	9.5
4. Arts and crafts	5.6	8.8
5. Raw silk	4.3	6.8
6. Pyrotechnical articles	3.2	5.0
7. Brooms, brushes, dusters	2.0	3.1
8. Essential oils, resinoids	1.5	2.4
9. Wood and resin chemical products	1.5	2.4
10. Animal hairs (excluding wool)	1.4	2.2
Total	**$40.5**	**63.6**
All Exports	**$63.7**	**100.0**

Source: U.S. Department of Commerce, reproduced in *China Trade Report*, vol. 12 (1974), p. 11.

TABLE 7
COMMODITY COMPOSITION OF CHINA—U.S. TRADE, 1974

TEN LEADING U.S. EXPORTS TO THE PRC, 1974

	$	Percent of All Exports
Wheat, unmilled, except relief	234,014,893	28.5
Cotton upland, 1 inch to 1-1/8 inch	157,411,015	19.2
Soybeans	140,482,966	17.1
Corn, unmilled, except seed and popcorn	95,671,435	11.4
Aircraft, passenger carrying, commercial, 33,000 pounds and over	33,695,195	4.1
Aircraft, passenger, transport 33,000 pounds and over	16,179,200	2.0
Cotton, upland 1-1/8 inch and over	15,226,079	1.9
Cotton, upland, under one inch	12,963,345	1.6
No. 1 heavy metal steel scrap except sheets	9,044,207	1.1
Tallow, inedible	7,538,854	0.9
Total Leading Ten Exports	722,227,189	87.8
Total All Exports	820,479,497	100.0

TEN LEADING U.S. IMPORTS FROM THE PRC, 1974

	$	Percent of All Exports
Piece Shirting NES White Cotton, not fancy, bleached or colored	11,364,491	9.9
Tin other than alloys, unwrought	9,395,564	8.2
Rosin, nonspecified	7,876,325	6.9
Antiques, nonspecified	6,764,925	5.9
Bristles, crude or processed	5,925,012	5.2
Shrimps and prawns, shell on	5,269,761	4.6
ABC Sheeting, White Cotton, not fancy, bleached or colored, ordinary	4,314,100	3.8
Silk, raw in skeins, etc. NES	2,576,034	2.2
Cigarette, leaf, not stemmed Burley	2,575,776	2.2
Twill NES White Cotton, not fancy, bleached or colored, ordinary	2,490,902	2.2
Total Leading Ten Imports	58,552,890	51.1
Total All Imports	114,689,406	100.0

Source: *U.S.—China Business Review, no. 2 (1975), p. 19.*

million metric tons by 1980.[18] If this projection is correct, China will be able to earn a large amount of foreign exchange from oil exports. Otherwise, the only way for China to expand its imports would be to accept foreign loans and investments. This leads to the third factor, the policy of self-reliance.

In light of its semi-colonial background, China's insistence on self-reliance is an understandable and sound policy.[19] However, economic realities may call for a re-examination of the policy, not in terms of returning to Nationalist practices of the first half of this century, but within the scope of self-reliance and its meaning in the context of a modern socialist economy. In his speech to the Sixth Special Session of the United Nations General Assembly on the problems of raw materials and development, April 10, 1974, then Vice-Premier Teng Hsiao-ping explained:

By self-reliance we mean that a country should mainly rely on the strength and wisdom of its own people, control its own economic lifelines, make full use of its own resources, strive hard to increase food production and develop its national economy step by step and in a planned way. The policy of independence and self-reliance in no way means that it should be divorced from the actual conditions of a country; instead, it requires that distinction must be made between different circumstances, and that each country should work out its own way of practicing self-reliance in the light of its specific conditions . . .

Self-reliance in no way means "self-seclusion" and rejection of foreign aid. We have always considered it beneficial and necessary for the development of the national economy that countries should carry on economic and technical exchanges on the basis of respect for state sovereignty, equality and mutual benefit, and the exchange of needed goods to make up for each other's deficiencies.[20]

On the basis of this definition, the vice-premier enunciated a set of principles concerning international economic and trade relations. These were, among others, that all developing nations are entitled to permanent sovereignty over their national resources and to the control and management of all foreign capital, particularly "transnational corporations," including nationalization; all countries have the right to participate in the decisions that effect international economic affairs, such as trade, shipping and monetary matters;improvement must be made in the terms offered developing nations

18. See Bobby A. Williams, "The Chinese Petroleum Industry: Growth and Prospects," in Joint Economic Committee of the U.S. Congress (1975), *op. cit.,* p. 225; Tatsu Kambara, "The Petroleum Industry in China," *China Quarterly,* no. 60 (1974), p. 696.

19. See Li Chiang, "New Developments in China's Foreign Trade," *China's Foreign Trade,* no. 1 (1974), p. 3.

20. See *Peking Review,* no. 16 (1974), pp. 6,9-10. Teng's speech is the latest thorough discussion of the policy of self-reliance. For similar views on earlier occasions, see Chou En-lai, "Address to the Third Session of the First National People's Congress, June 28, 1956," in *Jen-min shou-ts'e 1957,* pp. 182, 186; Nan Han-chen, "Firmly Carry Out the Struggle Against Imperialism and New Colonialism and Realize the Economic Liberation of the Afro-Asian People," in *Jen-min shou-ts'e 1965,* pp. 498, 501.

TABLE 8
ECONOMIC INDICATORS FOR CHINA, 1975
March 1975

Key Indicators	1952	1957	1958	1959	1960	1961	1962	1963
GNP (billion 1973 US $)	67	94	113	107	106	82	93	103
Population, mid-year (million persons)	570	641	657	672	685	695	704	716
Per capita GNP (1973 US $)	117	147	172	160	155	118	133	144
Industrial production index (1957 = 100)	48	100	145	177	184	108	114	137
Agricultural								
Grain (million metric tons)	154.0	185.0	200.0	165.0	160.0	160.0	180.0	185.0
Cotton (million metric tons)	1.3	1.6	1.7	1.2	0.9	0.8	1.0	1.2
Chemical fertilizers (million metric tons)								
Supply	0.4	2.1	3.2	3.3	3.6	2.9	4.0	6.6
Production	0.2	0.8	1.4	1.9	2.5	1.8	2.8	3.9
Imports	0.2	1.3	1.8	1.4	1.1	1.1	1.2	2.7
Industrial Production								
Crude steel (million metric tons)	1.35	5.35	11.1	13.4	18.7	8.0	8.0	9.0
Coal (million metric tons)	66.5	130.7	230.0	300.0	280.0	170.0	180.0	190.0
Electric power (billion kilowatt hours)	7.3	19.3	28.0	42.0	47.0	31.0	30.0	33.0
Crude oil (million metric tons)	0.44	1.46	2.3	3.7	5.5	5.3	5.8	6.4
Cement (million metric tons)	2.86	6.86	10.7	12.3	12.0	8.0	6.9	9.1
Machine tools (thousand units)	13.7	28.3	30.0	35.0	40.0	30.0	25.0	35.0
Trucks (thousand units)	0.0	7.5	16.0	19.4	15.0	1.0	8.4	16.8
Locomotives (units)	20.0	167.0	350.0	533.0	602.0	100.0	25.0	27.0
Freight cars (thousand units)	5.8	7.3	11.0	17.0	28.0	3.0	4.0	5.9
Cotton cloth (billion linear meters)	3.83	5.05	5.7	6.1	4.9	3.3	3.5	4.6

Source: *U.S.—China Business Review*, no. 3(1975), p. 15.

1964	1965	1966	1967	1968	1969	1970	1971	1972	1973	1974 (Prelim)
117	134	145	141	142	157	179	190	197	217	223
731	747	763	780	798	817	837	857	878	899	920
160	179	190	180	178	192	214	222	225	241	243
163	199	231	202	222	265	313	341	371	416	432
195.0	210.0	215.0	230.0	215.0	220.0	240.0	246.0	240.0	250.0	255.0
1.7	1.9	1.8	1.9	1.8	1.8	2.0	2.2	2.1	2.5	2.5
7.6	10.7	13.2	13.8	15.6	17.9	21.4	24.2	27.6	32.2	30.5
5.8	7.5	9.6	8.1	9.5	11.3	14.0	16.8	19.9	24.8	24.8
1.8	3.2	3.6	5.7	6.1	6.6	7.4	7.4	7.7	7.4	5.7
10.8	12.5	15.0	12.0	14.0	16.0	17.8	21.0	23.0	25.5	23.8
204.0	220.0	248.0	190.0	205.0	258.0	310.0	335.0	356.0	377.0	389.0
36.0	42.0	50.0	45.0	50.0	60.0	72.0	86.0	93.0	101.0	108.0
8.7	10.8	13.9	13.9	15.2	20.3	28.5	36.7	43.0	54.5	65.3
10.9	14.8	16.9	14.2	17.4	19.6	19.8	23.0	27.5	29.9	31.6
40.0	45.0	50.0	40.0	45.0	55.0	70.0	75.0	75.0	80.0	N.A.
20.3	30.0	43.0	32.0	27.0	60.0	70.0	86.0	100.0	110.0	N.A.
27.0	50.0	140.0	200.0	240.0	261.0	285.0	205.0	225.0	240.0	N.A.
5.7	6.6	7.5	6.9	8.7	11.0	12.0	14.0	15.0	16.0	N.A.
5.1	6.4	6.7	5.5	6.0	6.6	7.5	7.2	7.3	7.6	7.6

for their raw materials, primary products and semi-manufactured and man-ufactured goods; economic aid to the developing countries must be free of political strings, and loans to them free of interest or at low interest rates; deferred payment of capital and interest should be allowed, and reduction or cancellation of debts granted if necessary; and technology transferred to the developing nations must be practical, efficient, economical and convenient for use.

Thus, in keeping with its past practice, China does not reject foreign loans as a possible alternative means to expand its trade, and entertains the possibility of accepting foreign investments in joint ventures, as it did with the Soviet Union and some East European countries in the 1950s. However, consistent with Chinese policy, Teng insisted on the preservation of national sovereignty as the first and foremost condition for the acceptance of foreign financial and technical assistance. China's political relations with individual countries will have a decisive bearing on their future economic relations.

Trade and Diplomatic Relations

As noted earlier, Chinese leaders recognize the intimate link between trade and diplomacy. Commenting on Soviet trade with belligerents on both sides during World War II, Chairman Mao Tse-tung observed, ". . . even if one or several countries adopt an anti-Soviet attitude, the Soviet Union will not break off trade relations with them so long as they, like Germany before August 23, [1939], are willing to maintain diplomatic relations and conclude trade treaties with it and do not declare war on it.[21] Ten years later, Mao noted in a reply to a fictitious foreign businessman:

"We want to do business." Quite right, business will be done. We are against no one except the domestic and foreign reactionaries who hinder us from doing business and also from establishing diplomatic relations with foreign countries. When we have beaten the internal and external reactionaries by uniting all domestic and international forces, we shall be able to do business and establish diplomatic relations with all foreign countries on the basis of equality, mutual benefit and mutual respect for territorial integrity and sovereignty.[22]

However, when the Chinese Communist Party came to power in late 1949, it anticipated enormous difficulties in rehabilitating an economy that had been devastated by a hundred years of civil war and foreign invasion; it also foresaw the arduous task of winning diplomatic recognition for the new government because it was communist. In coping with this situation, the 1949

21. Mao Tse-tung, "The Identity of Interests Between the Soviet Union and All Mankind," *Mao Tse-tung hsüan-chi,* p. 583.
22. Mao Tse-tung, "On the People's Democratic Dictatorship," *ibid.,* p. 1478.

Common Program adopted two separate provisions as guidelines for the conduct of China's economic and political foreign affairs:[23]

The Central People's Government of the People's Republic of China may, on the basis of equality, mutual benefit and mutual respect for territory and sovereignty, negotiate with foreign governments which have severed relations with the Kuomintang reactionary clique and which adopt a friendly attitude towards the People's Republic of China, and may establish diplomatic relations with them. [Article 56]

The People's Republic of China may restore and develop commercial relations with foreign governments and peoples on a basis of equality and mutual benefit. [Article 57]

China's foreign trade policy is a strategy designed to deal with the economic and political realities of the world: to improve foreign relations through the expansion of trade and to promote trade through the conduct of diplomacy. It is apparent to Chinese policymakers that international trade cannot be normalized without some political and legal arrangements. But it is also evident to them that diplomatic relations do not guarantee the successful conduct of trade. In their judgment, diplomacy and trade are not ends in themselves but two complementary means to be used in fulfilling certain national goals. The record of China's foreign relations and trade patterns in the past twenty-five years clearly reveals a process of interaction between these two elements.

In the first decade of the People's Republic (1949-1959), China established diplomatic relations with 34 states (including Indonesia), 12 of them communist. At the same time it extended trade relations, involving fewer than 15 countries and regions in 1949-1950, to 93 in 1959.[24] In the following decade China exchanged diplomatic missions with 18 additional states while extending its trade relations to include 125 countries and regions.[25] The Cultural Revolution (1966-1969) held back further expansion in foreign relations; but from 1970 to 1975, China won diplomatic recognition and exchange with 56 more states, bringing the total to 107 states (excluding Indonesia) as of December, 1975. At the same time, China's trading partners also increased to a record high of more than 150 countries and regions (see table 9).[26]

23. In *FLHP 1949-1950*, vol. 1 (1952), p. 16.

24. Yeh Chi-chuang, "The Development of China's Foreign Trade in 1954," in MFT, ed., *Tui-wai mao-i lun-wen hsüan-chi* (1955), p. 20; Chao Chi-chang, "The Great Change and Development of Our Country's Foreign Trade in the Past Seven Years," in MFT, ed. *Tui-wai mao-i lun-wen hsüan*, vol. 3 (1957), p. 14; Yeh Chi-chuang, "China's Foreign Trade in the Past Ten Years," *Jen-min shou-ts'e 1960*, p. 91.

25. Lin Hai-yun, "China's Growing Foreign Trade," *Peking Review*, no. 1 (1965), p. 22.

26. Li Chiang, "New Developments in China's Foreign Trade," *China's Foreign Trade*, no. 1 (1974), p. 2.

TABLE 9

STATES WHICH HAVE DIPLOMATIC RELATIONS WITH THE PEOPLE'S REPUBLIC OF CHINA, AS OF DECEMBER 1975

Year	States	Year's total
1949	Albania, Bulgaria, Burma, Czechoslovakia, Germany (Democratic Republic), Hungary, India, Korea (Democratic People's Republic), Mongolia, Poland, Rumania, USSR, Yugoslavia[1]	13
1950	Afghanistan, Ceylon, Denmark, Finland, [Indonesia], Netherlands Norway, Pakistan, Sweden, Switzerland, United Kingdom, Vietnam (Democratic Republic)[2]	11
1955	Nepal	1
1956	Syria, United Arab Republic (Egypt), Yemen (Arab Republic)	3
1958	Cambodia, Iraq, Morocco, Sudan[3]	4
1959	Guinea	1
1960	Cuba, Ghana, Mali, Somali	4
1961	Tanzania[4]	1
1962	Algeria, Laos, Uganda[5]	3
1963	Burundi, Kenya[6]	2
1964	Congo, France, Tunisia, Zambia[7]	4
1965	Mauritania	1
1968	Mauritius, Yemen (People's Democratic Republic)[8]	2
1969	South Vietnam (Republic)[9]	1
1970	Canada, Chile, Equatorial Guinea, Ethiopia, Italy	5
1971	Austria, Belgium, Cameroon, Iceland, Iran, Kuwait, Lebanon, Nigeria, Peru, Rwanda, San Marino, Senegal, Sierra Leone, Turkey[10]	14
1972	Argentina, Australia, Chad, Cyprus, Germany (Federal Republic), Greece, Guyana, Jamaica, Japan, Luxemburg, Malagasy, Maldives, Malta, Mexico, New Zealand, Togo, Zaire	17
1973	Dahomey, Spain, Upper Volta	3
1974	Botswana, Brazil, Gabon, Gambia, Guinea-Bissau, Malaysia, Niger, Trinidad-Tobago, Venezuela	9
1975	Bangladesh, Comoros, Fiji, Mozambique, Philippines, Sao Tome & Principe, Thailand, Western Samoa	8

Source: *Jen-min jih-pao* and *Peking Review* for the years concerned.

1. Israel recognized the PRC on January 8, 1950, without receiving the latter's reciprocal recognition.

2. Indonesia recognized the PRC on April 13, 1950, but severed diplomatic relations in 1965. Ceylon is now called Sri Lanka.

3. Cambodia promulgated a new Constitution on January 5, 1976, and changed its formal name to "Democratic Cambodia" or "Democratic Kampuchea."

4. Tanzania is a merger of the two formerly independent states of Tanganyika and Zanzibar.

5. Uganda recognized the PRC on October 18, 1962, but later severed its diplomatic relations with Peking. The two states resumed normal relations in 1973.

6. Burundi recognized the PRC on December 23, 1963, but suspended its diplomatic relations with Peking in January 1965. The two states resumed normal relations in 1971.

7. Tunisia recognized the PRC on January 10, 1964, but the latter closed its embassy in Tunis on September 26, 1967, following the conclusion of an agreement for agricultural technical cooperation between the Tunisian and Taiwan governments on February 7 of the same year. In 1971, Tunisia and the PRC resumed their diplomatic relations.

8. Mauritius recognized the PRC on March 12, 1968, without exchanging diplomatic missions with Peking. The exchange took place in 1972.

9. The PRC recognized the National Front for Liberation of South Vietnam on June 14, 1969. Subsequently it exchanged diplomatic missions with the National Front which in official Chinese terminology is known as the Republic of South Vietnam.

10. Libya unilaterally announced its intention of recognition of the PRC in June 1971, without receiving the latter's reciprocal recognition.

The importance of the Soviet Union and East European countries in the early phase of the PRC's foreign trade operations was not due to their capability to satisfy China's economic needs but because of China's close political ties to them.[27] Later, as the Sino-Soviet dispute developed, the Soviet Union charged that China had reduced trade in order to undermine the common cause of communism, and offered to resume the supply of complete plants. In reply, the Chinese contended that the Soviets had always withheld the goods China urgently needed while insisting on the sale of goods China did not need at all.[28] In short, diplomacy, not economics, dominated trade during this period.

The number of countries having diplomatic intercourse with the People's Republic has not been a steady proportional of the number trading with it. The ratio between these two categories was about 1:3 in the PRC's first decade, 2:5 in the second, and 2:3 from 1970 to 1975. The American policy of containment of communism, of course, had a decisive bearing on China's foreign relations. This is evidenced by the fact that of the 107 states having diplomatic ties with the People's Republic in 1975, 56 established relations only after the American intention to reach a detente with Peking had become apparent. However, this does not mean that trade played no part in China's diplomacy until 1970. Indeed, it was largely in response to the

27. See "New Developments in Sino-Soviet Economic Cooperation," Editorial of *Jen-min jih-pao*, April 7, 1956, in MFT, ed., *Tui-wai mao-i lun-wen hsüan*, vol. 3 (1957), p. 30; Li Chiang, "The Achievements of China's Industrial Construction and the Development of Sino-Soviet Economic Cooperation," *ibid.*, p. 32; Huang Jun-ting, "The Constant Consolidation and Development of Sino-Soviet Trade," *ibid.*, p. 41.

28. Letter of the Central Committee of the Communist Party of the Soviet Union to the Central Committee of the Chinese Communist Party, November 29, 1963, in *Jen-min shou-ts'e 1964*, p. 196; letter of the CC/CCP to the CC/CPSU, February 29, 1964, *ibid.*, p. 192.

American containment policy that China used trade as a means to achieve a diplomatic "breakthrough".

In 1952, despite the continuing Korean War, China concluded $224 million worth of non-governmental trade agreements and contracts with 11 non-communist nations (five of them having no diplomatic relations with the People's Republic) at the International Economic Conference in Moscow. Although subsequently many of these transactions did not materialize because of the Western embargo, China widened the range of her commercial contacts with the non-communist world in spite of their political and ideological differences.[29]

Ceylon extended recognition to the People's Republic on January 6, 1950, but did not exchange diplomatic representatives with Peking until September 14, 1956.[30] In 1952, however, the two governments concluded an official trade agreement on the exchange of Chinese rice for Ceylonese rubber over the next five years.[31] Egypt's decision to exchange diplomatic missions with the People's Republic on May 16, 1956, was also preceded by a governmental trade agreement between the two countries.[32] High officials in Peking, including the late Premier Chou En-lai and the late Minister of Foreign Trade Yeh Chi-chuang, frequently cited both cases as practical examples by which nations can not only trade with each other in the absence of diplomatic relations but can, in effect, establish diplomatic relations through trade.[33]

Although India has never been an important commercial partner to China (the largest annual two-way trade amounting to less than $40 million in 1952) the famous Five Principles of Peaceful Coexistence, which underlie China's political and economic relations with other countries, were announced in the 1954 trade agreement with India.[34] And it was in the spirit of

29. Lei Jen-min, "New China's Trade with Capitalist Countries," in MFT, ed., *Tui-wai mao-i lun-wen hsüan-chi* (1955), p. 63. The 11 nations were: Belgium, France, Italy, Finland, the Netherlands, West Germany, the United Kingdom, Switzerland, Ceylon, Indonesia, and Pakistan. See "Achievements of the Chinese Delegation at the 1952 International Economic Conference," *Jen-min shou-ts'e 1952*, p. 293.

30. See Joint Communiqué of the Delegates of the PRC and the Ceylon Governments, *Jen-min shou-ts'e 1957*, p. 390.

31. For the text of the agreement, October 4, 1952, see *TYC 1952-1953*, vol. 2 (1957), p. 173; for a discussion of Sino-Ceylonese trade, see Szu Tung, "New Developments in Sino-Ceylonese Trade Relations," in MFT, ed., *Tui-wai mao-i lun-wen hsüan*, vol. 3 (1957), p. 78.

32. For the text of the agreement, August 22, 1955, see *TYC 1955*, vol. 4 (1960), p. 123.

33. Chou En-lai, "Address to the Third Session of the First National People's Congress, June 28, 1956," in *TWKH 1956-1957*, vol. 4 (1958), pp. 73, 80; Yeh Chi-chuang, "A New Stage in the Development of Economic Relations Between China and Egypt," in MFT, ed., *Tui-wai mao-i lun-wen hsüan*, vol. 2 (1956), p. 99; "Celebrating the Establishment of Diplomatic Relations Between China and Egypt," *ibid.*, p. 102; "China's Trade with Egypt," *ibid.*, vol. 3 (1957), p. 61; Yao-ting, "New Developments in Sino-Egyptian Economic Relations," *ibid.*, p. 64; Tsou Szu-i, "On Sino-Ceylonese Trade," *ibid.*, p. 81.

34. See Agreement with India on Trade and Intercourse Between Tibet Region of China

these principles that China played a leading role in the 1955 Asian-African Conference at Bandung, Indonesia, which paved the way for its economic cooperation with the developing nations and its leadership in the Third World.[35]

Ideological appeals apart, China's political relationship with developing or underdeveloped countries mainly takes on the form of economic cooperation through two interrelated programs, aid and trade. The aid program is directed toward small communist states and Third World countries. The principles governing the operation of this program as formulated by Chou En-lai in 1964, are as follows:

The Chinese government always bases itself on the principle of equality and mutual benefit in providing aid to other countries. It never regards such aid as a kind of unilateral alms but as something mutual;

In providing aid to other countries, the Chinese government strictly respects the sovereignty of the recipient countries and never attaches any conditions or asks for any privileges;

The Chinese government provides economic aid in the form of interest-free or low-interest loans and extends the time limit for the repayment when necessary so as to lighten the burden of the recipient countries as far as possible;

In providing aid to other countries, the purpose of the Chinese government is not to make the recipient countries dependent on China, but to help them embark step by step on the road of self-reliance and independent economic development;

The Chinese government tries its best to help the recipient countries build projects which require less investment while yielding quicker results, so that the recipient governments may increase their income and accumulate capital;

The Chinese government provides the best-quality equipment and material of its own manufacture at international market prices. If the equipment and material provided by the Chinese government are not up to the agreed specifications and quality, the Chinese government undertakes to replace them;

In giving any particular technical assistance, the Chinese government will see to it that the personnel of the recipient country fully master such technique;

The experts dispatched by the Chinese government to help in construction in the recipient countries will have the same standard of living as the experts of those countries; the Chinese experts are not allowed to make any special demands or enjoy any special amenities.[36]

---

and India, April 29, 1954, in *TYC 1954,* vol. 3 (1958), p. 1. For a discussion of the matter, see Lei Jen-min, "Our First Trade Agreement with India," *People's China,* no. 23 (1954), p. 9. The five principles are: mutual respect for each other's territorial integrity and sovereignty, non-aggression, non-interference in each other's internal affairs, equality and mutual benefit, and peaceful coexistence.

35. See Final Communiqué of the Asian-African Conference, April 24, 1955, in George McTurnan Kahin, *The Asian-African Conference,* p. 76.

36. These eight principles, Premier Chou En-lai's reply to the Ghana News Agency's questions, originally appeared in *Jen-min shou-ts'e 1964,* p. 392; English translation in Joint

In practice, from 1953 to 1971, China made a total commitment of at least $5,600 million in economic and military aid. Of this, about $3,100 million went to seven communist states, and the remaining $2,500 million to twenty-eight Third World countries (fourteen in Africa, three in East Asia, four in South Asia, five in the Middle East, and two in Latin America). Running at an annual cost of at least $400 million in recent years, a large share of this outlay consisted of semi-skilled labor, technical services, military goods, industrial materials, and simple machinery. About one-third of the total Chinese aid was delivered in the form of commodities and foreign exchange to finance the recipients' budgetary and trade deficits and to cover some of the local costs of Chinese aid projects. All Chinese credits were extended without interest and repayable in goods from ten to thirty years after grace periods of five to ten years.[37]

Like many other foreign aid programs, Chinese aid is tied to trade. However, as a matter of Chinese practice, diplomatic exchange with Third World countries is usually preceded by some kind of trade activity, such as direct commercial intercourse, exchange of trade delegations, or the conclusion of trade agreements. Only then are aid agreements contemplated. With Brazil, for example, diplomatic relations were established during a visit by Chinese Vice-Minister of Foreign Trade Chen Chieh in August, 1974. This was followed by the inauguration of a joint committee for economic cooperation and the conclusion of an accord for a three- to five-year bilateral trade contract, the establishment of operational contacts between the Bank of Brazil and the Bank of China, and the negotiation of a long-term trade agreement.[38] The significance of this lies not only in the fact that it opened the way for long-range economic cooperation between the two countries, but also in its demonstration of China's use of trade as an effective instrument of foreign policy. The present Brazilian government, the tenth in Latin America to exchange diplomatic missions with China, is the most anti-communist in that part of the world. It was under this military regime that nine citizens of the People's Republic representing the China Council for the Promotion of Internationl Trade and the New China News Agency were arrested in April,

---

Communiqué of China and Tanganyika-Zanzibar, June 19, 1964, *Peking Review,* no. 26 (1964), p. 12. China has not changed its position on these matters.

37. For a detailed discussion, see Leo Tansky, "Chinese Foreign Aid," in Joint Economic Committee of the U.S. Congress (1972), *People's Republic of China: An Economic Analysis,* p. 371. For a more recent study, see Carol H. Fogarty, "China's Economic Relations with the Third World," in Joint Economic Committee of the U.S. Congress (1975), *China: A Reassessment of the Economy,* p. 730.

38. "China and Brazil Establish Diplomatic Relations," *Peking Review,* no. 34 (1974), p. 4; "Brazil-China Ties Set Up," *Japan Times,* August 17, 1974, p. 3; "Brazil, China Ink Trade Pact," *ibid,* August 18, 1974, p. 8; "China-Brazil Joint Economic Committee Established," *Mei-chou hua-ch'iao jih-pao,* August 21, 1974, p. 1; "Brazil and China Set a Trade Commission," *New York Times,* August 18, 1974, p. 9.

1964 for alleged subversion, and were subsequently deported after serving one year of a ten-year sentence.[39] The Brazilian government's decision to enter into close economic cooperation with China as part of President Ernesto Geisel's "responsible pragmatism," regardless of their ideological and political differences, is likely to prompt the recognition of the People's Republic by other Latin American states.

In the case of Malaysia, relations with the People's Republic had long been cool because of racial incidents involving the large Chinese community in that country, and the alleged support of Malaysian communist insurgents by China. Trade between the two countries was carried out largely through middlemen in Singapore and Hong Kong. Then, under the impact of Sino-American detente in 1971, China and Malaysia agreed to establish direct trade contact. Pernas, the Malaysian state trading corporation, was given the China trade monopoly in October of that year, and trade missions were exchanged and agreements concluded for the direct interflow of goods.[40] The success of this commerce paved the way for a mutual understanding on the racial and political questions, which in turn led to Malaysia's recognition of the People's Republic in May, 1974.[41]

Unlike once-friendly Indonesia, which has been hostile to the People's Republic since their diplomatic break in 1965, all other members of the Association of Southeast Asian Nations have already moved in the direction set by Malaysia.[42] In late 1973, President Ferdinand Marcos of the Philippines granted an audience to a CCPIT trade mission which had come to Manila to reciprocate for two previous tours made by Philippine Chamber of Commerce delegations to China. Following that, Marcos' wife visited Peking in September, 1974, and a trade agreement was concluded between the two governments. Immediately thereafter, enough Chinese crude oil began arriving in Manila to satisfy about 10 percent of the Philippines' need. [43] Direct trade between the two countries leapt from none in 1972 to nearly $70 million in the fifteen months from May, 1973 to July, 1974, making China the Philippines' largest communist trading partner. On June 9, 1975, while President Marcos was on a state visit to Peking, the Philippines formally

39. "Protest Against Arrests and Torture of Chinese Citizens in Brazil," *Peking Review,* no. 16 (1964), p. 5. For a discussion of China's relations with Brazil at this time, including the incident mentioned above, see José Honório Rodrigues, "Brazil and China: the Varying Fortunes of Independent Diplomacy," in A. M. Halpern, ed., *Policies Toward China,* p. 457.

40. See *China Trade Report,* no. 8 (1971), p. 4; no. 9 (1971), p. 5; no. 10 (1971), p. 5; no. 12 (1971), p. 5; and no. 10 (1973), p. 7.

41. Joint Communiqué of the Government of the People's Republic of China and the Government of Malaysia, May 31, 1974, in *Peking Review,* no. 23 (1974), p. 8.

42. For a discussion of other Southeast Asian nations' reaction, see M. G. G. Pillai, "Blazing the Peking Trail," *Far Eastern Economic Review,* no. 23 (1974), p. 14.

43. See "Chinese Delegation Abroad," *China Trade Report,* no. 11 (1973), p, 14; "Madame Imelda Marcos' Visit to China Welcomed," *Peking Review,* no. 39 (1974), p. 3; "China Crude Oil Bound for R.P.," *Japan Times,* October 2, 1974, p. 10.

normalized relations with the People's Republic, and the two countries concluded an intergovernmental trade agreement (see Appendix F).[44] In Thailand, after a visit to China by Deputy Foreign Minister Chatichai Choonhavan, the government amended a fourteen-year-old ban on free trade with the People's Republic on January 1, 1974, so that the Thai state trading companies and approved private firms could do business with China through the latter's official representatives in Hong Kong. Meanwhile, Chinese diesel oil began to arrive in Bangkok. Eighteen months later, the Thai government established diplomatic ties with Peking.[45] Finally, Singapore's Prime Minister Lee Kuan Yew visited Peking in May, 1976, paving the way for mutual diplomatic recognition and closer trade cooperation in the future.[46]

The 1954 Geneva Conference, convened to discuss the problem of Korea and Indochina, provided the PRC with its first high-level opportunity to discuss trade with European states. Led by Premier Chou En-lai and Vice-Minister of Foreign Trade Lei Jen-min, the Chinese delegation held a series of meetings with leading businessmen from the United Kingdom, Italy, France, West Germany, Belgium, and the Netherlands. As a result, China exchanged visiting trade missions with the United Kingdom, Belgium, and Finland, which prompted the United Kingdom to remove the "China differentials" from the embargo list.[47] Until the United Kingdom acknowledged in March, 1972 Peking's claim that Taiwan is a province of the People's Republic, the overall relationship between the two countries was never a happy one. However, from the outset trade was a very important contributing factor in the British decision to recognize the People's Republic; it was also a means by which the two governments were able to maintain a degree of mutual accommodation and official communication.[48]

44. Joint Communiqué of the Government of the People's Republic of China and the Government of the Republic of the Philippines, June 9, 1975, *Peking Review*, no. 24 (1975), p. 7.

45. See Joint Communiqué on the Establishment of Diplomatic Relations Between the PRC and the Kingdom of Thailand, July 1, 1975, in *Peking Review*, no. 27 (1975), p. 8.

46. Singapore would establish diplomatic relations with China only after Indonesia had reached a rapprochement with Peking. See *Peking Review*, no. 22 (1976), p. 4; *Far Eastern Economic Review*, no. 22 (1976), p. 26.

47. See Chao Fan, "Trade Talks in Geneva," *Ching-chi tao-pao*, no. 15 (1954), p. 8; Wen Tao, "The Development of Trade Activities in Geneva," *ibid.*, no. 21 (1954), p. 6; Chou En-lai, "Diplomatic Report to the 33rd Session of the Council of the Central People's Government, August 11, 1954," *Jen-min shou-ts'e 1955*, p. 325; "Trade with the West," *People's China*, no. 16 (1954), p. 35; Ting Ming, "The Chinese Trade Delegation in London," *Ching-chi tao-pao*, no. 26 (1954), p. 14; "Attlee's Visit to Peking and Sino-British Trade," *ibid.*, no. 32 (1954), p. 10; and "British Labor Party Delegation in China," *People's China*, no. 18 (1954), p. 42.

48. Richard Harris, "Britain and China: Coexistence at Low Pressure," in A. M. Halpern, ed., *Policies Toward China*, p. 13; "China and Britain to Exchange Ambassadors," *Peking Review*, no. 11 (1972), p. 3.

Another important development during Chou's 1954 visit to Geneva was the improvement of trade relations with West Germany. This was made possible through East German Premier Otto Grotewohl's personal intercession, presumably because West Germany's trade with the East was largely tied to the so-called Ruble bloc. In a joint communiqué with the Chinese Premier, he formally urged Chou En-lai to support the efforts of West Germany to extend trade with the People's Reublic in the interest of the German people as a whole.[49] China did not seek immediate diplomatic ties with Bonn because of its official commitment to East Berlin and the lack of a peace treaty ending World War II with the whole of Germany. It was more than a year later that China unilaterally terminated the state of war with Germany and signed a treaty of friendship and cooperation with East Germany.[50] Pending a peaceful reunification of Germany, the East Berlin government welcomed a "normalization" of China's relationship with the Bonn government.[51] Thus the way was cleared for Peking to seek Bonn's formal diplomatic recognition.

At the Geneva conference, West German businessmen had been unsuccessful in seeking a trade agreement with the Chinese delegation because of the latter's insistence that any such agreement would have to be made at the governmental level. Subsequently, however, a delegation of the Eastern Committee of the German Economy did conclude a semi-official trade agreement with the CCPIT on September 27, 1957.[52] At that time, the Chinese obviously hoped that the agreement would lead to some form of normalization in both trade and diplomatic relations. But the Bonn government was not prepared to do this because of the Hallstein Doctrine, which precluded its recognition of any communist state except the Soviet Union, and when the trade agreement expired a year later, the Chinese refused to renew it. The two-way trade dropped steadily from a high of $220 million in 1958 to a low of $46 million in 1963, when negotiations for the exchange of trade missions, the use of West German credit facilities, and the conclusion of a formal trade agreement resumed. However, before the two parties were able to reach an accord, which was to include the sale of a $150 million (600 million *Deutschmark)* steel plant to China, the Bonn government backed out

49. See Communiqué on Sino-German Talks, July 25, 1954, Berlin, in Supplement to *People's China,* no. 17 (1954), p. 3.

50. "State of War with Germany Ends," *People's China,* no. 9 (1955), p. 40. For the text of the treaty, December 25, 1955, see *TYC 1955,* vol. 4 (1960), p. 7.

51. See Joint Statement of the Government of the People's Republic of China and the Government of the German Democratic Republic, December 25, 1955, in Supplement to *People's China,* no. 2 (1956), p. 1.

52. For the text of the agreement and related documents, see *TYC 1957,* vol. 6 (1958), pp. 323-329.

in the face of strong American opposition.[53] In spite of this incident, trade between the two countries rose again during the sixties because of China's traditional interest in German technology and machinery. Bonn's recognition of the People's Republic on October 11, 1972, boosted the 1973 two-way trade to a new high of $486 million, an increase of about 73 percent over 1972, with a German export surplus of about $168 million. A large West German industrial exhibition was inaugurated in Peking in 1975—an event that would not have been possible before the normalization of diplomatic relations.[54]

Although China's grain purchases in the last fifteen years have made Australia and Canada two of its most important trading partners, these deals were also not immune from politics. They caused a prolonged debate within the interest groups of the two grower countries as to whether such trade was consistent with their nonrecognition policy and their alliance with the United States: in short, whether trade could indeed be separated from politics.[55] And in view of its economic importance to Australia and Canada, the trade became a Chinese lever to move them toward granting the PRC diplomatic recognition. Following Canada's decision to establish diplomatic relations with the People's Republic in October 1970, which was in part prompted by the growing trade between the two countries, the Chinese government suddenly let it be known that for political reasons China would not purchase wheat from Australia, nor would it welcome any official trade delegation from Australia in the absence of normalized diplomatic relations.[56] To support this policy, the Chinese excluded Australian wheat dealers from their market soon after the last shipment of a 1969 contract was delivered in early 1971.[57] Needless to say, loss of such a large potential market immediately aroused intense debate among the various political factions in Australia. Under pressure, Prime

53. For a discussion of Sino-German trade and its political implications, see Bernhard Grossmann, "Peking-Bonn: Substantial Non-Relations," *Pacific Community,* no. 1 (1970), p. 224; and Arthur A. Stahnke, "The Political Context of Sino-West German Trade," in Arthur A. Stahnke, ed., *China's Trade with the West,* p. 135. In 1974, a West German consortium successfully regained the sale of the steel plant by signing two separate contracts totaling $260 million for its construction. See "China Inks Deal for Steel Plant," *Japan Times,* September 2, 1974, p. 9.

54. "F.R.G. Technical Exhibition in Peking," *Peking Review,* no. 38 (1975), p. 6.

55. For a discussion of these matters, see John Reynolds, "Recognition by Trade: The Controversial Wheat Sales to China," *Australian Outlook,* vol. 18 (1964), p. 117; J. Wilczynski, "Australia's Trade with China," *India Quarterly,* vol. 21 (1965), p. 156; "The Economics and Politics of Wheat Exports to China," *Australian Quarterly,* vol. 37 (1965), p. 44; "Sino-Australian Trade and Defense," *Australian Outlook,* vol. 20 (1966), p. 154; Henry S. Albinski, "Australia and the Chinese Strategic Embargo," *ibid.,* vol. 19 (1965), p. 117; Henry S. Albinski, "Canada's Chinese Trade in Political Perspective," in Arthur A. Stahnke, ed., *China's Trade with the West,* p. 89; John W. Holmes, "Canada and China: The Dilemmas of Middle Power," in A. M. Halpern, ed., *Policies Toward China,* p. 103.

56. *China Trade Report,* no. 4 (1971), p. 2; no. 7 (1971), p. 1; no. 8 (1971), p. 3.

57. *Ibid.,* no. 6 (1972), p. 9.

Minister William McMahon and his Foreign Minister Nigel Bowen finally announced in the spring of 1972 Australia's readiness to recognize the People's Republic, pending clarification of Taiwan's status.[58] By fall, when Canberra's decision to sever its ties with Taipei was acknowledged, China resumed the purchase of Australian wheat. And after Labor Party leader Gough Whitlam became prime minister at the end of 1972, Peking formally concluded a three-year general trade agreement the following summer with the Australian government (see Appendix E) and a separate agreement for the purchase of 4.7 million tons of wheat, worth $600 million, from 1974 to 1976.[59] The deal was the largest since 1969 and was obviously a reward for Canberra's diplomatic concession. However, even in these circumstances Peking retained a degree of control over the transaction for political reasons. According to Australian Minister for Overseas Trade J. F. Cairns, China would reexamine the wheat agreement with Australia if there was a change of government in Canberra in the next three years—a reference to the possible return of the conservative Australian leaders to power.[60]

The United States represents the final major porblem in China's continuing effort to win global recognition. In the 1950's, China repeatedly urged the United States to reopen direct trade because the embargo had far-reaching adverse effects on China's external economic and political relations.[61] The United States used the embargo first as a sanction against China for its participation in the Korean War and then as a bargaining lever to gain political concessions in the American-Chinese ambassadorial talks in Geneva and Warsaw.[62] By 1960 it had become apparent that discussion of the trade question would lead nowhere, and China reversed its position by insisting on the solution of such fundamental problems as the withdrawal of the United States forces from Taiwan as preconditions for the normalization of trade relations.[63] The Kennedy Administration showed some interest in improving relations with Peking but subsequently chose to wait until the next

58. *Ibid.*, no. 3 (1972), p. 7; no. 5 (1972), p. 3.

59. *Ibid.*, no. 9 (1972), p. 8; no. 10 (1972), p. 2. The wheat agreement was announced by Minister for Overseas Trade J. F. Cairns in October, 1973. See *China Trade Report*, no. 10 (1973), p. 2.

60. "China to Restudy Pact If Aussie Government Changes," *Japan Times*, October 16, 1973, p. 12. The Australian labor government collapsed in the winter of 1975, but it does not appear to have had any adverse effect on Australia's relations with China.

61. Nan Han-chen, "Address to the Moscow International Economic Conference, April 4, 1952," *People's China*, no. 9 (1952), p. 27; Lu Hsu-chang, "New China's Foreign Trade," *Jen-min shou-ts'e 1955*, p. 468; "Premier Chou En-lai's Interview with Forty-one American Youth Delegates," *People's China*, no. 20 (1957), p. 4; Hsu Yin, *Chin-yun i-ting yao ch'e-ti p'o-ch'an;* Gunnar Adler-Karlsson, *Western Economic Warfare 1947-1967.*

62. See "Control of Economic Relations with Communist China," Department of State, Bulletin, no. 28 (1950), p. 1004; Kenneth T. Young, *Negotiating with the Chinese Communists: The United States Experience, 1953-1967*, pp. 44-51 and 78-82.

63. "Chinese Statement on the Question of Exchanging Correspondents Between China and the U.S.," *Peking Review*, no. 37 (1960), p. 29.

generation of Chinese leaders emerged.[64] The Johnson Administration esca-
lated the Vietnam War and thereby eliminated any remaining possibility for
the restoration of direct commercial intercourse. In brief, mutual political
hostility impeded the resumption of bilateral trade throughout the first two
decades of the People's Republic.[65] After President Nixon's inauguration in
1969, however, the American government began to gradually reduce the
restrictions on trade with the People's Republic to match those applicable to
the Soviet Union. By the end of 1972, the government allowed American
vessels and aircraft to visit China on the same conditions it applied to most
East European countries.[66]

These developments notwithstanding, Sino-American trade from 1972
to 1974 was by no means balanced. The 1972 trade was more than 2:1 in favor
of the United States; the ratio for 1973 rose to 11:1; and that for 1974 about
7:1. In part, this was due to China's need for American technology and
equipment as well as its unfamiliarity with the American market. But more
fundamental were political problems. Because of the United States
government's continued recognition of the Republic of China on Taiwan, all
United States relations with the People's Republic, including the exchange of
liaison offices in May, 1973, are based on a special form of *de facto*
recognition which accords representatives of each government full diplomatic
immunities, while withholding certain privileges and rights accorded a state
recognized *de jure*.[67] One political-legal consequence of this special relationship is that it precludes the possibility of a formal treaty of friendship,
commerce and navigation—an instrument vital to the normalization of trade
relations in nearly all respects.

More important is the United States Trade Act of 1974, which affords
most-favored-nation status only to countries that adopt a policy of free
emigration (Section 402) and adhere to the Paris Convention for the Protection
of Industrial Property and the Universal Copyright Convention (Section
405).[68] The requirement for free emigration has its origin in Senator Henry A.

---

64. See "Assistant Secretary of State for Far Eastern Affairs Roger Hilsman's Speech on
China Policy to the Commonwealth Club, San Francisco. December 13, 1963 [Extracts]," in
Roderick MacFarquhar, ed., *Sino-American Relations, 1949-1971*, p. 201.

65. See Jerome Alan Cohen, "Chinese Law and Sino-American Trade," in Alexander
Eckstein, ed., *China Trade Prospects and U.S. Policy*, p. 27; Oliver M. Lee, "U.S. Trade Policy
Toward China: From Economic Warfare to Summit Diplomacy," in Arthur A. Stahnke, ed.,
China's Trade with the West, p. 33.

66. For a discussion of the current controls on exports to China, see Rauer H. Meyer,
"Control of Exports to the PRC," in William W. Whitson, ed., *Doing Business with China*, p.
126.

67. See Communiqué, February 23, 1973, in *Peking Review*, no. 8 (1973), p. 4; and
"Transcript of Kissinger's News Conference in Washington on His Asian Tour," *New York
Times*, February 23, 1973, p. 14. For a discussion of the difference between *de facto* and *de jure*
recognition, see L. Oppenheim, *International Law*, vol. 1, ed. by H. Lauterpacht, pp. 136-7.

68. See the Trade Act of 1974, Public Law 93-618, 93rd Congress, H.R. 10710, January
3, 1975 (Washington, D.C.: U.S. Government Printing Office, 1975).

Jackson's opposition to the Soviet government's restriction on the emigration of its Jewish nationals.[69] But ironically it places a limit on United States-China trade, for China considers its emigration policies a wholly domestic matter, and evaluation of domestic affairs by foreign—especially Western—standards is too reminiscent of the last century for China to accept. With respect to industrial property, China has so far acceded to neither convention. And as in the case of emigration, China also considers this a matter of domestic policy. Consequently, the U.S. Trade Act has in effect foreclosed the possibility of an intergovernmental trade agreement with China that would include most-favored-nation treatment, and Chinese exports to the United States will remain subject to very high tariff rates.[70]

China's difficulties in expanding its market in the United States are also compounded by a vestigial political roadblock. In the American market, China has to compete with Taiwan, among others, in the sale of basic exports such as foodstuffs, which in 1974 accounted for 32 percent ($2,100 million) of China's total exports ($6,515 million).[71] Since a large number of consumers of Chinese foodstuffs and other products are American-Chinese and Chinese residents, the competition has sharpened the political differences between rival factions in the American Chinese community, the largest outside Southeast Asia and a very important element in Sino-American trade. In addition, other Americans are by no means onlookers; various interest groups—political, economic, ideological, and religious—involved with Taiwan, China, or both, take sides on the issues for their own purposes. Sino-American detente has intensified the twenty-five-year struggle among these three groups, reflecting the deepening division between China and Taiwan, on the one hand, and the extremely unstable triangular relationship among Peking, Taipei, and Washington on the other. This state of affairs—a massive hangover from the cold war—is extremely counter-productive for Sino-American trade.

Last, but not least, there is the question of how to deal with the frozen assets in each country. The claims and counter-claims vary, depending on their legal validity, the method of calculation, and the length of time involved. Taking the United States government figures that American assets in China in 1950 were $196 million and the Chinese assets in the United States were $78 million, the Chinese debt to the Americans stands at $118 million without

69. Quoted in Christopher H. Phillips' testimony on the Trade Reform Act of 1973 before the Committee of Finance of the U.S. Senate, April 3, 1974. A summary of this testimony was published by the National Council for U.S.-China Trade, of which Mr. Phillips is president.

70. For an analysis of the tariff problem in Sino-American trade, see Harry A. Cahill, *The China Trade and U.S. Tariffs*, p. 79; for a detailed discussion of the Trade Act, see Jay F. Henderson, Nicholas H. Ludlow, and Eugene A. Theroux, "China and the Trade Act of 1974," in *U.S.-China Business Review*, no. 1 (1975), p.3.

71. Foodstuffs are also among Taiwan's major exports. See *Foreign Trade Quarterly*, no. 37 (Taipei, 1973), p. 44.

interest; it could go as high as $600 million at the end of 1975 if the 1950 balance was compounded yearly at an annual interest rate of 6½ percent. This is in itself an almost insoluble legal tangle.[72] The matter, however, is further complicated by two other factors. One is that the People's Republic, as the successor to the Republic of China, claims all of the latter's assets in the United States, which may amount to several hundred million dollars, if not more, although a large portion of the assets is known to have been transferred to "private" institutions incorporated in the United States by the Taiwan authorities, such as the New York branch of the International Commercial Bank of China.[73] The other is that before the frozen assets issue is settled,Chinese property even temporarily in the United States is subject to private legal attachment, thus precluding direct banking and shipping relations as well as the possibility of holding Chinese trade exhibitions in the United States or opening direct airline services between the two countries.[74]

In short, Sino-American trade has been carried out under abnormal and unfavorable conditions in spite of detente, and the basic cause of this abnormality has been a political problem: Taiwan. As in other cases, China has made no secret of its views on Sino-American trade. The Chou-Kissinger communiqué of November 14, 1973, stated: "Trade between the two countries has developed rapidly during the past year. The two sides held that it is in the interest of both countries to take measures to create conditions for further development of trade on the basis of equality and mutual benefit." At the same time, the People's Republic reiterated its position that "the normalization of relations between China and the United States can be realized only on the basis of confirming the principle of one China."[75] Until this problem is solved and a relative balance in trade between the two countries is achieved, the future of Sino-American trade is uncertain.

72. For a discussion see Charles Ford Redick, "The Jurisprudence of the Foreign Claims Settlement Commission: Chinese Claims," *American Journal of International Law* 67:728 (1973).

73. The progenitor of this institution was the Bank of China owned by the Nationalist government on Taiwan. Some details about its reorganization under the impact of the Sino-American detente are discussed in Chapter 4.

74. For reference to this and related issues, see William Clarke and Martha Avery, "The Sino-American Commercial Relationship," in Joint Economic Committee of the U.S. Congress (1975), *China: A Reassessment of the Economy*, p. 500; Eugene A. Theroux, "Legal and Practical Problems in the China Trade," *ibid.*, p. 535.

75. *Peking Review,* no. 46 (1973), p. 10.

3   The Case of Japan

UNTIL the Sino-Japanese rapprochement in September, 1972, Japan's basic diplomatic policy toward China was formulated within the general framework of United States policy in East Asia. In the economic field, however, Japan took a relatively independent course of action due to its traditional ties with both the mainland and Taiwan. Thus, in spite of its close alliance with the United States in strategic matters, and its long-standing role as a leading supplier of and investor in Taiwan, Japan has since 1965 become the top trading partner of the People's Republic.

Foreign trade requires institutional support. For this purpose, the Japanese government established a "trade liaison" relationship with the People's Republic, citing a euphemistic "separation of politics from economics" while maintaining full diplomatic intercourse with the Nationalist government on Taiwan. In the development of this triangular relationship, however, Japan has travelled a difficult path which no other nation has had to follow. At the heart of the problem was Japan's refusal to recognize Taiwan as an inalienable part of the People's Republic. The Japanese experience from 1952 to 1975 is highlighted by three major events: the Nagasaki flag incident, the Yoshida Letter, and the air transport and maritime agreements.

The Nagasaki Flag Incident

From 1952 to 1958, Japanese businessmen concluded four private trade agreements with China. Each of the first three agreements provided for a two-way trade of $167 million (60 million pounds sterling) for a period of one year.[1] Largely due to Japan's affiliation with the Western embargo organizations in Paris, known as COCOM and CHINCOM,[2] actual transactions under

---

1. See China-Japan Trade Agreement, June 1, 1952, in *TYC 1952-1953*, vol. 2 (1957), pp. 367-368. This agreement was originally for six months but was subsequently extended for another six months. China-Japan Trade Agreement, October 29, 1953, in *TYC 1952-1953*, vol. 2 (1957), pp. 369-371; China-Japan Trade Agreement, May 4, 1955, in *TYC 1955*, vol. 4 (1960), pp. 258-262.

2. "COCOM" stands for the Coordinating Committee of the Consultative Group, which was created in 1949 by the United States and certain European countries to control the trade of strategic goods with Communist areas. "CHINCOM" stands for the China Committee of the same Consultative Group. It was established in September, 1952, to enforce the control of exports to mainland China. Japan became a member of both committees in September, 1952. See Gunnar Adler-Karlsson, *Western Economic Warfare*, p. 51.

the first agreement (1952) amounted to only 5 percent of the total; under the second agreement (1953) to 39 percent; and under the third agreement (1955) to 75 percent.[3] The fourth agreement (1958) provided for slightly greater trade, $195 million (70 million pounds sterling) for the year.[4] However, when the Japanese government changed its mind and refused to approve the fourth agreement, China seized upon an incident in Nagasaki involving the PRC flag and discontinued commercial relations with Japan for more than four years. A classic example of the political and legal problems that can arise when trade takes place in a context of mutual nonrecognition, the case may be discussed in three respects: the negotiation of the agreement, third-state pressure, and the nullification of the agreement.

Negotiations for the fourth agreement started with the unresolved issues of the third agreement. These had included Chinese demands for a formal bilateral government trade agreement, the signing of a payments agreement between the two state banks, the exchange of permanent trade missions vested with diplomatic immunity, the abolition of Japan's embargo against China, and exemption from fingerprinting for Chinese trade officials visiting Japan for more than two months. To the Chinese, this last requirement was an insult to the People's Republic since the law had its origin in preventing smugglers of opium and other contraband from entering Japan after World War II.[5] The Japanese involved in the negotiations, however, had been unable to do much about Chinese demands due to the absence of diplomatic relations between the two countries. A compromise clause was finally introduced into the third agreement, stating that both parties would "urge their own governments to conduct intergovernmental negotiations as early as possible" for the conclusion of official agreements.[6]

Then, in July, 1957, the Japanese government removed 272 strategic items from its embargo list. With Prime Minister Nobusuke Kishi's approval, a Japanese delegation representing the Dietmen's League for the Promotion of Japan-China Trade, the Japan Association for the Promotion of International Trade, and the Japan Association for Japan-China Exports and Imports arrived in Peking on September 17, 1957 to open negotiations for the fourth agreement. Prior to their departure, the Japanese government provided the Japanese delegation, headed by senior Dietman Masanosuke Ikeda, with four

3. Tsao Chung-shu, "Perspectives of Sino-Japanese Trade as Viewed from the Japanese Trade Fair," in MFT, ed., *Tui-wai mao-i lun-wen hsüan*, vol. 3 (1957), p. 94.

4. See China-Japan Trade Agreement, March 5, 1958, in *TYC 1958*, vol. 7 (1959), pp. 197-201.

5. Lei Jen-min, "The Key to the Development of Sino-Japanese Trade, September 3, 1955," in *Jih-pen wen-t'i wen-chien hui-pien* (hereafter cited as *Jih-pen wen-t'i*), vol. 2 (1958), pp. 171 and 174; Commentator, "Trade and Fingerprinting," *Jen-min jih-pao*, August 7, 1957, reproduced in *Jih-pen wen-t'i*, pp. 182-184.

6. See China-Japan Trade Agreement, May 4, 1955, arts. 5, 10, 11, in *TYC 1955*, vol. 4 (1960), pp. 258-260.

specific instructions: first, five Chinese trade mission officials would be allowed entry without being fingerprinted; second, no formal diplomatic privileges would be granted to the trade mission members, but "every convenience" would be accorded them, including diplomatic treatment by the customs, the use of ciphers, and exemption from business and income taxes; third, the proposed trade missions should be established in the form of "trade offices"; and fourth, the volume of trade should be increased.[7]

On the basis of these instructions, Ikeda proceeded to negotiate with the Chinese. Three committees were established to discuss the pending issues. The first was in charge of "institutional arrangements," namely commodity inspection, arbitration, and the exchange of trade fairs and trade missions; the second, commodity classification; and the third, payments settlement.[8] As soon as the committees met, however, differences arose over the number and status of Chinese trade representatives in Tokyo. The Chinese insisted on giving official status to thirty.[9] Unable to resolve the difference, the Ikeda delegation decided to return home for consultation. Two days before their scheduled departure on November 1, however, the Chinese offered unexpected concessions in other aspects of the negotiations: an increase of the two-way trade from $167 million to $194 mllion (60 million to 70 million pounds sterling), and settlement of payments through correspondence contracts with private exchange banks until the conclusion of a payments agreement between the two state banks of China and Japan.[10] Thus, according to the Chinese chief negotiator, Vice-Minister of Foreign Trade Lei Jen-min, the remaining differences boiled down to the number of mission members to be exchanged, the fingerprinting of Chinese mission members, the guaranteeing of their physical safety, and the provision of work facilities for their activities. A joint statement was issued on the day the Ikeda delegation departed, November 1, announcing that both parties had discussed the draft of the fourth agreement proposed by the Chinese side and reached an accord on that document; both parties had agreed to a memorandum concerning the establishment of trade missions at the "people's" level and including the right to raise the national flag over a trade mission; and the Chinese side had consented to the Japanese proposal for adjournment of the meeting so that the Japanese could return home for consultation.[11]

After a nearly four-month consultation in Tokyo, the Ikeda delegation returned to Peking on February 25, 1958. Ikeda was under orders from the ruling Liberal Democratic Party not to compromise the Japanese

7. "Policy Fixed for Peiping Trade Talks," *Japan Times,* September 14, 1957, p. 6.
8. *Ta-kung pao* (Peking), October 18, 1957, p. 4.
9. *Japan Times,* November 1, 1957, p. 6.
10. *Ibid.,* October 31, 1957, p. 6.
11. See the Joint Statement of the CCPIT and the Visiting Japanese Official Trade Delegation, November 1, 1957, in *Jih-pen wen-t'i,* vol. 2 (1958), p. 184.

government's nonrecognition policy toward China, and to insist that the proposed Chinese trade mission in Tokyo not be turned into a base for political activities. In addition, he received a new four-point instruction for negotiations on the Chinese-drafted memorandum concerning "people's level" trade missions which was attached to the draft agreement. These points were: criminal jurisdiction over the proposed trade mission and its members should rest with the receiving state; the clause permitting the mission to raise its national flag should be deleted; the number of mission members should be limited to the minimum necessary for the performance of duties; and Japanese government appoval would be necessary for enforcing the trade agreement.[12]

When the Ikeda delegation arrived in Peking the Chinese suddenly announced the successful conclusion of a five-year barter agreement with a visiting delegation from the Japanese steel industry in the total amount of $556 million (200 million pounds sterling) both ways.[13] So smooth and swift were the negotiations for the agreement that it had taken less than twelve days to conclude the deal. And so reasonable were the terms of the agreement that both the Japanese government and the steel industry expressed great satisfaction.[14] No political strings were attached to the agreement.[15] On the contrary, Premier Chou En-lai had declared to the Japanese steel delegation that since his country was importing at least one million tons of steel products annually, in the future he would be willing to consider extension of the barter agreement from five years to ten without any specific conditions.[16]

Overwhelmed by Peking's combination of pressure and temptation, but restricted by Tokyo's four-point instruction, members of the Ikeda delegation were unable to meet with their Chinese counterparts in a full session for nearly a week after their arrival. In several individual sessions with Lei Jen-min, Ikeda tried to amend the clause of the draft memorandum that stipulated that the trade mission would have the right to fly its national flag. In his opinion, since the negotiations were held on a private, not official, basis, it was not proper to use the word "right." This proposal drew an immediate rebuttal from Lei, who declared that he could not accept it because he had previously reached an agreement with Premier Chou En-lai on this matter.[17]

Finally, on March 3, Lei held a press conference with Chinese and foreign correspondents in Peking and declared that, as evidenced by the joint statement of November 1, 1957, before their return to Tokyo for consultation

12. *Japan Times*, February 23, 1958, p. 1.

13. *Jen-min jih-pao*, February 27, 1958, p. 4.

14. *Japan Times*, February 27, 1958, p. 4.

15. See the text of the Barter Agreement of the China National Minerals Corporation and the China National Metals Import Corporation with the Japanese Steel Delegation, February 26, 1958, in *Jen-min jih-pao*, February 27, 1958, p. 4.

16. *Japan Times*, February 27, 1958, p. 1.

17. According to the Japanese, this was the first time that the Chinese negotiators quoted Chou in their trade talks. See *Japan Times*, March 2, 1958, p. 6.

the previous autumn, the Japanese had already accepted the draft fourth agreement, including the memorandum attached to it. The present delay in the signing of the document, Lei pointed out, was due to Japanese attempts to eliminate the memorandum clause affirming the right of the Chinese trade mission to fly its national flag; to evade the issue of guaranteeing Tokyo's enforcement of the agreement; and to limit the number of Chinese trade mission members. He warned that the whole matter was now "a test of the good faith of the official Japanese trade delegation."[18] Unable to resist the mounting pressure, and without prior consultation with Tokyo, Ikeda met with members of his delegation on the following day and decided to give in.[19]

Despite the active participation of high state officials in the negotiations, the fourth agreement, concluded in Peking on March 5, 1958, was nongovernmental in form: neither side had to concern itself with the procedures prescribed by the domestic law of each country for the approval of governmental commitments, such as treaties or other agreements.[20] The agreement dealt with three main subjects: trade, payments, and institutional arrangements. (See Appendix G for a partial text of the agreement). It provided for the establishment of trade missions at the "people's" level in Peking and Tokyo, the functions of which were described as follows: handling matters arising from the execution of the agreement, reporting the market conditions of each country, investigating and gathering information concerning the trade and market of the receiving state, assisting manufacturers and business firms of each country in the conduct of transactions, promoting technical intercourse between both states, and handling other commercial matters assigned to the trade missions by their appointing agencies.

In order to implement these functions, a memorandum of March 5, 1958—part of the fourth agreement—provided for protection for the physical safety of the trade mission and its members; choice of methods for settling legal disputes after agreement between the two parties; facilitation of the entry and exit of trade mission members; favorable treatment of mission members by customs authorities; freedom of travel for the purpose of carrying out trade activities; use of ciphers for the conduct of business; the right of the trade mission to fly its national flag on its buildings, and exemption from fingerprinting of trade mission members and their dependents. The number of mission members was left to each party to decide on the basis of its own needs.

18. *Jen-min jih-pao,* March 4, 1958, p. 4.
19. *Japan Times,* March 5, 1958, p. 1.
20. Under Japanese law, a treaty requires legislative ratification by the Diet, but executive agreements may be concluded independently by the cabinet under its general power to administer foreign relations. See *Constitution of Japan,* art. 73, paras. 3 and 4 (1946); also see Harold S. Quigley and John E. Turner, *The New Japan,* pp. 206-207. The procedures of Chinese law for ratification of treaties and agreements are similar to those of Japan.

It was these provisions for the exchange of trade missions that provoked strong reactions from Taipei and Washington. Taipei's principal charge against Tokyo was that the fourth agreement was nothing but a stepping stone toward the establishment of diplomatic relations with the People's Republic, and that the trade missions were simply functional substitutes for consulates.[21] While recognizing Japan's need for trade with the mainland as an economic necessity, the Nationalist authorities demanded that the Peking trade delegates be denied diplomatic privileges and the right to fly their national flag.[22] To demonstrate its determination, on March 13 the Nationalist cabinet called off the trade conference then being held in Taipei with Japan pending clarification of the issue by the Japanese government. When Tokyo showed no sign of yielding, the Nationalist authorities suspended all commercial negotiations and contracts with Japan, including credit letters and orders.[23] They also mobilized supporters at home and abroad (mainly those in Southeast Asia where memories of Japanese atrocities during World War II were still fresh) to boycott Japanese commodities. To add more weight to the pressure, Chiang Kai-shek personally warned Tokyo that his government would never accept Japan's *de facto* recognition of the Chinese government in Peking through the execution of the fourth trade agreement.[24]

The United States, too, exerted its influence in the development of this situation. The suspension of the Taipei-Tokyo trade conference coincided with the arrival in Taipei on March 14 of the U.S. secretary of state, the late John Foster Dulles, and his Assistant Secretary of State Walter S. Robertson. On the following day, when addressing the Association of Chinese Students Returned from the United States, Robertson delivered one of his strongest speeches condemning the Chinese on the mainland and declaring that his country would never recognize the People's Republic, whose existence was based on "bloody violence."[25] A week later, Undersecretary of Commerce Walter Williams, while visiting Tokyo, advised the Japanese to be "cautious" in their trade with mainland China.[26] At the same time, officials in Washington expressed their regret over the recent Taipei-Tokyo dispute and indicated their willingness to mediate it.[27] Finally, on April 9, the Committee

21. Editorial, "The Two Sides of Chinese Communist-Japanese Trade," *Chung-yang jih-pao* (Taipei), March 12, 1958, p. 2; Editorial, "A Re-Evaluation of Sino-Japanese Friendship," *ibid.*, March 17, 1958, p. 2.
22. Reports of Premier O. K. Yu and Vice-Minister of Foreign Affairs Shen Chang-huan to the Legislative Yuan, March 14, 1958, *ibid.*, March 15, 1958, p. 2.
23. Vice-Minister of Foreign Affairs Shen Chang-huan's report to the Legislative Yuan, March 18, 1958, *ibid.*, March 19, 1958, p. 1.
24. See Chiang's Interview with Associated Press correspondents, *ibid.*, April 6, 1958, p. 1.
25. *Ibid.*, March 16, 1958, p. 1.
26. *Ibid.*, March 21, 1958, p. 1.
27. *Ibid.*, March 22, 1958, p. 1.

of One Million, of which many United States senators and congressmen were members, published a full-page notice in the *Japan Times,* stating that Japan's trade with mainland China was "an act of insanity and potential national and international suicide."

The Japanese were not unaware of the political implications of the trade agreement and the difficulties in executing the document. But the need for trade seems to have overcome political considerations. In 1957, Japan's total trade amounted to about $7 billion, with an unfavorable balance of nearly $1.5 billion. Trade with China accounted for $140 million, with a deficit of $20 million; trade with Taipei, $150 million, with a surplus of $17 million; and trade with the United States, $2.2 billion, with a deficit of over $1 billion.[28] In that same year, Japan also suffered a depression in its domestic steel market.[29] Consequently, the fourth agreement and the five-year steel deal were very important for the Japanese.

When the first Chinese trade fair was held in Tokyo in 1955, the Japanese government had permitted the flying of the Chinese national flag. And Prime Minister Kishi, then a member of the Diet, had sponsored two joint resolutions in 1956 with the Socialist leader Inejiro Asanuma and others for the expansion of trade with the People's Republic.[30] It was also under the Kishi administration that the Japanese government successfully concluded a formal treaty of commerce with the Soviet Union on December 6, 1957, with an annex defining the juridical status of Soviet trade representation in Japan.[31] Failure to reach an accord with China on the terms of the fourth agreement would not only contradict Kishi's previous position, but might also jeopardize his re-election since the Japan Socialist Party held one-third of the seats in each house of the Diet and a general election was set for May, 1958.

For these reasons, Prime Minister Kishi was prepared to grant the Chinese trade mission all privileges provided in the memorandum of March 5, 1958, except for the right to fly its national flag in Japan—in this respect adhering to the second point of Tokyo's February instruction to the Ikeda delegation. At the end of March, in reply to Taipei's protests, he declared that flying a Chinese flag in Japan would not be recognized by the Japanese government as a right;[32] consequently, he could not protect the flag under article 92 of Japan's penal code, which provides that, "a person who, for the purpose of insulting a foreign state, damages, destroys, removes or defiles the national flag or other national emblem of that state shall be punished with

28. See Warren S. Hunsberger, *Japan and the United States in World Trade,* p. 106.
29. *Japan Times,* February 27, 1958, p. 1.
30. These resolutions were dated March 30, and December 12, 1956, respectively. In the Dietmen's League for the Promotion of Japan-China Trade, *Nichu kankei shryo shu,* pp. 23-24.
31. In *Japanese Annual of International Law,* vol. 2 (1958), p. 173.
32. *Japan Times,* March 30, 1958, p. 1.

imprisonment of forced labor for not more than two years or a fine of not more than 200 yen, but the crime shall be dealt with only on the request of the government of such state."[33] At the same time, however, Kishi equivocally pointed out that Japan did not have a law forbidding the hoisting of foreign flags.[34]

In response to American pressure against Japan's dealing with the People's Republic, Foreign Minister Aiichiro Fujiyama regretted "recent movements" in the United States to restrict Japanese imports, and declared, "I do not need to point out that Japan's trade with the United States is a matter of life and death to the Japanese people." He further noted that there was a need for Japan "to lessen the gap now existing in the 2:1 ratio in favor of the United States in the two countries' trade."[35] But neither Kishi's ambivalent attitude nor Fujiyama's appeal satisfied Taipei and Washington. On April 9, when the public notice of the Committee of One Million appeared in the *Japan Times,* Kishi issued a three-point statement in reply to a request from the three Japanese organizations which had signed the fourth agreement for approval of the accord. He denied the proposed PRC trade mission the right to fly its national flag, as well as diplomatic privileges and official status. While reassuring Peking that the Japanese government would support the agreement within the limits of Japan's domestic law, Kishi also reminded the Chinese of the fact of nonrecognition and Japan's consideration for existing relations with Taipei and Washington.[36] In a separate statement the same day, Kishi reiterated that in case of damage to the Chinese flag, the Japanese government would not invoke article 92 of the penal code to protect it; rather, he would consider such an act destruction of private property and handle the case accordingly.

The Nationalist government promptly accepted the statement and resumed normal trade relations with Japan. The People's Republic, however, refused to yield. When the three Japanese organizations forwarded Kishi's decision to Peking, the chief PRC signatory, Nan Han-chen, refused to accept it. Arguing that the Japanese government had failed to provide any assurance for the enforcement of the fourth agreement, Nan in a telegram to the Japanese signatories to the agreement, contended that Kishi's statement regarding the national flag of the People's Republic as private property not entitled to protection under article 92 of the penal code was discrimination in the application of Japan's domestic law. Nan, chairman of the CCPIT, apparently ignored the fact that application of that article was contingent upon the

33. In Supreme Court of Japan, *The Constitution of Japan and Criminal Statutes*, p. 73.
34. In *Chung-yang jih-pao,* March 31, 1958, p. 1.
35. *Japan Times,* April 8, 1958, p. 1.
36. *Japan Times,* April 10, 1958, p. 1.

existence of diplomatic relations between Japan and the foreign state in question. Nevertheless, it was on this basis that he raised the larger question as to whether or not the Japanese government really intended to protect other rights and privileges of the proposed trade mission, such as exemption from fingerprinting and protection of the mission members' physical safety.[37]

On the question of recognition, Nan declared that the basic spirit of the agreement was "friendship," but that the Japanese government's nonrecognition policy and pro-Nationalist attitude had destroyed that spirit. He attacked Kishi's policy of "separating trade from politics" as being hypocritical since the Japanese government had always linked the problem of trade with the People's Republic to the question of nonrecognition. Moreover, he pointed out that by unilaterally denying the Chinese trade mission the rights and privileges stipulated in the fourth agreement, the Japanese government had in fact violated the principles of equality, mutual benefit, and mutual respect, which the Japanese trade delegation then holding fairs in Wuhan and Kwangchow was enjoying—including the right to fly the Japanese national flag. With respect to Japan's consideration for international relations, Nan reminded Tokyo that the trade agreement was concluded with Peking, not with Taipei or Washington. Consequently, he contended that Japan should first of all consider its relations with the People's Republic and the enforcement of the agreement, so as to pave the way for the restoration of diplomatic relations between the two countries. He noted that China would not trade with Japan under any humiliating and unequal terms and that until all barriers created by the Japanese government were removed, China would not enforce the agreement.[38]

As the two sides were exchanging angry words across the sea, an incident involving the destruction of a Chinese flag occurred in Nagasaki. On May 2 in the Hamaya Department Store, at a Chinese postage stamp and paper cutting exhibition sponsored by the Nagasaki chapter of the Japan-China Friendship Association, two young Japanese, To Seki and Kiyoshi Ishibashi, ripped down one of the Chinese flags on display. The sponsor of the exhibition filed a complaint against Seki for destruction of private property. After questioning him on his motives, the local police released Seki, pending consultation with the Nagasaki district prosecutor's office.[39]

The People's Republic did not respond to the incident until May 7, when the Chinese government took three steps. First, it linked the flag

37. See Nan Han-chen's telegram to the three Japanese organizations, April 13, 1958, in *Jih-pen wen-t'i*, vol. 2 (1958), pp. 204-208.

38. *Ibid*. For Peking's further argument along these lines, see Observer's comment, "Who Is After All Destroying the Sino-Japanese Trade Agreement," *Jen-min jih-pao*, April 25, 1958, p. 5.

39. *Japan Times*, May 4, 1958, p. 3.

incident to the Nationalist protests of the fourth agreement, thus implying the existence of collusion between the Nationalists and the Japanese government.[40] Second, it seized fourteen Japanese fishing boats about a hundred miles north of Taiwan.[41] Third, it suspended all import and export licenses for Japan, discontinued all commercial negotiations with the Japanese at the trade fair in Kwangchow, and recalled the Chinese trade delegation that had been negotiating details in Tokyo for the conclusion of the steel deal.[42]

Following this, Nan Han-chen sent another telegram to his Japanese counterparts, holding the Kishi government responsible for the incident and "all the consequences arising therefrom"—the breakdown of Sino-Japanese trade, including trade under the fourth agreement and the steel deal.[43] At the same time, Foreign Minister Chen Yi issued a statement repeating Nan's charges.[44]

The Japanese businessmen quickly apologized for the "unfortunate" incident at Nagasaki.[45] The Japanese government, however, refused to change its policy on the flag issue. Instead, it expressed the view that since China "badly" needed iron and steel for its Second Five-Year Plan (1958-1962), its suspension of trade with Japan would not last very long. And in reply to Chen Yi's accusations, the Japanese government issued an "unofficial" statement saying that China either did not understand Japan's nonrecognition policy or deliberately misinterpreted Japan's stand for political reasons; Chen's accusations were not true because it was under Kishi that the Japanese government authorized the establishment of a Chinese trade mission in Japan for implementing the fourth trade agreement and waived fingerprinting requirements for the mission members—a controversial issue since the mid-fifties; the flying of a Chinese national flag in Tokyo had no direct relationship with trade; and China was trying to make a political issue out of the flag incident committed by an individual Japanese.[46] In addition, Prime Minister Kishi contended that it was against the principles of international law to treat the flag of a nation with which Japan had no diplomatic relations in a similar manner to that of a nation with which his country had formal relations.[47] Commenting on the Nagasaki flag incident, Chief Cabinet Secretary Kiichi Aichi explained that it was doubtful "whether the man responsible

40. *Jen-min jih-pao*, May 7, 1958, p. 5.

41. *Japan Times*, May 8, 1958, p. 1.

42. *Jen-min jih-pao*, May 11, 1958, p. 1; *Japan Times*, May 9, 1958, p. 1.

43. See the CCPIT's telegram to the three Japanese organizations, May 9, 1958, in *Jih-pen wen-t'i*, vol. 2 (1958), pp. 214-215.

44. Foreign Minister Chen Yi's Interview with Hsinhua Correspondents, May 9, 1958, in *ibid.*, pp. 87-89.

45. *Japan times*, May 9, 1958, p. 1.

46. *Ibid.*, May 11, 1958, p. 1.

47. *Ibid.*

could be punished under provisions of the penal code, even if diplomatic relations existed between the two countries."[48] He pointed out that the national flag of any country could not be treated as such unless it was flown by an official organization of that country.[49]

The Chinese maintained that the fourth agreement was actually "destroyed" by Kishi's statement of April 9, which denied the three Japanese organizations' request for approval of the entire agreement, including the flag clause. They believed the flag incident was the result of a Tokyo-Taipei plot: as such, it provided further evidence of the Japanese government's hostility toward the People's Republic. In the absence of friendly relations between the two countries and assurance that the Japanese government intended to fulfill the agreement, the Chinese said that they had no choice but to suspend trade relations with Japan to "maintain the dignity of an independent sovereign state and to protect its rights."[50]

The Yoshida Letter

After the fourth agreement was aborted, trade between the two countries was at a total standstill. Then in 1959, the All-China Federation of Trade Unions reached an understanding with the Japan Socialist Party and the General Council of Trade Unions (Sohyo) to resume trade on the basis of "special consideration" for those medium and small Japanese enterprises which depended upon the supply of such Chinese products as straw plait, lacquer, talc, and foods, for their operations.[51] A year later, Premier Chou En-lai formally enunciated "three trading principles" and "three political principles" for Sino-Japanese trade. The former called for the conclusion of both governmental agreements and private contracts, and for special consideration in individual cases involving friendly Japanese firms. The latter urged the Japanese government not to adopt a hostile attitude toward the Chinese government, not to follow the United States in the "two Chinas plot," and not

48. *Ibid.*, May 14, 1958, p. 1.
49. In spite of this view, To Seki, the man who destroyed the PRC flag in Nagasaki was fined 500 yen many months later under pressure from Peking. (This amount exceeded the 200 *yen* provided for in article 92 of the Japanese penal code. The difference arose from the devaluation of *yen* in the postwar period.) This, however, was too late to satisfy the Chinese who contended that the fine was nothing more than "lip service." See Observer's comment, "Kishi's Posture Cannot Deceive Any One," *Jen-min jih-pao,* February 16, 1959, reproduced in *Jih-pen wen-t'i,* vol. 3 (1961), pp. 42-45.
50. Commentator, "Why Was Sino-Japanese Trade Interrupted?" *Jen-min jih-pao,* May 20, 1958, reproduced in *Jih-pen wen-t'i,* vol. 2 (1958), pp. 216-220. For a more detailed analysis of the Nagasaki flag incident, see Gene T. Hsiao, "Nonrecognition and Trade: A Case Study of the Fourth Sino-Japanese Trade Agreement," in Jerome Alan Cohen, ed., *China's Practice of International Law,* pp. 129-153.
51. See Japan External Trade Organization, *How To Approach the China Market,* p. 75.

to obstruct the normalization of Sino-Japanese relations.[52] In accordance with these principles, China designated friendly Japanese firms as its trading partners and allowed them to attend the semi-annual trade fair in Kwangchow, and Japanese ships started serving China again in December, 1960.

Two years later, increasing mutual need for the other's goods finally brought about a semi-official Sino-Japanese trade accord, known as the L-T Memorandum concluded November 9, 1962 in the names of Liao Cheng-chih, president of the China-Japan Friendship Association, and of Ta-tsunosuke Takasaki, a senior LDP dietman and former minister of international trade and industry. It provided for an annual two-way trade of about $100 million, from 1963 to 1967. In a separate agreement concluded in December between the CCPIT and friendly Japanese trade organizations, provisions were also made for the increase of transactions on the basis of Chou's principles.[53] Unlike the abortive fourth agreement, the L-T Memorandum did not contain any provision for the exchange of trade missions and the enjoyment of diplomatic privileges by trade representatives. Instead, it indicated the desires of both parties to establish a deferred payment system for the sale of complete plants to China.[54]

In accordance with this arrangement, the Japanese government under Prime Minister Hayato Ikeda approved on August 20, 1963, the sale of a $20 million vinylon plant to China by the Kurashiki Textile Company on install-ment payments to be made over a period of five years, with a 25 percent down-payment and a grace period of five years after the delivery of the plant. To facilitate the transaction, the Ikeda cabinet instructed the government-owned Export and Import Bank of Japan to guarantee repayment of the full amount at an annual interest rate of 6 percent.[55]

The Nationalist ambassador to Japan, Chang Li-sheng, immediately

52. "Premier Chou En-lai on the Three Principles of Sino-Japanese Trade in an Interview with Managing Director Kazuo Suzuki of the Japan Association for the Promotion of Japan-China Trade, September 10, 1960," in *Jih-pen wen-t'i,* vol. 3 (1961), p. 135.

53. See the Protocol of Sino-Japanese Trade of the CCPIT with the Association for the Promotion of Japan-China Trade, the Japan Association for the Promotion of International Trade, and the Kansai Bureau of the Japan Association for the Promotion of International Trade, December 27, 1962, in *TYC 1962,* vol. 11 (1963), pp. 158-161.

54. The text of the memorandum in *TYC 1962,* vol. 11 (1963), pp. 157-158. The memorandum was concluded in accordance with the principles of a meeting on September 19, 1962, between Premier Chou En-lai and LDP Dietman Kenzo Matsumura, in which the premier restated the three trading and the three political principles but agreed with Matsumura that the two countries should adopt a "gradual and cumulative" formula to normalize their political and economic relations. See "Premier Chou En-lai's Restatement on the Principles of Sino-Japanese Relations, September 19, 1962," in *Jih-pen wen-t'i,* vol. 4 (1963), pp. 17-19.

55. See Japan External Trade Organization, *op. cit.,* p. 80; Soichiro Ohara, "Exportation of a Vinylon Plant to China," *Journal of Social and Political Ideas in Japan,* no. 2 (1964), p. 107; *Chung-yang jih-pao,* August 21, 1963, p. 2.

protested on the ground that the transaction was not a private deal, as the Japanese government sought to pretend, but was directly sponsored and approved by the Ikeda government. Allowing the use of state bank funds to finance the transaction, Chang argued, constituted a form of economic aid to Peking. The Japanese Foreign Office replied that the transaction was within the limits set by the United States embargo policy, and that the terms of installment payments under the agreement were no better than those Japan had granted to Southeast Asian countries.[56]

Obviously disappointed by the Japanese response, Taipei attacked Tokyo, just as Peking already had, for what it now claimed was a hypocritical policy of "separating politics from economics." Equating government financing with economic aid, the official organ of the ruling Kuomintang argued that "since the Industrial Revolution, economics has always been the precursor of.politics"; and inasmuch as the vinylon plant deal was officially approved by the Japanese government, how could it be said that the deal was nonpolitical?[57] To show its irritation, the Nationalist government recalled Chang Li-sheng for "consultation." Tension between Taipei and Tokyo continued to increase as Prime Minister Ikeda publicly denied the desirability of a "counterattack" against the mainland by the Nationalist authorities—a reference to the Nationalist commando attack upon the mainland the previous year.[58] Not long thereafter, an interpreter with a PRC oil hydraulics delegation visiting Tokyo, named Chou Hung-ching, deserted the group in an alleged attempt to seek political asylum. While there were many conflicting reports regarding the deserter's true intention, Taipei took the position that he was seeking Nationalist protection.[59] When the Japanese government decided to send the deserter back to the mainland, Taipei immediately accepted Chang Li-sheng's resignation and recalled all senior members of its Tokyo embassy.[60] But the Ikeda cabinet was determined to carry out its decision. It repatriated the deserter on January 9, 1964, under the escort of Kazuo Suzuki, managing director of The Japan-China Trade Promotion Association.[61]

56. *Ibid.*, August 29, 1963, p. 1.
57. Editorial, "A Reappraisal of Japan's Trade with the Chinese Communists: Economic or Political Transactions?" *ibid.*, August 30, 1963, p. 2.
58. *Ibid.*, September 20, 1963, p. 1; reports of Premier Chen Cheng and Foreign Minister Shen Chang-huan to the Legislative Yuan, September 20, 1963, in *ibid.*, September 21, 1963, p. 1.
59. "Red Chinese Defects to Soviets," *Japan Times,* October 8, 1963, p. 1; "Unhappy with Peiping," *ibid.,* October 9, 1963, p. 1; "Defector's Turnabout Laid to Leftists Here," *ibid.,* October 26, 1963, p. 1; *Chung-yang jih-pao,* October 8, 1963, p. 1; October 9, 1963, p. 1; October 26, 1963, p. 1.
60. *Ibid.,* December 31, 1963, p. 1.
61. Suzuki, the first Japanese to have formally discussed the three trading and the three political principles with Chou En-lai in 1960, was later to receive an audience with Chairman

Prime Minister Ikeda's refusal to turn the deserter over to Taipei did not mean that he was prepared for a showdown with the Nationalists. Earlier, before it was decided to return the deserter to the PRC, Ikeda had sent the vice-president of the LDP as his special envoy to Taipei, in the best East Asian tradition, to celebrate Chiang Kai-shek's seventy-seventh birthday on October 31, 1963.[62] After the repatriation of Chou Hung-ching, Ikeda appointed elder statesman and former prime minister Shigeru Yoshida as his special emissary to Taipei. Yoshida had three meetings with Chiang in four days and returned to Tokyo on February 27, 1964. Official reports disclosed nothing about the meetings except that Yoshida and Chiang had "reached important decisions" on certain anti-communist policies.[63]

The People's Republic watched the development of the situation with care. At the same time, it also stepped up its activities in Japan. In addition to cultural exchange between the two countries, a large trade delegation headed by Nan Han-chen visited Tokyo and held a three-week fair in April, 1964.[64] Despite Nationalist protests, the national flag of the People's Republic flew over the fair buildings. Meanwhile, a visiting Japanese delegation in Peking led by Dietman Kenzo Matsumura concluded agreements with the Chinese for the exchange of trade representatives and correspondents as well as for the establishment of liaison offices in each other's capital.[65] Trade between the two countries jumped to $310 million in 1964, from $137 million the previous year.[66] Encouraged by Kurashiki's successful vinylon plant deal, Japanese manufacturers continued to negotiate with the Chinese for additional sales. In September, 1964 the Dai Nippon Spinning Company signed a contract with the China Technical Import Corporation for the sale of a complete set of vinylon equipment. Two months later, the Hitachi Shipbuilding and Engineering Company concluded the first Japanese contract for the sale of a ten-thousand-ton freighter to the China National Machinery Import and Export Corporation. However, when the two Japanese companies applied for funds from the Export and Import Bank of Japan to finance their transactions, they were unexpectedly turned down by the government, now under Prime

---

Mao Tse-tung in honor of his friendship with China. See *Hsin-hua yüeh-pao,* no. 2 (1964), pp. 57-58.

62. *Chung-yang jih-pao,* October 30, 1963, p. 1.

63. *Ibid.,* February 24, 1964, p. 1; February 27, 1964, p. 1.

64. *Hsin-hua yüeh-pao,* no. 5 (1964), p. 160; no. 6 (1964), p. 206.

65. See Summary of Meeting Minutes between the Liao Cheng-chih Office and Takasaki Office for Exchange of Representatives and Liaison Offices, April 19, 1964, in *Jen-min shou-ts'e 1964,* p. 454; Summary of Meeting Minutes between the Liao Cheng-chih Office and Takasaki Office for Exchange of News Correspondents, April 19, 1964, *ibid.* The liaison offices were established in February 1965.

66. Japan External Trade Organization, *Foreign Trade of Japan 1966,* p. 185.

Minister Eisaku Sato, on the ground that such applications ran counter to the spirit of the Yoshida Letter.[67]

This was referring to a letter that Yoshida had written to Taipei's presidential secretary-general, Chang Chun, confirming a five-point agreement he had reached with Chiang Kai-shek in their February, 1964, meetings. While the full contents of the letter, dated April 4, 1964, have been kept secret until very recently, one point known to the public assured Taipei that the Japanese government would limit trade with mainland China to private circles, and that it would not provide the PRC with any economic assistance. It was on the basis of this promise that Sato refused to underwrite credit for the Dai Nippon and Hitachi transactions, and both contracts thus became ineffective.[68]

The Yoshida Letter was a major obstacle to the expansion of trade for a second, related reason. Financially, both China and Japanese exporters needed credit to expand trade, and the Yoshida Letter promised that the Japanese government would not guarantee such arrangements. Moreover, since the People's Republic was not a member of the International Monetary Fund and no international valuation existed for the *yuan,* it had to use British pounds and French francs to pay Japan. This meant that trade talks had to be suspended whenever an international monetary crisis threatened the stability of those currencies. To circumvent this, some Japanese firms adopted the "exchange contract method," fixing at the time of the agreement the rates of the pound or franc to be used for final settlement. A more desirable method, however, would have been to establish a *yen-yuan* exchange rate between the two countries, but this required the participation of Japan's state bank.[69] Without Japanese disavowal of the Yoshida Letter, significant improvement in trade relations between Japan and China could not be achieved.

The Chinese, as could be expected, demanded that the Yoshida Letter be abrogated; otherwise, they said, the Sato government would be responsible for "the destruction of Sino-Japanese trade."[70] The Japanese government ignored the protest, and its relations with Taipei remained calm for some time.

67. "The Yoshida Letter," *Peking Review,* no. 8 (1965), p. 31; "Sato Thwarts Trade with China," *ibid.,* no. 16 (1965), p. 28.

68. "Reply of the Liao Cheng-chih Office to the Takasaki Office in Japan on the Question of Destroying Sino-Japanese Trade by the Sato Government," *Jen-min jih-pao,* April 7, 1965, reproduced in *Jen-min shou-ts' e 1965,* p. 303; Commentator, "The Sato Government Must Assume the Responsibility for Destroying Sino-Japanese Trade," *Jen-min jih-pao,* May 10, 1965, reproduced in *ibid.*

69. Tomohiko Etoh, "What Money, What Rate?" *Far Eastern Economic Review,* no. 16 (1969), p. 178.

70. Commentator, "The Sato Government Must Abrogate the 'Yoshida Letter'," in *Hsin-hua yüeh-pao,* no. 3 (1965), p. 140.

Then in March, 1968, after the expiration of the L-T Memorandum, five Japanese business organizations renewed the trade agreement with the CCPIT for a one-year "memorandum trade" of $100 million. In so doing, however, they not only reaffirmed their commitment to Premier Chou En-lai's three political principles as a condition for trade but also vowed to remove the "artificial obstacles" created by the Japanese government and "U.S. imperialism" to the development of trade with China.[71]

Soon after the conclusion of this trade memorandum several members of the Sato cabinet denounced the Yoshida Letter. Some of them suggested that Japan should consider recognizing the People's Republic, and that the letter should be "buried" with Yoshida, who had passed away in October, 1967. Although Prime Minister Sato was quick to disavow the three political principles contained in the trade memorandum, he indicated to the House of Representatives of the Diet on April 12, 1968, that the Yoshida Letter was a "nongovernmental" agreement and therefore had no binding force. As for the use of state funds to finance transactions with Peking, he suggested that it should continue to be decided on the basis of individual cases, as it was in the sale of the Kurashiki vinylon plant.[72]

On Taiwan, Nationalist reactions were strong and angry. As on previous occasions, newspaper editorials and other public media began to criticize the Sato government. But unlike before, Taipei was now heavily dependent upon Japan's technological and financial assistance; in 1965, following the termination of United States economic aid, the Nationalist government received a five-year $150 million loan from Japan.[73] Trade with Japan also rose steadily from $280 million in 1964 to $576 million in 1968, with a balance decidedly in favor of Japan. Moreover, Japan ranked first in sending Taiwan tourists, and third in foreign investments.

It was in these heated circumstances that Chiang Kai-shek himself, on June 8, 1968, announced to a group of visiting Japanese correspondents that the Yoshida Letter came into being because he and the Japanese government, represented by Yoshida, felt that the 1952 peace treaty between Japan and Taiwan no longer covered all eventualities. Consequently, he noted, the Yoshida Letter was a supplement to the peace treaty. "Abrogation of the Yoshida Letter today would be tantamount to the scrapping of the peace treaty." Chiang added:

If the Japanese government should decide to establish diplomatic ties with the Chinese Communists, then Japan would have to break off its diplomatic relations with the

71. New China News Agency release, March 6, 1968; Minutes of Talks between the CCPIT and Five Japanese Organizations, March 19, 1968, in *Peking Review*, no. 13 (1968), p. 9.
72. Gene T. Hsiao, "The Role of Trade in China's Diplomacy with Japan," in Jerome Alan Cohen, ed., *The Dynamics of China's Foreign Relations*, pp. 41 and 52.
73. *China Yearbook 1965-1966* (1966), p. 229.

Republic of China first. In such an eventuality, I would declare the peace treaty null and void. . . . The problem of signing another peace treaty with the Chinese Communists would thereupon face the Japanese government. Any such second peace agreement would certainly involve questions of indemnity, Japan's continued adherence to the Japanese-American Treaty of Mutual Security and sovereignty over the Ryukyus [a group of islands between Japan and Taiwan].[74]

As mentioned earlier, the Yoshida Letter actually contained a five-point agreement between Chiang and the Ikeda cabinet. Aside from the point dealing with Japan's trade with the PRC, the other four points involved the "liberation" of the mainland Chinese people, the attainment of this goal through the joint effort of Taiwan and Japan, the rendering of Japanese moral support for such a Nationalist task, and Japan's opposition to any two-China scheme. Although legally this accord was merely an executive agreement, it did reinforce Japan's commitment to the defense of Taiwan under the "Far East clause" of the Japan-US mutual security treaty.[75] In fact, some informed sources reported that there actually existed "a secret but binding commitment" between the Nationalists and the United States tying the fate of Taiwan to that of Okinawa and therefore of Japan.[76]

Under this Nationalist pressure, Prime Minister Sato refused Peking's demand for the abrogation of the Yoshida Letter, despite his occasional ambivalent speeches on the subject. Instead, he signed a joint communiqué with President Nixon on November 21, 1969, designating a "sphere of influence" for Japan by specifying that "the security of the Republic of Korea was essential to Japan's own security" and that "the maintenance of peace and security in the Taiwan area was also a most important factor for the security of Japan."[77] This position, which amounted to submitting to Taipei's pressure for honoring the Yoshida Letter, was a direct challenge to Peking's claim of sovereignty over Taiwan, and immediately provoked a strong reaction from the People's Republic. At a mass rally in Pyongyang, North Korea, Premier Chou En-lai openly accused Japan of plotting to retake South Korea and Taiwan as colonies through economic expansionism.[78] Then after the conclusion of a trade memorandum for 1970, he presented the visiting Japanese delegation with four additional conditions of trade with Japan: China

74. *Chung-yang jih-pao,* June 11, 1968, p. 1; June 12, 1968, p. 1.

75. See Treaty of Mutual Cooperation and Security between the United States of America and Japan, January 19, 1960, arts. 4 and 6, in Department of State, *U.S. Treaties and Other International Agreements 1960,* vol. 11 (1961), part 2, TIAS 4509, pp. 1632 and 1634. For a discussion of the "Far East clause," see F. C. Langdon, *Japan's Foreign Policy,* pp. 39-41. The text of the Yoshida Letter is in *Chung-yang jih-pao,* December 18, 1976, p. 1.

76. C. L. Sulzberger, "An Okinawa-Taiwan Deal?" *New York Times,* November 18, 1970, p. 43.

77. The text of the joint communiqué in *New York Times,* November 22, 1969, p. 14.

78. "Speech by Premier Chou En-lai at Pyongyang Mass Rally," *Peking Review,* no. 15 (1970), p. 18.

would not trade with: firms that would help Taiwan invade the mainland, and South Korea invade North Korea; firms that had large investments in Taiwan and South Korea; firms that supplied arms and munitions for United States ''imperialism'' to wage aggression against Vietnam, Laos and Cambodia; and joint American-Japanese enterprises and American subsidiaries in Japan.[79]

In line with this general policy, the late Chen Yu, then chairman of the Kwangchow trade fair committee, specified that China would henceforth examine all transactions with Japan according to the four new conditions; would refuse to enter into any trade contract with Japan inconsistent with any of these conditions; and would even cancel already concluded contracts if they failed to conform to these conditions. To demonstrate the Chinese government's determination to enforce the policy, he disqualified four Japanese manufacturers, including a subsidiary of the U.S. Dow Chemical Company, from trading with China.[80] Furthermore, the Chinese government demanded that the so-called dummy firms set up by the four biggest Japanese trading companies to deal with China sever business ties with their parent companies, which had interests in Taiwan.[81] Many leading Japanese industrial firms and trading companies yielded to the Chinese demands; others which rejected them lost their contracts.[82]

The political and economic complications growing out of the Yoshida Letter were not resolved until July, 1972, when Prime Minister Kakuei Tanaka, who had already decided to seek a rapprochement with the People's Republic, overturned the publicized stipulations of the letter by approving the use of state funds to finance China's purchase of a $48 million (14,349 million *yen*) plant to manufacture ethylene gas. The first major plant sale to the PRC using the credits of the Export and Import Bank of Japan since 1963,[83] the contract, signed on December 29, 1972, provided that China would make a 20 percent down-payment, with the remainder to be paid within five years after completion of the plant at an annual interest rate of 6 percent. The bank granted the seller, Toyo Engineering Company, a low-interest loan in the

79. See ''Chou Attacks Japan Militarism,'' *Japan Times*, April 21, 1970, pp. 1 and 5; *Ta-kung pao* (Hong Kong), May 3, 1970, p. 2.

80. *Ibid.;*''Four Japanese Firms Barred from Red China Trade,'' *Japan Times*, May 3, 1970, p. 13. The four manufacturers were Sumitomo Chemical Co., Mitsubishi Heavy Industries, Teijin Ltd., and Asahi-Dow Co.

81. ''Fertilizer Firms OK Peking's Principles,'' *Japan Times*, May 12, 1970, pp. 1 and 5; ''Far East: So Long at the Fair,'' *Newsweek*, June 8, 1970, p. 82. These companies were Mitsubishi Shoji Kaisha, Ltd., Mitsui and Co., Marubeni-Iida Co., and C. Itoh and Co.

82. See ''Firms Cut Ties Due to Peking Pressure,'' *Japan Times*, May 8, 1970, p. 12; ''Sumitomo Metal Gives Red China Assurances,'' *ibid.*, May 10, 1970, p. 13; ''Two Firms Here Clarify Stand on Chou Rules,'' *ibid.*, May 13, 1970, pp. 1 and 5. As of December, 1970, nearly seven hundred Japanese companies had accepted Chou's conditions. See L. B. Weed, ''Japan Looks to China for Trade,'' *St. Louis Post Dispatch*, December 17, 1970, p. 13A.

83. ''Repayment Terms to be Decided on 'Quality' Basis,'' *Japan Times*, July 27, 1972, pp. 1 and 5.

amount of $27 million (8,065 million *yen*), or about 56 percent of the total price.[84] Also during the summer, the Bank of Tokyo concluded an agreement with the Bank of China on the settlement of accounts in both Japanese *yen* and Chinese *yuan*.[85]

These developments, which facilitated the restoration of Sino-Japanese diplomatic relations in the fall of 1972, had tremendous impact on the expansion of bilateral trade. The two-way trade reached the $2 billion mark in 1973, almost $3.3 billion in 1974, and $3.8 billion in 1975, more than three times that of 1972.[86] Furthermore, as a result of the expansion of trade, the People's Republic has begun to accept Japanese loans not only in the form of deferred payments but also in the form of deposits. Under this arrangement, the Bank of China and Japanese banks started mutually depositing third-country currencies in their London and Hong Kong branches after the Chinese agreed to pay interest on the amount of Japanese deposits in excess of the Chinese deposits. These surplus Japanese deposits would then be used by the Chinese to pay for their imports. Significantly, when the Japanese were short of foreign currencies, they borrowed from other sources in order to deposit.[87] In their opinion, this could promote further sales of complete plants and equipment to China.[88]

Without undermining China's self-reliance policy, as expounded in then Vice-Premier Teng Hsiao-ping's April, 1974 speech to the United Nations, this banking practice has undoubtedly benefited both countries in their mutual effort to expand trade and economic cooperation. It also testifies to the fact that international commerce can be successfully promoted between nations of different socio-political systems when artificial barriers, such as the Yoshida Letter, are removed.

The Air and Maritime Transport Agreements

The Sino-Japanese rapprochement in the fall of 1972 was achieved by Japan's compromise with three Chinese demands concerning Taiwan: recognition of the People's Republic as the sole legal government of China, acceptance of Taiwan as an inalienable part of the territory of the People's

84. "Bank Will OK Loan for Plant Export to China," *ibid.*, September 15, 1974, p. 9.
85. "Yen-yuan Settlement Accord Signed in Peking," *ibid.*, August 19, 1972, p. 1; "Japan, China Banks Start Yen-Yuan System," *ibid.*, September 13, 1972, p. 3; John Roberts, "Meeting in Peking," *Asia Yearbook 1973*, p. 182.
86. *Japan Economic Review*, no. 3 (1974), p. 12; no. 2 (1975), p. 10; no. 2 (1976), p. 8.
87. Susumu Awanohara, "When Japan Deposits, China Borrows," *Far Eastern Economic Review*, no. 24 (1974), p. 42.
88. The Export and Import Bank of Japan was expected to finance the export of six other industrial plants valued at $110 million (33,000 million *yen*) by the end of 1974. See *Japan Times*, September 15, 1974, p. 9. For a list of Japanese plant sales in 1973, see *U.S.-China Business Review*, no. 1 (1974), p. 36.

Republic, and abrogation of Japan's peace treaty with the Nationalists. The Japanese government accepted the first Chinese demand without reservation, expressed its "understanding and respect" for the second, and complied with the third by a press statement.[89] But because this rapprochement did not clear up all questions regarding the status of Taiwan, the Chinese government sought to eliminate the ambiguity through bilateral agreements with Japan.

The first such agreement that both countries agreed to negotiate was an air transport accord. In the opinion of many Chinese and Japanese officials, such an accord was essential to the promotion of trade and could lead to the conclusion of a treaty of peace and friendship—the final hallmark of full rapprochement.[90] Negotiations began in March, 1973, but after three rounds of preliminary discussions, the talks became bogged down because of Chinese opposition to the continued flights of Taiwan's China Airlines (CAL) to Japan. The gist of the Chinese argument was that Japan must stop treating Taiwan as a state. Since Taiwan is only a province of China, Peking argued, use of the name China and the Chinese nationalist flag by CAL was misleading and would inevitably contribute to the "two-China" illusion Peking opposed.[91] The PRC government demanded that the Japanese cancel the Japan-Taiwan route operated by CAL and Japan Airlines (JAL), or at least reroute CAL flights to Japanese airports other than Tokyo, such as Nagoya and Okinawa; oppose the use of the Nationalist flag on CAL planes; refer to CAL officially as something like Taiwan Airlines; and transfer CAL's branch office in Japan to a local agent. When the Japanese showed no sign of yielding to these demands, a Chinese economic delegation in Tokyo refused to initial a three-year intergovernmental trade agreement granting each party most-favored-nation treatment.[92] Adding to the pressure on Tokyo, the Nationalist authorities threatened to forbid Japanese airplanes to land in or fly over Taiwan's Air Defense Identification Zone should the Japanese government accept Peking's conditions.[93]

89. See the Sino-Japanese Joint Statement September 29, 1972, arts. 2 and 3, *Peking Review,* no. 40 (1972), p. 12; *Jen-min jih-pao,* September 30, 1972, p. 1; "Foreign Minister Masayoshi Ohira Holds Press Conference in Peking," *ibid.,* p. 2; *Peking Review,* no. 40 (1972), p. 15. For a detailed analysis of the rapprochement, see Gene T. Hsiao, "The Sino-Japanese Rapprochement: A Relationship of Ambivalence," *China Quarterly,* no. 57 (1974), p. 101. A longer version of this article appears in Gene T. Hsiao, ed., *Sino-American Detente,* p. 160.

90. See "A New Chapter in the Annals of Sino-Japanese Relations," *Jen-min jih-pao,* editorial, September 30, 1972, p. 2; "Japanese House of Representatives Adopted Unanimous Resolution Supporting Sino-Japanese Joint Statement," *ibid.,* November 11, 1972, p. 5.

91. The Chinese demands were first made by Premier Chou En-lai in his conversation with Minister of International Trade and Industry Yasuhiro Nakasone, in January, 1973. See *Japan Times,* January 20, 1973, p. 1. Details were later revealed by the Japanese government.

92. "Japan, China Officials Agree on Trade Rules," *Japan Times,* August 31, 1973, p. 1; Richard Halloran, "Chinese Return From Japan Talks," *New York Times,* September 3, 1973, p. 23.

93. "Japan Warned About Air Accord," *Free China Weekly,* no. 28 (1973), p. 1.

After further negotiations Japanese Foreign Minister Masayoshi Ohira finally concluded the most-favored-nation trade agreement with the Chinese government early in January, 1974 (along with a memorandum for the increase of resident correspondents in each country from five to eleven) on the basis of Japanese concessions involving the proposed air transport accord and the maintenance of the Taiwan route.[94] As was later revealed in Tokyo, the understanding consisted of six points: (1) the Japanese government would promptly conclude an air transport agreement with China on the basis of the Sino-Japanese joint statement of September 29, 1972, but present Japan-Taiwan air services would be maintained under a nongovernmental agreement; (2) the government would see to it that JAL would not serve the Japan-Taiwan route; (3) the government would not seek changes in the name and emblem of CAL against CAL's will, but would make clear its own view concerning the nature of CAL's name and emblem on another occasion, and would henceforth refer to CAL as "China Airlines (Taiwan)"; (4) Civil Aviation Administration of China (CAAC) aircraft would use the new Tokyo international airport in Narita, and those of CAL would use the old Tokyo international airport at Haneda (until the new international airport was opened, the government would permit both CAAC and CAL to use Haneda airport, alloting them different operational hours); (5) Japan and Taiwan would agree upon a second alternative airport for CAL; and (6) ground services for CAL would be transferred to local agents or a separate company. However, the government would give due consideration to ensure the operational safety of CAL's flights and guarantee a stable living situation for its employees.[95]

Immediately after the announcement of the proposed government plan, an ultranationalist group in the Diet named Seirankai (Blue Storm Society or Young Storm Association), reacted violently to the pending air transport agreement with China, arguing that continued cooperation with the Nationalists was "a matter of life and death" to Japan's security.[96] China responded to the Seirankai's challenge with a series of articles in its official organ, Jen-min jih-pao ("People's daily"), accusing the organization of being heir to the concept of the Greater East Asia Co-prosperity Sphere, and a

94. "Japan, China Ink Three-Year Most-Favored-Nation Reciprocal Trade Pact," *Japan Times,* January 6, 1974, p. 1; "Scribe Exchange Okayed," *ibid.,* January 6, 1974, p. 3.

95. "Government Announces Policy to Keep Up Air Service between Japan, Taiwan," *Japan Times,* January 18, 1974, pp. 1 and 4.

96. Koji Nakamura, "Seirankai, Forming the Battle Line," *Far Eastern Economic Review,* no. 8 (1974), p. 23; "Seirankai, the Young Turks Flex Their Muscles," Special Report on Japan in Asia 1974, in *ibid.,* no. 19 (1974), p. 21; Minoru Shimizu, "Rivalry Among Junior LDP Dietmen," *Japan Times,* January 17, 1974, p. 10; "Tanaka LDP Faction Gives Seirankai Return Blast," *ibid.,* February 21, 1974, p. 1; Kazushige Hirasawa, "LDP Factionalism," *ibid.,* March 8, 1974, p. 1; "Seirankai Nagoya Rally Blasts Ohira," *ibid.,* March 11, 1974, p. 1.

fascist-militarist force intending to recapture Taiwan and Korea.[97] Japanese Foreign Minister Ohira, who threatened to resign should the aviation accord with China fail, publicly opened the way for a resolution by insisting that the Nationalist flag and emblem carried by CAL were private identification marks that had nothing to do with Taiwan as a state.[98] Under pressure, the Japanese government resumed negotiations with China in March, 1974 on the basis of Ohira's earlier understanding with the Chinese authorities, and successfully concluded the air transport agreement on April 20, despite the strong rightist protests at home and Taiwan's consequent suspension of bilateral civil aviation relations with Japan.

Under the agreement, which consisted of 19 articles and an annex, JAL has landing rights at Peking and/or Shanghai, and CAAC at Tokyo and/or Osaka. From China JAL may fly to London via New Delhi, Bombay or Karachi; Teheran; Beirut, Cairo or Istanbul; Athens or another point in Europe; Rome or another point in Europe; and Paris. CAAC has the right to serve the following points beyond Japan: Vancouver, Ottawa, or another point in Canada; one point in North America excluding Canada; and four points in Latin America, including Mexico. The agreement also provided for most-favored-nation treatment concerning charges for the use of airports and other facilities, and stipulated that each country's aircraft, when flying over the territory of the other country, should use its own nationals as crews.[99] Following this, the two parties signed a separate technical agreement, and the first commercial flights took place on September 29, 1974, the second anniversary of the joint statement normalizing Sino-Japanese relations.[100]

Japan's acceptance of the Chinese terms for the air transport accord created a precedent for future negotiations with China on the conclusion of similar bilateral administrative agreements as stipulated in their 1972 joint statement. One such agreement was a 1974 navigation accord, which would permit Chinese and Japanese vessels to serve both countries on a regular basis. Negotiations for the agreement were suspended for three months because of China's insistence on the removal of the Nationalist flag from

97. Lin Po, "A Noteworthy Tendency," *Jen-min jih-pao*, February 2, 1974, p. 5; "Seirankai Calling for Closer Cooperation with the Chiang Gang," *ibid.;* "Japan: A Handful of Rightists Stage Anti-China Force," *Peking Review*, no. 10 (1974), p. 22; "Japan: Seirankai Militarists Denounced," *ibid.*, no. 12 (1974), p. 22.

98. "The Dirt Begins to Fly," *Far Eastern Economic Review*, no. 8 (1974), p. 5; Kazushige Hirasawa, "LDP Factionalism," *Japan Times*, March 8, 1974, p. 1.

99. "China-Japan Air Transport Agreement Signed in Peking," *Peking Review*, no. 17 (1974), p. 3; "Japan, China Ink Civil Air Pact," *Japan Times*, April 21, 1974, p. 1; "Outline of Japan-China Air Pact," *ibid.*, p. 2. The lower and upper houses of the Diet ratified the air transport agreement on May 7 and May 15, respectively. See "Japan-China Air Accord Okayed by Upper House," *ibid.*, May 16, 1974, p. 1.

100. "Japan-China Air Pact Technicalities Signed," *ibid.*, August 28, 1974, p. 1; "Regular China-Japan Air Service Inaugurated," *Peking Review*, no. 40 (1974), p. 13.

Taiwan's vessels calling on Japanese seaports. Japan was in a bind. To yield to the demand by again identifying the Nationalist flag as a private identification mark would probably result in breaking Japan's shipping lines with Taiwan, which in some respects are far more important than the air route in their bilateral trade. Conversely, to refuse to follow the precedent established in the air accord would inevitably impede the normalization of trade and political relations with China. However, before this dilemma developed into a deadlock, the Chinese government relented, and concluded the agreement in Tokyo on November 13, 1974 without insisting on the removal of Taiwan's flag.[101]

The Chinese made the concession for some practical reasons. First, the key to a final settlement of the Taiwan problem obviously lies in the United States, not in Japan. In his August 9, 1971 conversation with *New York Times'* James Reston, Premier Chou En-lai candidly stated that "it is for the doer to undo the knot."[102] Second, the Chinese leaders apparently realize that once Taiwan can no longer count on the United States for support, the possibility of cooperation between the Nationalist government and the Soviet Union cannot be entirely ruled out. Reports from Hong Kong indicate that in recent years Soviet representatives, including the well-known Soviet "journalist" Victor Louis, have visited Taiwan many times to discuss, among other things, the possibility of establishing direct trade relations.[103] Thus, Japan holds a pivotal position in the balance of power situation in East Asia. If China insists that Japan break away from Taiwan, the USSR will move into the vacuum, harming overall Chinese foreign policy objectives, of which the problem of Taiwan is only a collateral issue. In order to frustrate both the Soviet policy of encirclement and to prevent the resurgence of a predominant American military posture in that region, it is definitely in China's best interest to maintain a good neighborly relationship with Japan. Accordingly, on the conclusion of the air transport agreement, the Chinese issued a statement approving limited nongovernmental "regional intercourse" between Japan and Taiwan as a "transitional measure."[104]

101. See "Japan-China Shipping Pact Talks Suspended," *Japan Times,* August 2, 1974, p. 10; *Chung-yang jih-pao,* July 29, 1974, p. 1; "Japan and China Initial Agreement on Shipping," *Japan Times,* November 3, 1974, p. 1; "Japan, China Ink Shipping Pact," *ibid.,* November 14, 1974, p. 1.

102. See "Transcript of Reston Interview with Chou," in Frank Ching, ed., *Report from Red China,* p. 83.

103. *Far Eastern Economic Review,* no. 26 (1975), p. 5; *South China Morning Post,* July 21, 1975; *Mei-chou Hua-ch'iao jih-pao,* July 2, 1975, p. 1; August 2, 1975, p. 1.

104. *Jen-min jih-pao* commentator, "Greeting the Signing of China-Japan Air Transport Agreement," *Peking Review,* no. 21 (1974), p. 18. The Soviet policy to encircle China has been expressed in the Soviet-proposed collective security system for Asia. For a discussion, see Gene T. Hsiao, "Prospects for a New Sino-Japanese Relationship," *China Quarterly,* no. 60 (1974), pp. 720, 741-747.

For the Japanese, any decision on the "two-China" question will be based on considerations of the relative advantage of Japan's economic relations with China and Taiwan, and of Japan's security. Japan has been trading simultaneously with China and Taiwan since 1950, but with China Japan was unable to achieve a favorable balance until 1965, when she replaced the Soviet Union as China's leading trading partner.[105] Japan's favorable balance of trade with China from 1966 to 1975 exceeded $2.4 billion out of a total trade of over $14.3 billion; but in the same period Japan had a favorable balance of about $5.2 billion from her trade with Taiwan, which exceeded $13.5 billion (see table 10). Furthermore, by the end of 1974, Japan had a total investment of $174 million in 649 cases in Taiwan, and approximately $330 million outstanding in both government and private loans. The number of large Japanese trading companies in Taiwan totalled forty-eight, including such old *zaibatsu* as Mitsui and Mitsubishi. Many of them have acted as overseas agents for Taiwan's exporters and importers, sharing about 17 percent of Taiwan's total foreign trade—$12,620 million in 1974. In addition, Japan had over three hundred technical cooperation projects with numerous Taiwanese enterprises, outnumbering such United States projects by more than 4:1.[106]

Although these figures represented only a small fraction of Japan's overall foreign trade and overseas investments, Taiwan was nevertheless Japan's third greatest customer in 1973, and fourth in 1974, but slipped to seventh for 1975. It ranked eighth, with $174 million, among all Asian countries and areas which received private Japanese investments. By contrast, China ranked ninth among Japan's top customers in 1973, sixth in 1974, and third in 1975, but received no direct Japanese investments except for the short-term credits mentioned earlier (see tables 11 and 12). Since World War II, Japan has been almost obsessed with economic prosperity, and the importance of trade with Taiwan was self-evident. And it was for this reason that Japanese Foreign Minister Kiichi Miyazawa modified his predecessor's position on the Nationalist flag by saying that "nobody, including Japan, can deny the fact that the flag of blue sky and white sun is regarded as a national flag by those countries which recognize Taiwan."[107] Satisfied with this

105. In the fifteen years from 1950 to 1964, Japan's total trade with China amounted to $1,307 million with an import deficit of $257 million. Then in 1965, Japan achieved an export surplus of $21 million. See Robert F. Dernberger, "Prospects for Trade Between China and the United States," in Alexander Eckstein, ed., *China Trade Prospects*, Table A3, p. 288.

106. *Free China Review*, no. 4 (1975), p. 34; no. 3 (1975), p. 35; Chang Ching-sung, "The Development of Sino-Japanese Economic Relations," in *Chung-yang jih-pao*, January 30, 1974, p. 1. According to other sources, Japan's investments in Taiwan amounted to $200 million by the end of 1975. *Japan Times*, March 20, 1976, p. 5.

107. "Agreement Signed to Restore Japan-Taiwan Airline Flights," *Japan Times*, July 10, 1975, p. 1.

TABLE 10
JAPAN'S TRADE WITH CHINA AND TAIWAN, 1966-1975

Unit: one million U.S. dollars

	Trade with China					Trade with Taiwan			
Year	Export	Import	Total	Balance	Year	Export	Import	Total	Balance
1966	315	306	621	+ 9	1966	230	142	372	+ 88
1967	288	269	557	+ 19	1967	315	135	450	+ 180
1968	325	244	569	+ 81	1968	424	152	576	+ 272
1969	391	234	625	+ 157	1969	489	179	668	+ 310
1970	569	254	823	+ 315	1970	582	236	818	+ 346
1971	578	322	900	+ 256	1971	767	267	1,034	+ 500
1972	609	490	1,099	+ 119	1972	1,091	420	1,511	+ 671
1973	1,041	969	2,010	+ 72	1973	1,643	891	2,534	+ 752
1974	1,986	1,304	3,290	+ 682	1974	2,011	952	2,963	+1,059
1975	2,261	1,530	3,791	+ 731	1975	1,823	811	2,634	+1,012
Total	8,363	5,922	14,285	+2,441	Total	9,375	4,185	13,560	+5,190

Sources: *Far Eastern Economic Review, China Trade Report, Japan Economic Review,* and *Foreign Trade Quarterly* (Taipei) for the years in question. The figures for 1973, 1974, and 1975 were reported in *Japan Economic Review,* no. 3(1974), p. 12; no. 2(1975), p. 10; no. 2(1976), p. 8. All figures are approximate.

TABLE 11
JAPAN'S TEN TOP CUSTOMERS, 1973-1975

Unit: one million U.S. dollars

Country or Area	1973			1974			1975		
	Exports	Imports	Rank	Exports	Imports	Rank	Exports	Imports	Rank
USA	9,459	9,257	1	12,807	12,680	1	11,155	11,605	1
South Korea	1,790	1,214	2	2,656	1,570	2	2,252	1,311	4
Taiwan	1,643	891	3	2,011	952	4	1,823	811	7
Liberia	1,552	45	4	2,344	36	3	2,600	16	2
Britain	1,358	760	5	1,530	876	9	–	–	–
West Germany	1,272	1,112	6	1,500	1,459	10	1,660	1,139	9
Australia	1,195	3,496	7	2,000	4,027	5	1,740	4,156	8
Hong Kong	1,118	278	8	–	–	–	–	–	–
China	1,041	969	9	1,986	1,304	6	2,261	1,530	3
Canada	999	2,021	10	1,586	2,675	7	–	–	–
Singapore	–	–	–	1,568	618	8	–	–	–
Iran	–	–	–	–	–	–	1,857	4,978	5
Indonesia	–	–	–	–	–	–	1,851	3,432	6
USSR	–	–	–	–	–	–	1,628	1,169	10
Others	15,487	18,260	–	25,590	35,879	–	27,012	27,723	–
Total	36,914	38,303		55,578	62,076		55,839	57,870	

*Source: *Japan Economic Review*, no. 3 (1974), p. 12; no. 2 (1975), p. 10; no. 2 (1976), p. 8.

TABLE 12
JAPAN'S INVESTMENTS IN ASIA, 1951-1974

Unit: one million U.S. dollars

County or Area	FY 1973 No.	FY 1973 Amount	FY 1973 %	FY 1974 No.	FY 1974 Amount	FY 1974 %	FY 1951-1974 No.	FY 1951-1974 Amount	FY 1951-1974 %
Indonesia	143	341	9.7	113	376	15.7	443	1,190	9.4
South Korea	315	211	6.0	98	77	3.2	813	495	3.9
Hong Kong	216	123	3.5	148	51	2.1	819	274	2.1
Malaysia	117	126	3.6	78	48	2.0	374	250	2.0
Singapore	83	84	2.4	55	51	2.1	361	226	1.8
Thailand	76	34	1.0	60	31	1.3	468	194	1.5
Philippines	74	43	1.2	55	59	2.5	241	190	1.5
Taiwan	119	34	1.0	52	33	1.4	649	174	1.4
Brunei & others	22	5	0.2	23	5	0.2	208	129	0.1
Asia Total	**1,165**	**1,001**	**28.6**	**682**	**731**	**30.5**	**4,376**	**3,122**	**23.7**
World Total	**3,097**	**3,497**	**100**	**1,911**	**2,396**	**100**	**11,418**	**12,666**	**100**

Source: Japanese Ministry of International Trade and Industry, in Harvey Stockwin, "Japan: The Missing Link in ASEAN'S Blueprint,"*Far Eastern Economic Review*, no. 18 (1976) pp. 43, 46. The amount of investment is based on the number of cases approved; the figures for the period 1951-1974 are based on cumulative approvals.

face-saving remark, the Nationalist authorities promptly concluded a non-governmental aviation agreement with Japan on July 9, 1975. On that basis, CAL resumed its flights to Tokyo a month later and JAL reciprocated by setting up a dummy firm, called Japan Asia Airways (JAA), which began its flights to Taipei on September 15, 1975.[108] Peking registered no official protest. At the same time, trade between China and Japan was advancing steadily, as witness the 3½ times increase in the 1975 trade over 1972.[109] If this trend continues, Sino-Japanese trade might soon reach the $5 billion mark, as anticipated by many Japanese businessmen.[110] Moreover, the Japanese realize that the growth of their overseas sales could not continue at past rates as both the United States and Europe take protectionist postures. The Japanese markets in Southeast Asia might continue to expand but not enough to take up the slack. Taiwan's capacity is extremely limited due to the size of its population and territory, as well as its lack of natural resources. As table 10 shows, China in 1975 bought $438 million more from Japan than did Taiwan, while its two-way trade with Japan exceeded Taiwan's by over $1.1 billion. Taiwan's diplomatic isolation will be virtually complete after the recognition of the People's Republic by Singapore and Indonesia. Just as in the case of China's external trade before the Sino-American detente, so Taiwan will have to trade with foreign nations under very difficult circumstances, frequently subject to China's diplomatic pressure. Consequently, an increasing number of Japanese businessmen have begun to see the Chinese as their natural long-term partners. In particular, the oil crisis has compelled Japan to look for sources of supply other than the Middle East, and China's rising oil production promises to meet Japan's needs. China's oil export to Japan in 1975, which amounted to eight million metric tons, already constituted about 50 percent of its total exports to that country. And although estimates about China's future oil production and export vary, the Japan External Trade Organization recently predicted that it would reach 440 million tons by 1985; of this, Japan would probably import about 100 million tons, worth $9 billion at the current price of $12.85 per barrel, providing nearly 20 percent of its total oil consumption. In addition, Japan's imports of Chinese coal and natural gas are also expected to increase substantially.[111] Thus, Japan expects a huge deficit in trade with China in the coming decade, reversing the present balance of trade pattern, unless the Chinese correspondingly increase their imports of Japanese steel and plants.

108. "Japanese Airliner Leaves for Taiwan to Restore Link," *ibid.*, September 16, 1975, p. 1.

109. *Japan Economic Review,* no. 2 (1976), p. 8.

110. Masakatsu Kurita, "Normalization of Diplomatic Ties Spurs Trade Between China, Japan," *Japan Economic Review,* no. 2 (1974), p. 8.

111. Japan imported four million metric tons of Chinese crude oil at the price of $410 million in 1974. This accounted for about 30 per cent of China's total exports to Japan in that

On the question of security, it is generally agreed that the Sino-American detente and Japan's rapprochement with China have practically cancelled out the Chinese part of Japan's mutual secuirty treaty with the United States.[112] Consequently, for Japan the key to the maintenance of security and peace in East Asia no longer lies in her alliance with the United States versus China, but in keeping an equilibrium among the four involved powers: China, Japan, the Soviet Union, and the United States. Takeo Miki, when serving as deputy prime minister in the Tanaka cabinet, summarized Japan's position in the following words:

In the case of Japan, China and the United States, it is now possible to construct friendly triangular relations between the three countries as a result of the thaw in US-China relations and the restoration of Japan-China relations. But in the case of Japan, China and the Soviet Union, we cannot expect the same happy outcome because of the problems existing in China-Soviet relations. Concrete details of the Soviet Union's concept of Asian security have not as yet been revealed; but if that concept envisages a state of confrontation with China, it will fail to win China's approval. If, on the other hand, China's concept of Asian security includes policies aimed at checking the Soviet Union, it will not be acceptable to the Soviet Union. Japan must take full cognizance of these realities of China-Soviet relations, and must seek a path of friendship that does not favor one over the other. . . . . It could be that Japan might be able to play the role of a middleman in adjusting relations between the two countries.[113]

While this statement reflected the general mood of the Japanese people in regard to Japan's relationship with China and the Soviet Union, the role of a middleman in international power politics is exceedingly difficult, if not impossible. This is evidenced in the recent negotiations for a Japanese treaty of peace and friendship with the People's Republic which deadlocked mainly because of Soviet intervention. Reacting to a proposed clause opposing hegemony by any country in the Asia-Pacific region, a Chinese design to bring Japan into the anti-Soviet orbit, the Kremlin formally warned the Japanese government to take a "cautious stand" on the treaty question.[114] At the same time, private sources in Tokyo reported that the United States, while not objecting to the treaty in principle, had "privately" advised Foreign Minister Miyazawa to postpone the matter when he visited Washington in the spring of 1975 in view of its possible psychological effects on the rest of Asia

year. The value of Chinese oil exports to Japan in 1975 and its share in China's total exports to Japan are estimated on the basis of 1974 figures. See *Japan Economic Review*, no. 8 (1975), p. 12. Also see Young C. Kim, "Sino-Japanese Commercial Relations," in Joint Economic Committee of the U.S. Congress (1975), *China: A Reassessment of the Economy*, p. 607.

112. E.g., Mike Mansfield, "U.S. Foreign Policy in a Changing Pacific and Asia," *Pacific Community*, no. 4 (1974), p. 471.

113. Takeo Miki, "Future Japanese Diplomacy," *Japan Quarterly*, no. 1 (1973), pp. 21, 22.

114. "USSR Gov't Asks Japan to Take Cautious Stand," *Japan Times*, June 19, 1975, p. 1.

after the collapse of the U.S. effort in South Vietnam. Thus, considerations of security in Japan's relationship with China will not be determined solely on the basis of their bilateral interests; it depends on the development of the four-power relationship as a whole. And this, in turn, will affect the future of Sino-Japanese trade.

In sum, a degree of uneasiness will remain in Sino-Japanese relations because of the fluidity of international relations in general and Japan's unbroken marriage with Taiwan in particular. But Japan has certainly passed the most difficult period in the normalization of relations with China.

4   The Ministry of Foreign Trade

BENEATH the single aegis of China's Ministry of Foreign Trade lies a vast multi-level organization, operating both domestically and overseas, primarily commercial but with diplomatic and political functions as well—in short, a ministry of great importance for both the People's Republic and, increasingly, the world economy. It dates back to August, 1952, when the Division of Foreign Trade of the Ministry of Trade (later renamed Ministry of Commerce) was expanded into a full ministry, which was headed by Yeh Chi-chuang until his death in 1967. His long-time deputy, Lin Hai-yun, served as acting minister until replaced in 1970 by Pai Hsiang-kuo,[1] who was replaced in October, 1973 by the present Minister of Foreign Trade Li Chiang.[2] Specializing in engineering and telecommunications, Li has been a top trade official of the People's Republic since November, 1952, when he served as trade counselor in Moscow. Two years later, he became vice-minister of foreign trade, a post he held until his appointment as minister. In between, however, he twice left the MFT for other assignments. In the latter half of the 1950s he took positions in the Institute of Technology of the Chinese Academy of Sciences, the China Electronics Society, the Electronics Research Institute, the Sino-Soviet Joint Committee for Scientific and Technological Cooperation, and the Scientific Planning Commission of the State Council; and in the early 1960s he was assigned to the Commission for Economic Relations with Foreign Countries as vice-chairman (the commission later bacame a ministry).[3] His appointment as minister of foreign trade is indicative of China's increasing interest in the importation of Western technology.

According to the 1954 Organic Law of the State Council, the minister of foreign trade is assisted by an unspecified number of vice-ministers and assistant ministers.[4] In 1965, there were ten vice-ministers and two assistant ministers.[5] Then, under the impact of the Cultural Revolution and the

---

1. *China Trade Report*, no. 90 (1970), pp. 4,23; "New Foreign Trade Minister," in *ibid.*, no. 1 (1971), p. 6; "Premier Chou En-lai Meets Afghan Trade Delegation," *Peking Review*, no. 1 (1971), p. 7.
   2. See *Jen-min jih-pao*, October 23, 1973, p. 4.
   3. See Union Research Institute, *Who's Who in Communist China* (1969), p. 365.
   4. Adopted by the First NPC at its first session on September 21, 1954; promulgated by the Chairman of the People's Republic on September 28, 1954. In *FKHP 1954-1955*, vol. 1 (1956), pp. 119-121.
   5. The vice-ministers were Lei Jen-min, Li Chiang, Lin Hai-yun, Chiang Ming, Lu

concurrent program for the simplification of the administrative apparatus, many of these officials were either removed or transferred.[6] When the new Constitution was promulgated in January, 1975, there were five vice-ministers (Chai Shu-fan, Chen Chieh, Chen Shu-fu, Chou Hua-min, and Yao I-lin) and two assistant ministers (Liu Hsi-wen and Tu Yu-yun). Of these top officials, Li Chiang is concurrently one of the 195 members of the Tenth Central Committee of the CCP, and Vice-Minister Yao I-lin an alternate member.[7] Prior to Yao's appointment as vice-minister he served in various capacities as vice-minister of trade and, later, commerce (1949-1959); minister of commerce (1959-1965); and concurrently as deputy director of the Office of Finance and Trade under the State Council and director of the Department of Finance and Trade under the Central Committee of the CCP.[8] His transfer to the new portfolio, nominally a demotion, suggests a measure of closer coordination between the internal and external aspects of China's commercial policy as the socialization of private commerce is almost complete.

Before 1966, the Ministry of Foreign Trade worked in close coordination with the Department of Finance and Trade of the Central Committee of the CCP and the Office of Finance and Trade under the State Council. After the reorganization of the CCP and the State Council during the Cultural Revolution, it is no longer certain whether these two offices are still in existence. As of 1971, the Ministry of Foreign Trade consisted of five regional bureaus dealing with the Soviet Union and Asiatic socialist states, East Europe, West Europe and Oceania, Afro-Asian nations, and Latin America; three functional bureaus handling import, export and planning affairs; two administrative offices managing personnel and accounting matters; two specialized agencies for customs affairs and commodity inspection; a political department in charge of ideological and security affairs; an international market research institute; a foreign trade personnel training school; and several foreign trade, transportation, and publication corporations.[9] A later

---

Hsu-chang, Pai Hsiang-yin, Yang Hao-lu, Fu Sheng-ling, Chou Hua-min, and Chia Shih; the assistant ministers were Li Cho-chih and Liu Hsi-wen. See *Jen-min shou-ts'e 1965*, p. 126.

6. For a general discussion, see Richard K. Diao, "The Impact of the Cultural Revolution on China's Economic Elite," in *China Quarterly*, no. 42 (1970), pp. 65, 73.

7. See *Hung-ch'i*, no. 9 (1973), pp. 34-35.

8. See the respective volumes of *Jen-min shou-ts'e*.

9. See Japan External Trade Organization, *How to Approach the China Market*, p. 24; Feng-hwa Mah, *The Foreign Trade of Mainland China*, pp. 4-5. Before the Cultural Revolution, there were several foreign trade personnel training schools in Peking, Shanghai and other places. Whether all these schools are still functioning is not known. For the establishment of the Political Department, see *Ta-kung pao* (Peking), June 7, 1964, p. 1; December 10, 1964, p. 1. As reported by these sources, political departments were initially established in the ministries of commerce, food, and foreign trade, as well as several banking and commercial institutions. Later they were founded in all government agencies.

reorganization took place, reducing the regional bureaus to four by incorporating the Latin American Bureau into the Bureau in charge of West European, American and Oceanian affairs. The import and export bureaus were probably abolished, but other administrative units, such as planning, personnel, accounting, and personnel training, still exist.[10] The political department was strengthened, and the national foreign trade corporations now number nine, in addition to several foreign trade related organizations.

According to the 1975 Constitution, the Ministry of Foreign Trade remains under the jurisdiction of the State Council. The MFT exercises direct supervision over its local branches, called foreign trade bureaus, and works in close coordination with other government agencies concerned with foreign trade, such as the CCPIT, the Ministry of Finance, the People's Bank of China, the Bank of China, various insurance companies, the State Planning Commission, the Ministry of Economic Relations with Foreign Countries, the Ministry of Communications, and the Ministry of Foreign Affairs. Outside China, the MFT is responsible for the appointment of commercial counselors and attachès to Chinese diplomatic missions abroad, the assignment of permanent or visiting official trade delegations overseas, the development of trade relations and technical cooperation with foreign states, and the conclusion of trade treaties and agreements with foreign governments on behalf of the People's Republic. The internal functions of the MFT include planning, licensing, customs work, quality control, trade operation, the role of the CCPIT, and the Kwangchow trade fair.

Planning

In China foreign trade is an integral part of national economic planning. The 1954 Constitution provided: "By economic planning, the state directs the growth and transformation of the national economy to bring about the constant increase of productive forces, in this way enriching the material and cultural life of the people and consolidating the independence and security of the country" (article 15). Under the 1954 Constitution the National People's Congress was vested with the power "to decide on the national economic plan" (article 27) and the State Council was charged with formulating and executing the plans under the supervision of the Standing Committee of the NPC. In practice, this legal formality was waived after the adoption of

10. There are conflicting reports concerning the internal structure of the MFT, and even the consolidation of the Latin American Bureau is uncertain, given China's emphasis on its role in the Third World. In a 1975 United States government publication, entitled "Foreign Trade Organizations of the PRC," the existence of these administrative units and the Political Department was not mentioned. The publication has no author identification and is distributed through the Library of Congress.

the First FYP in 1955.[11] Acting under the authority of the Central Committee of the CCP, the State Council assumed all basic responsibilities for economic planning. According to the 1975 Constitution, "The state . . . promotes the planned and proportionate development of the socialist economy. . . . " (article 10). Under this fundamental law, the National People's Congress is again vested with the authority to "approve the national economic plan" (article 17) on the basis of the draft prepared by the State Council.

Prior to 1956, the principal agency responsible for the preparation of both long-range and annual economic plans was the State Council's State Planning Commission, which was created in 1952 and formalized in 1955.[12] Under its 1955 operational rule, the Commission consisted of two staff offices, one research and editing office, and twenty-three planning bureaus in charge of various sectors of the national economy, including foreign trade. Then in May, 1956 a new State Economic Commission was founded, taking over from the State Planning Commission the responsibility of making annual plans on the basis of the five-year and other long-range plans prepared by the latter.[13] Organizationally and functionally, these two commissions had their counterparts in all central and local government and production units.[14] More recently, having absorbed the State Economic Commission and the State Statistical Bureau, the State Planning Commission is again designated as the sole national agency responsible for both long-range and annual plans.[15] A similar reorganization took place at the local level.

In the area of foreign trade, as in other sectors of the economy, the State Planning Commission makes preliminary estimates and issues initial control figures of imports and exports for long-range and annual plans respectively on the basis of the overall economic goals and the statistical

11. The first FYP was adopted by the First NPC at its second session, July 30, 1955, in *FKHP 1955*, vol. 2 (1956), p. 129. The second and third FYPs were adopted without formal legislative enactments. The last report of the State Council on the National Planning Conference and the 1970 National Economic Plan was approved by the Second Plenum of the Ninth Central Committee of the CCP. See the Plenum's communique, September 6, 1970, in *Jen-min jih-pao,* September 10, 1970, p. 1. The fourth FYP went into effect in 1971 obviously by similar procedures.

12. Central People's Government Council decision of November 15, 1952, in *FLHP 1952* (1954), p. 37; Provisional Operational Rule for the State Planning Commission, approved by the State Council on October 26, 1955, in *FKHP 1955*, vol. 2 (1956), p. 72.

13. Proposal of the Premier for Reorganization of the Finance and Economic Departments under the State Council, May 11, 1956, ratified by a resolution of the Standing Committee of the NPC, May 12, 1956, in *FKHP 1956*, vol. 3 (1956), p. 79.

14. Provisional Organic Rule for Planning Committees of the Local People's Councils, February 18, 1956, in *FKHP 1956*, vol. 3 (1956), p. 54.

15. Audrey Donnithorne, "Recent Economic Developments," *China Quarterly*, no. 60 (1974), p. 772. For a discussion of the work of the State Statistical Bureau before its absorption by the State Planning Commission, see Choh-Ming Li, *The Statistical System of Communist China*.

information it has received from various sources. These control figures go to the MFT, which maps out general import and export plans in accordance with the PRC's political relations with and existing contractual commitments to foreign trading partners; the nature of import and export commodities involved; world market conditions; domestic demand and export capability; and the amount of foreign currencies and external credits available.[16] These general plans are then transmitted to the national foreign trade corporations as guidelines for their specific import and export plans. After review by the MFT, these become part of the general trade plans which, in turn, are part of the national economic plan. Finally, after approval of the national plan by the State Council, the MFT assumes the ultimate responsibility of supervising the national foreign trade corporations in executing their specific plans.[17]

Licensing

The basic purpose of licensing is to protect the national economy against old foreign interests in China and to facilitate socialist economic planning through the control of foreign trade operation. The 1949 Common Program provided: "The People's Republic of China must abolish all the prerogatives of imperialist countries in China" (article 3); and "All legitimate public and private trade shall be protected. Control shall be exercised over foreign trade and the policy of protecting trade shall be adopted" (article 37). Thus, all import and export firms were required to register with local foreign trade bureaus. In the case of foreign firms, such registration was to be recommended by a local department of foreign affairs and approved by the MFT (prior to 1952, by the Ministry of Trade) before the firms could operate at a designated place.[18] Imports and exports were each classified into several general categories, and permits were issued on this basis.[19] Unless otherwise

16. The earliest regulation empowering the Ministry of Trade to make general foreign trade plans is in Government Administration Council Decision on the Enforcement Rules for Unification of State Trading Throughout the Country, March 10, 1950, in *FLHP 1949-1950*, vol. 2 (1952), p. 326. Subsequently, however, no other statutory information on the subject has been made available.

17. Feng-hwa Mah, *The Foreign Trade of Mainland China*, pp. 6-12; Nai-Ruenn Chen and Walter Galenson, *The Chinese Economy Under Communism*, p. 199; Japan External Trade Organization, *How to Approach the China Market*, p. 9. For more recent works on the question of planning in general, see Audrey Donnithorne, *The Budget and the Plan in China: Central-Local Economic Relations;* Nicholas R. Lardy, "Economic Planning in the People's Republic of China: Central-Provincial Fiscal Relations," in Joint Economic Committee of the U.S. Congress (1975). *China: A Reassessment of the Economy*, p. 94.

18. Provisional Regulation for the Control of Foreign Trade, December 8, 1950, arts. 3 and 4, in *FLHP 1949-1950*, vol. 2 (1952), p. 337.

19. The PRC's classification of import and export goods has changed several times over the years in accordance with the changing conditions of the national economy. The regulation of

approved by the authorities concerned, all payments were to be made through designated official foreign-exchange banks. Persons in violation of these and other related provisions were subject to "education," warning, suspension of business operations, and, in serious cases, formal legal punishment through court trials.[20]

Due to these and other measures of socialist transformation, such as the control of payments, bank credits, sources of supply, and labor, virtually all foreign firms were out of business by 1956. Observers outside China interpreted this as a result of Chinese nationalization or confiscation of foreign property, but, China has never passed a law confiscating alien interests. High officials of the Peking government attributed the discontinuation of foreign business in China primarily to the abolition of "imperialist privileges" in China by the Chinese government; the United States embargo which cut off supplies to China and thus paralyzed the operation of many foreign firms; the transfer of alien property to the Chinese government through voluntary sale or abandonment; and the freezing of American assets in China in retaliation for United States government control of Chinese assets in areas under American jurisdiction.[21]

December 8, 1950, cited above, provided for four categories of imports and exports, to be controlled by ordinary permits, the national foreign trade corporations, the Ministry of Trade and its successor the MFT, and the state itself. For reference to these early classifications, see Kwangchow Foreign Trade Control Bureau, ed., *Tui-wai mao-i shou-ts'e,* pp. 41-90.

The first FYP specified forty-six major industrial products, five food grains, six technical crops, and seven kinds of animals for planned production without mentioning their control in foreign trade. See the First Five-Year Plan for the Development of the National Economy 1953-1957, in *FKHP 1955,* vol. 2 (1956), pp. 156-158, 200 and 208.

In 1959, a list of commodities, divided into three categories, was released. Category 1 embraced 38 items to be absolutely controlled by the State Council through administration by the ministries of food, commerce, foreign trade, light industry, and public health. Category 2 consisted of 293 items to be managed by the ministries of commerce, food, foreign trade, marine products, and public health according to policy laid down by the State Council. Category 3 consisted of all items not included in the other two categories or specifically mentioned in government regulations; these were to be managed primarily by the ministries of commerce and public health. See Report of the Ministries of Commerce, Food, Foreign Trade, Public Health, Marine Products, and Light Industry on the Regulation for Control of Commodities by Category, February 6, 1959, endorsed by the State Council on February 12, 1959, in *FKHP 1959,* vol. 9 (1959), pp. 158-163.

These classifications, however, were basically for planning purposes. Since the socialization of the foreign trade sector of the national economy in 1956, all imports and exports have been licensed except those specifically exempted by the MFT, which are discussed below.

20. Provisional Regulation for the Control of Foreign Trade, December 8, 1950, arts. 5-11. The system of import and export permits was not put into effect until November, 1953. During the interim, the People's Republic retained the old system of "customs declaration" to control foreign trade. See "National Customs Affairs Conference," in *Jen-min shou-ts'e 1953,* p. 412; "The Kwangtung Customs House Adopted the System of Import and Export Permits," in *Ching-chi tao-pao,* no. 50 (1953), p. 18.

21. Hsueh Mu-chiao, Su Hsing and Lin Tse-li, *The Socialist Transformation of the National Economy in China,* p. 33. Aside from three joint shipping companies that China has set

Chinese-owned private import and export firms and industries, like other private concerns, were by 1956 converted to joint state-private operation—a Chinese form of state capitalism. Under this arrangement the state took full control of the management of a private import and export business while permitting its shareholders to receive fixed dividends at a rate of 5 percent annually of their original investment and irrespective of the actual earnings or losses of the enterprise.[22] Payment of such dividends continued for about ten years, but the practice was not renewed when the last term expired in 1965.

Socialization of the foreign trade sector of the Chinese economy, basically accomplished by 1956, was followed a year later by a new Regulation Governing the Issuance of Export and Import Permits.[23] According to this regulation, which superseded all previous regulations on the subject, permits are required for the importation and exportation of all goods except those exempted by the MFT.[24] (Twenty-three categories of imports and seventeen categories of exports are exempt from licensing; see below.) Traders are classified into three general groups: foreign trade corporations exclusively owned by the state or under state-private joint management; Chinese or foreign private traders; and other enterprises, state organs, social groups, schools, and individuals. Procedures for the application of import or export permits are basically the same for all three groups: each applicant must fill out an import or export form to be approved by an MFT bureau or a local foreign trade bureau. With this approval, he then prepares another application, known as Schedule of Import or Export Goods, for the examination and release of his cargo by the customs office. In the case of a private merchant, endorsement of his application by a local branch of the Bank of China is necessary.

The application must be accompanied by specified documents for customs inspections. In the case of imports, these normally are: bills of lading, invoices and their duplicate copies, packing lists, contracts, manufacturer's invoices, certificates of origin, and certificates of provenance.

---

up with Albania, Poland and Tanzania, there are currently only two private foreign firms in Shanghai: the Hong Kong and Shanghai Bank, and the Chartered Bank. Both banks limit their operations to transactions involving the British and Chinese governments.

22. State Council regulation of February 8, 1956, in *FKHP 1956,* vol. 3 (1956), p. 282; State Council decree of July 28, 1956, in *FKHP 1956,* vol. 4 (1957), p. 355.

23. The promulgation was made by an order of the MFT on January 23, 1957, in *FKHP 1957,* vol. 5 (1957), p. 163.

24. The previous regulations were: Enforcement Rules for the Provisional Regulation for the Control of Foreign Trade, promulgated by the Ministry of Trade on December 28, 1950; MFT Decision on the Handling of Import Goods without Permits by the Customs, March 20, 1953; Enforcement Rules for the System of Import and Export Trade Permits, promulgated by the MFT on November 16, 1953.

In the case of exports, the specified documents are: shipping orders or consignment notes, invoices, packing lists, contracts, and testing certificates.[25] Expired permits must be renewed or surrendered to the issuing bureau. The customs may detain goods leaving or entering the country without permits or sufficient documentary proof. The cargo-owner may claim the goods within three months after receiving the customs' notice of detention by submitting the required permits and documents; otherwise, the goods will be disposed of by the customs.[26]

Customs Work

In accordance with the government's established policy of control and protection, the customs was assigned a critical role in the operation of foreign trade. Speaking to a May Day rally in 1950, Liu Shao-chi, then Vice Chairman of the People's Republic, declared:

Imperialism has been ousted from China, and its prerogatives in China have been abolished. New China's customs policy and foreign trade policy have become important instruments to protect its industrial development. This is to say, we have put the key to China's front door in our own pocket, instead of putting it in the pockets of imperialism and its running dogs, as happened in the past. From now on, China's industries will no longer suffer from the competition of imperialism's low-priced commodities. China's raw materials will be first allocated to meet the needs of her own industries. In this way, one of the greatest obstacles to the development of China's industries during the past one hundred years will be eliminated.[27]

Prior to the founding of the People's Republic, there were a total of 173 customs houses in China with a staff of twelve thousand, including 234 Europeans and Americans, who all held important administrative positions. The head of the staff was Inspector-General L. K. Little, an American citizen. In addition to its normal duties, the customs was also responsible for coastal

25. Also see Provisional Customs Law, March 23, 1951, arts. 106, 107, in *FLHP 1951*, vol. 1 (1953), p. 198.

26. The proceeds of the sale, after deducting expenses incurred, are used to defray the payment of duty, taxes and other expenses connected with the impounded goods in the following order: customs duty; other taxes and dues collected by the customs; customs fines and late payment fees; freight and miscellaneous charges; and warehouse and sundry charges. The balance, if any, may be refunded to the cargo-owner on application within six months, provided no violation of the trade control regulations has been found by the customs; it is remitted to the national treasury if not claimed in six months. See Chen Ti-pao, "Supervision and Control of Imports and Exports by the Chinese Customs Administration," *Foreign Trade of the PRC*, no. 2 (1963) pp. 2-3. Also see Customs Regulation for the Handling of Forfeited Articles, November 6, 1958, in *FKHP 1958*, vol. 8 (1959), p. 212.

27. In *Jen-min jih-pao*, May 1, 1950, p. 1. For other references concerning the reform of the customs, see "Customs Offices Throughout the Country Undertake Reform," *ibid.*, July 24, 1950, p. 2; Yang Po, "New China's Customs Policy and Foreign Trade," *ibid.*, August 18, 1950, p. 5; Chen Ti-pao, "The Levying Task of the People's Customs," *ibid.*, August 18, 1950, p. 5; Kung Yuan, "Summary Report of the National Customs Conference to the Central People's Government, October 6, 1950," *ibid.*, November 12, 1950, p. 2.

security, administration of harbor affairs, waterways, light houses, and buoys, preparation of weather reports; disposal of the customs revenues; and collection of war indemnities. In fact, customs revenues were held by the foreign powers in China as securities against the payment of indemnities and loans owed by the pre-1949 Chinese government.[28]

Under the new government, all these extra functions of the customs were either abolished or transferred to other government agencies, and the 173 customs houses were reduced to 70, of which 26 were district customs offices, 9 were branches, and 35 were sub-branches. (In 1961, four district customs offices and four branches were established in Tibet, bringing the total to 78 customs houses.)[29] The General Customs Administration was made an independent unit of the Government Administration Council in 1949 with one director and several deputy directors, and ten divisions in charge of staff work, tariff control (including the drafting of international tariff agreements), supervision of cargo movements, investigation of smuggling, maritime affairs, financial affairs, foreign trade statistics, inspection, personnel, and general administrative work.[30]

In order to meet the needs of the First FYP, a government decision of January 9, 1953, placed the customs under the direct jurisdiction of the MFT and merged the foreign trade bureaus in trading ports with the local customs houses.[31] This unusual practice did not last very long, and the foreign trade bureaus soon resumed their separate duties. The General Customs Administration has, however, remained a subordinate unit of the MFT.[32] The organizational establishment, alteration, or abolition of its branches and sub-branches has remained within the sole jurisdiction of the MFT, subject only to the

28. Moh Ju-chien, "New China's Customs Administration," in *People's China*, no. 2 (1951), p. 13; "National Customs Affairs Conference," in *Jen-min shou-ts'e 1951*, p. 50 (wei); Ting Kuei-tang, "The Key to China's Front Door Is Truly in the Chinese People's Hands," in *Jen-min jih-pao*, September 20, 1954, p. 3.

29. Government Administration Council Decision on Tariff Policy and Customs Work, January 27, 1950, in *FLHP 1949-1950*, vol. 2 (1952), pp. 347-348; Government Administration Council Directive on the Principles of Establishing Customs Offices and Adjusting the Structure of the Customs Throughout the Country, December 14, 1950, in *FLHP 1949-1950*, vol. 2 (1952), p. 350; State Council Decision to Establish Customs Houses in Tibet, December 15, 1961, in *FKHP 1960-1961*, vol. 12 (1962), p. 83.

30. Experimental Regulation for the Organization of the General Customs Administration, December 30, 1949, in *FLHP 1949-1950*, vol. 2 (1952), p. 343; Provisional Customs Law, March 23, 1951, arts. 7-9, in *FLHP 1951*, vol. 1 (1953), pp. 185-6. For a discussion of the Customs' foreign trade statistical work, which is an important part of foreign trade planning, see Chen Chih-shih and Liu Po-wu, *Tui-wai mao-i t'ung-chi hsüeh*.

31. Government Administration Council Decision on the Consolidation of the Customs with Foreign Trade Control Institutions, January 9, 1953, ratified by a resolution of the Central People's Government Council, January 14, 1953, in *FLHP 1953* (1955), pp. 7-8. At the central level, the General Foreign Trade Control Bureau within the MFT was also merged with the General Customs Administration. Later, this bureau was abolished.

32. State Council Notice on Adjusting Local Customs Assignments and Leadership Relations, September 5, 1955, in *FKHP 1955*, vol. 2 (1956), p. 594.

advice and consent of the ministries of finance and public security and the local governments concerned.[33] Operationally, local customs offices, like local foreign trade bureaus, work under the dual leadership and supervision of local governments and the MFT.[34]

Like licensing, the collection of duties is used to control the nature and volume of China's foreign trade. The People's Republic has adopted a protective tariff policy providing either low rates or exemptions for capital equipment, industrial raw materials, agricultural machinery, grain seeds, fertilizers, and other things which China produces only in limited quantities or cannot produce at all. On the other hand, China imposes high duty rates on goods abundantly produced or manufactured in the country and on manufactures and semi-manufactures not amply produced in the country at present but which may be developed in the future. For luxuries and non-essentials, China stipulates even higher duty rates. In addition, the government provides reduced duty rates for imports purchased and shipped from countries having "mutually beneficial" trade treaties or agreements with China, while general duty rates are levied on imports from countries which do not have such treaties or agreements with China.[35] The reduced duty rates for imports range from 5 to 150 percent, and the general duty rates from 7.5 to 400 percent.[36]

Imports are classified into 17 groups, including 89 types encompassing 939 items. Customs valuations are on the basis of CIF (cost, insurance, and freight) prices: normal wholesale market value of the goods in the country of origin plus foreign export duties and all charges incurred before discharge at the place of importation in China, such as packing charges, freight, insurance premiums, and commissions (subject to verification and approval by the customs). For export from China, all but 96 items are exempt from duties. The dutiable value of these items is assessed on the basis of FOB (free on board) prices, excluding export duty, if any, and subject to verification and approval by the customs. If the normal wholesale market value for imports or the FOB value for exports cannot be ascertained, the dutiable value shall be determined by the customs.[37] Beyond those provided for in the tariff, duty

33. Provisional Customs Law, March 23, 1951, art. 13, in *FLHP 1951*, vol. 1 (1953), p. 183; State Council reply to the MFT, January 26, 1962, in *FKHP 1962-1963*, vol. 13 (1964), p. 147.

34. State Council notice of September 5, 1955, in *FKHP 1955*, vol. 2 (1956), pp. 594-5.

35. Government Administration Council Decision on Tariff Policy and Customs Work, January 27, 1950, in *FLHP 1949-1950*, vol. 2 (1952), pp. 347 and 349; Provisional Enforcement Rules for the Customs Import and Export Tariff, May 4, 1951, art. 4, in *FLHP 1951*, vol. 2 (1953), p. 344.

36. Customs Import and Export Tariff, May 4, 1951, in *FLHP 1951*, vol. 2 (1953), p. 213. Tibet has its own tariff. See Provisional Regulation for the Collection of Import and Export Duties by Customs Houses in Tibet Region, adopted by the State Council on December 15, 1961, in *FKHP 1962-1963*, vol. 13 (1964), pp. 148-153.

37. Customs Import and Export Tariff, May 4, 1951; Provisional Enforcement Rules for

exemptions are accorded to certain imports and exports: (1) advertising matter and trade samples for free distribution, having no other use and no commercial value; (2) items such as dutiable samples, exhibition articles, theatrical costumes and paraphernalia, and engineering equipment, which are temporarily imported to be exported abroad within six months or which are temporarily exported to be returned within a fixed period of time; (3) machinery and other goods imported from or exported abroad for repairs or for installing additional parts, to be exported or returned within a prescribed time limit (import duty is charged on the cost of repairs, and/or additional parts installed abroad); (4) exports of Chinese origin returned from abroad for any justifiable reason, if importation is applied for by the original shipper with supporting documentary evidence covering original export, subject to verification by the customs; (5) fuel and stores used in means of conveyance proceeding abroad, and provisions for the crew and passengers on board; (6) other cases such as damaged cargo, which are granted duty exemptions in accordance with customs regulations or on special authority.[38]

The power to decide tariff interpretation, tariff classification of goods and the dutiable value of goods rests with the customs house concerned. Should the consignee or shipper or his agent disagree with its decision he may file a protest in writing with the customs house within fourteen days from the date of the duty valuation memo. On receipt of the protest, the customs house shall review the case within seven days and may modify the original decision. If the original decision is not modified, the customs house shall transmit the protest, together with its comments, to the General Customs Administration for review. If the original decision is modified and the petitioner is still not satisfied, he may protest again to the same customs house within seven days after receiving the modified decision. The customs house is required to transmit within seven days the new protest to the General Customs Administration. In either case, however, the latter's decision is final.[39]

---

the Customs Import and Export Tariff, May 4, 1951, arts. 5 and 8, in *FLHP 1951*, vol. 2 (1953), pp. 344-5.

38. See Chen Ti-pao, "Supervision and Control of Imports and Exports by the Chinese Customs Administration," in *Foreign Trade of the PRC*, no. 2 (1963), pp. 2, 3; Regulation for the Exemption of Import and Export Duties for Cultural and Educational Articles, amended and promulgated by the MFT and the Ministry of Finance on February 16, 1959, in *FKHP 1959*, vol. 9 (1959), p. 190; Customs Regulation for the Supervision of Import and Export Trade Samples and Advertising Matter, second amendment, promulgated by the MFT on March 27, 1959, in *FKHP 1959*, vol. 9 (1959), p. 192.

39. Provisional Enforcement Rules for the Customs Import and Export Tariff, May 4, 1951, arts. 13 and 14, in *FLHP 1951*, vol. 2 (1953), p. 346. For reference to other functions of the customs, see Provisional Customs Law, March 23, 1951, in *FLHP 1951*, vol. 1 (1953), p. 183; Customs Regulation Awarding the Investigation of Smuggling, promulgated by the MFT on January 9, 1958, in *FKHP 1958*, vol. 8 (1959), p. 179.

Quality Control

For the purpose of developing foreign trade and protecting standards of domestic production, the government convened in May, 1950 a national conference to discuss the questions of quality control, weight survey, and packing.[40] This resulted in the adoption of a regulation establishing a national Bureau for the Inspection and Testing of Commodities with branches in main trading ports and producing areas.[41] In 1953, a new regulation, superseding the former, extended the organization of these bureaus to key transport centers and inland areas where import and export goods were concentrated and distributed. Within the MFT itself, a General Administration for the Inspection and Testing of Commodities was also established to oversee the work.[42] By 1966, in step with the steady development of foreign trade, the number of the local bureaus and their branches had increased to twenty-seven throughout the country.[43]

The local bureaus and their branches are equipped with modern apparatus and instruments, and staffed by experienced technicians to meet particular requirements. Inspectors are frequently sent to industrial plants to make a field inspection of goods as they are being manufactured or processed. In the case of major export commodities (such as cotton textiles, frozen meat, canned goods, egg products, rubber and canvas shoes, and sewing machines), the bureaus assign technical representatives to reside at the production units. In addition, every industrial plant producing commodities for export has its own technical supervision organization, with equipment and personnel, to examine the raw materials and semi-finished and finished products. The national foreign trade corporations also station resident technical personnel in these plants to maintain a field check.[44]

Under the 1950 regulation, export goods subject to inspection and testing consisted of 27 classes and 215 types; among import goods, there were 9 classes and 29 types.[45] The 1953 regulation provided "legal inspection and testing" for: export and import commodities that are officially listed by the government for testing; that are required to be tested by the foreign trade contracts of state enterprises; that may have suffered damage by insects or

40. "The Ministry of Trade Convened the Conference on Commodity Inspection and Testing," in *Jen-min jih-pao,* May 27, 1950, p. 2.
41. Provisional Regulation for the Inspection and Testing of Commodities, November 15, 1951, art. 4, in *FLHP 1951,* vol. 2 (1953), p. 448.
42. Provisional Regulation for the Inspection and Testing of Export and Import Commodities, December 17, 1953, art. 2, in *FLHP 1954* (1955), pp. 71-2.
43. Liao Ti-jen, "Inspection of China's Export Commodities," in *China's Foreign Trade,* no. 1 (1966), p. 20. Liao was then Director of the General Administration for the Inspection and Testing of Commodities.
44. *Ibid.*
45. The list was published by the Ministry of Trade in *Jen-min jih-pao,* May 27, 1950, p. 2.

pests; and that may have been adulterated. While no new official list of goods subject to inspection and testing has been made available, an authoritative source has stated that they have increased to "several thousand" types.[46] The standards and methods of inspection and testing are either those stipulated by the MFT or by individual foreign trade contracts.

If the seller, purchaser, or any interested party to a foreign trade deal disagrees with the result of the inspection, he may, under the 1953 regulation, apply for reinspection. If after reinspection he still disagrees with the result, he may submit a petition to the local government which has jurisdiction over the inspecting bureau to review the case. The applicant or petitioner is responsible, however, for all consequences arising from the delay in delivery and all expenses incurred during the reinspection or the review.

The Bureau for the Inspection and Testing of Commodities, at the request of the concerned foreign trade corporation, also determines the weight of export merchandise and inspects the quality of the materials used in packing, and the packing itself. To insure that packing conforms to the terms specified in a contract, meets the prescribed standards so as to be capable of protecting the quality of merchandise, and is suitable for long-distance transport, a China National Export Commodities Packing Corporation was created in 1974 under the general supervision of the MFT.[47]

In addition, the bureau handles all notary work relating to a foreign trade transaction. Upon receiving an application from a direct or interested party to the transaction, it can, for example, certify the actual state of delivery. In all, the bureau issues four types of documents: Certificate of Origin, Certificate of Inspection and Testing, Survey Report for Weight, and Notary Certificate. Unless otherwise specifically approved by the MFT, permit applications for all goods subject to inspection and testing must be supported by these documents before they will be allowed to leave or enter the country by the customs.

Finally, the bureau is empowered to discipline its inspectors and notary workers who made mistakes because of negligence; and it can send them to a local judicial organ for prosecution and trial if they are suspected of malfeasance. If a person applying for inspection and testing has altered purchasing or sales documents; changed the inspected goods or the quality or quantity of the inspected goods; intentionally altered, removed, or extinguished the bureau's stamps, seals, or any other marks on the inspected package or goods; he is subject to a maximum fine of not more than 20 percent

46. Liao Ti-jen, "Inspection of China's Export Commodities," *loc. cit.*, p. 22.

47. For a discussion of quality, weight and packing conditions, see Shanghai Foreign Languages Institute, Department of Foreign Languages for Foreign Trade, *Tui-wai mao-i shih-wu*, pp. 3, 7, and 17. For reference to packing work, see "New Improved Packaging and Packing for Light Industrial Goods from Shanghai," in *Foreign Trade of the PRC*, no. 4 (1963), p. 9.

of the total value of the goods recorded in the inspection certificate. The bureau may request a local judicial organ to handle the case if the delinquent person does not make the payment or refuses to accept the imposition of the fine.

On the whole, China has shown great concern for the quality of its products. The state requires all producers to fulfill both the quantitative and qualitative targets set forth by the economic plans and contracts. The importance of adherence to standards is seen as going beyond mere trade to involving China's national reputation.[48]

The National Foreign Trade Corporations

China began its state trading operations with six national corporations under the Ministry of Trade in 1950.[49] After a long process of expansion, merger, and reorganization, there are now a total of sixteen trade and related corporations, including the National Export Commodities Packing Corporation mentioned earlier. Of these, eight are engaged in regular merchandise trade, and cover: cereals, oils, and foodstuffs; chemical products; light industrial products; machinery; technical import; metals and minerals; native produce and animal by-products; and textiles. The China National Complete Plant Export Corporation is under the jurisdiction of the Ministry of Economic Relations with Foreign Countries, but because the activities of this corporation are part of Chinese aid programs, which in turn are tied to trade, it is technically regarded as a foreign trade corporation supervised by the MFT. There are four literary, film, and stamp corporations: the National Publications Center, responsible for the export of books, periodicals, and newspapers of various languages published in China; the National Publications Import Corporation, newly split from the National Publications Center, for the purchase of foreign publications to enhance China's knowledge of the international scene; the National Film Distribution Corporation, for the import and export of foreign and Chinese films; and the National Stamp Export Corporation, for the export of Chinese stamps. Judging from the nature of their business, these four corporations are probably all connected with the

48. For reference to early PRC inspection work, see State Council Instruction to Industrial Departments and the Ministry of Foreign Trade, in *Jen-min jih-pao,* July 18, 1956, p. 3; Kuo Chung-yen, *Hsin Chung-kuo ti kung-yeh-p'in ch'u-k'ou mao-i,* p. 44. For more recent references, see "The Problem of Quality Is a Problem of the [Political] Line," in *Jen-min jih-pao,* April 6, 1972, p. 2; "Raise the Quality of Products to the First Place," in *ibid.,* April 19, 1972, p. 2; Chang Ming, "Inspection of China's Export Commodities," *China's Foreign Trade,* no. 1 (1974), pp. 9, 41.

49. Government Administration Council Decision on the Enforcement Rules for Unification of State Trading Throughout the Country, March 10, 1950, art. 1, para. 3, in *FLHP 1949-1950,* vol 2 (1952), pp. 325-6.

Ministry of Culture although they operate under the general guidance of the MFT. Finally, there are two shipping agencies: the National Chartering Corporation, which handles the chartering of vessels and the booking of shipping space for Chinese import and export cargoes, as well as doing similar business on behalf of principals abroad, and canvassing cargoes for ship owners; and the National Foreign Trade Transportation Corporation, which arranges customs clearance and delivery of import and export cargoes by land, sea and air, or by post. Both of these corporations are assisted by six other transportation agencies under the Ministry of Communications: the China Ocean Shipping Company, China Ocean Shipping Agency, the Sino-Albanian Joint Shipping Company, the Sino-Polish Joint Shipbrokers Company, the Sino-Tanzanian Joint Shipping Company, and the Civil Aviation Administration of China—the flag carrier of the People's Republic.[50]

A foreign trade corporation, unlike an MFT bureau which is a state organ and usually does not participate in civil law activities, engages directly in trade and is responsible for its own losses and profits according to the system of "economic accountability."[51] As such, it assumes juristic personality and implements the foreign trade plan through the formation of contracts with both domestic and foreign partners.[52] However, since China does not have a corporation law, it is impossible to determine the exact legal nature of such a juristic person and its capacity to assume liabilities. The only authoritative source on the subject is the civil law textbook published by China's leading law school, in Peking in 1958, according to which a juristic person must meet four requirements. First, it must be an organization approved by the state and governed by a charter (i.e., articles of incorporation). Second, it must possess a property separate from its own members and other organizations and independently controlled by its own will. Third, it must be able to assume property liabilities in civil matters; the treasury of the state is not responsible for its obligations. Fourth, it must be able to use its own name to participate in civil lawsuits as plaintiff or defendant.[53]

These four requirements are essentially the same as those the USSR requires of Soviet juristic persons.[54] However, unlike their Soviet counterparts, the Chinese corporations have never published their charters. From a

50. *Hsiangkang ching-chi nien-chien 1976*, Part V, pp. 133-134. Information concerning corporations not in this source was obtained through interviews.

51. Government Administration Council Decision, March 10, 1950, art. 3, in *FLHP 1949-1950*, vol. 2 (1952), p. 327.

52. For reference to the domestic contracts, see Gene T. Hsiao, "The Role of Economic Contracts in Communist China," *California Law Review* 53: 1029 (1965).

53. Central Political-Legal Cadres School, Teaching and Research Institute of Civil Law, ed., *Chung-hua jen-min kung-ho-kuo min-fa chi-pen wen-t'i*, p. 68.

54. James Henry Giffen, *The Legal and Practical Aspects of Trade with the Soviet Union*, p. 153.

purely legal point of view, the lack of a corporation law and the secrecy of the corporate charters, if any, may become a hazard in transactions with the Chinese corporations. For like its Soviet counterpart, a Chinese corporation is legally .capable of entering into transactions only in accordance with the purposes specified by its charter and to the extent that its assets permit. Transactions inconsistent with the charter may be invalid, and claims in excess of the corporation's capital may not prevail. However, in practice, the Chinese have publicized each corporations's "scope of activities" or the type of business each corporation is permitted to do.[55] As to the question of corporate assets, the Chinese have also let it be known unofficially that the state treasury supports all corporation business activities, including liabilities arising from foreign claims. Thus, it is possible that the Chinese have simply abandoned the legalistic approach of the Soviet Union to the status and activities of trade corporations.

Officially, a Chinese corporation is not a consuming or producing unit but a middleman in the planned economy. As such, it does not possess fixed assets such as factories and machines. Its only asset is working capital appropriated to it by the state.[56] As in the case of all other state enterprises, this working capital is controlled by the People's Bank of China, formally an independent unit of the State Council, but placed under the direct supervision of the Ministry of Finance in 1970.[57] For transactions with socialist countries, all payments, clearing accounts, and exchange quotations are managed by the People's Bank of China according to the agreements between the parties concerned. In trade with non-socialist countries, the Bank of China serves as the principal foreign exchange agent.[58]

The Bank of China was originally a state-private bank and a leading foreign exchange agency of the pre-1949 Chinese government. In 1950, the People's Republic took over the two-thirds share which had been held by the Nationalist government, but allowed the private shareholders, except those classified as "war criminals," to retain the remaining one-third.[59] But this confiscation of the Nationalist state investment was incomplete because a substantial amount of the Bank's assets had been moved to Taiwan the

---

55. A 1950 government decision authorized the national foreign trade corporations to decide on their own organizational arrangements and personnel subject only to approval by the Ministry of Trade. In *FLHP 1949-1950*, vol. 2 (1952), p. 326. Since then no mention has been made of corporate charters, except in the civil law textbook cited above.

56. Central Political-Legal Cadres School, *op. cit.*, p. 138.

57. *China Trade Report*, no. 91 (1970), p. 3. For a general discussion of the bank's functions, see Japan External Trade Organization, *How to Approach the China Market*, p. 26.

58. Chung Yung, "Foreign Exchange Work in China," in *Foreign Trade of the PRC*, no. 2 (1960), p. 10.

59. Government Administration Council order of March 22, 1950, in *FLHP 1949-1950*, vol. 1 (1952), p. 303.

previous year. Moreover, those branches of the bank which were located in countries maintaining diplomatic ties with Taipei, such as the one in New York, remained under the control of the main office in Taipei. In December, 1971, obviously in response to the changing international situation, the Taipei authorities—by presidential decree—made that part of the Bank of China under their control a "private" bank with a total investment of $25 million and renamed it "The International Commercial Bank of China."[60] The People's Republic protested, calling it an "illegal selling" of the bank's stocks, and has publicly reserved its right to recover them.[61]

Now there is only one Bank of China, subordinate to the People's Bank of China, with headquarters in Peking, branches in London, Singapore, and Hong Kong, and a vast network of correspondent relationship with other major banks around the world. Chen Hsi-yu, former vice-minister of finance, was appointed president of the People's Bank of China in October, 1973; Chiao Pei-hsin, who had been acting president of the bank from the late 1960s until Chen's appointment, remains acting board chairman and president of the Bank of China.[62] In theory, this bank is still one-third privately owned, as it was in 1950; in practice, no mention has ever been made of its private shareholders. At the end of 1973, the bank's assets were reported at $8.9 billion; its principal liabilities were those under letters of credit and guarantee (for China's foreign trade) which amounted to over $3.2 billion.[63] These figures, however, probably do not include assets held by approximately a dozen "private" Chinese commercial banks in Hong Kong which serve as the Bank of China's agents in the international monetary market. They are: Bank of Communications, Kwangtung Provincial Bank, Sin Hua Trust, Savings and Commercial Bank, Kingcheng Banking Corporation, Nanyang Commercial Bank, Yien Yieh Commercial Bank, China and South Sea Bank, National Commercial Bank, the China State Bank, and Po Sang Bank. Most are incorporated in the PRC. Except for the first two banks, which were owned by

60. The International Commercial Bank of China Act, December 15, 1971, promulgated by a presidential order on the same day, in *Chung-yang jih-pao,* December 16, 1971, p. 1.

61. See Statement by Spokesman of the People's Bank of China Head Office, March 13, 1972, in *Peking Review,* no. 11 (1972), p. 3.

62. When the People's Republic took over the Bank of China in 1950, there were nineteen branches abroad. Eleven of them accepted Peking's leadership. See "The Bank of China Held Its Board Meeting," in *Jen-min jih-pao,* April 11, 1950, p. 1. In the following years, eight of these branches were closed.

As of 1960, Peking's Bank of China had kept business connections with 574 foreign banks (not including their branches) in ninety-three countries and regions. See Chung Yung, "Foreign Exchange Work in China," in *Foreign Trade of the PRC,* no. 2 (1960), p. 10. Since then, the bank's business connections with other countries have greatly expanded as a result of the development of China's foreign trade and diplomatic relations. For reference to Chen Hsi-yu's appointment, see *Kuang-ming jih-pao,* October 4, 1973, p. 2.

63. Dick Wilson, "The Bank of China's Expanding Role in International Finance," *U.S.-China Business Review,* no. 6 (1974), p. 21.

the Nationalist government before 1950, they were originally private corporations, converted into state-private enterprises in the 1950s.[64] In addition, the Bank of China branch in Hong Kong, together with the New China News Agency, plays a quasi-diplomatic role in the absence of formal governmental representation in the British Crown Colony. Since the U.S.-China detente in 1971, quite a few American banks have expressed interest in establishing direct working relations with the Bank of China. However, this cannot be done before the frozen assets issue is solved.

Another important element in China's trade operation is the insurance business. In 1949, the government set up a Chinese People's Insurance Company to engage in various types of insurance business.[65] Like the People's Bank of China, which has a number of semi-governmental banks serving as its foreign exchange agencies, the Chinese People's Insurance Company is also assisted in its foreign operation by two major state-private joint establishments: the China Insurance Company, Ltd., and the Tai Ping Insurance Company, Ltd., the latter being incorporated in Hong Kong. Together they maintain an extensive network throughout the world (except those countries where the People's Repubic does not have diplomatic representation), and write policies such as Ocean Marine, Land Transportation, Aviation, Postal Sendings, and Hulls. The scope of coverage includes: All Risks, which covers all loss or damage arising from accidents; W.A., under which all particular average losses are recoverable; F.P.A., which covers total loss as well as total or partial loss in consequence of accidents; and various classes of reinsurance. Extraneous risks such as theft, pilferage, and non-delivery may be included according to the nature of commodities. Claims are generally paid at the shipment's destination in the currency specified in the policy.[66] A uniqueness of China's foreign trade insurance business lies in the fact that it is not governed by statutory law. In most cases, the validity of a claim depends on the contractual terms of the policy.

The China Council for the Promotion of International Trade

In 1952 the People's Republic was recognized by only twenty-five countries, and the Western embargo was in full force. In response to this

64. A Hong Kong source suggests that there are two additional banks in this category: Chiyu Banking Corporation and Hua Chiao Commercial Bank. See "Banking the People's Way," *China Trade Report*, vol. 12 (1974), p. 9.

65. Directive of the Commission on Financial and Economic Affairs of the Government Administration Council, December 23, 1949, in *FLHP 1949-1950*, vol. 1 (1952), p. 306.

66. "The Foreign Insurance Business of the People's Republic of China," in *Foreign Trade of the PRC*, no. 1 (1963), p. 6. Keng Tao-ming, president of the Chinese People's Insurance Company, is also vice-president of the Bank of China.

situation, following the establishment of an international committee for "expanding trade between countries on a basis of equality and with due regard to the needs of the industrialization of underdeveloped countries" under the 1952 International Economic Conference in Moscow,[67] China founded its national counterpart, the China Council for the Promotion of International Trade on May 4, 1952.[68]

The main function of the CCPIT is to handle trade with non-socialist countries, especially those having no diplomatic relations with Peking. Toward this end, it undertakes a number of important activities: entering into nongovernmental trade agreements with foreign partners whose countries do not recognize the People's Republic;[69] representing China's foreign trade organization in these countries;[70] sending trade delegations to both recognized and unrecognized states for goodwill visits; receiving foreign trade delegations in China; participating in international trade fairs; holding Chinese commodity exhibitions overseas; rendering services to foreign exhibitions in China; and collecting and disseminating information concerning international trade. On behalf of the People's Republic, for example, it took an active part in the Council of the Afro-Asian Organization for Economic Cooperation.[71] In addition, the CCPIT also handles the registration of foreign trademarks and foreign trade and maritime arbitration cases involving socialist and non-socialist countries.

Initially, the governing body of the CCPIT consisted of seventeen prominent bankers, economists, and trade unionists, with Nan Han-chen, then president of the People's Bank of China, as chairman,[72] and at the end of the 1950s its membership was expanded to twenty-three. The decree or corporate charter creating the CCPIT has never been made public; even in official literature its status is ambiguous. To foreign readers the CCPIT is identified as "a public body and an independent legal person . . . composed of the state trade enterprises, representatives of joint state-private exporters and importers, economic, trade and legal experts and foreign trade workers."[73] In

---

67. The conference brought together 471 participants from forty-nine countries; its Committee for the Promotion of International Trade consisted of seventeen members, including both China and the U.S. See Communiqué of the International Economic Conference in Moscow, April 12, 1952, in *New Times,* no. 16 (1952), p. 3.

68. See *Jen-min jih-pao,* May 15, 1952, p. 1; *New Times,* no. 16 (1952), p. 6.

69. The first such arrangement was the China-Japan Trade Agreement, December 31, 1952, in *TYC 1952-1953,* vol. 2 (1957), p. 367.

70. The CCPIT had representation in Japan, Italy, Austria, Chile, Peru—and other countries—beofre their recognition of the People's Republic.

71. E.g., Hsiao Fang-chou, "Ten Years of the China Council for the Promotion of International Trade," in *Foreign Trade of the PRC,* no. 2 (1962), p. 2.

72. *Jen-min shou-ts'e 1953,* pp. 269-270.

73. See "China's Foreign Trade Organizations," in *Peking Review,* no. 28 (1958), p. 13. Also see Gene T. Hsiao, "Communist China's Foreign Trade Organization" in *Vanderbilt Law*

Chinese publications the CCPIT as a "legal person" is never mentioned, and it is defined as a "permanent agency performing duties similar to those of the Chamber of International Commerce in other countries."[74] The discrepancy between these two descriptions, however, is not a serious issue in view of the fact that the CCPIT does not engage in direct transactions, and its agreements are all private pre-contract arrangements without binding legal force upon the parties. Moreover, the composition of the CCPIT leadership clearly indicates that it is more a component of China's state foreign trade organization—an intermediary of the MFT in its relations to foreign partners—than a public body like a chamber of international commerce.

High officials of the CCPIT recently disclosed to some American guests that the organization is led by the CCP, which decides on all key appointments (as with every other governmental agency). Traditionally, the personnel of the CCPIT have been interchangeable with those of the MFT, the Ministry of Foreign Affairs, and other interested governmental and social organizations. During the Cultural Revolution Assistant Minister of Foreign Trade Liu Hsi-wen replaced Nan Han-chen as acting head of the CCPIT, a position he held until 1973 when Wang Yao-ting, a former high official of the China National Textiles Import and Export Corporation, became chairman.[75] At the same time, death and retirement among vice-chairmen of the CCPIT brought about the appointment of six new vice-chairmen: Hsiao Fang-chou, Li Chuan, Li Hsi-fu, Li Yung-ting, Liu Hsi-wen and Wang Wen-lin.[76] At present, the twenty-three-person governing body of the CCPIT is not filled.[77]

Directly subordinate to the governing body is a staff, headed by a secretary-general and a deputy secretary-general, and consisting of the following units:

General Administrative Office, responsible for daily administrative, financial, secretarial and personnel work; Department of Liaison, responsible for establishing contacts with Chinese and foreign corporations and trade institutions, organizing overseas tours in connection with trade, economic and

---

Review 20:303 (1967); "The Organization of China's Foreign Trade," U.S.-China Business Review, no. 3 (1974), p. 9.

74. See "A Brief Introduction to the China Council for the Promotion of International Trade," in Chung-hua jen-min kung-ho-kuo Tui-wai mao-i, no. 1 (1959), p. 1. Hereafter cited as Tui-wai mao-i.

75. Wang's earlier career is not known. One article signed with his first name, Yao-ting, "New Developments in Sino-Egyptian Economic Relations," in MFT, ed., Tui-wai mao-i lun-wen hsüan, vol. 3, p. 64, suggests that he is probably a veteran official of the MFT. Also see "Council Delegation in Peking: The Exchanges Begin," U.S.-China Business Review, no. 1 (1973), p. 3.

76. See Jen-min jih-pao, April 3, 1972, p. 5; April 6, 1972, p. 5; April 10, 1972, p. 6; June 3, 1972, p. 1.

77. For reference to an old, but representative, membership list, see Chung-kuo kuo-chi mao-i ts'u-chin wei-yuan hui.

technical affairs, receiving foreign visitors, and handling private trade agreements and protocols signed in the name of the CCPIT; Department of Overseas Exhibitions, responsible for organizing and operating economic and trade exhibitions overseas; Department of Foreign Exhibitions in China, responsible for assisting foreign institutions in operating exhibitions in China; Department of Publicity, responsible for publishing foreign trade periodicals and other information concerning China's trade and economy; Department of Legal Affairs, responsible for handling legal and administrative problems in connection with foreign trade and maritime affairs as well as registration of foreign trademarks; Department for Average Adjustment, responsible for the administration of the Provisional Rules for General Average Adjustment promulgated on January 1, 1975 (see Appendix T); and Department for Technical Exchange, responsible for the exchange of technical information with foreign countries and presumably working in cooperation and collaboration with the Chinese Scientific and Technical Association.

In addition to the above, the CCPIT has branches in Hangchow, Harbin, Kwangchow, Nanking, Shanghai, Shenyang, Taiyuan, Talien, Tientsin, and Wuhan, each consisting of a governing body and a staff similar to those of the CCPIT in Peking; it also has a Foreign Trade Arbitration Commission and a Maritime Arbitration Commission.[78] In the years ahead, as more countries recognize the People's Republic, the diplomatic function of the CCPIT is likely to diminish and its purely trade activities increase.

The Kwangchow Trade Fair

Since the spring of 1957, China has held a semi-annual trade fair in Kwangchow (formerly Canton), officially known as the "Chinese Export Commodities Fair," under the joint sponsorship of the national foreign trade corporations.[79] Selection of this city was meaningful in several respects. Historically, Kwangchow was for more than a century China's only major trading port with the outside world.[80] The First Opium War (1839-42) started there, providing a political reminder to both Chinese and foreign traders today.[81] Geographically, since the fair is basically export-oriented, the city's

78. These commissions are discussed in chapter 6. See *Kuo-chi mao-i chih-shih* (1973), pp. 66-7. For reference to documents creating the two arbitration commissions, see Government Administration Council decision of May 6, 1954, in *Chung-hua jen-min kung-ho-kuo fa-kuei hsüan-chi* (1957), p. 470; State Council decision of November 21, 1958, in Supplement to *Tui-wai mao-i*, no. 1 (1959).

79. "More and Better Things for Export," *People's China*, no. 3 (1957), p. 40.

80. See the Kwangchow Branch of the CCPIT, "Kwangchow—An Important Port on the Shore of South China Sea," in *Chung-kuo Tui-wai mao-i*, no. 2 (1974), p. 46.

81. For example, in 1965 China published an article on the fair by the author of *From the Opium War to Liberation*, Israel Epstein, entitled "The Chinese Export Commodities Fair in

proximity to Hong Kong provides fair visitors easy access to the Chinese market. Militarily, the city's distance from China's strategic and industrial centers assures the Chinese government and people a sense of security.

At the outset, the fair was an experiment to promote the sale of Chinese products. Subsequently, as China began to increase both the variety and quantity of its exports, the fair was institutionalized as a part of China's overall foreign trade organization. Its principal objectives are: to hold a full exhibition of all major Chinese export items for examination and selection; to conduct negotiations for the conclusion of both export and import contracts; to discuss business problems that are difficult to solve through correspondence; to provide businessmen from other countries a personal opportunity to get acquainted with the Chinese market; to exchange technical experience and knowledge; to establish and widen business contacts between Chinese trade representatives and their foreign counterparts; and to explain China's foreign trade policy to the rest of the world.[82]

The fair is held from April 15 to May 15 and from October 15 to November 15 each year. Although the internal organizational structure of the fair is not known, it is supervised by the local authorities: the late Chen Yu, vice-chairman of the Kwangtung Provincial Revolutionary Committee (equivalent to deputy governor) served as chairman of the working committee of the fair from 1967 until his death in March, 1974.[83] Lin Li-ming, vice-chairman of the Kwangtung Provincial Revolutionary Committee (and concurrently Secretary of the Kwangtung Provincial Party Committee as well as alternate member of the Tenth Central Committee of the CCP) succeeded Chen as the fair's committee chairman. Lin is assisted by a number of vice-chairmen, among them: Chang Ken-sheng, vice-chairman of the Kwangtung Provincial Revolutionary Committee; Lo Fan-chun, vice-chairman of the Kwangchow Municipal Revolutionary Committee; Wang Jun-sheng; and

Kwangchow," in *Chung-kuo ch'u-k'ou shang-p'in chiao-i-hui t'e-k'an,* supplement to *Ching-chi tao-pao,* no. 2 (1965), p. 22. It was translated into Chinese from the original English, which was in *China Reconstructs,* no. 8 (1965).

82. An important example of this last objective was Chou En-lai's announcement to Japanese businessmen through the chairman of the 1970 spring fair, of the four conditions for Sino-Japanese trade. See *Chung-kuo ch'u-k'uo shang-p'in chiao-i-hui t'e-k'an,* no. 3 (1970), p. 10. Also see Yen Yi-chun, "The Chinese Export Commodities Spring Fair 1959," *Foreign Trade of the PRC,* no. 2 (1959), p. 8; Liang Hsu-feng, "The Chinese Export Commodities Autumn Fair 1959," *ibid.,* no. 1 (1960), p. 12; "The Chinese Export Commodities Fair in Canton," *ibid.,* no. 3 (1962), p. 2; Tsou Szu-yee (vice-chairman of the Working Committee of the Chinese Export Commodities Fair), "Fifteen Chinese Export Commodities Fairs," *ibid.,* no. 3 (1964), p. 6.

83. See "The Opening Session of the Chinese Export Commodities Autumn Fair 1967," *Chung-kuo ch'u-k'uo shang-p'in chiao-i-hui t'e-k'an,* no. 2 (1976), p. 18. Tseng Sheng, mayor of Kwangchow before the Cultural Revolution, served as vice-chairman of the working committee.

Cheng Shao-kang, who serves concurrently as secretary-general of the fair's committee.[84] Operationally, the fair is controlled by the MFT with the CCPIT's assistance. Each interested national foreign trade corporation is represented at the fair in order to conduct negotiations with visitors. The fair also provides its visitors a great variety of services, including banking, insurance, post and telecommunications, translation, transportation, and tourism.[85]

From 1957 to 1975 the exhibition floor space increased from twelve-thousand to one-hundred-ten-thousand square meters; export samples from twelve-thousand to more than thirty-thousand; and attendance from twelve hundred persons representing about twenty countries and regions to more than twenty-thousand from over one hundred countries and regions.[86] The value of transactions at the first session of the fair in 1957 was reported at $55 million (20 million pounds sterling). It reached about $1 billion (400 million pounds sterling) at the eighteenth session of the fair in autumn 1965.[87] Although no official figures have been made available since then, informed sources reported that the turnover in the spring fair of 1975 was estimated at about $1.7 billion.[88]

Generally, the fair is only open to those who are invited by a Chinese national foreign trade corporation with which they have business connections. The procedures for attending the fair can be briefly described as follows: if the visitor is residing in a country where the People's Republic is represented by a diplomatic mission, an office of a chargé d' affaires, or a consulate, he should apply to that office for a visa; if the visitor is residing in a country where the People's Republic is not as yet represented, he should apply for a visa to one of these offices in a neighboring country or to the China Travel Service in Hong Kong. The applicant must present his passport and the invitation card issued to him by a Chinese national foreign trade corporation. In case he applies to the China Travel Service, he should also send three passport-size photographs. Those who do not have an invitation but wish to attend the fair may write to the Chinese national foreign trade corporations with which they have business connections, to the commercial officer of the Chinese diplomatic or consular mission in their country or a neighboring country. The invitation cards cannot be transferred on the initiative of the invited. In the

84. See *Ta-kung pao* (Hong Kong), April 16, 1975, p. 1; April 20, 1975, p.4.

85. See *Trade and Tour* (Hong Kong), spring 1971; *ibid.*, spring 1972.

86. Wang Yao-ting, "China's Foreign Trade," *Peking Review*, no. 41 (1974), p. 18; Chu Shang, "The Development of China's Export Trade Reflected by the Chinese Export Commodities Fair," *China's Foreign Trade*, no. 1 (1974), p. 42.

87. See *People's China*, no. 3 (1957), p. 40; Tseng Sheng, "The Chinese Export Commodities Fair," *China's Foreign Trade*, no. 2 (1966), p. 12.

88. *South China Morning Post* (Hong Kong), Business News, March 31, 1975.

event that the invited firms are unable to appoint their own representatives to attend the fair but find it necessary to authorize other firms to act on their behalf, such authorization must be approved by the Chinese host corporations in advance.[89] Without a special permit, the fair visitor is not allowed to travel beyond the city limits of Kwangchow. (For quick reference to China's foreign trade organization, three charts are attached, showing the Organizational Structure of the Ministry of Foreign Trade, the Organizational Structure of the CCPIT, and China National Foreign Trade and Related Corporations.)

89. "How to Attend the Fair," *Chung-kuo ch'u-k'ou shang-p'in chiao-i-hui t'e-k'an* (spring 1965), p. 14; *ibid.*, no. 1 (1966), p. 16. For further reference, see *U.S.-China Business Review,* which provides useful information about the fair and travel to China in general.

Footnote to CHART 1

PRINCIPAL SOURCES: Japan External Trade Organization, *How to Approach the China Market* (1972), p. 24; U.S. Government, "Foreign Trade Organizations of the People's Republic of China" (1975).

NOTE: The Central Committee of the CCP consists of 195 members and 124 alternate members. Its daily work is carried out by the Central Political Bureau, which consists of 21 members and four alternate members. The Standing Committee of the Central Political Bureau, comprising nine members, is the highest decision-making body in China. See *Hung-ch'i,* no. 9 (1973), pp. 34-36.

The Standing Committee of the National People's Congress is the permanent organ of the highest body of state power, comprising a chairman, 22 vice chairmen, and 145 members.

The State Council consists of a premier, 12 vice premiers, and 29 ministries and commissions. Vice Premier Li Hsien-nien is in charge of financial and economic affairs, including foreign trade.

Top officials of the Ministry of Foreign Trade are already mentioned in the text. Some secondary officials are: Wang Pin, director of the First Bureau; Cheng To-pin, director of the Third Bureau, assisted by deputy directors Peng Chin-po and Sun So-chang and United States Affairs Section chief Li Shu-te; Wu Shu-tung, director of the Fourth Bureau.

CHART 1

ORGANIZATIONAL STRUCTURE OF THE MINISTRY OF FOREIGN TRADE

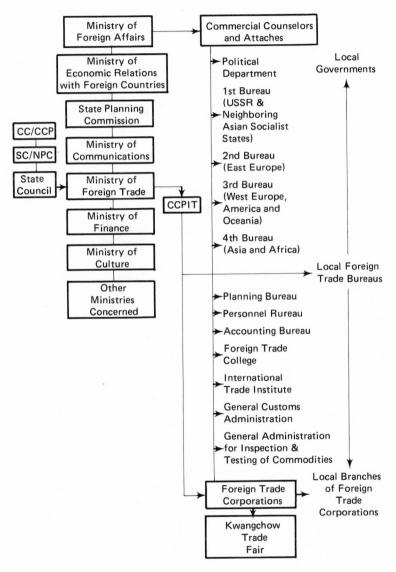

CHART 2
ORGANIZATIONAL STRUCTURE OF THE CCPIT

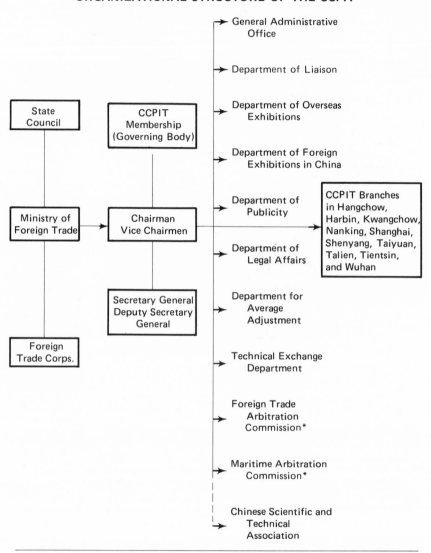

*These two commissions are independent units.

Footnote to CHART 2

PRINCIPAL SOURCES: *Kuo-chi mao-i chih-shih* (1973), pp. 66-67; U.S. Government, "Foreign Trade Organizations of the People's Republic of China" (1975); *Chung-kuo kuo-chi mao-i ts'u-chin wei-yuan-hui* (1959).

NOTE: A list of names of the responsible officials of the CCPIT and its subordinate departments follows. Sources: U.S. Government, *op. cit.; China's Foreign Trade,* no. 3 (1975), p. 51.

Officials of the CCPIT

Chairman: Wang Yao-ting
Vice Chairmen: Hsiao Fang-chou, Li Chuan, Li Hsi-fu, Li Yung-ting, Liu Hsi-wen, Wang Wen-lin
General Administrative Office: Director, not available
Department of Liaison: Director Tung Chao, Deputy Director Chang Feng, Chief of American Section Kuo Szu-mien
Department of Overseas Exhibitions: Director, not available
Department of Foreign Exhibitions in China: Director Kung Fan-cheng
Department of Publicity: Director Sung Fang
Department of Legal Affairs: Jen Chien-hsin (or Jen Tsien-hsin)
Department for Average Adjustment: Director, not available
Department for Technical Exchange: Director Li Chao-li
Foreign Trade Arbitration Commission: Chairman Hsiao Fang-chou
Maritime Arbitration Commission: Chairman Wang Wen-lin
Chinese Scientific and Technical Association: Director, not available

CHART 3
CHINA NATIONAL FOREIGN TRADE AND RELATED CORPORATIONS

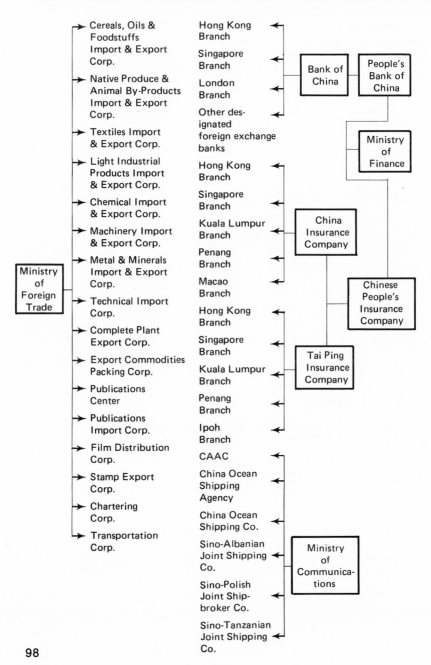

Cereals, Oils & Foodstuffs Import & Export Corp.

Native Produce & Animal By-Products Import & Export Corp.

Textiles Import & Export Corp.

Light Industrial Products Import & Export Corp.

Chemical Import & Export Corp.

Machinery Import & Export Corp.

Metal & Minerals Import & Export Corp.

Technical Import Corp.

Complete Plant Export Corp.

Export Commodities Packing Corp.

Publications Center

Publications Import Corp.

Film Distribution Corp.

Stamp Export Corp.

Chartering Corp.

Transportation Corp.

Ministry of Foreign Trade

Hong Kong Branch

Singapore Branch

London Branch

Other designated foreign exchange banks

Hong Kong Branch

Singapore Branch

Kuala Lumpur Branch

Penang Branch

Macao Branch

Hong Kong Branch

Singapore Branch

Kuala Lumpur Branch

Penang Branch

Ipoh Branch

CAAC

China Ocean Shipping Agency

China Ocean Shipping Co.

Sino-Albanian Joint Shipping Co.

Sino-Polish Joint Ship-broker Co.

Sino-Tanzanian Joint Shipping Co.

Bank of China

People's Bank of China

Ministry of Finance

China Insurance Company

Chinese People's Insurance Company

Tai Ping Insurance Company

Ministry of Communications

Footnote to CHART 3

PRINCIPAL SOURCES: *Hsiangkang ching-chi nien-chien* 1976, Part V, pp. 131-135; U.S. Government, "Foreign Trade Organizations of the People's Republic of China" (1975).

NOTE: A list of names of the corporations, their cable and mailing addresses follows:

China National Cereals, Oils and Foodstuffs Import and Export Corporation
82 Tung An Men Street, Peking
Cable: CEROILFOOD PEKING
Sixteen branches in thirteen cities and provinces
Hong Kong Agent: Ng Fung Hong
                  Bank of China Building
                  Hong Kong
                  Cable: NG FUNG HONG KONG
Macao Agent: Nam Kwong Trading Company
                  Rua Alm. Sergio Nos. 94-98
                  Macao
                  Cable: NAMKWONG MACAO

China National Native Produce and Animal By-Products Import and Export Corporation
82 Tung An Men Street, Peking
Cable: CHINATUHSU PEKING
Seventeen branches and eighteen subbranches in twelve cities and provinces
Hong Kong Agents: Teck Soon Hong Ltd. (for tea and native produce)
                  37 Connaught Road West
                  Hong Kong

                  Hua Yuan Company (for animal by-products)
                  37 Connaught Road West
                  Hong Kong
Macao Agent: Nam Kwong Trading Company

China National Textiles Import and Export Corporation
82 Tung An Men Street, Peking
Cable: CHINATEX PEKING
Eight branches in six cities and provinces
Hong Kong Agent: China Resources Company
                  Bank of China Building
                  Hong Kong
Macao Agent: Nam Kwong Trading Company

China National Light Industrial Products Import and Export Corporation
82 Tung An Men Street, Peking
Cable: INDUSTRY PEKING
Twenty branches in ten cities and provinces
Hong Kong Agent: Hua Yuan Company
Macao Agent: Nam Kwong Trading Company

China National Chemical Import and Export Corporation
Erh Li Kou, Hsi Chiao, Peking
Cable: SINOCHEM PEKING
Six branches in six cities and provinces
Hong Kong Agent: China Resources Company
Macao Agent: Nam Kwong Trading Company

99

Footnote to CHART 3 *(continued)*

China National Machinery Import and Export Corporation
Erh Li Kou, Hsi Chiao, Peking
Cable: MACHIMPEX PEKING
Five branches in five cities
Hong Kong Agent: China Resources Company
Macao Agent: Nam Kwong Trading Company

China National Metals and Minerals Import and Export Corporation
Erh Li Kou, Hsi Chiao, Peking
Cable: MINMETALS PEKING
Six branches in six cities and provinces
Hong Kong Agent: China Resources Company
Macao Agent: Nam Kwong Trading Company

China National Technical Import Corporation
Erh Li Kou, Hsi Chiao, Peking
Cable: TECHIMPORT Peking

China National Complete Plant Export Corporation
Fu-Wai Street, Peking
Cable: COMPLANT PEKING

China National Export Commodities Packing Corporation
Address not available

China National Publications Center *(Guozi Shudian)*
P. O. Box 399, Peking
Cable: GUOZI Peking

China National Publications Import Corporation
P. O. Box 88, Peking

China Film Distribution Corporation
Hsin Wai Ta Street, Peking
Cable: CFDCORP PEKING
Hong Kong Agent: Nan Fang Film Company

China Stamp Export Corporation
28 Tung An Men Street, Peking
Cable: CHINASTAMP PEKING

China National Chartering Corporation
Erh Li Kou, Hsi Chiao, Peking
Cable: ZHONGZU PEKING
Six branches in six ports

China National Foreign Trade Transportation Corporation
Erh Li Kou, Hsi Chiao, Peking
Cable ZHONGWAIYUN PEKING
Nine branches in nine ports

Bank of China Head Office
Address not available
Cable: HOCHUNGKUO PEKING
Thirty branches in thirty cities
Branches in Hong Kong, Singapore, and London

Chinese People's Insurance Company
34 Fan Ti Road, Peking
P. O. Box 2149 Peking
Cable: 42001 PEKING
Six branches in six cities and seven sub-branches in seven cities

China Insurance Company, Limited
P. O. Box 20, Peking
Cable: CHINSURCO PEKING
Branches in Hong Kong, Singapore, Kuala Lumpur, Penang, Macao.

Tai Ping Insurance Company
Address not available
Cable: TAIPINGING PEKING
Branches in Hong Kong, Singapore, Kuala Lumpur, Penang, Ipoh.

China Ocean Shipping Agency
6 Tung Chang An Street, Peking
Cable: PENAVICO PEKING
(Note: This agency handles international ocean-going ships engaged in passenger and/or cargo services calling at Chinese coastal ports.)

China Ocean Shipping Company
6 Tung Chang An Street, Peking
Cable: COSCO PEKING

Sino-Albanian Joint Shipping Company
Address not available

Sino-Polish Joint Shipbrokers Company, Limited
Address not available
Cable: CHIPOLBROK PEKING

Sino-Tanzanian Joint Shipping Company
Address not available
Cable: SINOTASHIP PEKING

5   Trade Treaties and Agreements

THE Chinese government regards trade accords as an important form of economic cooperation and a conventional legal instrument for the advancement of diplomatic interests. Economically, a trade accord is useful in at least five respects. First, it can provide information about future supply and demand which is necessary for the compilation of foreign trade plans. Second, it can provide some legal assurance that the trading partner involved will fulfill his obligations. Third, it can provide negotiated prices that will remain fixed for a period of time to come—and in turn provide an element of stability for planning. Fourth, consummation of a trade accord can help normalize economic relations between contracting states and promote their commercial intercourse. From the Chinese point of view such accords, based on the principles of equality and mutual benefit, are particularly important in trade with countries which adopt discriminatory tariff policies. Fifth, a trade accord can coordinate the development of the Chinese economy with other planned economies. Specifically, it can play a major role in Chinese aid programs to the Third World which are generally tied to trade.[1]

Diplomatically, a trade agreement can provide China with a legal safeguard for the protection of its national sovereignty and the rights of its trade representatives overseas.[2] More generally, Chinese leaders believe that the lack of formal diplomatic relations between states need not impede the conclusion of intergovernmental trade agreements; rather, such agreements should lead to the normalization of diplomatic relations.[3] Chinese writers cited as a historical precedent Britain's 1921 trade agreement with Soviet

1. Chao Chi-chang, "Overall Planning of Foreign Trade and Conclusion of Long-Term Trade Agreements," MFT, ed., *Tui-wai mao-i lun-wen hsüan,* vol. 2 (1956), p. 151; Tsou Szu-i, "The Efforts Made by China in the Execution of the Afro-Asian Conference's Resolution on Economic Cooperation," *ibid.,* p. 80; Yeh Chi-chuang, "Address to the Eighth National Congress of the Chinese Communist Party," *ibid.,* vol. 3 (1957), p. 5; Ting Ke-chuan (deputy director of the General Office of the Ministry of Foreign Trade), "Long-Term Trade Agreements," *Peking Review,* no. 20 (1958), p. 12; Yeh Chi-chuang, "On Foreign Trade," address to the Fourth Session of the First NPC, July 11, 1957, in *Jen-min shou-ts'e 1958,* p. 557; Yeh Chi-chuang, "China's Foreign Trade in the Past Ten Years," *Foreign Trade of the PRC,* no. 3 (1959), p. 2.
2. Wang Yao-tien, *Kuo-chi mao-i t'iao-yüeh ho hsieh-ting,* pp. 111-118, 135-136.
3. See "Premier Chou En-lai's Interview with Ikuo Oyama, Chairman of the Japanese Committee for the Promotion of Peace, September 28, 1953," in *TWKH 1951-1953,* vol. 2 (1958), p. 150; Chou En-lai, "Address to the Third Session of the First NPC, June 28, 1956," in *Jen-min shou-ts'e 1957,* pp. 182, 186.

Russia, which preceded the British government's *de jure* recognition of the Soviet regime on February 2, 1924.[4]

Accordingly, over a period of twenty-five years the People's Republic has concluded about one thousand bilateral economic treaties and agreements with more than sixty states.[5] Although these figures are incomplete and approximate (due to the lack of official statistical information and a unified nomenclature and stable criteria for the classification of treaties) they reflect the importance of foreign trade agreements in China's treaty practice. According to the Chinese government's classification, treaties fall into fourteen major categories: political, legal, border problems, frontier problems, economic, cultural, scientific and technological, agricultural and forest, fishing, public health, postal service and telecommunications, communications and transport, rules of war, and military.[6] Within the economic category, there are six groups: (1) commerce and navigation; (2) economic aid, loans, and technical cooperation; (3) trade and payments; (4) general conditions for delivery; (5) registration of trademarks; and (6) miscellaneous.[7] Although most of these categories touch in one way or another upon China's foreign trade, for purposes of this discussion their importance and roles can best be shown by focusing on several basic aspects: the general principles of trade treaties; trade representation abroad; national treatment of aliens; most-favored-nation status; and the protection of industrial property.

General Principles

China's trade treaties and agreements are formulated according to general principles established in the first twelve years of the People's

4. Trade Agreement between His Britannic Majesty's Government and the Government of the Russian Socialist Federal Soviet Republic, March 16, 1921, in *League of Nations Treaty Series,* vol. 4 (1921), p. 128; Wang Yao-tien, *op.*'*cit.,* p. 17.

5. From 1949 to 1964 China concluded 408 bilateral economic treaties and agreements with forty-eight states out of a total number of 762 bilateral treaties and agreements which China reached with fifty-three states and the United Nations. See Gene T. Hsiao, "Communist China's Trade Treaties and Agreements, 1949-1964," in *Vanderbilt Law Review* 21:626, 656-658 (1968). Since 1964 the Ministry of Foreign Affairs has suspended the publication of its official treaty series, *TYC.* In consequence, no reliable figures are available. The figures cited above are based on two sources. First, Douglas M. Johnston and Hungdah Chiu estimate that from 1949 to 1967, China concluded over 2,000 agreements with more than seventy states, of which a total of 620 were trade agreements. In *Agreements of the People's Republic of China, 1949-1967: A Calendar,* Table 1, pp. 218-9. Second, a semi-official Chinese source in Hong Kong, *Hsiangkang ching-chi nien-chien,* listed 138 economic and trade agreements from January 1, 1972 to May 31, 1973 in its 1973 yearbook; 35 from June 1, 1973 to May 31, 1974 in its 1974 yearbook; and 82 from June 1, 1974 to May 31, 1975 in its 1975 yearbook. The number of foreign states concluding such agreements with China has risen to more than 60 as of October 1975. See Tung Sheng, "The Development of Our Country's Trade and Economic Relations," in *Ching-chi tao-pao,* no. 38 (1975), p. 39.

6. See *TYC 1962,* vol. 11 (1963), pp. 227-284.

7. *Ibid.,* pp. 237-268.

Republic.[8] (The PRC has never acceded to the Vienna Convention on the Law of Treaties.)[9] To date, the People's Republic has concluded seven formal treaties of trade and navigation with six socialist states and Yemen. The bulk of the remaining economic agreements concern trade and payments, and the rest are economic aid and technical cooperation accords, general conditions for delivery, agreements on the registration of trademarks, and miscellaneous others.

Definition and Designation

Borrowing from the writings of F. I. Kozhevnikov, a Soviet jurist, the Peking Foreign Trade College defined a treaty as "a document between two or more states concerning the establishment, amendment, or termination of their sovereign rights and obligations," and "a typical and most widespread legal form in the realm of political, economic, and other relations between states."[10] On the basis of this general definition, a trade treaty or agreement is described as "a written agreement between two or more sovereign states concerning the regulation of the mutual economic and trade relations of natural and juristic persons of the contracting states as well as those relations between the governments of the contracting states themselves."[11]

From among a dozen treaty designations defined by Soviet jurists,[12] the Chinese have enumerated and elaborated upon six: (1) treaty *(t'iao-yüeh),* a most important international document regulating the political, economic, or other relations of the contracting states; (2) agreement *(hsieh-ting),* a treaty regulating certain special or temporary problems of the contracting states; (3) convention *(kung-yüeh)* or pact *(chuan-yüeh),* a multilateral agreement concerning certain specific problems; (4) declaration *(hsüan-yen),* a general statement concerning the international relations and the general principles of international law recognized by the interested states, sometimes including concrete obligations (such as the 1856 Paris Declaration on the Abolition of Privateering, and the December 1, 1943, Cairo Declaration);[13] (5) protocol

8. See Hungdah Chiu, *The People's Republic of China and the Law of Treaties.*

9. The text of the convention is in *American Journal of International Law* 63:875 (1969).

10. Wang Yao-tien, *op. cit.,* p. 9; F. I. Kozhevnikov, "Nekotorye voprosy teorii i praktiki mezhdunarodnogo dogovora," *Sovetskoe Gosudarstvo i pravo,* no. 2 (1954), pp. 62-76; translated in *Hsien-tai kuo-chi-fa shang ti chi-pen yüan-tse ho wen-t'i,* pp. 223 and 227. In another source, Kozhevnikov is reported to have defined a treaty as "a typical and most widespread legal form of *struggle* or cooperation in the realm of political, economic, and other relations between states." (Emphasis added.) See J. Triska and R. Slusser, *The Theory, Law, and Policy of Soviet Treaties,* p. 38. In the Chinese version of the above definition the word "struggle" is omitted.

11. Wang Yao-tien, *op. cit.,* p. 15.

12. These are: treaty, convention, agreement, covenant or charter, protocol, exchange of notes, declaration, gentlemen's agreement, modus vivendi, cartels, concordats, and compromise. See J. Triska and R. Slusser, *op. cit.,* pp. 39-40.

13. Although the Cairo Declaration is not listed in the U.S. Department of State's

(I-ting-shu), an agreement on individual problems, sometimes amending, interpreting, or supplementing certain provisions of a treaty; and (6) exchange of notes *(huan-wen)* defining certain matters already agreed upon by the parties.[14]

The omission by the Chinese of other treaty designations known in international treaty law does not mean that the People's Republic has ignored their existence or usefulness; rather, the Chinese government has generally confined its trade practice to the use of four of the six types mentioned above. Thus, for example, of the 408 economic arrangements that China had made with other nations before 1964, 7 assumed the title "treaty of trade and navigation," 393 took the titles "agreement," "protocol," and "exchange of notes," and the remaining eight took miscellaneous designations. China has also used such formal and informal titles as "communiqué," "joint statement," "exchange of letters," "memorandum," and "minutes of talks." The use of "general conditions for delivery" as a treaty designation has been limited to socialist states and Finland, which had two such arrangements with the People's Republic in the early 1950s.[15]

Form and Language

China's practice suggests that all treaties must be written; no oral treaties have been reported. A formal trade treaty usually consists of three parts: the preamble states the names of the contracting parties, the general purpose of the treaty, and the plenipotentiaries empowered to sign the treaty; the main text contains substantive provisions concerning natural and juristic persons, goods, vessels, and arbitration; and the concluding part stipulates ratification, entry into force, duration, and the authenticity of languages. An example of the standard form is the Treaty of Trade and Navigation with the Soviet Union, April 23, 1958 (see Appendix B).[16]

A trade agreement with a socialist state also contains three parts but is less rigid in form and more specific in content. The exchange in the preamble of credentials bearing "full powers" and other formalities is omitted; the main text deals with such problems as goods, price, payment, currency, enforcement, and the manner in which tariff duties are to be paid. The third and concluding part concerns duration and language. As a matter of practice, the agreement is usually accompanied by an export schedule of goods for each party.[17] Following the conclusion of a trade agreement, a protocol containing

---

Treaties in Force, the People's Republic has always considered it a treaty. See *Kuo-chi t' iao-yüeh chi 1934-1944,* vol. 3, (1961) p. 407.

14. Wang Yao-tien, *op. cit.,* p. 12.

15. In *TYC 1952-1953,* vol. 2 (1957), p. 372; *TYC 1954,* vol. 3 (1958), p. 197.

16. The Chinese text of the treaty is in *TYC 1958,* vol. 7 (1959), p. 42.

17. An example of the standard form for this document is the Trade Agreement with the

the general conditions for delivery is also reached, specifying rules for the form of contracts, terms of delivery, quantity and quality of goods, packing and marking, inspection of goods, methods of payment, adjustment of disagreements, penalties, *force majeure,* and arbitration (see Appendix C).[18] The basic function of the general conditions for delivery is to simplify the procedures for the making of individual contracts; in essence, the document is a general contract of the Soviet type. In recent years, there has been a tendency among members of the Council for Mutual Economic Aid (COM-ECON) to use this document as an instrument for unification of socialist international trade law.[19] However, since China is not a COMECON member, the effect of such a tendency on China's treaty and contract practices remains to be seen.

The official languages of both contracting parties are equally authentic in China's trade treaties and agreements with the USSR, Outer Mongolia, North Korea, North Vietnam, and Cuba.[20] In trade agreements with all East European countries except Yugoslavia, the authentic languages are usually the official languages of the contracting parties and Russian; in the case of a dispute arising from the interpretation of the languages, Russian prevails. However, it should be noted that this practice is limited to trade agreements, protocols, and general conditions for delivery, and does not apply to formal treaties of trade and navigation. China's first trade agreement with Yugoslavia, dated February 17, 1956, accepted both Chinese and Serbo-Croatian as the authentic languages; no reference was made to any third language.[21]

Government of the USSR, April 19, 1950, in *TYC 1949-1951,* vol. 1 (1960), p. 47; English translation in *Chinese Law and Government,* no. 2 (1972), p. 8.

18. An outline of these terms is in Wang Yao-tien, *op. cit.,* pp. 126-132. For reference to another sample, see Protocol on the General Conditions for Delivery between the Foreign Trade Organizations of the PRC and the USSR for the Year 1950, April 19, 1950, in *TYC 1949-1950,* vol. 1 (1960), p. 51; English translation in *Chinese Law and Government,* no. 2 (1972), p. 14.

19. Thomas W. Hoya, "The Common General Conditions—A Socialist Unification of International Trade Law," *Columbia Law Review* 70:253 (1970); Harold J. Berman, "Unification of Contract Clauses in Trade between Member Countries of the Council for Mutual Economic Aid," *International and Comparative Law Quarterly* 7:659 (1958); Thomas W. Hoya and John B. Quigley, Jr., "COMECON 1968 General Conditions for the Delivery of Goods," *Ohio State Law Journal* 31:1 (1970).

20. See, e.g., Protocol on the General Conditions for Delivery with the USSR for the Year 1957, April 10, 1957, in *TYC 1957,* vol. 6 (1958), pp. 77, 78; Treaty of Trade and Navigation with the USSR, April 23, 1958, in *TYC 1958,* vol. 7 (1959), pp. 42, 46; Protocol on the Mutual Supply of Goods with the People's Republic of Mongolia for the Year 1959, January 30, 1959, in *TYC 1959,* vol. 8 (1960), pp. 102, 103; Protocol on the Mutual Supply of Goods with the Democratic People's Republic of Korea for the Year 1960, February 29, 1960, in *TYC 1960,* vol. 9 (1961), pp. 121, 123; Agreement on the Mutual Supply of Goods and Payments with the Democratic Republic of Vietnam for the Year 1959, February 18, 1959, in *TYC 1959,* vol. 8 (1960), pp. 104, 105; Trade and Payments Agreement with Cuba, July 23, 1960, in *TYC 1961,* vol. 10 (1962), pp. 238, 243.

21. In *TYC 1956,* vol. 5 (1958), pp. 113, 115.

However, in their ten succeeding trade agreements, beginning with the agreement of January 4, 1957, both parties agreed to use English as the prevailing language.[22] Since there was no official explanation, one can only guess English was chosen for political reasons, or perhaps for convenience.

Outside the socialist world, China has only one formal treaty of commerce, with Yemen, January 12, 1958.[23] Although the general form of this instrument is similar to the trade treaties with socialist states, its content differs in two respects: first, it provided an export schedule for each party as the basis of their transactions—a provision that does not appear in formal trade treaties with socialist states, but only in trade agreements. Second, the treaty required natural and juristic persons of one party in the territory of the other to strictly respect local religions, customs and habits, and not to interfere in the domestic affairs of the other country. Presumably, this stipulation, also omitted in trade treaties with socialist states, was made in special consideration of social conditions in Yemen. In addition, the Chinese Ministry of Foreign Affairs has classified four arrangements with Cambodia, Denmark, Finland, and Pakistan—all in the form of exchange of notes for the mutual grant of most-favored-nation treatment in matters relating to navigation and tariffs—as being trade and navigation treaties.[24]

Trade agreements with non-socialist states also differ significantly from China's socialist-partner trade agreements. Instead of dealing with specific problems, in many cases these non-socialist trade agreements provide such general principles as "equilibrium" in the volume of trade, most-favored-nation treatment, the establishment of a joint trade committee or the exchange of trade missions and exhibitions, methods of payment, and means of settling disputes. While most of these agreements were concluded with those states which maintain formal diplomatic relations with China,[25] there are exceptions, such as the agreement with Peru, the so-called Minutes of Lima Talks (see Appendix I). It was signed on April 28, 1971—about six months before Peru's *de jure* recognition of the People's Republic—by Chinese Vice-Minister of Foreign Trade Chou Hua-min, and Carlos Garcia Bedoya, Secretary-General of the Ministry of Foreign Affairs of the Republic of Peru,

22. In *TYC 1957,* vol. 6 (1958), pp. 164, 165.

23. In *TYC 1958,* vol. 7 (1959), p. 28.

24. See *TYC 1962,* vol. 11 (1963), pp. 237-8; Exchange of Notes with Finland, March 31, 1956, in *TYC 1956,* vol. 5 (1958), p. 61; Exchange of Notes with Denmark, December 1, 1957, in *TYC 1957,* vol. 6 (1958), p. 45; Exchange of Notes with Pakistan, December 24, 1957, April 9, 1958, October 4, 1958, in *TYC 1958,* vol. 7 (1959), pp. 35-36; Exchange of Notes with Cambodia, October 20, 1959, *TYC 1959,* vol. 4 (1960), p. 95.

25. See, e.g., Trade Agreement with the Government of the Republic of Syria, November 30, 1955, in *TYC 1955,* vol. 4 (1960), p. 118; Trade Agreement with the Government of Australia, July 24, 1973, in Appendix E. The actual date of signing does not appear in the agreement; the date above is based on a press statement given by Australian Minister for Overseas Trade J. F. Cairns.

in the presence of Peruvian Foreign Minister Edgardo Mercado Jarrin.[26] A preamble stating the common desire of both parties for developing trade relations and friendship was followed by provisions for the exchange of goods on the basis of one export schedule for each party; the mutual granting of most-favored-nation treatment for exports and imports listed in the schedules, customs duties, other taxes and customs procedures, navigation, and the qualifications of actual trading parties; the possible establishment of commercial offices; and the Chinese government's support of the actions which Peru and other Latin American countries have taken to exercise their sovereign rights over 200-nautical-mile territorial waters, and to establish more impartial, realistic and lasting international order on the sea. In subsequent "minutes of talks" signed between the Peruvian Minister of Fisheries and his Chinese counterpart in Peking, the Chinese government reiterated its support of Peru's claim of territorial waters and its agreement to purchase Peruvian products. In addition, both sides agreed to exchange commercial offices.[27] These minutes constitute a form of *de facto* mutual recognition between the two governments as well as an intergovernmental agreement that combines the elements of both a commercial and a political treaty.[28]

Another feature of trade with non-socialist countries is the so-called private, nongovernmental, or semi-governmental agreement concluded between the CCPIT or a Chinese trade delegation and private or semi-governmental foreign organizations. To the Chinese, foreign trade is basically a sovereign function of the state, and the delegations that conclude these agreements are invariably representatives of the state's overall foreign trade organization.[29] Those who conclude such agreements with China are doubtless aware of the fact that they are doing business with the Chinese state, not with private corporations or individuals, and that, even in non-socialist

26. Peru extended the recognition to China in November, 1971. See "Joint Communique on Establishment of Diplomatic Relations between China and Peru," *Peking Review*, no. 45 (1971), p. 5.

27. See "Peruvian Minister of Fisheries Visits China," *ibid.*, no. 26 (1971), p. 4; and "Trade Delegations of China and Peru Hold Talks," *ibid.*

28. A more recent example is China's first trade agreement with the Philippines, which was an exchange of letters between officials of the two governments in the presence of Vice-Premier Li Hsien-nien and Madame Imelda Romualdez Marcos in Peking. See "Madame Marcos' Visit to China Welcomed," *Peking Review*, no. 39 (1974), pp. 3-5. For reference to some earlier agreements concluded by China with foreign states before the establishment of diplomatic relations, see Trade Agreement with the Government of Ceylon, October 4, 1952, in *TYC 1952-1953*, vol. 2 (1957), p. 173; Trade Agreement with the Government of the Republic of Egypt, August 22, 1955, in *TYC 1955*, vol. 4 (1960), p. 123.

29. China's frontier trade is not monopolized by the state. However, the amount involved in this type of trade is exceedingly small; for example, in each frontier transaction with the North Vietnamese, the amount was limited to ten *yuan* or about $5.00. See Protocol with the Democratic Republic of Vietnam Concerning Small Transactions in the Border Areas of the Two Countries, July 7, 1955, in *TYC 1955*, vol. 4 (1960), pp. 154, 155.

countries, they themselves are either connected with or supported by their own governments. The fourth Sino-Japanese trade agreement is an example. It was signed on March 5, 1958 by the Chinese in the name of the CCPIT and by the Japanese in the name of the Dietmen's League for the Promotion of Japan-China Trade and two private organizations.[30] But when the agreement broke off in May, 1958 as a result of the Nagasaki flag incident, Chinese Vice-Premier and Foreign Minister Chen Yi, together with the chief Chinese signatory Nan Han-chen, openly held the Japanese government, not the Japanese signatories, responsible for its nullification.[31] Moreover, as a matter of practice, the Chinese Ministry of Foreign Affairs included most of these nongovernmental agreements in its official treaty collection, *TYC*, thus lending the agreements a treaty character.[32] Although legally speaking, such inclusion is a unilateral act not binding upon the governments of China's foreign trading partners, a breach of such an agreement is not without consequences, as seen in the case of the fourth Sino-Japanese trade agreement. At the same time, it should be pointed out that China used this special form of agreement with certain foreign countries not by choice, but when required for lack of diplomatic relations—under normal circumstances, this form is unnecessary.

In trade agreements with non-socialist states, the official languages of the contracting parties are equally authentic, a practice based on the principle of equality. Upon agreement of the contracting parties a third language, usually English or French, is sometimes used, either for reference or as the basis for interpretation.[33] The Treaty of Commerce with Yemen, January 12, 1958, in which Arabic prevails, is an exception, unlike the Trade Agreement with Egypt, August 22, 1955, where Arabic, Chinese, and English are all accepted as being equally authentic.[34]

Treaty-Making Power and Ratification

The 1954 Constitution contained three provisions regarding the treaty-making power: article 31 provided the Standing Committee of the NPC

---

30. See *TYC 1958*, vol. 7 (1959), pp. 197-203.

31. See Vice-Premier Chen Yi's statement to Hsinhua correspondents on recent Sino-Japanese relations, May 9, 1958, in *Jih-pen wen-t'i*, vol. 2 (1958), p. 87; the CCPIT's telegram to the three Japanese organizations, May 9, 1958, in *ibid.*, pp. 214-215.

32. See, e.g., Trade Agreement between the CCPIT and the Eastern Committee of the German Economy, September 27, 1957, *TYC 1957*, vol. 6 (1958), p. 323; official letters of the governmental departments of the PRC and the Federal Republic of Germany concerning the realization of trade agreements, August 20, 1956, September 26, 1957, and September 27, 1957, in *ibid.*, pp. 325-327.

33. See, e.g., Trade Agreement with the Government of Finland, June 5, 1953, in *TYC 1952-1953*, vol. 2 (1957), pp. 35, 37; Trade Agreement with the Government of Syria, November 30, 1955, *TYC 1955*, vol. 4 (1960), pp. 118, 120.

34. *TYC 1958*, vol. 7 (1959), pp. 28, 30; *TYC 1955*, vol. 4 (1960), pp. 123, 124-125.

with the power "to decide on the ratification or abrogation of treaties concluded with foreign states"; article 41 stipulated: "the Chairman of the People's Republic of China represents the People's Republic of China in its relations with foreign states, receives foreign diplomatic representatives and, in pursuance of decisions of the Standing Committee of the National People's Congress, appoints or recalls plenipotentiary representatives to foreign states and ratifies treaties concluded with foreign states"; and article 49 authorized the State Council "to direct the conduct of external affairs." The 1975 Constitution abolished the chairmanship of the People's Republic and in article 18, empowers the Standing Committee of the NPC to "dispatch and recall plenipotentiary representatives abroad, receive foreign diplomatic envoys, [and] ratify and denounce treaties concluded with foreign states."

In practice, of the seven formal treaties of trade and navigation that China has concluded with foreign states, one was signed by Premier Chou En-lai, three by Vice-Premier Li Hsien-nien, and three by the late Minister of Foreign Trade Yeh Chi-chuang—all acting as plenipotentiaries of the chairman of the PRC.[35] In formal economic and trade agreements *(hsieh-ting)*, Vice-Premier Li Hsien-nien, the minister of foreign trade, or vice-ministers of foreign trade signed as plenipotentiaries of the government of the PRC or the State Council.[36] In other trade agreements, vice-ministers of foreign trade acted either as representatives of the State Council or the plenipotentiaries of the Ministry of Foreign Trade.[37] In still other trade documents, lesser officials signed as representatives of the Ministry of Foreign Trade without "full powers" of the ministry or the Chinese government.[38] The Ministry of Foreign Affairs or its authorized officials sometimes acted on behalf of the Ministry of Foreign Trade, as in the Exchange of Notes with Pakistan for the Mutual Grant of Most-Favored-Nation Treatment to the Other Party's Goods,

35. See, respectively, treaties with Yemen, January 12, 1958, *TYC 1958*, vol. 7 (1959), pp. 28, 30; the Democratic Republic of Germany, January 18, 1960, *TYC 1960*, vol. 9 (1961), pp. 134, 139; Albania, February 2, 1961, *TYC 1961*, vol. 10 (1962), pp. 290, 294; the Democratic People's Republic of Korea, November 5, 1962, *TYC 1962*, vol. 11 (1963), pp. 92, 97; the USSR, April 23, 1958, *TYC 1958*, vol. 7 (1959), pp. 42, 46; the People's Republic of Mongolia, April 26, 1961, *TYC 1961*, vol. 10 (1962), pp. 361, 365; and the Democratic Republic of Vietnam, December 5, 1962, *TYC 1962*, vol. 11 (1963), pp. 100, 104.

36. See, e.g., two agreements with the Republic of Ghana, August 18, 1961, *TYC 1961*, vol. 10 (1962), pp. 250-251; and *ibid.*, pp. 252, 255 (English translation of both agreements in Appendix H). Also see Trade Agreement with the Government of the Republic of Iraq, May 25, 1960, *ibid.*, pp. 266, 267; Agreement with the People's Republic of Hungary on the Exchange of Goods and Payments for the Year 1959, March 17, 1959, *TYC 1959*, vol. 8 (1960), pp. 33, 36.

37. See, e.g. Trade Agreement with the Government of the Republic of Finland, August 8, 1955, in *TYC 1955*, vol. 4 (1960), pp. 43, 45; Protocol on the General Conditions for Delivery with the USSR, February 12, 1955, in *ibid.*, p. 46.

38. See, e.g., Protocol on the General Conditions for the Delivery of Goods between the Foreign Trade Organizations of the PRC and the People's Republic of Romania of 1961, July 7, 1961, in Appendix C.

December 24, 1957 and April 9, 1958, made between the Pakistani embassy in China and the Chinese Ministry of Foreign Affairs in Peking without naming individual signatories.[39] In another exchange of notes with Cambodia on a similar subject, the Chinese chargé d' affaires in Phnom Penh signed the document.[40] And in China's most recent trade agreement with Japan, Minister of Foreign Affairs Chi Peng-fei signed as representative of the Government of the PRC—an act unprecedented in China's trade treaty practice (see Appendix D).

In sum, the level of representation parallels the rigidity of form in Chinese practice. The four main classes of representatives empowered to make trade treaties and agreements are plenipotentiaries of the Standing Committee of the NPC for formal trade treaties *(t'iao-yüeh);* plenipotentiaries or authorized representatives of the State Council for formal trade agreements *(hsieh-ting);* authorized representatives of the Ministry of Foreign Trade for other trade agreements or protocols *(I-ting-shu),* general conditions for delivery, and other trade documents which are less formal and permanent than those in the first two classes; and authorized representatives of the Ministry of Foreign Affairs or the MFT. Those who signed semi-governmental or nongovernmental agreements for China in the name of the CCPIT or other organizations are not official representatives of the People's Republic under either international law or the Chinese Constitution, although in practice such agreements are usually respected by the Chinese government.[41]

According to Chinese law, all treaties and agreements with foreign states require ratification or approval. A decision of the Standing Committee of the NPC provides:

The following types of treaties concluded by the People's Republic of China with foreign states are to be ratified in accordance with the provisions of Article 31, paragraph 12, and Article 41 of the Constitution of the People's Republic of China: peace treaties; treaties of non-aggression; treaties of friendship, alliance and mutual assistance; and all other treaties, including agreements, which contain stipulations that they are to be submitted for ratification.

Agreements and protocols which do not fall under the above categories are to be approved by the State Council.[42]

All seven formal trade treaties that China has concluded with foreign states provided for ratification and the exchange of instruments of ratification

39. *TYC 1958,* vol. 7 (1959), pp. 35-36.

40. In *TYC 1959,* vol. 8 (1960), p. 96.

41. For an analysis of China's treaty performance in general, see Luke T. Lee, "Treaty Relations of the People's Republic of China: A Study of Compliance," *University Of Pennsylvania Law Review* 116:244 (1967).

42. Adopted by the Standing Committee of the NPC at its first session on October 16,

before entering into force.[43] In some trade agreements, stipulations were made for approval by the respective governments of the contracting parties; in other agreements, no such provisions were made.[44] As far as Chinese law is concerned, however, both types of agreements fall under the jurisdiction of the State Council, and require its approval.[45]

Trade Representation Abroad

Reasoning that Hong Kong and Macao are Chinese territory, the Chinese government does not consider its trade representation and operation there relevant to its trade treaty relations with other countries (except Britain, with which China has a reciprocal banking arrangement). The Chinese prohibit citizens of any foreign nationality from operating trading firms in China. In essence, then, Chinese state-owned firms incorporated in Hong Kong can establish branches in other countries without obligating the Chinese government to reciprocate.[46] China's state monopoly of foreign trade and its refusal to accept private foreign investment and commercial representation in Chinese territory has minimized the role played by individuals in its foreign trade, and increased the importance of official trade representation abroad. Over the years the Chinese government has adopted three basic forms of such representation: semi-official trade missions in unrecognized states; formal official trade missions in recognized states; and commercial counselors and

---

1954, in *FKHP 1954-1955,* vol. 1 (1956), p. 207.

43. With Yemen, January 12, 1958, art. 12, *TYC 1958,* vol. 7 (1959), p. 30; the USSR, April 23, 1958, art. 17, *ibid.,* p. 46; the Democratic Republic of Germany, January 18, 1960, art. 17, *TYC 1960,* vol. 9 (1961), p. 138; Albania, February 2, 1961, art. 17, *TYC 1961,* vol. 10 (1962), p. 294; Mongolia, April 26, 1961, art. 14, *ibid.,* p. 364; the Democratic People's Republic of Korea, November 5, 1962, art. 16, *TYC 1962,* vol. 11 (1963), p. 96; the Democratic Republic of Vietnam, December 5, 1962, art. 16, *ibid.,* p. 104.

44. See, e.g., Trade and Payments Agreement with Cuba, July 23, 1960, art. 23, in *TYC 1961,* vol. 10 (1962), p. 243; Trade Agreement with Sudan, May 23, 1962, *TYC 1962,* vol. 11 (1963), pp. 56-58.

45. For further reference to the Chinese law of treaties, see Jerome Alan Cohen and Hungdah Chiu, *People's China and International Law,* vol. 2 (1974), Part VIII, pp. 1111-1282.

46. In a pioneering effort Nippon Steel Corporation is currently seeking Chinese permission to open an office in Wuhan and another in Peking in order to implement a $217 (65,000 million *yen*) contract, under which the Japanese will help the Chinese build a strip mill capable of producing three million tons of hot rolled steel a year and an additional facility with an annual production capacity of seventy thousand tons of silicon steel plate. By mutual agreement, a total of 300 Chinese engineers will receive training in Japan, a total of 150 Japanese engineers will periodically stay at the construction site in Wuhan, and about 360 Japanese technicians will work on the entire project over a period of ten years. The proposed Japanese office in Peking is intended to function as a branch of the corporation to negotiate further exports of Japanese steel products to China. Whether the Chinese government will comply with the Japanese request remains to be seen. See "Japanese Firms Will Export Steel Plant to China," *Japan Times,* June 5, 1974, p. 8; "Largest Contract Is for Steel Plants," *Economic Salon,* July 1974, p. 19; "Nippon Steel Seeks Offices in China," *ibid.,* p. 20.

attachés, visiting trade delegations, and joint trade committees. The idea of establishing trade missions abroad *(torgpredstov)* as official representatives of the state originated in Soviet Russia. Prior to 1933, their status was defined in a number of international conventions which the Soviet government entered into with other countries.[47] Then on September 13, 1933, a statute was promulgated authorizing the trade missions to exercise abroad "the rights of the Union of the Soviet Socialist Republics pertaining to the monopoly of foreign trade enjoyed by the Union."[48] As distinguished from corporate bodies, these trade missions are not legal entities; rather, they are part of the corresponding diplomatic missions of the Soviet Union abroad and enjoy the latter's privileges. In addition to their various functions relating to the operation and regulation of Soviet foreign trade, they are authorized to conclude in the name of the Soviet state all kinds of contracts and legal transactions, and the treasury of the Soviet state is liable for obligations incurred by the trade missions.[49]

China does not have a domestic law defining the nature and functions of its trade representation abroad. In practice, it has used the Soviet idea with certain modifications. In trade agreements with unrecognized states, a clause for the exchange of "trade missions" or "trade representative offices" *(shang-wu tai-piao ch'u)* was first included in an agreement with Japan.[50] A memorandum attached to the second Sino-Japanese trade agreement, October 29, 1953, stated: "The Contracting Parties agreed to exchange trade missions; Japan will establish her permanent trade mission in China when China's permanent trade mission has been established in Japan."[51] The third agreement, May 4, 1955 specified the locations of the trade missions and provided these missions and their members with "diplomatic treatment and rights" (article 10).[52] The agreement did not say how such treatment and rights could be granted in the absence of diplomatic relations between the two countries and a direct and open commitment by their governments. It merely added: "The Contracting Parties agreed to work for the realization [of this provision] as early as possible." Then the fourth agreement, March 5, 1958, provided

47. Protocol on the Legal Status of the Trade Representation of the USSR in Lithuania, August 29, 1931, in T. A. Taracouzio, *The Soviet Union and International Law,* p. 431.

48. Statute Concerning Trade Missions and Trade Agencies of the USSR Abroad, September 13, 1933, section 1, in Vladimir Gsovski, *Soviet Civil Law,* vol. 2 (1949), p. 347.

49. *Ibid.,* at pp. 348-352.

50. A Chinese dictionary on foreign trade translated the Russian word *torgpredstov* as *shang-wu tai-piao ch'u* or "trade representative office." See *Chien-ming tui-wai mao-i tz'u-tien,* p. 101. In other publications, however, the Russian word has been variously translated as "trade mission," "trade bureau," etc. For the sake of consistency, the Chinese phrase *shang-wu tai-piao ch'u* is hereafter translated as "trade mission," as distinguished from "trade agency" *(shang-wu tai-li ch'u)* and "trade delegation" *(mao-i tai-piao t'uan).*

51. In *TYC 1952-1953,* vol. 2 (1957), p. 372.

52. In *TYC 1955,* vol. 4 (1960), pp. 258, 260.

quasi-diplomatic treatment of the proposed trade missions and their members in detail.

After the aborted fourth agreement resumption of Sino-Japanese trade relations—first under the L-T agreement (1963-1967) and then through the annual memorandum trade accords (1968-1973)—did not include defining the formal legal status of either party's trade mission, officially known as a "trade liaison office." It was well known, however, that the Chinese representatives in Tokyo were all state officials and their Japanese counterparts in Peking were mostly employees of the Japanese government "temporarily on leave."[53] The matter was not officially resolved until after the Sino-Japanese rapprochement in September, 1972 when the Japanese government formally granted the Chinese trade office diplomatic status pending the exchange of ambassadors.[54]

Under both L-T practice and the memorandum trade arrangements, actual transactions were carried out through a double channel. On one hand, trade with friendly firms or "friendly trade" was based on Premier Chou En-lai's three political principles and three trading principles. Any Japanese company desirous of entering into business with China had to be recommended by the three Japanese organizations which had sponsored the agreements (The Japan-China Trade Promotion Association, the Japan Association for the Promotion of International Trade, and the Kansai Headquarters of the Japan Association for the Promotion of International Trade) for approval by their Chinese counterparts. Once the status of "friendly firm" was granted, the company could then attend the Kwangchow trade fair or occasional trade exhibitions to transact business. On the other hand, the L-T trade was based on a five-year barter agreement for the exchange of major commodities with provisions for deferred payments as well as the establishment of liaison offices for the coordination of trade activities. Under this arrangement, representatives of the L-T trade liaison offices on both sides met at the beginning of every fiscal year to formulate tentative trade plans for the following year. Actual negotiations were always conducted in Peking with officials of the CCPIT and the Ministry of Foreign Trade.[55] Later under the memorandum trade arrangement, both sides followed the same procedures except that the agreement operated on a yearly basis.[56] (Thus, in the economic field the Chinese trade office in Tokyo merely exercised a liaison function, as

53. For example, Hsiao Hsiang-chien who served as chief of the Chinese trade mission, formally known as the Tokyo Liaison Office of the China-Japan Memorandum Trade Office, from July, 1972 to January, 1974, has since become counselor of the Chinese embassy.

54. See *Far Eastern Economic Review*, no. 42 (1972), p. 5.

55. See Japan External Trade Organization, *How to Approach the China Market*, pp. 124-130.

56. "Chinese and Japanese Trade Organizations Signed Minutes of Talks in Peking," *Peking Review*, no. 13 (1968), p. 9.

distinguished from the functions prescribed in the 1933 Soviet statute for its trade missions abroad.)

Chinese trade missions in other unrecognized states functioned in a similar manner. Italy, for example, exchanged trade missions with China in 1965, five years before its recognition of the People's Republic.[57] During the interim, only a few contracts were actually signed by the Chinese mission in Rome and none was signed by the Italian mission in Peking. The majority of contracts were drafted and concluded outside both trade missions, either in Italy or in China, often at the autumn and spring trade fairs in Kwangchow.[58]

Unlike their Soviet counterparts, Chinese trade representatives abroad have never been accused of espionage. (In the 1964 Brazilian case, mentioned earlier, the Chinese government did not claim diplomatic immunity or official status for the nine employees of the CCPIT and the New China News Agency arrested by the Brazilian government, even though one of them, Wang Yao-ting, was a vice-president of the China National Textiles Import and Export Corporation. The Brazilian authorities were unable to prove their charges against the Chinese in a year-long trial and appeal).[59] In sum, the basic political functions of the Chinese trade missions in unrecognized states have been to maintain a degree of semi-official communication with the host governments, and to win the latter's diplomatic recognition of the People's Republic.

The second form of Chinese trade representation involves those states which maintain diplomatic relations with the People's Republic and have agreements with it for the exchange of trade missions, such as India and the

57. "Sino-Italian Trade Bureaux to be Established," *ibid.,* no. 50, (1964), p. 25.

58. Gabriele Crespi Reghizzi, "Legal Aspects of Trade with China: the Italian Experience," *Harvard International Law Journal* 9:85, 92-93 (1968). Other countries which exchanged trade missions with China before the establishment of diplomatic relations included Egypt, Lebanon, and Peru. See Trade Agreement with Egypt, August 22, 1955, art. 6, in *TYC 1955,* vol. 4 (1960), p. 124; Trade Agreement with Lebanon,·December 31, 1955, in *TYC 1955,* vol. 4 (1960), p. 159; "Trade Delegations of China and Peru Hold Talks," *Peking Review,* no. 26 (1971), p. 4. However, both Egypt and Peru extended formal recognition to the People's Republic soon after their agreement for the exchange, providing no information for a meaningful analysis. In the case of Lebanon, the agreement quoted above provided that each party has the right to establish a trade mission in the capital of the other; however, it did not specify the functions of the trade missions.

59. The Chinese government first identified the nine as "citizens." See "Protest Against Arrests and Torture of Chinese Citizens in Brazil," *Peking Review,* no. 16 (1964), p. 5. Then, in a formal protest to the Brazilian military tribunal the Chinese government simply called the nine individuals as Chinese *jen-yüan,* which was officially translated as "personnel." See Statement of the Government of the PRC Concerning the Brazilian Authorities' Illegal Judgement of Chinese Personnel, December 23, 1964, in *Cheng-fa yen-chiu,* no. 1 (1965), p. 1; English translation of the statement in *Peking Review,* no. 1 (1965), p. 22. Also see Statement of the International Lawyers' Delegation Observing the Court Martial of the Nine Chinese Personnel in Brazil, January 31, 1965, in *Cheng-fa yen-chiu,* no. 1 (1965), p. 2. Wang Yao-ting's identity was mentioned in this statement. According to Heraclito Sobral Pinto, then president of the Institute of Lawyers in Brazil defending the nine Chinese, the Brazilian government's charge against his

Soviet Union.[60] According to the Agreement with India on Trade and Intercourse between Tibet Region of China and India, April 29, 1954, the two parties agreed to exchange "trade agencies," rather than missions.[61]

What matters, of course, is not semantics but the actual status and functions of each type of trade representation. The Sino-Indian accord provided the trade agents of both parties with freedom from arrest while exercising their functions and with the right to enjoy freedom from search in respect to themselves, their wives, and dependent children. The agreement also provided the trade agencies of both parties with privileges and immunities for couriers, mail bags, and communications in code. The trade agents of both parties, in accordance with the laws and regulations of the local governments, had access to their nationals involved in civil or criminal cases.[62] Chinese trade agencies were established in New Delhi, Calcutta, and Kalimpong, whereas the Indian representation was confined to Yatung, Gyantse, and Gartok, in accordance with the titular limitation of the agreement to Tibet.[63] However, the agreement did not mention the commercial functions of the agencies, such as their ability to conclude business transactions; in fact, the Chinese Ministry of Foreign Affairs formally classified the agreement with India as a political treaty.[64]

In contrast to the agreements with India and Japan, China's 1958 agreement with the Soviet Union provides for exchange of trade missions between states who already recognize each other. The Annex to this Treaty of

---

clients was made in the "total absence of genuine proofs and evidence." See José Honório Rodrigues, "Brazil and China, the Varying Fortunes of Independent Diplomacy," in A. M. Halpern, *Policies Toward China* pp. 457, 474.

60. For reference to other countries, see Trade Agreement with Syria, November 30, 1955, in TYC 1955, vol. 4 (1960), p. 118; Protocol Modifying the Trade and Payments Agreements with Syria, July 3, 1957, in *TYC 1957*, vol. 6 (1958), p. 161; Agreement with Nepal on Trade and Intercourse, September 20, 1956, in *TYC 1956*, vol. 5 (1958), p. 4. In the Exchange of Notes with the Government of Sudan Concerning the Trade Problems of the Two Countries, April 12, 1956, it was provided that the contracting states agreed in principle "to encourage the exchange of trade delegates in order to develop the economic and trade relations between the two states." In *TYC 1956*, vol. 5 (1958), p. 59.

61. The 1933 Soviet statute stipulates that the People's Commissar for Foreign Trade may establish independent trade agencies for the countries in which there are no trade missions of the USSR or for individual districts within the countries in which trade missions are located. See Vladimir Gsovski, *Soviet Civil Law,* vol. 2, (1949), p. 352. The Chinese have offered no explanation as to the distinction between these two types of trade representation.

62. Exchange of Notes with India, April 29, 1954, in *TYC 1954,* vol. 3 (1958), pp. 4, 5. Similar provisions can be found in the Agreement with Nepal on Trade and Intercourse, September 20, 1956, and the Exchange of Notes with Nepal on the same date. In *TYC 1956,* vol. 5 (1958), pp. 4-10.

63. Agreement with India, April 29, 1954, art. 1, in *TYC 1954,* vol. 3 (1958), p. 1. It should be noted that the local status of the Indian representation is consistent with the title of the agreement which is limited to Tibet Region of China. The agreement expired in 1962, and India refused to renew it. See *Jen-min shou-ts'e 1962,* p. 147.

64. See *TYC 1954,* vol. 3 (1958), p. 1.

Trade and Navigation with the Soviet Union (see Appendix B) stipulates the functions of their trade missions as follows: promoting the development of trade and economic relations between the two states; representing the interests of its own state in the other state in all matters relating to foreign trade; regulating trading transactions with the other state on behalf of its own state; and carrying on trade between the two states. The trade mission forms an integral part of the embassy of its own state and thus enjoys certain rights and privileges accorded to a diplomatic mission, including: diplomatic immunity for the trade mission chief and his deputies; extraterritoriality for the premises occupied by the trade mission and its branches; the right to use ciphers; waiver of commercial registration by the trade mission and its branches; and exemption from taxation of its employees who are citizens of the state to which the mission belongs. Represented by its trade mission, the government is responsible for foreign commercial contracts concluded or guaranteed on behalf of the trade mission in the receiving state and signed by authorized persons. The names of such authorized persons are to be published by the government of the receiving state. Finally, the trade mission enjoys all the immunities to which a sovereign state is entitled, and which relate also to foreign trade, with two exceptions:

Disputes regarding foreign commercial contracts concluded or guaranteed under article 3 by the Trade Delegation in the territory of the receiving state shall, in the absence of a reservation regarding arbitration or any other jurisdiction, be subject to the competence of the courts of the said state. No interim court orders for the provision of security may be made;

Final judicial decisions against the Trade Delegation in the afore-mentioned disputes which have become legally valid may be enforced by execution, but such execution may be levied only on the goods and claims outstanding to the credit of the Trade Delegations. [Article 4]

China has made no such detailed treaty arrangements with any other state except for the People's Republic of Mongolia which is virtually a puppet state of the Soviet Union.[65] This legalistic approach to the status and functions of trade missions in the Sino-Soviet treaty was a Chinese concession to the Soviet tradition rather than an established Chinese practice. Since the conclusion of the treaty in 1958, there has been no official information as to whether

65. The text of the annex regarding Chinese trade representation in Mongolia and Mongolian trade representation in China is exactly the same as that China has had with the Soviet Union. See *TYC 1961*, vol. 10 (1962), pp. 365-366. China's arrangement with Syria accorded the trade missions diplomatic status without specifying their trading functions and legal capacities. China's arrangement with Nepal for exchange of trade agencies, like that with India, was officially classfied as political rather than commercial. See, respectively, Trade Agreement with Syria, November 30, 1955, art. 8, in *TYC 1955*, vol. 4 (1960), pp. 118, 119; Protocol Modifying Trade and Payments Agreements with Syria, July 3, 1957, art. 1, in *TYC 1957*, vol. 6 (1958), pp. 161, 162; Agreement with Nepal on Trade and Intercourse between Tibet Region of China and Nepal, September 20, 1956, in *TYC 1956*, vol. 5 (1958), p. 4.

the trade missions have actually functioned in accordance with the provisions described in the treaty annex.

The third form of China's trade representation consists of commercial counselors or attachés, visiting trade delegations, and joint trade committees. The counselors and attachés are all appointed by the Ministry of Foreign Trade and attached to the Chinese diplomatic missions abroad. Like their foreign counterparts in China, they gather information concerning the local markets in their receiving states; disseminate information concerning the Chinese market; assist local importers and exporters in establishing business contacts with Chinese foreign trade corporations, and vice versa; arrange with local business organizations for the exchange of exhibitions; and attend to other matters relating to foreign trade. The exchange of these commercial counselors and attachés is usually not provided for by a trade treaty but is based on a reciprocal diplomatic agreement. Generally, they enjoy diplomatic status and immunities and are not engaged in actual business transactions. In countries where Chinese consular officers are present, they are also assisted by these officers, whose status and functions are usually stipulated in treaties concluded for such purposes.[66] The Chinese commercial counselor's office is sometimes staffed by representatives of Chinese national foreign trade corporations in order to provide the counselor with the kind of special assistance and knowledge he needs. The actual status of such personnel is, however, determined by their official credentials.

While commercial counselors and attachés constitute China's resident trade representatives in most of the foreign states with which the People's Republic maintains diplomatic relations, visiting Chinese trade delegations are sent abroad for ad hoc purpose, such as inspecting important factory equipment and technology, negotiating for trade agreements and contracts, goodwill tours, and commodity exhibitions.[67] These visiting Chinese delegations and their foreign counterparts in China (in addition to those attending the Kwangchow trade fair) are responsible for a substantial portion of China's annual trade. From 1972 to 1974, for instance, China held exhibitions and took part in thirty-nine international fairs in thirty-eight developing countries in Asia, Africa, Latin America and other regions; in addition, it held twenty-nine exhibitions in twenty-seven countries in northwestern Europe,

66. See, e.g., Consular Treaty with the USSR, June 23, 1959, in *TYC 1959*, vol. 8 (1960), p. 20; Consular Treaty with the Democratic Republic of Germany, January 27, 1959, in *TYC 1959*, vol. 8 (1960), p. 26; Consular Treaty with the Republic of Czechoslovakia, May 7, 1960, in *TYC 1960*, vol. 9 (1961), p. 52. In November 1974, Peking announced the establishment of a consulate-general in Vancouver, the first in the Western Hemisphere. See *Mei-chou hua-ch'iao jih-pao*, November 23, 1974, p. 4.

67. See "Chinese Commercial Officials Make First Major Tours of the US Sponsored by National Council," *U.S.-China Business Review*, no. 5 (1974), p. 18.

East Europe, North America, Oceania and Japan. During the same period, seventeen countries sponsored twenty-nine exhibitions in Peking, Shanghai and Tientsin.[68]

Although occasionally the exchange of visiting trade delegations can be arranged through informal contacts, it is usually agreed upon by the parties in a formal trade document. For example, the 1973 Sino-Australian trade agreement (see Appendix E) provides: "Each Contracting Party will promote the interchange of trade representatives, groups and delegations between the two countries, encourage the commercial exchange of industrial and technical expertise, and will facilitate the holding of trade exhibitions and other trade promotion activities in its country by organizations of the other in accordance with general customary practice" (article 7). The status of these delegations is dependent upon their official identity and composition as well as their arrangements with the receiving states. Generally, the head of a Chinese delegation is an official of the Ministry of Foreign Trade, the CCPIT, or a national foreign trade corporation, and its members are specialized personnel of the national foreign trade corporations concerned, and of relevant consuming or producing industries. Their treatment and reception in foreign states are usually cordial; every possible convenience is accorded them in entry and customs clearance; and security protection is also provided in countries where such precautionary measures are needed.[69] In return, foreign delegations visiting China receive equal treatment.

The institution of a joint trade committee, invariably based on an official or semi-official trade agreement, developed from a provision in the 1950 Sino-Soviet trade agreement which required the trade representatives of each party to examine the implementation of the agreement every six months and, when necessary, to submit appropriate suggestions regarding the mutual supply of goods and the maintenance of balance of payments as stipulated in the agreement.[70] Then, in a 1955 trade agreement with Syria, provisions were made for the establishment of a "mixed" committee, to be convened at the request of either contracting party, for the purpose of supervising the implementation of the agreement, solving any difficulties that might arise, and making proposals for the improvement and development of economic and trade relations between the two states.[71] The establishment of such a joint trade committee has become a standard provision in China's trade agreements

---

68. Wang Yao-ting, "China's Foreign Trade," *Peking Review,* no. 41 (1974), p. 18.
69. See details of former Minister of Foreign Trade Pai Hsiang-kuo's visit to Canada in 1972, in *China Trade Report,* no. 8 (1972), p. 15.
70. In *TYC 1949-1951,* vol. 1 (1960), p. 48.
71. In *TYC 1955,* vol. 4 (1960), pp. 119-120.

with many other countries, including Australia, Japan, and Brazil.[72] For example, the 1973 Sino-Australian trade agreement provides:

In order to facilitate the implementation of this Agreement, the two Contracting Parties establish a joint trade committee consisting of their respective designated representatives.

The committee shall meet once a year, unless otherwise mutually agreed, alternately in Canberra and Peking. When necessary, special meetings to discuss matters of mutual interest may be arranged through consultations between the two Contracting Parties.

The committee shall be assigned the task of examining the implementation of this Agreement, exploring measures for the expansion of mutually beneficial trade, improving understanding of the trade and related commercial policies of each country, and seeking solutions to problems which may arise in the course of the development of trade between the two countries. [Article 8]

The mutually beneficial merits of this institution obviously lie in the fact that regular meetings of such committees not only provide solutions for trade problems, but can also serve in the preparation of future trade plans and agreements. Moreover, from the Chinese point of view, the establishment of such an institution can also reduce the commercial counselor's work load, thus avoiding the need for a large resident staff in his office or a permanent special trade mission.

Semi-official Chinese trade representation in unrecognized states came into being as a matter of expediency, and is about to become obsolete as the People's Republic gains more recognition in the international community. Formal trade mission representation in recognized states, which is based on the legalistic Soviet model, is not likely to win wider acceptance because of its rigid formality and unconventional methods. Consequently, the use of commercial counselors and attachés along with visiting delegations and joint trade committees, because it provides a considerable degree of flexibility in state trading operations, will in all likelihood become the dominant form of official Chinese trade representation abroad.

National Treatment of Aliens

China recognizes the status of alien individuals and corporate bodies in both its international treaties and domestic legislation. In dealing with the status of alien individuals the Chinese government has simply followed the principle of territorial supremacy in the sense that it requires all aliens with the exception of those enjoying diplomatic immunities to abide by its laws. The 1949 Common Program is very specific on this point: "The Central People's

72. See the Sino-Australian Trade Agreement, art. 8, in Appendix E; Agreement on Trade between Japan and the PRC, art. 9, in Appendix D; and "Brazil and China Set a Trade Commission," *New York Times*, August 18, 1974, p. 9.

Government of the People's Republic of China protects law-abiding foreign nationals in China'' (article 58). A law of March 13, 1964, dealing with the entry into, exit from, and transit through the national boundaries of the People's Republic by foreign nationals, as well as their residence and travel within China, is also emphatic that they all "observe the laws and decrees of China."[73] (See Appendix J.) (At the same time, the Chinese government urges its own citizens abroad not only to obey the laws of their host states but also to respect local customs.)

The treatment afforded such law-abiding aliens, however, is conditioned by the Chinese economic and political system. This can be best explained through an analysis of the Chinese government's application of national treatment, defined by a textbook of the Peking Foreign Trade College as follows: "According to this principle, either contracting state guarantees to the nationals, enterprises, or vessels of the other contracting state in its territory the same treatment as it is accorded to its own nationals, enterprises, and vessels.[74] It also noted that this principle generally applies to the economic rights of foreign citizens and enterprises, internal taxation, the treatment of vessels, railway transport and transit, and civil suits.[75] However, the Chinese have insisted that extensive application of the national treatment principle by capitalist nations in their trade treaties and agreements with small and weak nations constitutes a legal basis for the former to encroach upon the latter's economies.[76] Accordingly, the Chinese government has limited its use of national treatment clauses to the question of "humanitarianism," as found in the 1958 Treaty of Trade and Navigation with the Soviet Union:

If a vessel of one Contracting Party is in distress or is wrecked on the coast of the other Contracting Party, such vessel and its cargo shall enjoy the same advantages and immunities as are granted under the laws of the latter State to its own vessels in similar circumstances. The necessary aid and assistance shall be afforded at all times, and in the same measure as in the case of national vessels in the same situation, to the master, crew and passengers, and to the vessel and its cargo. Where there are special agreements on such matters, aid shall likewise be afforded in accordance with such agreements. [Article 9]

Such treatment of nationals is, however, limited to socialist countries which have such agreements with the People's Republic.[77] In agreements

73. For further reference to aliens in China, see Jerome Alan Cohen and Hungdah Chiu, *People's China and International Law,* vol. 1 (1974), pp. 503-741.

74. Wang Yao-tien, op. cit., p. 23.

75. *Ibid.*

76. *Ibid.;* Wei-liang, "A Brief Comment on International Treaties After World War II," in *Kuo-chi t' iao-yüeh chi 1953-1957,* vol. 7 (1961), pp. 660, 671. Wei-liang is believed to be the first name of Shen Wei-liang, who was Deputy Director of the Department of International Treaties and Law in the Ministry of Foreign Affairs. See *Jen-min jih-pao,* April 28, 1972, p. 2.

77. The Democratic Republic of Germany, January 18, 1960, in *TYC 1960,* vol. 9

with non-socialist states, it has been provided that a vessel of either contracting party in distress or otherwise endangered in the territorial waters of the other party is to receive ''all possible aid and assistance'' within the limits of the latter's law.[78] Since a nation cannot be expected to treat aliens better than its own citizens, China's denial of national treatment to foreign individuals in matters concerning trade other than shipwreck is basically consistent with its domestic system and international practice. China has not yet promulgated a nationality law and will not be able to do so until the problem of nationality of those Chinese residing abroad with or without foreign citizenships —approximately forty million—is solved.

In 1955, China concluded a treaty with Indonesia concerning the problem of dual nationality. According to that document, China agreed to offer the Chinese residents in Indonesia a choice of nationality: if one chose to adopt the nationality of Indonesia, he lost the nationality of the People's Republic, and vice versa.[79] However, this treaty was never satisfactorily implemented because of the intrinsic nature of the problem inherent in the mutual discrimination between native Indonesians and Chinese residents. Since the Sino-American detente, China has begun to develop a new nationality policy: all Chinese under Nationalist rule (sixteen million) and those living in Hong Kong and Macao (over four million) are now referred to as ''compatriots'' (t'ung-pao); those in foreign countries without being naturalized as ''overseas Chinese'' (hua-ch' iao); and those who have adopted

---

(1961), pp. 134, 137; Albania, February 2, 1961, in *TYC 1961*, vol. 10 (1962), pp. 290, 293; the Democratic Republic of Vietnam, December 5, 1962, in *TYC 1962*, vol. 11 (1963), pp. 100, 103; the Democratic People's Republic of Korea, November 5, 1962, in *TYC 1962*, vol. 11 (1963), pp. 92, 95.

78. See Maritime Transport Agreements: with Ceylon, July 25, 1963, art. 5, in *TYC 1963*, vol. 12 (1964), pp. 251, 252; Ghana, March 26, 1963, art. 5, in *TYC 1963*, vol. 12 (1964), pp. 234, 235; Congo (Brazzaville) October 2, 1964, art. 5, in *TYC 1964*, vol. 13 (1965), pp. 366-367. The Maritime Transport Agreement with Italy, October 8, 1972, article 5 provides: "Should merchant vessels of either Party referred to in Article 1 be involved in maritime perils or encounter any other danger in the territorial waters or ports of the other Party, both Parties shall mutually render all possible salvage and protection to such vessels, crew, cargo and passengers in peril or in danger." The Maritime Transport Agreement with Norway, October 9, 1974, article 9, provides: "Should vessels of either Party referred to in Article 1 .of the present Agreement be involved in maritime casualties or encounter any other danger in the territorial waters or ports of the other Party, the latter shall give all possible assistance and attention to the vessels, crew, cargo and passengers in danger, and notify the appropriate Authorities of the Party concerned in the quickest way. No discrimination shall be exercised in the collection of charges incurred." The texts of both agreements are in National Council for U.S.-China Trade Special Report no. 10, *China Shipping Manual*, ed. by Nicholas H. Ludlow, 1974, pp. 30-34.

79. The treaty was not ratified by the Chairman of the People's Republic until February 10, 1958, and by the President of Indonesia until January 11, 1959. The instruments of ratification were exchanged on January 20, 1960. In *TYC 1959*, vol. 8 (1960), pp. 12-17. For a discussion of the matter, see Tao-tai Hsia, "Settlement of Dual Nationality between Communist China and Other Countries," in *Osteuropa-Recht*, no. 1 (1965), p. 27. Hsia's article is published in English in the above journal.

foreign citizenships as "foreigners."[80] Then in the joint communiqué establishing diplomatic relationship with Malaysia, the Chinese government formally renounced the principle of *jus sanguinis* (the right of blood) and dual nationality[81] (which has been vigorously enforced by the Nationalists in competition for the allegiance of overseas Chinese).[82]

The PRC policy still leaves many questions unanswered. As of 1975, Taiwan still maintained diplomatic relations with some twenty countries in addition to quasi-consular representation in more than a hundred foreign states either in the name of news agencies or through such "academic" institutes as the Sun Yat-sen Center in Spain. Because of their personal or business ties with Taiwan, many Chinese living, trading, or studying in these countries bear Nationalist passports. If the PRC government is to conclude a treaty with one of these states granting certain privileges to citizens of both contracting parties, it would be forced to make a difficult decision as to whether the Nationalist Chinese should be legally included in its citizenry and protected accordingly. This uncertainty in the status of Chinese residing abroad has already caused a massive "desertion" in some countries. In Japan alone, for example, there were about fifty thousand Chinese residents in 1972. As a result of the Sino-Japanese rapprochement, nearly twenty thousand of them renounced their Chinese nationality—rejecting both Taiwan and the People's Republic—in order to protect their property in Japan, and to avoid possible political harassment. Only about one half of them have been approved for naturalization; the rest have become stateless.[83]

The People's Republic is a socialist state; no law or treaty has ever provided aliens with the right to own or lease productive property or to establish a gainful private enterprise in China.[84] Britain maintains two

80. For a principal reference to this policy, see "Comrade Yeh Chien-ying's Speech," *Peking Review,* no. 40 (1972), p. 8. For a study of China's policy before the detente, see Stephen Fitzgerald, *China and the Overseas Chinese.* The total number of Chinese in the last two categories is estimated to be over twenty million.

81. Article 5 of the Joint Communiqué, March 31, 1974, reads in part: "Both the Government of the People's Republic of China and the Government of Malaysia declare that they do not recognize dual nationality. Proceeding from this principle, the Chinese government considers any one of Chinese origin who has taken up of his own will or acquired Malaysian nationality as automatically forfeiting Chinese nationality." *Peking Review,* no. 23 (1974), p. 8.

82. See Nationality Act, February 19, 1929, in Chang Chih-pen, ed., *Tsui-hsin liu-fa ch'üan-shu* (1960), p. 833. For reference to Nationalist policy towards Chinese abroad, see Committee for the Compilation of the Annals of Overseas Chinese, ed., *Hua-ch'iao chih: tsung-chih.*

83. "10,000 Ethnic Chinese Lack Any Nationality," *Japan Times,* November 24, 1974, p. 2.

84. The only exception to forbidding private investment up to the time of the Cultural Revolution was in the case of overseas Chinese, whom the government encouraged to establish a number of state-private companies in Kwangtung and Fukien in the early 1950s. By March 1955, in line with the government's policy of socialist transformation, many of these companies were incorporated into a single State-Private Joint Overseas Chinese Investment Company, Ltd., with a

banking offices in Shanghai, each with a single officer, for handling payments for Chinese exports and intergovernmental transactions, but their exact legal status is not known.[85] Presumably this is a Chinese concession in exchange for the privilege of operating Bank of China branches in Hong Kong and London. Tanzania operates a joint shipping company with China, obviously tied to Chinese aid to that country for the building of a railway. Among socialist states, all Soviet and certain East European shares in a few government joint stock corporations were liquidated in the early 1950s;[86] only Albania and Poland still operate joint shipping companies with the People's Republic.[87] However, like Tanzania, they cooperate with China on a governmental basis.

At this stage of development China is not prepared to receive large numbers of alien residents, or to offer them national treatment. It welcomes aliens who visit the country for business purposes or sightseeing, but not as permanent residents. In fact, aside from several hundred diplomats, staff members and their dependents, as well as some three thousand Japanese who have chosen to remain in China since the end of World War II,[88] only a handful of alien individuals have been permitted to live there for a prolonged

---

total capital of about $50 million in one million shares. The scope of business was confined to investment in industrial enterprises, foreign trade, and service industries especially established to serve overseas Chinese. Under the company's charter, each shareholder was guaranteed to receive a minimum dividend of 8 percent of his original investment, irrespective of the company's gains or losses. In 1957, a law was promulgated granting overseas Chinese preferential treatment with respect to their investment in various state-owned overseas Chinese investment companies, including the right to withdraw their investment after a minimum of twelve years and the right to continue to hold their shares in these state companies even after the completion of socialist construction. Since the Cultural Revolution, the status of those state-private joint investment companies is no longer known. It is generally assumed that the private shareholders still retain their rights in accordance with the 1957 law. See State-Private Joint Overseas Chinese Investment Company, Ltd., Charter (in Chinese), 1955, published by the company in Kwangchow. Also see Kuo Jui-jen, "The Development of Fukien Investment Company," *Ching-chi tao-pao*, nos. 37-38 (1955), p. 14; and Regulation for the Preferential Treatment of Overseas Chinese Investment in State-Owned Overseas Chinese Investment Companies, August 1, 1957, passed at the 78th meeting of the Standing Committee of the NPC, in *FKHP 1957*, vol. 6 (1958), p. 570. The commercial advertisement regularly published by the State-Private Joint Overseas Chinese Investment Company was last seen in *Chung-kuo ch'u-k'ou shang-p'in chiao-i hui t'e-k'an*, no. 1, April 15, 1966, no page number.

85. See "U.K. Banks in Shanghai Now Busy," in *Japan Times*, June 8, 1972, p. 11. These banks are the Hong Kong and Shanghai Bank and the Chartered Bank.

86. For reference to the transfer of Soviet shares in four joint stock corporations in China, see Sino-Soviet Joint Communiqué, October 12, 1954, in *TWKH 1954-1955*, vol. 3 (1958), p. 179.

87. The Sino-Albanian Shipping Company, Ltd., was established in 1962 with a branch in Kwangchow. See *Jen-min jih-pao*, April 2, 1972, p. 5. The date of establishment of the Sino-Polish Shipping Company is not known, but there is a joint committee managing the affairs of the company. *Ibid.*, May 9, 1972, p. 5; May 13, 1972, p. 6.

88. The figures were released by the Japanese embassy in Peking. See *Japan Times*, November 17, 1974, p. 4.

period. And since most Chinese go abroad not for their own business purposes but on government assignments, they do so in accordance with officially established practices. At private levels, the Chinese authorities issue approximately one hundred exit permits a day to those who wish to leave for Hong Kong. But this is considered an "interflow" of individuals between two Chinese localities, not as a form of emigration (although Chinese residents in Hong Kong and Macao working for the People's Republic can easily travel to other countries by virtue of their residence in those colonies).

Most-Favored-Nation Status

In contrast to its attitude toward national treatment, the Chinese government has employed the most-favored-nation clause as a fundamental principle of its trade treaties and agreements. Reflecting a classic Western analysis of the clause, a textbook of the Peking Foreign Trade College described its five basic forms: (1) conditional or unconditional: the conditional form implies that concessions shall be generalized only upon the reciprocal payment of equivalent compensation, whereas the unconditional form lays down no conditions under which concessions granted by contracting states should be generalized; (2) mutual or unilateral: the mutual form consists of the reciprocal grant of most-favored-nation treatment, whereas the unilateral form provides one contracting state with most-favored-nation treatment while denying it to the other; (3) limited or unlimited: the limited form confines the application of the clause to certain specified objects or territories, whereas the unlimited form imposes no restrictions on the scope of application; (4) positive or negative: the positive form requires that either contracting state undertakes to grant the other all privileges, favors, and immunities it has granted or may hereafter grant to any third state, while the negative form stipulates that neither contracting state shall treat the other less favorably than it does any third state; and (5) simple or complex: the simple form contains a general statement providing most-favored-nation treatment, whereas the complex form defines the clause in greater detail and usually consists of four parts concerning its general purpose, interpretation, limitations, and exceptions.[89] In practice, China has favored the unconditional, mutual, and limited forms and rejected the conditional form as being "out-of-fashion" and the unilateral and unlimited forms as unequal. In this connection, of course, the Chinese had in mind the experience of China's treaty relations with foreign powers in

89. Wang Yao-tien, *op. cit.* pp. 28-33; cf. Richard Carlton Snyder, *The Most-Favored-Nation Clause* (1948), pp. 20-21, 52, 58. In addition to Snyder's classic work, Wang also used Stanley Kuhl Hornbeck, "The Most-Favored-Nation Clause," *American Journal of International Law* 3:395, 619 (1909); and "The Most-Favored-Nation Clause in Commercial Treaties," *Bulletin of the University of Wisconsin,* no. 343 (1910), pp. 5-121.

which the most-favored-nation clause applied unilaterally to foreigners in China, without providing reciprocal treatment for the Chinese in foreign countries.[90] With respect to the forms in the fourth and fifth categories, they are considered a matter of technicality, rather than principle.

Given the nature of the Chinese economy, in which all individuals work for the state and collectives, it is not surprising that application of the clause to the status of natural and juristic persons is very limited. Of China's six trade treaties with socialist states, only five provide most-favored-nation treatment for such persons. A standard clause, providing "simple" and "negative" application, is found in the 1958 Treaty of Trade and Navigation with the Soviet Union: "Juristic and natural persons of either Contracting Party shall in all respects enjoy in the territory of the other Party treatment no less favorable than that accorded to juristic and natural persons of any third State" (article 14).[91] In the treaty with the Democratic Republic of Germany, January 18, 1960, most-favored-nation treatment is accorded only to juristic persons of either contracting state, and the status of natural persons is not mentioned.[92] In trade agreements with non-socialist states, except Yemen and some of China's neighboring states where frontier trade is involved,[93] there are no provisions defining the legal status and rights of natural and juristic persons. Instead, in some instances a formula relying on each other's foreign trade system is used, as in the 1973 Sino-Australian trade agreement:

The exchange of goods and technical services under contracts and agreements entered into between the two countries shall, subject to the laws and regulations in force in each country, be at reasonable international market prices and shall be carried out by Australian legal and physical persons and state-owned import and export corporations of the People's Republic of China. [Article 3]

Without mentioning the legal nature of Chinese corporations and how their representatives and the Australian persons visiting each other's country should

90. For a study on this subject, see Tsung-yu Sze, *China and the Most-Favored-Nation Clause.*

91. In *TYC 1958,* vol. 7 (1959), pp. 42, 46. The other four treaties in which a similar provision can be found are: Albania, February 2, 1961, art. 14, in *TYC 1961,* vol. 10 (1962), pp. 290, 294; the People's Republic of Mongolia, April 26, 1961, art. 12, in *TYC 1961,* vol. 10 (1962), pp. 361, 364; the Democratic People's Republic of Korea, November 5, 1962, art. 13, in *TYC 1962,* vol. 11 (1963), pp. 92, 96; the Democratic Republic of Vietnam, December 5, 1962, art. 13, in *TYC 1962,* vol. 11 (1963), pp. 100, 104.

92. In *TYC 1960,* vol. 9 (1961), pp. 134, 138.

93. The Treaty with Yemen, January 12, 1958, art. 7, requires natural and juristic persons of either contracting state to respect the existing local laws and regulation, etc. In *TYC 1958,* vol. 7 (1959), pp. 28, 29. For reference to frontier trade, see Agreement with India, April 29, 1954, in *TYC 1954,* vol. 3 (1958), pp. 1, 3; Exchange of Notes with India, April 29, 1954, in *TYC 1954,* vol. 3 (1958), pp. 4-7; and Agreement with Nepal on Trade and Intercourse between Tibet Region of China and Nepal, September 20, 1956, in *TYC 1956,* vol. 5 (1958), p. 4.

be treated in the execution of the agreement, the two parties agreed to grant each other most-favored-nation treatment only "in the issue of import and export licenses and the allocation of foreign exchange connected therewith, as well as in all respects concerning customs duties, internal taxes or other charges imposed on or in connection with imported goods, and customs and other related formalities, regulations and procedures" (article 4).[94] Another example is found in the Sino-Japanese trade agreement, January 5, 1974 (see Appendix D), limiting the most-favored-nation treatment of the natural and juristic persons of either contracting party to matters relating to "payments, remittances and transfers of funds or financial instruments between the territories of the two Contracting Parties as well as between the territories of the other Contracting Party and of any third country" (article 4).

While the Chinese government restricts the application of the most-favored-nation clause to the status of natural and juristic persons, it favors extensive use of the clause in matters relating to navigation and commerce proper. This policy first appeared in the Trade Agreement with Egypt, August 22, 1955, which provided mutual most-favored-nation treatment in the issuance of import and export licenses and customs duties.[95] Soon after the agreement with Egypt, China reached similar agreements with no less than ten countries; and the scope of application was widened to include taxes and other charges imposed on goods, the warehousing of goods, customs regulations and procedures, and navigation.[96] But the most sweeping application of the clause is found in the 1958 Treaty of Trade and Navigation with the Soviet Union: of the seventeen articles in the treaty, ten deal with most-favored-nation treatment. Beginning with a general statement granting the contracting parties "most-favored-nation treatment in all matters relating to trade, navigation and other economic relations between the two states" (article 2), the treaty proceeds to specify the objects to which the clause applies. These

94. For similar examples in China's earlier trade agreements with other countries, see Trade Agreement with Finland, June 5, 1953, art. 1, in *TYC 1952-1953*, vol. 2 (1957), p. 35; Agreement for the Exchange of Goods and Payments with Afghanistan, July 28, 1957, art. 4, in *TYC 1957*, vol. 6 (1958), pp. 139, 140; Trade Agreement with the Republic of Tunis, September 25, 1958, art. 4, in *TYC 1958*, vol. 7 (1959), pp. 96, 97; Trade and Payments Agreement with the Republic of Ghana, August 18, 1961, art. 5, in *TYC 1961*, vol. 10 (1962), pp. 252, 253; and Trade and Payments Agreement with Congo (Brazzaville), July 23, 1964, art. 1, in *TYC 1964*, vol. 13 (1965), p. 281.

95. In *TYC 1955*, vol. 4 (1960), p. 123.

96. Syria, November 30, 1955, in *TYC 1955*, vol. 4 (1960), p. 118; Lebanon, December 31, 1955, in *TYC 1955*, vol. 4 (1960), p. 159; Yugoslavia, February 17, 1956, in *TYC 1956*, vol. 5 (1958), p. 113; Finland, March 31, 1956, in *TYC 1956*, vol. 5 (1958), p. 61; Indonesia, November 3, 1956, in *TYC 1956*, vol. 5 (1958), p. 56; Ceylon, September 19, 1957, in *TYC 1957*, vol. 6 (1958), p. 203; Sweden, November 8, 1957, in *TYC 1957*, vol. 6 (1958), p. 181; Denmark, December 1, 1957, in *TYC 1957*, vol. 6 (1958), p. 45; Pakistan, December 24, 1957, in *TYC 1958*, vol. 7 (1959), p. 35; and Yemen, January 12, 1958, in *TYC 1958*, vol. 7 (1959), p. 28.

include: all customs matters relating to the importation or exportation of natural and manufactured products of either contracting party (articles 3 and 4); internal taxation or charges (article 6); restrictions on importation or exportation for reasons such as national security and public health (article 7); vessels and their cargoes (article 8); conveyance of goods, passengers and baggage by internal railways, roads or waterways (article 11); goods in transit (article 12); the legal status of natural and juristic persons (article 14); and exceptions to the clause in frontier trade (article 15).

Subsequent to the Soviet Union's conclusion of this treaty, many other countries followed suit. But the absence of the clause in China's trade agreements with some countries, such as Switzerland, should not be construed as a phenomenon of restraint of trade; rather, it is a question of their individual relations. For example, it is well known that China is seeking an official trade agreement with the United States which would include the most-favored-nation treatment of goods and customs procedures. However, as noted earlier, the 1974 United States Trade Act has, for the present, foreclosed the possibility of such an agreement.

Industrial Property

The protection of industrial property has been one of the most controversial subjects in China's treaty relations with foreign states since the late nineteenth century.[97] At the heart of the problem lies the fact that China is a very late comer to the industrial world; by denying full protection to the inventions of technologically advanced nations, China had much to gain but very little to lose. Historical evidence is abundant. In spite of enormous pressure by foreign powers, the Chinese government, first under the Manchus and then the Nationalists, did not promulgate a copyright law until 1928, a trademark law until 1930, and a patent law until 1944.[98] Even then, these

97. For reference to some of the principal provisions regarding the protection of industrial property in China, see Supplementary Treaties on Commerce and Navigation with: Great Britain, September 5, 1902, art. 7, in *Chung wai chiu yüeh-chang hui-pien,* Set II (1901-1919), pp. 101, 103; the United States, October 8, 1903, arts. 9 and 10, in *ibid.,* pp. 181, 186; Japan, October 8, 1903, art. 5, in *ibid.,* pp. 192, 193. For an English translation of these treaties, see John V. A. MacMurray, ed., *Treaties and Agreements With and Concerning China 1894-1919,* vol. 1 (1894-1911), pp. 344-345, 412-413, 429, respectively.

98. See Copyright Law, May 14, 1928, in Chang Chih-pen, ed., *Tsui-hsin liu-fa ch'üan-shu* (1960), p. 876; Trademark Law, May 6, 1930, in *ibid.,* p. 1122; Patent Law, May 29, 1944, in *ibid.,* p. 1105. For a discussion of the development of these laws, see Chang Kuei-chuan, *Shang-piao fa yao-i;* Wang Shu-ming, *Shang-piao fa;* Chin Chung-chi, *Shang-piao fa lun;* Chin Hung-chi, *Chuan-li chih-tu kai-lun;* and Robert T. Bryan, Jr., "American Trademarks, Trade Names, Copyrights and Patents in China," *China Law Review* I.1:424 (1924).

laws did not work to the satisfaction of foreign interests. Piracy of foreign works in Taiwan, for example, remained an international problem until recently.

The People's Republic has never adopted a copyright law. It has recognized "authorship" in individual contracts with the state-owned publishing houses, and a standard contract required the author to assign his "copyright" to the publisher during the contract period. However, this arrangement was not a recognition of copyright law in the typical sense (although the word *copyright* was used), but part of the state monopoly in the field of publishing.[99] Foreign works were not expressly protected. With respect to foreign inventions and trademarks, the state granted some limited protection along the general principles established in the Soviet Union.

Inventions

The concept of patent law generally consists of two essential elements: the exclusive right to make, use, and vend the invention; and the novelty of the invention itself. In the Chinese case, as in the Soviet case upon which it is modelled, this concept is broadened to include "suggestions for technical improvements" and "suggestions for rationalization of production techniques and/or procedures."[100] A law of August 11, 1950, vaguely defined invention as "the discovery of new production methods which can truly raise production efficiency or manufacture new products, can truly increase the use-value [of a thing]" (article 3).[101] Under the law, an inventor might apply to the government for recognition of the rights of invention or patent rights in the form of a certificate of authorship or a patent certificate for a period of three to fifteen years (articles 4 and 9). In the former case, the author would be entitled to receive various kinds of prizes and remunerations and to bequeath the rights of invention to his heirs except for the right to use and dispose of the invention, which belonged to the state (article 6). In the latter case, the patent owner was entitled to make exclusive use of his invention. All alien individuals residing in China might apply for certificates of authorship or patents in accordance with the law on the same footing as Chinese nationals (article 18).

99. For a sample contract with Jen-min ch'u-pen-she (People's Press) and Chi-hsieh kung-yeh ch'u-pen-she (Machine Industry Press) as well as the rules for payment of fees, see Chinese People's University, Teaching and Research Institute of Civil Law, ed., *Chung-hua jen-min kung-ho-kuo min-fa ts'an-k'ao tzu-liao,* vol. 3 (1957), pp. 533-546.

100. For a discussion of Soviet patent law, see Vladimir Gsovski, *Soviet Civil Law,* vol. 1 (1948), p. 592.

101. Provisional Act for the Protection of the Rights of Invention and Patent Rights, August 11, 1950, approved by the Government Administration Council at its 45th meeting, in *FLHP 1949-1950,* vol. 2 (1952), pp. 359-362.

While this law was a simplified version of a 1941 Soviet statute and therefore did not provide details, a separate act, promulgated on May 6, 1954, defined suggestions for technical improvements as those which would improve the construction of mechanical equipment or the technical processes of production used in an enterprise, and rationalization of production procedures as a proposal that would improve production processes by means of more effective use of mechanical equipment, materials, and manpower. Together with the inventions defined in the 1950 law, the 1954 act provided a schedule of remunerations for three types of authorships (as distinguished from patents).[102]

The socialization of private ownership necessitated adjustment of the patent laws. Accordingly, the State Council on November 3, 1963, promulgated two acts dealing with authorship and remuneration, superseding laws from 1950 and 1954. The first act,[103] providing remuneration for inventions, abolished private patent rights in the 1950 law and redefined invention as 'a new scientific or technological achievement' which simultaneously meets three requirements: the invention is new and previously unknown, or if the invention does exist in a foreign country it has not been made public; it can be put to practical use or one can be found through experimentation; and it is more advanced than what exists at present (article 2). The State Commission on Science and Technology (since abolished) was charged to lead inventive work, to supervise the use of inventions throughout the country, and to certify all inventions except those for the exclusive use of national defense. The state awards inventors five types of certificates of authorship and cash prizes ranging from five hundred *yuan* to 10,000 *yuan,* but an invention of extraordinarily great significance merits special awards to be determined by the State Commission on Science and Technology and the State Council (article 17). All inventions belong to the state; and all state agencies, including collective units, may use the inventions they need. When an invention is sold to a foreign country because of the need for external trade or other reasons, the transaction shall be handled by the Ministry of Foreign Trade. Chinese residing abroad, and alien individuals or institutional units, may apply for certificates of authorship and receive remunerations in accordance with the

---

102. See Provisional Act Regarding Remuneration for Inventions and Suggestions for Technical Improvements and Rationalization of Production [Procedures], May 6, 1954, arts. 4 and 5, in *FLHP 1954* (1955), pp. 53-57; cf. Instruction Regarding Remuneration for Inventions, Technical Improvements, and Suggestions for Rationalization of Procedures, November 27, 1942, approved by the USSR Council of People's Commissars, in Vladimir Gsovski, *Soviet Civil Law,* vol. 2 (1949), pp. 385-397; for reference to the 1941 Soviet statute, see Statute Concerning Inventions and Technical Improvements, March 5, 1941, in *ibid.,* pp. 361-384.

103. Act Regarding Remuneration for Inventions, November 3, 1963, in *FKHP 1962-1963,* vol. 13 (1964), pp. 241-246.

law. Thus, like other private property rights in China, patent rights are also socialized.

The second act,[104] providing remuneration for technical improvements, redefined the "suggestions for rationalization of production procedures" into one general category: any suggestion that leads to "greater, faster, better, and more economic" achievement in production or work in an institutional unit, through experimental research and practical use, is a technical improvement (article 2). The State Commission on Science and Technology was charged to direct the work of technical improvement throughout the country (article 6). Collective units or individual persons, including aliens residing in China, are entitled to receive cash awards of less than a hundred *yuan* to a thousand *yuan* if their suggestions have been accepted for use (articles 19 and 20).[105]

Although thus far China has made no agreement with any foreign country for the protection of patents, the 1963 act does provide "special awards" for an invention of extraordinary significance.[106] In practice, some foreign corporations have obtained sizable amounts of money from the Chinese government for transactions involving highly sophisticated technology. For example, Nippon Steel Corporation will receive nearly $17 million (5 billion *yen*) out of its $217 million (65 billion *yen*) sale of a steel mill to China for "technical service."[107]

Trademarks

Although trademarks are traditional competitive devices of the capitalist world, the Chinese government considers them useful to socialist construction. Thus, the Government Administration Council promulgated a provisional act for the registration of trademarks as early as July 28, 1950, in order to remove "the vestiges of colonialism" and to insure the quality of products.[108] Under this act, registration was to be made with the Central Administration for Private Enterprises (article 2). Eight general categories of trademarks bearing certain words or drawings were not eligible for registra-

104. Act Regarding Remuneration for Technical Improvements, November 3, 1963, in *FKHP 1962-1963,* vol. 13 (1964), pp. 246-251.

105. For a discussion of this law, see Kuan Huai, "Legal Measures Supporting and Promoting Inventions and Technical Improvements," *Cheng-fa yen-chiu,* no. 3 (1964), p. 16.

106. It was said that the mutual supply of technical data among socialist states did not involve any compensation except for the actual cost of design papers. See Wang Tung-nien, "Our Scientific and Technological Cooperation with the Soviet Union and People's Democracies," in MFT, ed., *Tui-wai mao-i lun-wen hsüan,* vol. 2 (1956), p. 44.

107. See "Japan Firms Will Export Steel Plant to China," *Japan Times,* June 5, 1974, p. 8.

108. Passed at its 43rd meeting. In *FLHP 1949-1950,* vol. 2 (1952), pp. 528-531.

tion, including those using foreign words. However, there were two exceptions: trademarks using foreign words or drawings for export merchandise or on imported goods, and those already registered with the Nationalist government before the founding of the People's Republic. In the latter event, the trademark owners must re-apply for registration and if approved, the right of exclusive use would be limited to a period of two years (article 4). Merchants of those countries which had established diplomatic relationships and had concluded commercial treaties with China might petition for registration of their trademarks, if they desired to secure the right of exclusive use of such marks, within the limits of those treaties and according to the present act (article 5). If approved, the right of exclusive use of a trademark was valid for a period of twenty years, and this period could be extended (article 18). Disputes arising from the registration of a trademark might be adjudicated by the Central Administration for Private Enterprises, which was later superseded by the Central Administration for Industry and Commerce (article 26). If a disputing party disagreed with the Administration's decision, he might appeal to its supervisory organ for review. In case the right of exclusive use of a trademark had been violated, the injured party could institute a lawsuit in the people's court (articles 27-29).

In 1957, the CCPIT was appointed as the official agent of the Central Administration for Industry and Commerce for registration of trademarks by foreigners.[109] Six years later, a new Act for the Control of Trademarks was promulgated to replace the 1950 law.[110] Under this legislation, trademarks with "derogatory political influence" are excluded from registration, along with those marks identical with or similar to symbols such as the national flag; use of foreign words is also prohibited except as a supplement to a Chinese trademark on export merchandise (article 5). A registered trademark may be revoked if the trademarked commodity failed to meet its quality requirements, if the trademark has been altered without proper permit, or if the trademark has not been put to use for a full year without permission to retain it (article 11). Diplomatic recognition of the People's Republic and the conclusion of a commercial treaty is no longer a requirement for registration of foreign trademarks. Instead, the new act copies a provision of the Soviet Statute Concerning Trademarks and Trade-Signs of March 7, 1936,[111] by stipulating that a foreign petitioner may apply for registration of a trademark if his country has concluded a reciprocal agreement on the registration of

109. Central Administration for Industry and Commerce opinion, (no date), approved by the State Council on January 17, 1957, in *FKHP 1957*, vol. 5 (1957), p. 217.

110. This act was passed at the 100th meeting of the State Council on April 29, 1960, but was not promulgated until 1963. In *FKHP 1962-1963*, vol. 13 (1964), pp. 162-164. See Appendix K.

111. In Vladimir Gsovski, *Soviet Civil Law*, vol. 2 (1949), pp. 37, 39.

trademarks with the People's Republic. The new law also repealed the earlier provision which gave exclusive right to the use of a foreign trademark for a twenty-year period and replaced it with another Soviet concept—the trademark whose registration is petitioned for must already be duly registered under the name of the petitioner in his own country, and the duration of its valid Chinese registration is to be determined by the Central Administration for Industry and Commerce.

A separate rule for the enforcement of the act, promulgated by the Central Administration for Industry and Commerce on April 25, 1963,[112] reaffirms the CCPIT as its official agent for registration of foreign trademarks (article 15). It also requires a foreign petitioner to submit the following: a certificate of nationality, an application, an authorization statement, a duplicate copy of the certificate of registration of the trademark in his home country, twenty samples of the trademark, and a fee of twenty *yuan*. The duration of validity of a registered trademark may be extended if the application is filed before the expiration of the current registration (article 17), and registered trademarks may be altered or transferred or revoked in accordance with due procedures (articles 18-19). All documents used by a foreign petitioner to apply for the registration of trademarks must be written in Chinese; documents in foreign languages, such as the nationality certificate and the certificate of registration in his home state, must be accompanied by Chinese translations.

The 1963 trademark acts have replaced the 1950 law's "right of exclusive use" with "registration." The purpose of registration is, of course, to acquire the right of exclusive use. But registration is a process, not a right. To what extent a registered foreign trademark is protected is not specified in the acts. Related to this the 1963 acts are silent on the question of a foreign trademark owner's right to institute a lawsuit if and when his rights have been violated. Presumably a foreign petitioner can make special contractual arrangements with the CCPIT for the concrete protection of his rights. But even then, the question remains as to how important it is to register a foreign trademark in China, whose imports are mostly industrial plants and materials, and where all commodities, Chinese or foreign, are basically distributed by the government, not marketed by private firms. In fact, the intention of the acts is obviously to use a trademark to foster "competition" among domestic socialist enterprises, not between these enterprises and their foreign counterparts. But left unclear is the meaning of those agreements between China and a few capitalist nations for the reciprocal protection of trademarks.[113] Since

---

112. In *FKHP 1962-1963*, vol. 13 (1964), pp. 164-170.

113. For reference to China's exchange of notes with foreign states for the reciprocal protection of trademarks, see, e.g., Britain, April 13, 1956, and June 1, 1956, in *TYC 1956*, vol.

vast differences exist in the purpose of their respective trademark laws, as well as in the nature of their economies, the real advantage of these agreements seems to favor the Chinese, whose exports are mostly marketed in non-socialist countries and therefore need protection more than do foreign commodities in China.

---

5 (1958), p. 68; Switzerland, April 14, 1956, and March 8, 1957, in *TYC 1957,* vol. 6 (1958), p. 178; Sweden, April 6, 1957, and April 8, 1957, in *TYC 1957,* vol. 6 (1958), p. 180; Denmark, March 25, 1958, and April 12, 1958, in *TYC 1958,* vol. 7 (1959), p. 37. Since the end of the Cultural Revolution, China has concluded additional reciprocal agreements for the registration of trademarks with several other states. These include: Italy, January 8, 1973, in *Hsiangkang ching-chi nien-chien 1973,* p. 30; Norway, November 8, 1974, Belgium, the Netherlands, and Luxemburg, April 14, 1975, and Greece, April 19, 1975, in *ibid.* (1975), pp. 54, 56. For an additional discussion of China's patents, invention law, and trademarks, see Eugene A. Theroux, "Licensing Operations in the People's Republic of China," *Patent and Trademark Review* 73:339, 387 (1975); 74:14 (1976).

6   Trade Contracts and
       Means of Settling Disputes

NATIONS may enter into trade treaties and agreements to define and regulate their general commercial relations, but actual transactions are always concluded on the basis of contracts. In the Chinese case, trade contracts are also important for the implementation of export and import plans.[1] Whereas a trade agreement can provide the planner with a general idea about a trade relationship, a contract specifies the details of a given transaction and contains procedures for their execution. Thus, for example, the 1974 Sino-Japanese trade agreement (see Appendix D) stipulates:

In accordance with the principle of equality and mutual benefit and on the basis of reasonable international market prices, the trade between the two Contracting Parties shall be carried out through the conclusion of contracts by juridical or natural persons having the capacity to engage in foreign trade under the laws and regulations of Japan on the one hand, and foreign trade organizations having the capacity to engage in foreign trade under the laws and regulations of the People's Republic of China on the other. [Article 5].

As China has thus far concluded intergovernmental trade agreements with only sixty foreign countries, long-term trade contracts can replace official trade accords with other countries in the overall planning process. For these reasons Chinese officials are emphatic about the importance of fulfilling contractual obligations.[2]

In practice, the Chinese have had a considerable number of disputes with trading partners due to the nature of merchandise transactions, the inherent ambiguity of some contractual provisions, and differences in trade customs and legal concepts. However, because most of these disputes are confidential, neither the Chinese nor their partners have released any concrete case for public analysis. The following discussion of such disputes is therefore illustrative, based on fragmentary information and circumstantial evidence. The analysis of the institution of trade contracts, on the other hand, is based on Chinese publications and examination of about one hundred

1. See Shanghai Foreign Languages Institute, Department of Foreign Languages for Foreign Trade, *Tui-wai mao-i shih-wu,* p. 101.
2. See Yeh Chi-chuang, "Working for the Development of Normal International Trade," MFT, ed., *Tui-wai mao-i lun-wen hsüan,* vol. 2 (1956), p. 7.

Chinese trade contracts with Australia, Britain, Canada, France, West Germany, Italy, Japan, the United States, and some Third World countries. They cover a period of ten years, from 1965 to 1974. Some of them are reproduced in this volume as appendices; others are cited in the text. The names of the foreign parties and the statements concerning objects, specifications, prices, and specific dates are all omitted.

The Institution of Contracts

China's trade contracts can be divided into two general categories: those with socialist countries and those with non-socialist countries.

Socialist Contracts

The form and content of contracts concluded between China's foreign trade corporations and their socialist counterparts are governed by a general governmental contract, known as the General Conditions for Delivery. (See, for example, Appendix C.) This document was, as indicated earlier, designed to simplify procedures for the formation of individual contracts, to serve as a legal basis for the delivery of goods, to supervise the execution of individual contracts, and to provide a means of escaping from the application of municipal law.[3] Unless circumstances require unusual terms in a given individual contract, it provides uniform principles and terms for the exchange of goods between socialist states. These principles and terms are legally binding upon the contracting parties, who are subject to penalties in case of violation.[4]

A standard form of this document usually consists of twelve sections.[5] Aside from the two sections dealing with the adjustment of disagreements and arbitration, which will be discussed later, the sections may be summarized as follows:

Formation of Contracts. This section stipulates that individual contracts for the exchange of goods, for making payments, and for fulfilling other obligations shall be made according to the General Conditions for Delivery.

3. For a discussion of this matter, see Aleksandar Goldstajn, ''International Conventions and Standard Contracts As Means of Escaping From the Application of Municipal Law,'' in Clive M. Schmitthoff, ed., *The Sources of the Law of International Trade,* p. 103.

4. See Wang Yao-tien, *Kuo-chi mao-i t'iao-yüeh ho hsieh-ting,* p. 127.

5. For a discussion of the General Conditions for Delivery, see Wang Yao-tien, *op. cit.,* pp. 126-131. For reference to other examples of this document in English, see *Chinese Law and Government,* no. 2 (1972), *passim.* CIF and C & F price quotations appear in the Trade Agreement with the Government of the Republic of Finland, June 21, 1954, in *TYC 1954,* vol. 3 (1958), p. 43; Trade Agreement with the Government of the Republic of Finland, June 5, 1953, in *TYC 1952-1953,* vol. 2 (1957), p. 35; General Conditions for Delivery with Finland Concerning China's Exports, June 17, 1954, in *TYC 1954,* vol. 3 (1958), p. 197.

The authorized representatives of the foreign trade organizations (usually corporations) of the contracting states sign the contract, which shall specify the denomination of the goods and the quantity, quality, specifications, price, total value, shipping marks, packing conditions, the date and place of delivery, and other conditions not in the General Conditions for Delivery. Amendments and/or supplements to the contract must be agreed upon in writing by both parties.

Terms of Delivery. This section specifies the means of transportation (sea, land, air, or postal service) and the place where the transfer of ownership of the goods will take place. Responsibilities for expenses and risks incidental to the goods are also determined on this basis. With the few exceptions where CIF and C & F terms are used, the price quotations are generally based on FOB terms.

Date of Delivery. Unless otherwise specified in individual contracts, delivery shall be made within the period to which the General Conditions for Delivery applies.

Notice of Delivery. This section requires the contracting parties to notify each other of the detailed procedures of delivery required in the execution of individual contracts. For example, if the delivery is made by sea transportation, the seller must issue a notice to the buyer forty-five days before the goods arrive at the loading port. Within fifteen days after receiving the notice, the buyer must in turn notify the seller by telegram of the name of the vessel and the date of its arrival at the loading port.

Late or Early Delivery and Penalties. Generally there is a grace period for late delivery—thirty days for ordinary goods and forty-five to sixty days for machinery and equipment. Further delay requires agreement by both parties. If the seller fails to make delivery after the grace period or the agreed period of delay, he is subject to a penalty of no more than 8 percent of the total value of the delayed goods. Early delivery (delivery ahead of schedule) may be made after agreement by both parties.

Quantity and Quality. Quantity and/or weight are generally accepted as set forth by the bill of lading. Quality must conform to the standard of the producing state or to the technical conditions specified in the individual contract and must be certified by the commodity inspection administration of the selling party's country.

Packing and Marking. Unless otherwise specified in the individual contract, both packing and marking must conform to international standards.

Guaranty. If necessary and if both parties agree, the seller must guarantee for a given period of time the quality of certain types of goods delivered. The length of the period is specified in the individual contracts.

The Method of Making Payments. All payments are settled through the state banks of the contracting parties. Generally there are two ways of making payments: a payment may be settled through the clearing accounts of the state banks or the seller may get his payment directly from his country's state bank, which then debits it to the clearing accounts of the buyer's state bank. Either state bank has the right to refuse payment if the papers (such as the bill of lading) submitted to the bank by the seller are not consistent with the contract terms.

Force Majeure. This section describes the effect of various circumstances beyond the control of either party, such as fire, flood, drought, plague, earthquake, blockade, and war.

Non-Socialist Contracts

Outside the socialist world, China has intergovernmental trade agreements with about fifty countries.[6] While many of these trade agreements have served as the basis for the formation of individual contracts, they do not provide uniform contractual rules such as are embodied in the General Conditions for Delivery used with socialist states. As reported by official Chinese sources, there are seven types of contracts with non-socialist countries:

1. *Straight sale, straight purchase,* or the combined form, called *reciprocal trade*. Under the straight sale formula, export is not conditioned by import; likewise, under the straight purchase formula, import is not conditioned by export. In either case, a contract is deemed concluded when the seller and buyer have reached an agreement on the quality, quantity, specifications, and prices of a given commodity as well as the date of delivery and the terms of payment. Under the reciprocal trade formula, these terms are mutually binding: a sale is conditioned by a purchase and vice versa.

2. *Barter*. Under this formula sale and purchase are carried out at the same time: one kind of commodity is exchanged for another, or given amounts of merchandise are exchanged. In either case, a relatively even balance of trade is maintained.

3. *Consignment*. Under this formula, an export corporation or consignor entrusts a reliable agent or consignee abroad to sell certain types of goods in accordance with terms agreed upon by both parties, and the consignee may claim a given amount of commissions for his service. In general, this formula only applies to the sale of new commodities totally unknown to the external market; or commodities not yet well known to foreign consumers; or delicate items such as jade, when transactions can take place only after the customer has actually inspected the object. The price of a

---

6. For reference, see *Hsiangkang ching-chi nien-chien 1975*, pp. 52-56; *ibid.* (1974), pp. 71-74; *ibid.* (1973), pp. 25-32. These are the most recent examples and do not include all of the agreements that China has signed with non-socialist states.

consigned commodity is determined either by the consignor or by the consignee on the basis of actual market conditions or by special agreement between the consignor and consignee. Since consigned commodities are delivered to the consignee before payments are made, the amount involved is usually limited and the contract specifies terms for payments settlement, commissions, and other related matters.

4. *Sole or general agency.* Under these formulas, an export corporation entrusts a selected firm abroad to sell a given type of commodity or commodities with a specific trademark in a designated area within a given period of time. In the case of sole agency, the export corporation or principal is not allowed to sell to other distributors the type of commodities that have been entrusted to its agent, or to appoint sub-agents within the designated area during the stipulated period of time, unless otherwise provided for in the contract. General agency is a special form of sole agency, under which the principal may appoint sub-agents and the general agent may share commissions with the sub-agents.

The principal terms of an agency contract usually specify the foundation and purposes of the contract; commodity descriptions, quality and specifications; the minimum amount of goods to be sold; the area and time period of agency; remunerations for the agent or agents; prices, payments settlement, delivery conditions; and procedures for claims and arbitration. (See Appendix O.) An agency contract also provides that the agent must protect the principal's rights, including the trademarks, the brands, and the minimum amount of goods to be sold; the agent shall study and investigate market conditions, actively promote sales, and submit reports on these activities to the principal on a regular basis; unless otherwise agreed upon by the principal, the agent shall not sell similar or competitive goods, or privately accept claims for compensation or assume obligations in the name of the principal; the principal's direct trade with the government of the country where the agent is located is not restricted by the agency contract; and the agent shall be obligated to assist the principal's representatives in the conduct of business.

Generally the commodity prices involved in an agency contract are determined by the principal and the commission is a percentage of sales. In some cases, the agent receives a discount price and is then responsible for his own profits or losses. The average period of agency for a new agent ranges from three months to a year, and it may be extended on the basis of the agent's satisfactory performance.

5. *Ching-hsiao* (conditional agency). As with the institution of agency, this contract also provides the agent a commission, or profits above his cost, for the sale of certain commodities for an export corporation. The only difference between these two types of agency is that under a *conditional*

agency contract the agent must make a deposit of security money with the principal, refundable upon satisfactory execution of the contract.

6. *Pao-hsiao* (distributorship). Under this formula, a single firm or a group of firms abroad undertakes to buy commodities from an export corporation for resale within a designated area during a given period of time. While the buyer is responsible for his own gains or losses, the seller undertakes not to sell the same type of commodities to a third party within that area during the stipulated period of time. The terms of payment are negotiable. If the buyer failed to fulfill the contract due to objective circumstances, a settlement may be made in accordance with the principle of "mutual benefit." Otherwise, he is obligated to compensate the seller's losses. (See Appendix P.)

7. *Ting-hsiao* (fixed distributorship). A formula based on relatively long-term large transactions, a *ting-hsiao* contract assures the buyer a supply of certain types of commodities for a stipulated period of time. The prices for these commodities are generally lower than for the same commodities sold to buyers without a *ting-hsiao* contract. Resale of these commodities by the buyer is not restricted by area or time, and the seller is free to market the same commodities in any area at any time. Under this contract, the buyer is responsible for his own gains or losses.[7]

Because of the obvious advantages for those who sell Chinese products abroad under the last five types of contracts (consignment, agency, *ching-hsiao, pao-hsiao,* and *ting-hsiao*) they are usually awarded to overseas Chinese, Chinese residents in Hong Kong and Macao, and friendly alien firms which have a special ability to develop the market for the Chinese commodities involved. Aliens of Chinese descent have been denied such contracts since 1974 when the People's Republic adopted a new nationality policy renouncing the principle of *jus sanguinis.*[8] However, like friendly alien firms, aliens of Chinese descent may be awarded these contracts if they can prove themselves "friendly" to the People's Republic. The barter contracts and the reciprocal trade formula are used only when feasible; consequently, the most commonly used contracts in China's foreign trade are those of straight sale and straight purchase.

Formation of Sales and Purchase Contracts

Like its domestic commerce and its trade with socialist countries,

7. See Shanghai Foreign Languages Institute, Department of Foreign Languages for Foreign Trade, *Tui-wai mao-i shih-wu,* pp. 164-166; Hong Kong *Ta-kung pao,* ed., *Tao Kwangchow tso sheng-i,* pp. 5-8. Also see Gene T. Hsiao, "Chinese Trade Contracts," in Howard M. Holtzmann, ed., *Legal Aspects of Doing Business with China,* pp. 137-182.

8. For further information on this subject, see Huang Yun-chi, "Teng Hsiao-ping on China's Future and Overseas Chinese Policy, Part II," in *Shih-tai pao,* December 18, 1974, pp. 1, 3.

China's trade with non-socialist nations is governed by a set of export and import plans.[9] The export plan consists of subordinate plans for the purchase of export commodities from domestic producers, for the coordination of activities with other state export corporations, and for the processing of certain types of goods.[10] Since the basic purpose of exporting is to enable China to import products needed for the expansion of production and industrialization, the export plan is considered the key to the entire foreign trade plan. The import plan involves the classification of products needed by various domestic consumers; the clarification of commodity specifications in order to meet international standards; the search for substitutes on the domestic market in order to save foreign exchange; the coordination of planning processes with domestic consumption; and the development of a file system on importing.[11]

Planning is facilitated by and coordinated with bilateral trade agreements, if any, and a process of market investigation, calculation of costs and prices, and selection of suitable foreign buyers and sellers.[12] When all this is done, the negotiation of transactions begins. Since both Chinese sales and purchases are carried out through the semi-annual Kwangchow trade fair, exhibitions in foreign countries or foreign exhibitions in China, visiting trade delegations, and individual contacts, negotiations for these transactions take various forms. In general, they are conducted by correspondence and/or face-to-face bargaining. In the case of correspondence, the contract is concluded in one of the following ways. (1) In accordance with the terms agreed upon by both parties, the seller makes out a contract in two copies, one for himself and the other for the buyer. The contract takes effect when both parties have signed it. (2) When the buyer has accepted the seller's offer and the seller has confirmed the acceptance by correspondence, the contract is deemed concluded. The correspondence between the parties and the seller's final confirmation of the buyer's acceptance serve as the legal basis of the contract. (3) When the seller has accepted the buyer's order and conditions by mail or telegram and has sent back to the buyer a confirmation of the order, the contract is also considered concluded. (4) When an agreement has been

9. See Gene T. Hsiao, "The Role of Economic Contracts in Communist China," *California Law Review* 53:1029 (1965); Chao Chi-chang, "Overall Planning of Foreign Trade and Conclusion of Long-Term Trade Agreements," in MFT, ed., *Tui-wai mao-i lun-wen hsüan* (1956), p. 151.

10. See Shanghai Foreign Languages Institute, *op. cit.*, pp. 45-47.

11. *Ibid.*, pp. 84-86.

12. This process is carried out by the various research units in the Ministry of Foreign Trade, the CCPIT, and national foreign trade corporations. In addition, the Chinese maintain a Center for Literature Concerning New Foreign Products (P.O. Box 615, Peking) and a Chinese Scientific and Technical Association (P.O. Box 640, Peking). The former receives product literature from foreign countries and the latter scientific and technical information from American and other foreign universities and technical institutes under the aegis of exchange programs. See "Technical Product Libraries in Peking," *U.S.-China Business Review,* no. 6 (1974), p. 58.

reached through correspondence containing both parties' signatures, the agreement is considered to be a contract.[13]

China's 1972 purchase of ten Boeing 707s involved correspondence in the preliminary stages, and face-to-face negotiations to conclude the sale. In March, 1972, after President Nixon's China trip, Boeing wrote the China National Machinery Import and Export Corporation (Machimpex) and received an invitation to attend the Kwangchow trade fair, and to visit Peking. Out of this developed a summer of negotiations in Peking between Machimpex and Boeing representatives on general contractual principles as well as specific technical and financial aspects of the proposed sale of the ten aircraft. After Boeing obtained the requisite U.S. Department of Commerce export license, Machimpex and Boeing signed a contract on September 9, 1972, for delivery to Shanghai of the ten planes for $125 million.[14]

On the heels of the Boeing sale, and related to it, came a transaction wrought entirely by correspondence. Early in 1973 Machimpex cabled the Clark Equipment Company of Buchanan, Michigan, to inquire about terms for a single Clark tractor suitable for towing airport baggage carts. Clark replied, and subsequent letters and cables arranged for the sale of twenty tractors at a discounted total price of $150,000. In August the tractors were put on board a Japanese freighter bound for Shanghai, without seller and buyer ever meeting.[15]

A case of face-to-face negotiations with no prior contact, written or otherwise, involved the largest sale to date of American mining equipment to China. Anxious to make a sale, the Bucyrus-Erie Company of Milwaukee, Wisconsin charged a private consultant, about to attend the fall 1972 Kwangchow trade fair, with contacting Machimpex on their behalf. Machimpex was sufficiently impressed to invite the consultant to Peking for further talks, and after several more visits by the consultant and some Bucyrus-Erie personnel, a contract was signed in December, 1973, for the sale of $20 million worth of blast hole drills and power shovels.[16] Contracts concluded on these and other occasions, of course, vary, but they share one common legal problem: in nearly one hundred sales and purchase contracts that China has signed with eight of its major trading partners (Australia, Britain, Canada,

13. See Shanghai Foreign Languages Institute, *op. cit.*, p. 69.

14. For details of the deal, see "Exporting to China, Two Examples of Timing, Boeing and Clark Equipment," *U.S.-China Business Review*, no. 4 (1974), p. 5. For additional information concerning contract negotiations with Chinese through correspondence and the forms of correspondence, see Harutaka Yano, ed., *Chunichi boeki tsushin bun;* Masahira Kumano, *Shin Chugoku shogyo tsushin bun;* Ting Hsiu-shan and Yoshitaro Shibagaki, *Saishin Nichu boeki tsushin bun;* Teruo Sumida, *Chugoku gendai shogyo tsushin bun.*

15. For details, see *U.S.-China Business Review*, no. 4 (1974), p. 5.

16. See "Negotiating the Sale of Mining Equipment in Peking," *U.S.-China Business Review*, no. 6 (1974), p. 47. For additional information concerning the promotion of sales to China, see *ibid.*, no. 4 (1974), p. 3; Harned Pettus Hoose, "How to Negotiate with the Chinese of the PRC," in William W. Whitson, ed., *Doing Business with China*, p. 449.

France, West Germany, Italy, Japan, and the United States) in the last few years, there appears no reference to the legal system that is to govern these contracts. A British lawyer observed:

The matter has always been left open or vague, deliberately so in many cases such as the large wheat deals which the P.R.C. has negotiated in the past with Australia and Canada, and there is, no doubt, scope for the rules of private international law to determine the proper law of the contract. In many cases it would be extremely difficult to predict with confidence which legal system a court would hold to have the closest connection with the contract, *e.g.,* in the case of the sale to the P.R.C. of Canadian wheat, f.o.b. Vancouver, the contract having been concluded in Hong Kong between China Resources [Company] and the Canadian Wheat Board and with a provision for arbitration in Switzerland. If P.R.C. civil law is to govern it will be difficult to discover the appropriate rules in the absence of any authoritative, reported court decisions or any published Code.[17]

Another related problem concerns the place of contract formation, which is important in determining the proper law of the contract and the jurisdiction of a government over it. The Chinese seem to be aware of this question, and have signed most of their trade contracts in China in order to avoid the interference of foreign jurisdictions. However, a few were concluded through their agents in foreign territories, as for example, a 1971 sales contract between China Resources Company (seller) and an Australian firm (buyer). The deal was concluded in Hong Kong, but the shipment was to be effected from a Chinese port and a confirmed, irrevocable, and without-recourse letter of credit was to be made in favor of the China National Machinery Import and Export Corporation, Shanghai Branch. The fact that the contract did not mention the seller acting as an agent leaves unclear who is liable for the transaction in the case of a breach of contract.[18]

Principal Terms of Contracts

Chinese trade contracts are all written in Chinese for internal use of the foreign trade corporations and for transactions with their Japanese partners. For transactions with all other non-socialist foreign partners, the contracts are translated into English with equal force, though occasionally the English version of a particular contract may also contain the original Chinese text.[19] Large transactions have occasionally been preceded by pre-contract agreements (see Appendix L). In the case of Sino-Japanese trade contracts, they were conditioned by a preamble reciting the three trading principles set forth by Premier Chou En-lai in the aftermath of the Nagasaki flag incident.[20]

17. See Alan H. Smith, "Standard Form Contracts in the International Commercial Transactions of the People's Republic of China," *International and Comparative Law Quarterly* 21:133, 138 (1972).

18. For a discussion see *ibid.,* p. 137.

19. See Shanghai Foreign Languages Institute, *op. cit.,* p. 102.

20. For an example of this type of contract, see Gene T. Hsiao, "Communist China's

Later, as a result of the Sato-Nixon communiqué, November 21, 1969, the Japanese were further required to acknowledge the four conditions of trade with Japan announced by Premier Chou in 1970.[21] Aside from this Japanese experience, which was unique in many respects and has been discontinued since the Sino-Japanese rapprochement, the principal terms of Chinese trade contracts vary, depending on the foreign party's individual relationship with the Chinese party, the time of contract signing, the nature of merchandise, and the correlation of both parties' bargaining strength. Generally these terms include: payment, shipping and insurance, commodity inspection, quality guarantee, penalty for late delivery, *force majeure,* and arbitration.

Payment. The terms of payment in Chinese trade contracts with non-socialist nations fall into two general categories: those with developing nations and those with "developed" nations. In the former case, China's policy appears to have been designed to coordinate with its aid programs in Third World countries and for this purpose, the terms of payment are more generous than those with other nations. For example, in the Trade and Payments Agreement with Ghana, August 18, 1961 (see Appendix H), it was agreed that the national banks of the two contracting parties should establish "non-interest bearing and free of charge clearing accounts in Ghana Pound" for the settlement of payments (article 7); "if the par value of the Ghana Pound in terms of gold, being 2.48828 grams of fine gold per currency unit, is altered, the balance of the accounts referred to in Article 7 of this Agreement shall be adjusted accordingly on the date of the alteration" (article 8).

In settling payments with "developed" nations or industrialized countries, the terms are complex and generally favor China whether exporting or importing. Two sections of a 1972 Chinese export sales confirmation (see Appendix M) provide:

A usual trade margin of 5% plus or minus of the quantities confirmed shall be allowed. Where shipment is spread over two or more periods, the above-mentioned trade margin of plus or minus 5% shall, when necessary, be applicable to the quantity designated by the Buyers to be shipped each period.

Unless otherwise agreed to by the Sellers, payment is to be made against sight draft drawn under a Confirmed, Irrevocable, Divisible and Assignable Letter of Credit, Without Recourse for the full amount, established through a first class bank acceptable to the Sellers. The Letter of Credit in due form must reach the Seller at least 30 days before the month of shipment stipulated in this Sales Confirmation, failing which the Sellers shall not be responsible for shipment as stipulated; in case the Buyers' credit still fails to reach the Sellers after the expiry of the shipping period, the Sellers shall

Foreign Trade Contracts and Means of Settling Disputes," *Vanderbilt Law Review* 22:503, 521-525 (1969).

21. For reference to this type of contract, see Japan External Trade Organization, *How to Approach the China Market,* p. 149.

have the right to cancel this Sales Confirmation and claim for damage against the Buyers.

When China was importing, a purchase contract provided the following payment terms:

The Buyers, upon receipt from the Sellers of the delivery advice specified in Article 14 hereof, shall, in 15-20 days prior to the date of delivery, open an irrevocable Letter of Credit with the Bank of China, in favor of the Sellers, for an amount equivalent to the total value of the shipment. The Credit shall be payable against the presentation of draft drawn on the opening bank and the shipping documents specified in Article 13 hereof. The Letter of Credit shall be valid until the 15th day after the shipment is effected.[See Appendix N.]

The discrepancies between these two types of payment terms are obvious. First, the letter of credit must be confirmed when China is selling, but is not confirmed when it is buying. Second, the letter must be "irrevocable, divisible, assignable, and without recourse" in a Chinese sales contract but only "irrevocable" in the case of a Chinese purchase contract. Third, the letter must reach the Chinese as sellers thirty days before shipment, whereas in the case of Chinese purchase, the letter is to be opened only fifteen to twenty days before shipment. Fourth, a Chinese sales contract generally requires "a usual trade margin of 5% plus or minus of the quantities confirmed," while in purchase China insists on full payment, the total value of the shipment. Fifth, when selling, the Chinese usually require the buyers to open a letter of credit payable in China, but when buying, stipulate that payment will not be made until all documents have reached the opening bank in China. Last, but not least, the Chinese expressly retain the right to cancel their sales contract and claim for damage against the buyers if the letter of credit fails to reach them before the expiry of the stipulated period, but the same right is not expressly assured foreign sellers in the same situation.[22]

When the American embargo and other related regulations concerning the China trade were in full force, this asymmetrical practice could have ensured the full consummation of all sales and purchases without third-party interference. Before the Sino-American detente the Chinese required foreign sellers of certain embargoed goods to deposit a "performance bond," a percentage of the total value of shipment, in a bank designated by the PRC in Hong Kong. If the sellers failed to make the delivery, the Chinese had the right to the deposit.[23] Since the relaxation of the embargo, there seems to be

22. For a detailed discussion of the relative disadvantages of this Chinese practice to foreign traders, see Katherine Schwering, "Financing Imports from China," *U.S.-China Business Review*, no. 5 (1974), pp. 36, 40. An opening bank is that bank which opens a Letter of Credit on behalf of a customer. For reference to other related terms, see *ibid.*, p. 38.

23. See Shanghai Foreign Languages Institute, *op. cit.*, p. 29.

no justification for the continuation of this practice. It should be pointed out, however, that the practice, though common, is by no means absolute or universal. At least one American importer has arranged with the Chinese to postpone opening a letter of credit until the Chinese goods are ready for shipment. Another found that the Chinese would accept a check drawn on an American bank, instead of a letter of credit, for a shipment of goods to be made.[24]

Due to the changing international monetary situation, the currencies that China has used to settle trade payments have also varied from time to time. In its trade agreement with the Soviet Union, concluded on April 19, 1950, China agreed to use the American dollar as one of the three basic means for payments.[25] Shortly thereafter, however, the People's Republic officially discontinued use of the dollar because of the U.S. Foreign Assets Control Regulations and instead, chose sterling as the basic unit in its dealings with non-socialist countries.[26] The devaluation of the pound sterling in the late 1960s compelled China to use Swiss francs, French francs, German marks, and Hong Kong dollars more frequently than before. Another European monetary crisis, involving the mark and the Swiss franc in 1970-1971, led China to negotiate with the British for dual use of sterling and China's renminbi ("people's currency") in their transactions. By the fall of 1974 China reportedly stipulated the use of renminbi in many of its trade contracts with more than sixty countries.[27] Since August, 1974, the People's Bank of China in Peking has published the renminbi's daily exchange rates with fifteen major foreign currencies at the fixed theoretical value of .3610 grams of gold per yuan.[28]

It is generally recognized that the yuan is strong and stable and that the record of China's trade payments is almost impeccable. Accordingly, acceptance of renminbi by foreign traders in settlement of payments is really not surprising. However, as the world monetary market continues to fluctuate, China has begun to modify its policy on yuan as a settlement currency in order to protect its trade interests. An outstanding example is China's agreement

24. See Katherine Schwering, loc. cit., pp. 36-37.
25. See TYC 1949-1951, vol. 1 (1960), p. 47. The other two means were gold and pound sterling.
26. See Chung Yung, "Foreign Exchange Work in China," Foreign Trade of the PRC, no. 2 (1960), p. 10; The Bank of China, "The Bank of China's Work of International Settlements," Foreign Trade of the PRC, no. 1 (1962), p. 4.
27. See "The Renminbi and the Dollar," U.S.-China Business Review, no. 1 (1974), p. 50; Mei-chou hua-ch'iao jih-pao, September 11, 1974, p. 1; Ta-kung pao (Hong Kong), March 8, 1975, p. 9.
28. The yuan is an alternative term for the renminbi, analogous to "pound" and "sterling." The yuan is divided into 10 chiao and 100 fen.

with Japanese oil and fertilizer industries in early 1975 to quote prices in American dollars, in spite of an earlier agreement between the Bank of China and the Bank of Tokyo to settle trade payments in *yuan* or *yen*. In the case of Chinese oil prices, the change in currency was based on a Japanese request because the quotation in *yuan* would cost Japanese importers about $1.10 per barrel more than if they bought Indonesian crude, and this would hinder the expansion of Chinese oil exports to Japan.[29] In the case of Japanese fertilizer prices, the change was requested by the Chinese because the interest rates of *yen* as a settlement currency were considerably higher than those in the Eurodollar market which the Chinese could obtain.[30]

A special problem confronts U.S. importers of Chinese goods. As Chinese sales are now mostly quoted in *renminbi*, it sometimes becomes necessary for importers to obtain forward contracts for the Chinese currency. These contracts, however, are not obtainable in the United States owing to the lack of full correspondent relations between banks in the United States and the Bank of China. As a result, American importers can make these contracts only through London, Hong Kong, or other foreign cities where third-country banks are authorized by the Chinese bank to sell *renminbi* to Americans having purchase contracts with Chinese national foreign trade corporations. Recently, however, it has been reported that a few American companies well known to the Bank of China have been permitted to conclude forward contracts directly with the bank.[31]

Shipping and Insurance. In order to protect their state insurance and shipping interests, terms of Chinese sales to non-socialist countries are almost always CIF, very rarely C & F, and almost never FOB; whereas Chinese purchases from those countries are mostly FOB, sometimes C & F, and almost never CIF. Generally, under the terms of a CIF contract, the seller is responsible for chartering a vessel or freight space in a vessel, and bears all risks until after the goods have been actually loaded on board the vessel within the date or period stipulated in the contract. He is also obligated to pay the freight to the port of destination, to buy adequate insurance to cover the sum specified in the contract, to obtain the export license, to assist the buyer in obtaining other necessary papers issued by the exporting country, and to provide the buyer with the clean bill of lading, insurance policies, invoices, and other documents specified in the contract. The buyer's obligations are to accept the documents presented by the seller, to pay expenses provided for in

29. See "China Said Agreeable on Oil Quotes in $," *Japan Times*, January 27, 1975, p. 9; "Japan Inks China Oil Import Pact," *ibid.*, February 20, 1975, p. 10.

30. See "China Agrees to Pay in U.S. Dollars," *South China Morning Post*, Business News Section, February 15, 1975, p. 5.

31. See Katherine Schwering, *loc. cit.*, p. 40.

the contract, to handle all procedures for the unloading of the goods at the port of destination, and to bear all risks from the moment the goods have actually been loaded on board the vessel in the port of shipment.[32]

In an FOB contract the seller is generally obligated to deliver the goods on board a vessel and to assume all risks until that delivery has been made. He also pays all export duties and is responsible for the export license and other related expenses. The loading port and the date of delivery are specified in the contract. Only when he has agreed to charter a vessel or freight space in a vessel for the buyer must the seller procure the bill of lading. The buyer's usual obligations are to charter a vessel or freight space in a vessel, to buy insurance for the goods, to notify the seller of the name of the vessel, to pay all expenses incidental to the goods, and to bear all risks from the moment the goods have actually been placed on board the vessel in the port agreed upon by the parties.[33]

A standard form CIF sales confirmation of the China National Textile Import and Export Corporation (see Appendix M) provides the following shipping and insurance terms:

Shipment may be made from any Chinese port, the date of Bill of Lading shall be taken as the date of shipment. Any change of destination should be agreed to by the Sellers beforehand. Extra freight and/or insurance premiums thus incurred are to be borne by the Buyers.

The Buyers are requested to refrain from SPECIFYING ANY PARTICULAR SHIPPING LINE, NAME OF STEAMER, or INSURANCE COMPANY in the Letter of Credit. To facilitate negotiation of the credit by the Sellers, the validity of the Letter of Credit shall be so stipulated as to remain valid for at least 10 days (expiring in China) after the last day of shipment and the amount, quantity of the credit shall allow plus or minus 5%. The buyers are requested always to stipulate in the Letter of Credit that TRANSHIPMENT AND PARTIAL SHIPMENT ARE ALLOWED.

The Sellers are to cover insurance at invoice value plus 10% thereof of the goods sold on CIF basis. If the Letter of Credit stipulates that the goods after arrival at the port of destination are to be transported to an inland city or some other ports, the Sellers will cover insurance up to that city or ports, and the Buyers are to be responsible for payment of this additional premium.[34]

In many other standard form Chinese CIF sales contracts, however, these provisions for shipment are either omitted or left in very vague terms. For example, a 1973 sales contract of the China National Chemicals Import and Export Corporation simply provided general stipulations for the shipping documents to be presented by the sellers; the negotiation of payment;

32. See Shanghai Foreign Languages Institute, *op. cit.,* pp. 16-17.
33. See Shanghai Foreign Languages Institute, *op. cit.,* pp. 15-16.
34. For a sample Chinese insurance contract, see Appendix Q.

commodity inspection, *force majeure,* discrepancy and claim; arbitration; and obligations.

In a 1974 Chinese sales contract, for the sale of seafood to an American company, the Chinese used the rare C & F terms, stipulating that insurance was "to be effected by the Buyers," presumably for the reason that the Chinese did not want to assume the risk of insurance for such a commodity. The shipment's bill of lading, invoice, commodity inspection certificate on quality and weight, and insurance policy were required for the negotiation of payment. Otherwise, the contract provided no shipping terms except that the sellers were obligated to deliver a "shipping advice" to the buyers concerning "credit, quantity, and name of vessel" immediately after the completion of loading. Of all the Chinese sales contracts with non-socialist countries that I have examined, none was made on FOB terms, although the existence of such contracts cannot be ruled out, especially in China's trade relations with Third World countries or when the transactions involved are of such a nature that it requires FOB arrangements. One most recent example is the contracted sale of nearly eight million tons of Chinese crude oil to Japan in 1975: the price, $12.10 per barrel, was quoted on FOB terms probably because China did not have enough tankers to deliver the oil.[35]

The specific terms of a standard form Chinese purchase contract, usually FOB, are more elaborate than those of the usually CIF Chinese sales contract. A 1972 purchase contract of the China National Light Industrial Products Import and Export Corporation (see Appendix N) provided, in case of C & F terms, that "the Sellers shall ship the goods within the shipment time from the port of shipment to the port of destination. Transhipment is not allowed. The carrying vessel shall not fly the flag of USA or shall her captain be USA nationality nor shall she call en route at any port of USA or in the vicinity of Taiwan." The clause prohibiting United States flag ships or ships with American captains to carry cargo to Chinese ports was, of course, a reaction to United States embargo regulations, and the mention of Taiwan was obviously based on Chinese political and security considerations. After the Sino-American detente the Chinese dropped the American restriction in all their C & F purchase contracts, but retained certain qualifications for shipping as well as the Taiwan proviso. A 1974 contract of the China National Chemicals Import and Export Corporation (see Appendix N) reads in part: "Transhipment en route is not allowed without the Buyers' consent. The goods shall not be carried by vessels flying the flags of the countries not acceptable to the Buyers. The carrying vessel shall not call or stop over at the

35. See "Japan to Double Oil Imports from China," *Japan Times,* March 11, 1974, p. 9.

port/ports of Taiwan Province and the port/ports in the vicinity of Taiwan Province prior to her arrival at the port of destination as stipulated in the Clause (11) of this Contract."[36]

Commodity Inspection and Quality Guarantee. In Chinese sales contracts, the commodity inspection clause is vague and usually mixed with the provisions for quality and/or quantity discrepancies and claims. The simplest clause is found in a standard form sales contract of the China National Cereals, Oils and Foodstuffs Import and Export Corporation which merely states that "Quality and Weight certified by the China Commodity Inspection Bureau as per their respective certificates are to be taken as final." In one sales contract of the China National Chemicals Import and Export Corporation, the inspection clause stipulates that "the Certificate of Quality, Quantity/Weight issued by [a commodity inspection bureau] shall be taken as the basis of delivery." It does not mention the scope of such basis, nor the nationality of the inspection bureau. In another sales contract (in the author's possession) of the China National Cereals, Oils and Foodstuffs Import and Export Corporation, the inspection clause was replaced by a claims clause, which reads as follows:

Should the quality, quantity, and/or weight be found not in conformity with those stipulated in this Contract, aside from those usual natural changes of quality and weight in transit and losses within the responsibility of the shipping company and/or insurance company, the Buyers shall have the right within 30 days after the arrival of the goods at the port of destination, to lodge claims concerning the quality, quantity or weight of the goods. Claims for perishable goods are to be put forward immediately after arrival of the goods at destination, but the Buyers should provide the Sellers with the Certificates issued by the concerned Inspection Organization.

While this provision recognizes the right of the buyers to reinspect the goods, "the concerned Inspection Organization" could have differing interpretations. A sales contract of the China National Metals and Minerals Import and Export Corporation, however, required that "claims must be accompanied by Survey Reports of Recognized Public Surveyors agreed to by the Sellers." And a standard form sales contract of the China National Machinery Import and Export Corporation stipulates merely that: "The Sellers are only responsible for claims against bad workmanship or faulty materials. Claims concerning quality shall be made within 2 months after the arrival of the goods at destination."

Under China's commodity inspection law of 1953, any interested party to a foreign trade deal has the right to apply for reinspection if he is not

36. In an agreement with Finland on the General Conditions for Delivery, June 5, 1953, the Chinese also prohibited any vessel flying American or Japanese flags or sailing with an American or Japanese master to carry cargo to China. See *TYC 1952-1953,* vol. 2 (1957), p. 372. The Japanese restriction was dropped after the cessation of the Korean War.

satisfied with the result of the initial inspection, and to request a review of the entire case if he is still not satisfied with the result of the reinspection.[37] In light of the foregoing discussion, this regulation apparently does not automatically or unconditionally apply to all Chinese sales contracts. Moreover, the Chinese seem to have tailored the inspection clauses in their sales contracts to fit the merchandise involved, limiting their responsibility accordingly.

By contrast, in all Chinese purchase contracts that I have studied, the foreign sellers are invariably required to guarantee the quality of goods, or the right of the Chinese buyers to reinspect the goods by a Chinese commodity inspection bureau, and sometimes both.[38]

A comparison of the differences between these Chinese sales and purchase contracts demonstrates that the Chinese, as either sellers or buyers, are better protected than their foreign partners. For example, guarantees against "bad workmanship" and "faulty materials" in the sales contract of the China National Machinery Import and Export Corporation are hardly equivalent to stipulations for "the best materials" and "first class workmanship" found in some purchase contracts of the same corporation. Japanese traders, among others, have shown displeasure at this kind of uneven protection, as well as with Chinese methods of weighing and inspection.[39] However, due to the lucrative nature of the transactions, they have accepted the Chinese terms without registering serious complaints.

Late Delivery and Force Majeure. When exporting, the Chinese usually insist on provisions that could justify late delivery or non-delivery due to either *force majeure* causes or the buyers' failure to forward the letter of credit to the sellers in time for shipment. Chinese sales contracts provide no specific penalties for late delivery or non-delivery except the right to cancel the transaction. But Chinese purchase contracts, with the exception of *force majeure* causes, generally stipulate a penalty of no more than 5 percent of the total value of the goods involved for late delivery. A standard clause reads as follows:

Should the Sellers fail to make delivery on time as stipulated in the Contract, with the exception of Force Majeure causes specified in Clause 13 of this Contract, the Buyers shall agree to postpone the delivery on condition that the Sellers agree to pay a penalty

37. See Provisional Regulation for the Inspection and Testing of Export and Import Commodities, December 17, 1953, art. 9, in *FLHP 1954* (1955), pp. 71, 72.

38. See, for example, the purchase contract of the China National Chemicals Import and Export Corporation in Appendix N. Sources for the contracts and their provisions quoted or paraphrased above and below cannot be documented without being reproduced as sections of Appendices M and N. Since this is not feasible, documentation in these discussions is omitted. For reference to similar contract materials, see National Council for United States-China Trade, Special Report no. 13 *Standard Form Contracts of the People's Republic of China,* (1975).

39. See Japan External Trade Organization, *How to Approach the China Market,* pp. 129, 147-48.

which shall be deducted by the paying bank from the payment under negotiation. The penalty, however, shall not exceed 5% of the total value of the goods involved in the late delivery. The rate of penalty is charged at 0.5% for every seven days, odd days less than seven days should be counted as seven days. In case the Sellers fail to make delivery ten weeks later than the time of shipment stipulated in the Contract, the Buyers shall have the right to cancel the contract and the Sellers, in spite of the cancellation, shall still pay the aforesaid penalty to the Buyers without delay.[40]

Although the Chinese rely on and accept *force majeure* as a justifiable cause for late delivery or non-delivery in both export and import transactions, in some instances they do not define the concept, and in cases where a definition is available, it is not always conclusive. As in the case of commodity inspection and other important contractual terms discussed above, there is always a difference between Chinese sales and purchase contracts in the use of the *force majeure* clause. When the Chinese are selling, the procedures for reporting a *force majeure* incident are usually simple and vague, if included at all. A sales contract of the China National Light Industrial Products Import and Export Corporation merely stipulates: "The Seller shall not be held liable for failure or delay in delivery of the entire lot or a portion of the goods under this Sales Confirmation in consequence of any Force Majeure incidents." Another sales contract, concluded between the China National Cereals, Oils and Foodstuffs Import and Export Corporation and a European firm, provides:

Should the Sellers fail to deliver the contracted goods or effect the shipment in time by reason of war, flood, fire, storm, heavy snow or any other causes beyond their control, the time of shipment might be duly extended, or alternatively a part or whole of the Contract might be cancelled without any liability attached to the Sellers, but the Sellers have to furnish the buyers with a certificate attesting such event or events.

When the Chinese are buying, two standard clauses are used. A China National Chemicals Import and Export Corporation purchase contract (see Appendix N) reads:

The Sellers shall not be held responsible for late delivery or non-delivery of the goods owing to generally recognized "Force Majeure" causes. However, in such case, the Sellers shall immediately cable the Buyers [of] the accident and airmail to the Buyers within 15 days after the accident, a certificate of the accident issued by the competent government authorities or the chamber of commerce which is located at the place where the accident occurs as evidence thereof. With the exception of late delivery or non-delivery due to "Force Majeure" causes, in case the Sellers fail to make delivery within the time as stipulated in the Contract, the Sellers should indemnify the Buyers for all losses and expenses incurred to the latter directly attributable to late delivery or failure to make delivery of the goods in accordance with the terms of this Contract. If the "Force Majeure" cause lasts over 60 days, the Buyers shall have the right to cancel the Contract and/or the undelivered part of the Contract.

40. A similar clause can be found in Appendix N.

The other clause, found in a purchase contract of the China National Machinery Import and Export Corporation, obligates the sellers to deliver the goods in spite of any *force majeure* incident:

The Sellers shall not be held responsible for the delay in shipment or non-delivery of the goods due to Force Majeure, which might occur during the process of manufacturing or in the course of loading or transit. The Sellers shall advise the Buyers immediately of the occurrence mentioned above and within fourteen days thereafter, the Sellers shall send by airmail to the Buyers for their acceptance a certificate of the accident issued by the competent Government Authorities where the accident occurs as evidence thereof. *Under such circumstances the Sellers, however, are still under the obligation to take all necessary measures to hasten the delivery of the goods.* In case the accident lasts for more than ten weeks the Buyers shall have the right to cancel the Contract. [Emphasis added]

If *force majeure* is an "act of God" beyond man's control, it is noteworthy that the sellers could still be held liable for delivery. In view of the fact that the contract was signed by the Chinese machinery corporation, it may be assumed that the object involved in the transaction was important to the development of Chinese industry, and to ensure delivery the Chinese required the sellers to make good the deal even in *force majeure* circumstances. Left unclear is the Chinese position on government intervention and strikes as elements of *force majeure*. It has been generally assumed that the Chinese would follow Soviet practice in regarding acts of governments as valid *force majeure* causes, but evidence suggests the contrary.[41] In a transaction with an American firm, the Chinese buyers reportedly insisted on a provision which would exclude the sellers' inability to obtain an export license from the United States government as an element of *force majeure*. In another instance, in which the China National Metals and Minerals Import and Export Corporation was the seller, the contract provided: "Buyers' failure to obtain the relative Import License is not to be treated as Force Majeure."

China, like other socialist countries, was reported to have refused to accept strikes as a *force majeure* cause. However, for the first time in the PRC's history the 1975 Constitution provides all Chinese citizens with the "freedom of strike" (article 28). Whether this significant development in China's domestic policy will have any impact on its foreign trade policy and practice remains to be seen.

41. The Soviet provision defining "acts or demands of the [Soviet] government" as elements of *force majeure* is in contracts between certain Soviet and Israeli corporations. See Martin Domke, "The Israeli-Soviet Oil Arbitration," *American Journal of International Law* 53:787 (1959). In *Jordan Investment Ltd. v. Soiuznefteksport,* a case growing out of the 1956 Arab-Israeli War, the Foreign Trade Arbitration Commission of the Soviet Union ruled that Moscow's denial of an export license for the defendant, a Soviet state enterprise, to supply the plaintiff Israeli company Soviet oil was an act of *force majeure,* and thus voided the defendant's obligation to fulfill the contract. See Harold Berman, "Force Majeure and the Denial of an Export License under Soviet Law," *Harvard Law Review* 73:1128 (1960).

Means of Settling Disputes

Before 1911 China had a comprehensive code of substantive law, but lacked a fixed and elaborated procedural code. Influenced by the Confucian view of social and ethical conduct embodied in the concept of *li* (propriety) Chinese society found the settlement of a pecuniary matter before a magistrate very distasteful, and considered lawyers who encouraged court litigation as pettifoggers undeserving of community respect. While legal avenues were always open for the adjudication of disputes, conciliation and mediation were the preferred methods.

The People's Republic seems to have followed traditional practice in the settlement of commercial disputes. In nearly all agreements with socialist countries, there are provisions in the General Conditions for Delivery for the direct adjustment of disagreements between the parties with regard to quantity and quality of the goods. Usually, the buyer must present a complaint to the seller within a given period, stating the quantity and quality of the goods that differ from those stipulated in the individual contract. Upon receiving the complaint, the seller is obligated to reply within a specified period of time. Failure to reply is considered acquiescence to the buyer's claim, and automatically requires the seller to make up the differences and to pay for all expenses involved.[42] In some instances a review board, organized by representatives of the buyer's state organs which have no direct interest in the transaction, examines the validity of the complaint to facilitate the settlement.[43] In trade agreements with non-socialist countries, too, there are provisions for settling contractual disputes primarily through "friendly negotiation" between the parties.[44]

China's preference for amicable settlement is, however, not uniquely Chinese; for example, the International Chamber of Commerce has also encouraged conciliation as an option to arbitration. What is typically Chinese

42. *E.g.,* Protocol on the General Conditions for Delivery with the Foreign Trade Organization of the People's Republic of Hungary for the Year 1962, March 30, 1962, art. 23, in *TYC 1962,* vol. 11 (1963), pp. 40, 50-52.

43. See, for example, Protocol on the General Conditions for Delivery with the Ministry of Foreign Trade of the People's Republic of Poland for the Year 1959, December 31, 1959, art. 22, in *TYC 1959,* vol. 8 (1960), pp. 56, 66-67.

44. See Appendix D, the 1974 Sino-Japanese trade agreement, art. 8. For reference to similar provisions in other trade agreements, see Trade Agreement with the Government of the Republic of Finland, June 5, 1953, art. 7, in *TYC 1952-1953,* vol. 2 (1957), pp. 35, 36; Sino-Japanese Trade Agreement, October 29, 1953, art. 7, in *TYC 1952-1953,* vol. 2 (1957), pp. 369, 370; Trade Agreement for the Exchange of Goods between the China Import and Export Corporation and the French Industrial and Commercial Trade Delegation, June 5, 1953, art. 7, in *TYC 1952-1953,* vol. 2 (1957), pp. 377, 378; Trade Agreement with the Republic of India, October 14, 1954, art. 8, in *TYC 1954,* vol. 3 (1958), pp. 28, 30; Agreement on the Exchange of Goods and Payments with the Kingdom of Afghanistan, July 28, 1957, art. 5, in *TYC 1957,* vol. 6 (1958), pp. 139, 140; Trade Agreement between the China Council for the Promotion of International Trade and the Eastern Committee of the German Economy, September 27, 1957, art. 9, in *TYC 1957,* vol. 6 (1958), pp. 323, 324.

is the lack of concern for formal procedures in the settlement of disputes. None of China's trade agreements and contracts stipulate the process by which an amicable settlement may be obtained. So far as is known, the Chinese have adopted three formulas for non-arbitrary settlement of disputes, officially called *yu-hao hsieh-shang chieh-chüeh* (settlement through friendly negotiation), *tzu-hsün* (consultation), and *t'iao-chieh* (conciliation).[45] Under the first formula, the parties engage in direct negotiations without involving an official Chinese arbitration organ. Under the second formula, the dispute is brought to the attention of either the Foreign Trade Arbitration Commission (FTAC) or the Maritime Arbitration Commission (MAC), depending on the nature of the dispute, for consultation. The arbitration organ will not recommend a solution, but will assist the parties in finding a solution between themselves. Under the third formula, the arbitration organ will act as a conciliator at the request of either party, making a "concrete suggestion" in a special written form or ordinary correspondence to the parties; the suggestion, however, is not binding. Under any of these formulas, the settlement can be carried out through either face-to-face discussion or correspondence. Jen Tsien-hsin (Chien-hsin), director of the Department of Legal Affairs of the CCPIT, reported that in 1974 the two Chinese arbitration organs settled twelve cases by conciliation and over one hundred cases through consultation.[46] The number of cases of friendly negotiation is not mentioned, obviously because they did not involve either arbitration organ.

With Americans, the Chinese seem to be very cooperative and successful in resolving potential or existing disputes through friendly negotiations. One example is the Chinese cancellation of two orders for nearly one million tons of American wheat and 233,000 bales of American cotton in 1975. In both instances it was reported that the Chinese paid the difference between the high prices prevailing when the contracts were concluded and the much lower rates quoted on the wheat and cotton markets when the contracts were cancelled. According to one expert, "the effect is the same as if the Chinese accepted delivery of the cotton and then resold it to the American dealers at the low current price."[47] American official sources indicated that

45. The first term is universally used in Chinese trade contracts where the method of settling disputes is provided for; the second and the third are in Jen Tsien-hsin, "Foreign Trade and Maritime Arbitration in China," *Chung-kuo tui-wai-mao-i,* no. 3 (1975), p. 50. The English version of this article is in *China's Foreign Trade,* no. 3 (1975), p. 50. The article is the first written explanation on the subject since the early sixties.

46. *Ibid.* The procedures for consultation and conciliation are not described in the article but come from Jen Tsien-hsin's interviews with two prominent lawyers, Donald B. Straus and Howard M. Holtzmann, who represented the American Arbitration Association on a January 1975 visit to the CCPIT in Peking. See Howard M. Holtzmann, "Resolving Disputes in U.S.-China Trade," in Howard M. Holtzmann, ed., *Legal Aspects of Doing Business with China,* p. 83.

47. See "China Cancels Cotton Orders," *South China Morning Post,* Business News Section, March 8, 1975, p. 9.

the amount of money involved in the settlement of the cotton case was "very substantial."

A second case involved the Chinese failure to comply with American law and mark the country of origin on a consumer product shipped to the United States. The American importer was faced with two options: either to return the goods to China or to have them re-marked in the United States. He chose the second option, and the Chinese promptly paid all the costs on presentation of the bills from the various parties involved in re-marking the goods. In another Chinese sale to an American importer, a problem arose from mutual misinterpretation of a commodity description ". . . with both parties having properly executed their respective ends of the contract. [Although] market conditions were unfavorable . . . the matter was eventually resolved by the sellers instructing the U.S. representative of one of their third country agents for this commodity to purchase and dispose of the goods from us."[48]

Given China's conciliatory approach to dispute resolution, it would seem that a clause dealing with arbitration is unnecessary in Chinese trade contracts. One veteran China trader went so far as to advise: "Forget about going to arbitration. You will find the Chinese to be the fairest and most ingenious conciliators in the world of commerce."[49] Yet, there is an arbitration clause in virtually every Chinese trade contract and their use is not unknown. According to an East German source, as of 1960 the Chinese foreign trade arbitration organization in Peking had been called upon "to hand down rulings in sixty-one cases" involving Chinese enterprises and their foreign business partners from Britain, Switzerland, Finland, Greece, the United Arab Republic, India, Ceylon, Canada, and Singapore.[50] In 1973 and 1974, some private Canadian, European and Japanese sources reported that as in the Cultural Revolution, the Chinese were sometimes late in making deliveries and payments, supposedly due to shortages in supply and foreign exchange reserves.[51] Although not many of these incidents have developed into serious disputes and China's three "non-arbitrary" formulas have worked well, arbitration will continue to be necessary in some cases.[52]

48. See David Cookson, "Two Dispute Settlement Problems with the PRC Encountered by a U.S. Trading Firm," in National Council for United States-China Trade Special Report no. 4, *Arbitration and Dispute Settlement In Trade with China* (1974), pp. 28-30.

49. See "Hans Schneider, the China Hand's China Hand," in *U.S.-China Business Review*, no. 5 (1974), p. 4.

50. See H. Fellhauer, "Foreign Trade Arbitral Jurisdiction in the People's Republic of China," United States Commerce Department Joint Publications Research Service translation no. 8612 (1960), p. 6.

51. The speculation arose from Chinese trade deficits of $567 million and about $1,000 million in 1973 and 1974 respectively. However, then Vice-Premier Teng Hsiao-ping assured Japan that China would pay on time. See "China Promises to Pay Japan on Time," *Japan Times,* January 22, 1975, p. 1.

52. In his article cited in note 45, Jen Tsien-hsin reported that there was only one

Arbitration Organs and Procedures

Jen Tsien-hsin has explained the principles of arbitration as follows:

Under the guidance of Chairman Mao's proletarian revolutionary line, the FTAC and MAC carry out their work in accordance with the policy of maintaining China's independence and taking the initiative in hand, and the policy of equality and mutual benefit, while taking into account the custom of international practice. In handling disputes, they stress that once a contract is signed, the parties must seriously enforce it—a principle that requires both parties to respect contractual provisions and honor promises, that emphasizes the importance of equality among all nations regardless of their size and economic strength. Both arbitration commissions are firmly opposed to the practice of hegemony in international trade and maritime transport: wanton encroachment on the rights of others, deception and extortion, the bullying of the small by the big, and the suppression of the weak by the strong. They are resolutely opposed to great-power chauvinism and national egoism by making use of arbitration as a means to protect the party of one's own nationality.[53]

When the CCPIT was established in 1952, a Department of Arbitration was set up under its supervision.[54] The Government Administration Council, on May 6, 1954, replaced the Department of Arbitration with the FTAC, and adopted a set of arbitral procedures.[55] Twenty-one trade officials, economists, industrialists, transportation experts, insurance agents, and international lawyers were elected members of the FTAC,[56] which was empowered to arbitrate virtually any and all trade disputes to which a Chinese enterprise was a party, over a wide range of commercial activity. According to Jen Tsien-hsin, the FTAC now arbitrates three types of cases: (1) disputes arising from contracts and transactions in foreign trade, including contracts for commissioning agencies to purchase or sell merchandise; (2) disputes arising from transportation, insurance or safe-keeping of merchandise; and (3) disputes arising from other matters of business in foreign trade. Jen's explanation left uncertain whether the FTAC would still arbitrate a controversy between two foreign parties or between two Chinese parties, as it could under its original mandate. Omission of the latter instance, however, is consistent with Peking's current policy toward disputes between domestic economic or commercial organizations, where the Soviet practice of arbitration has been abandoned in favor of administrative solutions.

---

arbitration case in 1974.

    53. See note 45. The translation is mine.

    54. See *Jen-min shou-ts'e 1953*, p. 270.

    55. Both the decision and the rule are in *Chung-hua jen-min kung-ho-kuo fa-kuei hsüan-chi*, (1957), pp. 470-478, and translated in Appendix R. Also see *Jen-min jih-pao*, May 13, 1954; *ibid.*, April 7, 1956; and *Ta-kung-pao* (Tientsin), April 7, 1956, p. 1.

    56. Chi Chao-ting, then secretary-general of the CCPIT, was named chairman, and international lawyer Chou Keng-sheng became vice-chairman. After Chi's death in 1963, Hsiao Fang-chou, who had served as his deputy secretary-general in the CCPIT, was appointed chairman. Ordinarily the term of membership is two years, but the Cultural Revolution interrupted the bi-annual selection and a new membership was not announced until the summer of

The Provisional Rules of Procedure are silent as to whether exhaustion of non-arbitrary remedies embodied in the three formulas is a precondition for arbitration; the rules merely provide that an arbitration tribunal or the FTAC will immediately dismiss a case if it has been settled by "conciliation." In practice, there is a clause in virtually every Chinese arbitration agreement which states: "All disputes in connection with this Contract or the execution thereof shall be settled through friendly negotiations. In case no settlement can be reached, the case may then be submitted for arbitration . . ."[57] It is on the basis of this clause that the FTAC will arbitrate if one party insists; but it must also be satisfied that other means are to no avail.[58]

A formal arbitration proceeding begins with the filing of a written application by a disputing party, providing the following information: (1) the name and address of the plaintiff, and of the defendant; (2) the claim of the plaintiff and the facts and evidence on which the claim is based; and (3) the name of an arbitrator chosen by the plaintiff from among the members of the FTAC or a statement authorizing the chairman of the FTAC to appoint an arbitrator for the applicant. (See Appendix R.) (Biographic information concerning the twenty-one members of the FTAC is made available to the parties upon request.) A copy of the arbitration clause from the contract in question is required, as is a filing fee equivalent to 0.5 percent of the claim. This serves as a deposit for the required arbitration fee, which cannot exceed 1 percent of the claim.

An arbitration tribunal consists of an arbitrator chosen by each party from the FTAC, and an umpire chosen by the arbitrators from among their fellow members; or, by mutual agreement, the parties may jointly choose, or

---

1975. Its principal officers were: Chairman Hsiao Fang-chou (vice-chairman of the CCPIT); Secretary General Jen Tsien-hsin (Chien-hsin) (director of the Department of Legal Affairs of the CCPIT); and Deputy Secretary General Liu Shao-shan (deputy director of the Department of Legal Affairs of the CCPIT). Its members, and their fields of expertise, were Feng Tieh-cheng, trademarks and packing; Liu Ting, lecturer in the Department of Law, Peking University; Liu Meng, law; Liu Shao-shan, deputy director of the Department of Legal Affairs at the CCPIT; Jen Tsien-hsin (Chien-hsin) director of the Department of Legal Affairs at the CCPIT; Hsu Nai-chiung, economics; Li Fan-ju, foreign trade; Juan Ke-ming, foreign trade; Hsiao Fang-chou, vice-chairman of the CCPIT; Ho Ko-chung, insurance; Yang Shi-meng (Hsi-meng), foreign trade; Chang Ming, commodity inspection and testing; Liu Ku-shu, deputy director of the Department of Legal Affairs at the CCPIT; Nyi Tsung-yuh (Ni Cheng-yu), law; Ku Wei-tao, foreign trade; Kao Tso, customs; Shang Kuang-wen, economics; Huang Kuo-kuang, commodities; Tsao Ying-fang, foreign trade; Tan Ting-tung, foreign trade; Tan Shu-an, banking. The names are arranged in order of the number of strokes in Chinese surnames, as printed in *Chung-kuo tui-wai mao-i*, no. 3 (1975), p. 51, and translated in *China's Foreign Trade*, no. 3 (1975), p. 51. The romanizations are taken from the original, and, when different from the Wade-Giles system, the latter usage is indicated in parentheses. For reference to the FTAC's old membership, see *Chung-kuo kuo-chi mao-i ts'u-chin wei-yuan-hui*, p. 27.

57. The wording varies; this clause is representative and is taken from a 1974 purchase contract of the China National Machinery Import and Export Corporation.

58. Jen Tsien-hsin, *op. cit.*, at p. 50; Howard M. Holtzmann, *op. cit.*, p. 82.

entrust the FTAC chairman to appoint, a sole arbitrator. Hearings are normally open but can be held in closed sessions at the request of either party. A disputing party may confer with the FTAC on the proceedings either in person or through a Chinese or foreign ''attorney'' *(tai-li-jen)*.

The Chinese term literally means ''agent'' and may be translated as attorney in the most general sense of the word; attorney appears in the official English version of the Provisional Rules of Procedure. However, *tai-li-jen,* or agent, is not identical with *''lü-shih,''* or ''attorney-at-law,'' who holds a practising license.[59] Moreover, since the promulgation of the rules in 1956, the FTAC has not offered any explanation as to the qualifications of such attorneys or *tai-li-jen,* their nationalities if not citizens of China, or the country of the foreign parties involved, and whether Chinese attorneys can be made available to serve foreign parties.

The decision of the tribunal, decided by majority vote, is final. In difficult cases the tribunal may approach the entire FTAC for advice as to the fairness of the settlement to be awarded, and the FTAC may look into the substance of the award to make certain that it is reasonable.[60] Underlying this practice is the belief that procedures are designed to serve principles. Execution of the award is to be implemented by the parties themselves; if one party fails to comply with the decision, the other may petition the people's court to enforce it.

The Maritime Arbitration Commission, the FTAC's sister organization, was created by a State Council decision of November 21, 1958, to handle disputes arising from maritime salvage, collisions, marine insurance, and shipping documents (see Appendix S). The State Council Decision provided that the MAC be composed of from twenty-one to thirty-one members;[61] and the procedures of the MAC are similar to those of the

59. For a discussion of the official legal terms, see State Council regulation for fees charged by lawyers, May 25, 1956, in *FKHP 1956,* vol. 4 (1957), p. 235; Huang Yuan, *Wo-kuo jen-min lü-shih chih-tu.*

60. See Howard M. Holtzmann, *op. cit.,* pp. 92-3.

61. In the early years of the MAC, Sun Ta-kuang, a transport expert and member of the CCPIT, served as chairman and Hsiao Fang-chou as vice-chairman. A 1975 article on the MAC revealed a new membership of thirty-one, with principal officers, Chairman Wang Wen-lin (vice-chairman of the CCPIT); Secretary General Jen Tsien-hsin (Chien-hsin) (director of the Department of Legal Affairs and Secretary General of the FTAC); and Deputy Secretary General Liu Shao-shan (deputy director of the Department of Legal Affairs at the CCPIT and deputy secretary general of the FTAC). Other members of the MAC, and their fields of expertise, were: Wang Hsiu-wen, navigation; Wang En-shao, insurance; Shih Yun-sheng, transport; Szu Yu-cho, navigation; Hsu Chan-fu, navigation; Liu Meng, law; Liu Liang, transport; Liu Shuang-en, transport; Liu Ting-hua, transport; Sun Jui-lung, marine transport; Hsiao Feng, navigation; Shen Chih-cheng, transport; Yang Chi-yuan, navigation; Li Sheng-min, economic geography; Shao Yi-li, transport; Shao Shun-yi, international private law; Tsou Yung-cheng, transport; Chen Ming, foreign trade; Chen Jung, marine insurance; Yao Shiu-tsai, engineering; Chang Chien-chen, ship machinery; Yu Ying-sheng, captain; Nyi Tsung-yuh (Ni Cheng-yu), law; Kao Tso, customs; Kao Chung-lai, maritime law; Chia Chen-chih, foreign trade; Cheng Hsi-meng,

FTAC.[62] In addition, the MAC works closely with the newly created Department for Average Adjustments of the CCPIT (see Appendix T).

Forms of the Arbitration Clause

Chinese insistence on using arbitration only as a last resort takes into account the disadvantages of a lawsuit growing out of a contract dispute. And in the rare contracts where a formal arbitration clause does not exist, there are at least two alternative provisions. One is found in a sales confirmation of the China National Textiles Import and Export Corporation, which states: "claims for damage should be filed by the Buyers with the Sellers within 30 days after arrival of the goods at destination and supported by sufficient evidence for Sellers' reference so that claims can be settled through friendly negotiation." The other appears in a sales confirmation of the China National Light Industrial Products Import and Export Corporation, which made no mention of arbitration or conciliation, but contained a simple clause about claims that might arise from "quality and quantity discrepancy."

But when needed, the arbitration clause is important for a number of reasons. First and foremost, in specifying a location it assigns jurisdiction, determining which party's tribunal will hear and decide the dispute. This in turn involves the question as to whose law, both substantive and procedural, is to apply. (The attitude of the general public, too, where the hearing is conducted sometimes has an important bearing on the outcome of the arbitration.)[63] Second, the convening of a tribunal for the adjudication of a dispute involves the choice of arbitrators and an umpire, and although all arbitrators and umpires are supposed to be impartial judges, it is a fact of life that the inherited instincts, traditional beliefs, and acquired convictions of a judge have a great deal to do with his decisions. In some instances, national arbitration laws expressly require the observance of local justice and customs by arbitrators.

In arbitration with corporations of the People's Republic, these problems are compounded by the Chinese belief that all economic, political, legal and social institutions in a given country serve the interests of its ruling class, and as a result, that it is impossible to obtain a fair hearing and an equitable arbitration award from a non-socialist country.[64] Thus, the Chinese have always preferred Peking or other Chinese locales for arbitration, although if

---

international law; and Tai Hung-tuan, marine insurance. Sources are the same as for the FTAC, note 56.

62. Both the MAC and the FTAC are copies of their counterparts in the USSR Chamber of Commerce. See Vladimir Gsovksi, *Soviet Civil Law,* vol. 2, (1949), pp. 641-659.

63. See Richard N. Gardner, "Economic and Political Implications of International Commercial Arbitration," in Martin Domke, ed., *International Trade Arbitration,* p. 15.

64. See Shanghai Foreign Languages Institute, *Tui-wai mao-i shih-wu,* p. 109.

the other party insists, and if the transaction is important, the Chinese will compromise on the site.

To date, seven forms of the arbitration clause have appeared in Chinese trade documents. In all forms the arbitration clause, like other important provisions in a Chinese sales contract, is generally less precise than the same clause in a Chinese purchase contract. But both usually specify that expenses for arbitration are borne by the losing party in a dispute. The first and simplest form appears in a sales contract of the China National Cereals, Oils, and Foodstuffs Import and Export Corporation, and specifies neither the location of the hearing nor the composition of the tribunal. It simply reads as follows: "Should there be any disputes between the contracting parties, they shall be settled through negotiation. In case no settlement can be reached, the case under dispute may then be referred to arbitration."

The second form, used in the first two semi-governmental trade agreements with Japan, in 1952 and 1953, provides for arbitration within the territorial boundaries of China regardless of which party is the defendant. No mention was made of the composition of the tribunal, nor the method by which the arbitrators were to be selected.[65]

The third form found in a sales contract of the China National Chemicals Import and Export Corporation, provides for arbitration exclusively in Peking in accordance with the established procedures of the Chinese FTAC, regardless of which party is the defendant. The fourth form provides for arbitration at the port of destination. The arbitration tribunal consists of two arbitrators appointed by the disputing parties and an umpire chosen by the arbitrators. This provision is said to be formulated according to international custom.[66] No actual examples of this form can be found, however, in Chinese foreign trade contracts to substantiate this claim. The fifth form provides for arbitration in another socialist country if China's capitalist trading partner refuses to accept China as the location of arbitration. However, no details are available.

The sixth form provides for arbitration in the country of nationality of the defendant. This follows the Soviet model, and is the standard clause in all of China's trade agreements with socialist countries, and is used in many with non-socialist states. The composition of the arbitration tribunal varies. With socialist countries, each party is entitled to choose a number of arbitrators from among the members of the defendant country's national foreign trade arbitration commission. These then choose an umpire from the remaining members of the arbitration commission. Or, by mutual agreement, the

65. See China-Japan Trade Agreement, June 1, 1952, art. 6, in *TYC 1952-1953*, vol. 2 (1957), pp. 367, 368; China-Japan Trade Agreement, October 29, 1953, art. 7, in *ibid.*, pp. 369, 370.

66. See Shanghai Foreign Languages Institute, *Tui-wai mao-i shih-wu*, p. 109.

disputing parties may jointly choose, or entrust the chairman of the arbitration commission to appoint, a sole arbitrator. Both the arbitrators and the umpire are thus nationals of the country of the defendant.[67]

With non-socialist countries several methods are used. According to the Trade Agreement with Finland, June 5, 1953, each party was entitled to appoint one arbitrator and the umpire was to be chosen by agreement of the two arbitrators so appointed. Both the arbitrators and the umpire must be citizens of either China or Finland.[68] In the Trade Agreement with the French Trade Delegation, June 5, 1953, a more detailed provision was adopted. While accepting the defendant's country as the location of arbitration, the agreement stipulated that if the arbitration was conducted in France, each party was entitled to appoint an arbitrator of French nationality, and an umpire was to be chosen by agreement of the arbitrators. If the arbitrators could not agree, the umpire was to be appointed by the president of the civil court of Seine Province. The nationality of the umpire, appointed either by the arbitrators or the Court, was not mentioned.[69] If the arbitration was conducted in Peking, the prevailing rules were to be those of the FTAC. Similarly, in the third and fourth semi-governmental trade agreements with Japan, in 1955 and 1958, as well as in private contracts with Japanese firms in subsequent years, the Chinese accepted the country of "domicile" of the defendant as the location of arbitration and agreed that if the arbitration was conducted in Japan the rules of the Japan International Commercial Arbitration Association would prevail.[70] However, the arbitrators whom the parties might choose were not limited to those listed by the association; they might be Chinese, Japanese or persons of a third country agreed upon by the parties.[71]

The seventh form, and perhaps the one most frequently used in China's important trade contracts with capitalist countries, provides for arbitration in a third country agreeable to both parties. An early example of this is the Trade Agreement with the Eastern Committee of the [West] German Economy, September 27, 1957, which designated Zurich as the location of arbitration, irrespective of the nationality of the defendant.[72] In selecting

67. See the pertinent arbitration laws of the socialist countries in CCPIT, ed., *Tui-wai mao-i chung-tsai shou-ts'e*, 2 vols. (1957). English translation in *Commercial Arbitration and the Law Throughout the World*.

68. In *TYC 1952-1953*, vol. 2 (1957), pp. 35, 36.

69. In *TYC 1952-1953*, vol. 2 (1957), pp. 377, 378.

70. "Domicile" and "nationality" are not identical. Presumably what the Chinese and Japanese actually meant in these agreements and contracts was nationality, not domicile.

71. See Gene T. Hsiao, "Communist China's Foreign Trade Contracts and Means of Settling Disputes," *Vanderbilt Law Review* 22:521-525 (1969). Also see Commercial Arbitration Rules of the Japan Commercial Arbitration Association, revised on June 14, 1963; Arbitration Procedures, Extract, from *The Code of Civil Procedures, Japan* (1962).

72. In *TYC 1957*, vol. 6 (1958), pp. 323, 324.

arbitrators, the third country's rules were not binding upon the parties; although under a supplemental agreement between the Chinese and the West Germans, if one of them failed to appoint an arbitrator within a month, the local Chamber of Commerce could appoint an arbitrator for that party upon the request of the other party. Likewise, the chamber of commerce could appoint the umpire upon the request of either party when the arbitrators themselves failed to agree on an umpire.[73]

While in most cases the third-country is usually in Europe (often Sweden or Switzerland), for the first time in their trade relations with the United States, the Chinese recently agreed to accept Toronto as the location of arbitration. More significant is that arbitration in Toronto is to be under the rules of the International Chamber of Commerce; any disputes arising from this method are subject to resolution under Canadian law.[74]

73. Exchange of Notes between the China Council for the Promotion of International Trade and the Eastern Committee of the German Economy Concerning the Procedure of Arbitration, September 27, 1957, in *TYC 1957*, vol. 6 (1958), pp. 328-329.

74. See "Negotiating the Sale of Mining Equipment in Peking," *U.S.-China Business Review*, no. 6 (1974), p. 47. The Chinese would not accept arbitration in the U.S. in the absence of formal diplomatic ties.

7   Conclusion

CHINA is moving into the last quarter of the twentieth century with great confidence and pride. In his 1975 ''Report on the Work of the Government'' to the Fourth National People's Congress, the late Premier Chou En-lai promised that the Chinese would build their nation into ''a powerful modern socialist country . . . before the end of the century.''[1] Quoting Chairman Mao, he characterized the period from 1965 to 1980 as the first major stage of development for the building of an independent and relatively comprehensive industrial and economic system, and the period from 1981 to 2000 as the second major stage, ''to accomplish the comprehensive modernization of agriculture, industry, national defense and science and technology . . . so that our national economy will be advancing in the front ranks of the world.'' Seeing the next ten years as the most crucial decade for accomplishing what has been envisaged for the second stage, he reaffirmed the ordering of China's priorities for the period as they have been set for the last ten years: agriculture, light industry, heavy industry. Within the context of this economic strategy, foreign trade will continue to play a dynamic role in supporting the development of industrialization and agricultural production. While the basic commodity composition of China's trade is not likely to undergo any drastic change, growing Chinese oil exports may reduce its present heavy reliance on exports of agricultural products and textiles and increase imports of plants and equipment. Efforts will be continued to achieve an even balance, if not a surplus, in trade; however, adverse balances may be expected before oil exports become a significant factor.[2]

In the diplomatic arena, China has formally proclaimed the demise of the ''socialist camp'' and announced a foreign policy in accordance with its own vision of a trichotomous universe consisting of the Soviet Union and the United States as the First World; the developing countries in Asia, Africa, Latin America, and other regions as the Third World; the developed countries between the two as the Second World or the Intermediate Zone.[3] Underlying

1. See *Hung-ch'i,* no. 2 (1975), pp. 20, 27.
2. China's oil export capability may be limited by its increasing need for internal use. Externally, its export effort has already met with some resistence. According to sources in Japan External Trade Organization, the international oil consortiums, which have a large stake in the Japanese oil industry, have recently interfered with the latter's import plan for more Chinese crude oil.
3. See Teng Hsiao-ping's speech to the Sixth Special Session of the United Nations

this concept is the Chinese perception that both the Soviet Union and the United States are contending for world hegemony while colluding with each other for the redivision of the world into spheres of influence. According to Chou En-lai, the contention is absolute and protracted, whereas the collusion is relative and temporary—dialectically serving "the purpose of more intensified contention."[4] In this situation, he pointed out, Europe is the immediate strategic target of the two superpowers in their competition for world domination, and the task of China is to form a broad international united front with all other developing nations and the Second World against superpower hegemonism. Barring certain unlikely events, such as a Sino-Soviet rapprochement, this grand strategy is to guide the next generation of Chinese leadership in conducting foreign affairs.

Taken together, these economic and diplomatic determinants will shape the future of Chinese trade. Japan is likely to remain China's top trading partner, both as a large consumer of Chinese crude oil and raw materials and as a leading supplier of complete plants, machinery, and equipment. This is not only because of their geographic proximity, cultural affinity, and experiences in each other's market, but also because of the enduring Sino-Soviet conflict in which China is actively seeking Japanese support.[5] For the foreseeable future, Hong Kong and Southeast Asia will continue to be the principal sources of China's foreign exchange income because of their heavy imports of Chinese goods, while economic cooperation with Africa and Latin America is likely to expand as Chinese influence in these regions gains momentum. Commercial relations with Western Europe may continue to improve, especially with West Germany, whereas trade with Eastern Europe and the Soviet Union will probably stay at present levels.

Trade with the United States will depend partly on how the question of Taiwan is resolved, and partly on whether a trade agreement including most-favored-nation treatment can be worked out. No immediate change can be expected, since China will not modify its policy on Taiwan or alter its emigration policy and property system in exchange for a trade agreement with the United States. Conversely, the United States is not likely to yield to Chinese political demands simply to improve trade relations. The value of bilateral trade in 1975 already dropped to $460 million, and officials of the Bank of America predicted that the annual turnover will not until 1980 regain the $1 billion mark—approximately one-half of 1 percent of the total United

General Assembly to study the problem of raw materials and development, April 10, 1974, in *Peking Review,* no. 16 (1974), p. 6.

4. See Chou En-lai, "Report to the Tenth National Congress of the Communist Party of China," *Peking Review,* no. 36 (1973), pp. 17, 22.

5. For a discussion of this matter, see Gene T. Hsiao, "Prospects for a New Sino-Japanese Relationship," *China Quarterly,* no. 60 (1974), pp. 720-749.

States trade for 1975.[6] This gloomy forecast, however, need not be true if both parties can find some ways and means to resolve their outstanding issues as the process of normalization is carried forward.

The structure of China's foreign trade organization and its practices have been established through twenty-six years of experimentation, and are not likely to change without a major policy reversal in domestic and external affairs. A decisive factor lies in China's special relationship with Hong Kong. Over the years China has built a large commercial network in the British Crown colony, which has become an integral part of the overall Chinese foreign trade apparatus.[7] China uses Hong Kong to receive foreign visitors, thus avoiding foreign cultural and political penetration. And, through Hong Kong, Chinese trade representatives in various official and private capacities can reach virtually every corner of the commercial world. Legally, Hong Kong frees China from obligations of reciprocity, and consequently from the burden of enacting related domestic legislation. China can authorize its agents in Hong Kong to conduct a great variety of trade activities, including the establishment of companies, branch offices, and correspondent relationships, in foreign countries without being legally obligated to reciprocate in kind, since these agents technically operate from a British colony. British laws form a component part of present Chinese foreign trade practice in the sense that all Chinese trade, banking, shipping, and insurance transactions in Hong Kong are technically subject to the colony's regulations.

Thus, preservation of the present structure of China's foreign trade organization requires the maintenance of the status quo in Hong Kong, a commercial gold mine but a political humiliation for the People's Republic. For a socialist country to enjoy such a relationship with an ultra-capitalistic colony is historically embarrassing, diplomatically one-sided, and ideologically inconsistent. Repossession of Hong Kong, however, will necessitate a reorganization of the whole foreign trade apparatus, including the creation of a modern infrastructure of Chinese trading ports; the opening of a part of China to foreign residence; and the enactment of laws necessary to the conduct of foreign trade and the accommodation of foreign visitors and

6. See *U.S.-China Business Review,* no. 2 (1976), p. 30; *Mei-chou hua-ch'iao jih-pao,* October 1, 1975, p. 1.

7. The exact extent of China's commercial network in Hong Kong is not known, but judging from the fact that the colony has one registered local or foreign company for nearly every hundred residents, the number of establishments involved in China's trade operations must be very great. At the end of 1974, Hong Kong had 74 licensed banks with a total of 631 banking offices, in addition to 66 representative offices of foreign banks; 35,416 local companies of all kinds; 870 foreign companies registered from 46 countries, including 226 from the United States; and 268 insurance companies, including 88 local companies. During the same year, aircraft arrivals and departures numbered about fifty-three thousand, carrying a total of about three and a half million incoming and outgoing passengers, compared with eighteen thousand passengers

residents—in short, reliving some of the experiences of old China before 1949. Alternatively, China could make Hong Kong a Chinese free port separate from the rest of the country and governed by a different system. All this constitutes a serious dilemma for the People's Republic. Until the expiration of the lease for Hong Kong's New Territories in 1997, it appears that the colony's fate is to a certain extent tied to that of other territories claimed by China. Foremost among these is Taiwan, which, in both strategic and economic terms, is far more important than Hong Kong. Next in line are Macao and Nansha (Spratly) Islands, which are partly occupied by the Nationalist Chinese and partly claimed by Vietnam and the Philippines. Since Peking reportedly rejected Portugal's recent offer to return Macao to China,[8] and since neither the solution of the Taiwan problem nor the recovery of Nansha Islands is in sight,[9] Hong Kong will doubtless continue as a Chinese trading "outpost" administered by the British for some time to come.

Meanwhile, there is some indication that China may adopt some formal laws relating to foreign trade to make up for deficiencies in the present system; and it may even accede to certain international conventions, such as the United Nations Convention on the Recognition and Enforcement of Foreign Arbitral Awards of 1958: on the promulgation of the 1975 Constitution, Chairman Mao was quoted as saying, "An organization must have rules, and a state also must have rules."[10] Such laws, if promulgated, will be in conformity with established Chinese patterns, although some Soviet elements may continue to be used where there are no suitable Chinese alternatives. Above all, the new laws will be principally technical and administrative, completely devoid of personal economic interests (as the late Soviet jurist E. B. Pashukanis predicted);[11] they will still provide a maximum degree of flexibility for China to protect its national interests.

---

through Peking International Airport. Hong Kong's population is about four and a half million, over 98 percent of them being ethnic Chinese. See Anthony Tobin, ed., *Hong Kong 1975*, pp. 24, 31, 188, 248. Figures for Peking are taken from *Jen-min jih-pao*, January 30, 1975, p. 5.

8. See David Binder, "Macao Offer Was Rejected," *South China Morning Post*, April 2, 1975, p. 1.

9. Near the end of 1975, the two leading Chinese national newspapers, *Jen-min jih-pao* and *Kuang-ming jih-pao*, published a significant article by Shih Ti-tsu on "South China Sea Islands, Chinese Territory Since Ancient Times," foreshadowing a possible early Chinese action to recover Nansha and other islands in the South China Sea before they become a serious dispute with Vietnam and the Philippines. For English translation of this article, see *Peking Review*, no. 50 (1975), pp. 10-15.

10. Quoted in Chang Chun-chiao, "Report on the Revision of the Constitution, January 13, 1975," *Hung-ch'i*, no. 2 (1975), p. 15.

11. According to Pashukanis, under the conditions of a planned economy, "bourgeois law" based on private property institutions would die and "technical regulation" or "economic law" would take its place. In "The General Theory of Law and Marxism," Hugh W. Babb, trans., *Soviet Legal Philosophy*, introd. John N. Hazard, pp. 122, 136-37, 147.

Accordingly, China is not likely to make any major concessions to foreign states in the form of long-term, rigid trade treaties—an institution the Chinese government has ceased to use since the early 1960s. Instead, China will place emphasis on medium-range trade agreements of from three to five years, exclusively regulating matters concerning commerce proper and, if necessary, navigation—the type of trade, air, and maritime transport agreements that China has concluded with Japan and some other countries in recent years. At the operational level, contracts will continue to be essential in China's trade transactions. At least for the time being, many of the gaps in Chinese trade agreements and domestic legislation, such as patent law, can be made up only through contracts. For example, although China and Japan do not have an agreement on visas and the status of visiting individual citizens, in 1973 alone over ten thousand Japanese, most of them businessmen, visited the People's Republic. And today thousands of Japanese are working in China as technicians on both temporary and relatively permanent bases. All this was made possible through contractual arrangements.

But despite their usefulness in China's future trade, contracts may have to undergo certain changes to facilitate trade expansion. So far the Chinese, as others, have made sales terms vaguer than purchase terms to protect their interests. Foreigners trading with China have accepted this, both because competition for the Chinese market was keen, and because they felt they could rely on the integrity of Chinese trade officials to protect their interests: *caveat emptor* was a condition of doing business with China, and it was accepted as such. However, it should be remembered that one of the reasons underlying the conflicts between old China and the West lay in the misunderstanding of their legal norms and values. In retrospect, perhaps such misunderstanding and therefore conflicts were historically inevitable given their enormous cultural differences and lack of communications. Today, however, technology has made the world smaller than ever before. Increased economic interdependence among nations will sooner or later bring about a universal commercial code. Moreover, the most fundamental task of contracts is to avoid controversy through careful preparation of their provisions based on the autonomy of wills and the meeting of minds. It is true that such preparation can be more expensive than standard form contracts, in terms of both time and money. Nevertheless, as the volume and value of China's trade continue to grow, the Chinese may eventually find it desirable to do away with the imbalance between the terms of sale and those of purchase so as to set an example of true equality and mutual benefit for other nations to follow. Foreigners, on the other hand, should learn more about Chinese society, which, after generations of revolution under the combined impact of internal decay and Western mercantilism, Christian movements, as well as Marxism-

Leninism, is becoming a more perplexing culture than it was one hundred-fifty years ago. In short, mutual accommodation in trade and other matters can be achieved only through mutual understanding and compromise. This need not sacrifice the principles of any nation, but it does require a degree of mutual trust and a conscientious effort by both the Chinese and foreigners in the development of their relations.

Appendix A

The Constitution of the People's Republic of China*

(Adopted on January 17, 1975 by the Fourth National People's Congress of the People's Republic of China at its First Session)

Contents

PREAMBLE

Preamble

The founding of the People's Republic of China marked the great victory of the new-democratic revolution and the beginning of the new historical period of socialist revolution and the dictatorship of the proletariat, a victory gained only after the Chinese people had waged a heroic struggle for over a century and, finally, under the leadership of the Communist Party of China, overthrown the reactionary rule of imperialism, feudalism and bureaucrat-capitalism by a people's revolutionary war.

For the last twenty years and more, the people of all the nationalities in our country, continuing their triumphant advance under the leadership of the Communist

*Published in one volume by the Foreign Languages Press, Peking, in 1975. Translation is official.

Party of China, have achieved great victories both in socialist revolution and socialist construction and in the Great Proletarian Cultural Revolution, and have consolidated and strengthened the dictatorship of the proletariat.

Socialist society covers a considerably long historical period. Throughout this historical period, there are classes, class contradictions and class struggle, there is the struggle between the socialist road and the capitalist road, there is the danger of capitalist restoration and there is the threat of subversion and aggression by imperialism and social-imperialism. These contradictions can be resolved only by depending on the theory of continued revolution under the dictatorship of the proletariat and on practice under its guidance.

We must adhere to the basic line and policies of the Communist Party of China for the entire historical period of socialism and persist in continued revolution under the dictatorship of the proletariat, so that our great motherland will always advance along the road indicated by Marxism-Leninism-Mao Tsetung Thought.

We should consolidate the great unity of the people of all nationalities led by the working class and based on the alliance of workers and peasants, and develop the revolutionary united front. We should correctly distinguish contradictions among the people from those between ourselves and the enemy and correctly handle them. We should carry on the three great revolutionary movements of class struggle, the struggle for production and scientific experiment; we should build socialism independently and with the initiative in our own hands, through self-reliance, hard struggle, diligence and thrift and by going all out, aiming high and achieving greater, faster, better and more economical results; and we should be prepared against war and natural disasters and do everything for the people.

In international affairs, we should uphold proletarian internationalism. China will never be a superpower. We should strengthen our unity with the socialist countries and all oppressed people and oppressed nations, with each supporting the other; strive for peaceful coexistence with countries having different social systems on the basis of the Five Principles of mutual respect for sovereignty and territorial integrity, mutual non-aggression, non-interference in each other's internal affairs, equality and mutual benefit, and peaceful coexistence, and oppose the imperialist and social-imperialist policies of aggression and war and oppose the hegemonism of the superpowers.

The Chinese people are fully confident that, led by the Communist Party of China, they will vanquish enemies at home and abroad and surmount all difficulties to build China into a powerful socialist state of the dictatorship of the proletariat so as to make a greater contribution to humanity.

People of all nationalities in our country, unite to win still greater victories!

Chapter 1. General Principles

Article 1. The People's Republic of China is a socialist state of the dictatorship of the proletariat led by the working class and based on the alliance of workers and peasants.

Article 2. The Communist Party of China is the core of leadership of the whole

Chinese people. The working class exercises leadership over the state through its vanguard, the Communist Party of China.

Marxism-Leninism-Mao Tsetung Thought is the theoretical basis guiding the thinking of our nation.

Article 3. All power in the People's Republic of China belongs to the people. The organs through which the people exercise power are the people's congresses at all levels, with deputies of workers, peasants and soldiers as their main body.

The people's congresses at all levels and all other organs of state practise democratic centralism.

Deputies to the people's congresses at all levels are elected through democratic consultation. The electoral units and electors have the power to supervise the deputies they elect and to replace them at any time according to provisions of law.

Article 4. The People's Republic of China is a unitary multi-national state. The areas where regional national autonomy is exercised are all inalienable parts of the People's Republic of China.

All the nationalities are equal. Big-nationality chauvinism and local-nationality chauvinism must be opposed.

All the nationalities have the freedom to use their own spoken and written languages.

Article 5. In the People's Republic of China, there are mainly two kinds of ownership of the means of production at the present stage: socialist ownership by the whole people and socialist collective ownership by working people.

The state may allow non-agricultural individual labourers to engage in individual labour involving no exploitation of others, within the limits permitted by law and under unified arrangement by neighbourhood organizations in cities and towns or by production teams in rural people's communes. At the same time, these individual labourers should be guided onto the road of socialist collectivization step by step.

Article 6. The state sector of the economy is the leading force in the national economy.

All mineral resources and waters as well as the forests, undeveloped land and other resources owned by the state are the property of the whole people.

The state may requisition by purchase, take over for use, or nationalize urban and rural land as well as other means of production under conditions prescribed by law.

Article 7. The rural people's commune is an organization which integrates government administration and economic management.

The economic system of collective ownership in the rural people's communes at the present stage generally takes the form of three-level ownership with the production team at the basic level, that is, ownership by the commune, the production brigade and the production team, with the last as the basic accounting unit.

Provided that the development and absolute predominance of the collective economy of the people's commune are ensured, people's commune members may farm small plots for their personal needs, engage in limited household side-line production, and in pastoral areas keep a small number of livestock for their personal needs.

Article 8. Socialist public property shall be inviolable. The state shall ensure the consolidation and development of the socialist economy and prohibit any person from undermining the socialist economy and the public interest in any way whatsoever.

Article 9. The state applies the socialist principle: "He who does not work, neither shall he eat" and "from each according to his ability, to each according to his work."

The state protects the citizens' right of ownership to their income from work, their savings, their houses, and other means of livelihood.

Article 10. The state applies the principle of grasping revolution, promoting production and other work and preparedness against war; promotes the planned and proportionate development of the socialist economy, taking agriculture as the foundation and industry as the leading factor and bringing the initiative of both the central and the local authorities into full play; and improves the people's material and cultural life step by step on the basis of the constant growth of social production and consolidates the independence and security of the country.

Article 11. State organizations and state personnel must earnestly study Marxism-Leninism-Mao Tsetung Thought, firmly put proletarian politics in command, combat bureaucracy, maintain close ties with the masses and wholeheartedly serve the people. Cadres at all levels must participate in collective productive labour.

Every organ of state must apply the principle of efficient and simple administration. Its leading body must be a three-in-one combination of the old, the middle-aged and the young.

Article 12. The proletariat must exercise all-round dictatorship over the bourgeoisie in the superstructure, including all spheres of culture. Culture and education, literature and art, physical education, health work and scientific research work must all serve proletarian politics, serve the workers, peasants and soldiers, and be combined with productive labour.

Article 13. Speaking out freely, airing views fully, holding great debates and writing big-character posters are new forms of carrying on socialist revolution created by the masses of the people. The state shall ensure to the masses the right to use these forms to create a political situation in which there are both centralism and democracy, both discipline and freedom, both unity of will and personal ease of mind and liveliness, and so help consolidate the leadership of the Communist Party of China over the state and consolidate the dictatorship of the proletariat.

Article 14. The state safeguards the socialist system, suppresses all treasonable and counter-revolutionary activities and punishes all traitors and counter-revolutionaries.

The state deprives the landlords, rich peasants, reactionary capitalists and other bad elements of political rights for specified periods of time according to law, and at the same time provides them with the opportunity to earn a living so that they may be reformed through labour and become law-abiding citizens supporting themselves by their own labour.

Article 15. The Chinese People's Liberation Army and the people's militia are the workers' and peasants' own armed forces led by the Communist Party of China; they are the armed forces of the people of all nationalities.

The Chairman of the Central Committee of the Communist Party of China commands the country's armed forces.

The Chinese People's Liberation Army is at all times a fighting force, and simultaneously a working force and a production force.

The task of the armed forces of the People's Republic of China is to safeguard the achievements of the socialist revolution and socialist construction, to defend the sovereignty, territorial integrity and security of the state, and to guard against subversion and aggression by imperialism, social-imperialism and their lackeys.

Chapter 2. The Structure of the State

Section I. The National People's Congress

Article 16. The National People's Congress is the highest organ of state power under the leadership of the Communist Party of China.

The National People's Congress is composed of deputies elected by the provinces, autonomous regions, municipalities directly under the Central Government, and the People's Liberation Army. When necessary, a certain number of patriotic personages may be specially invited to take part as deputies.

The National People's Congress is elected for a term of five years. Its term of office may be extended under special circumstances.

The National People's Congress holds one session each year. When necessary, the session may be advanced or postponed.

Article 17. The functions and powers of the National People's Congress are: to amend the Constitution, make laws, appoint and remove the Premier of the State Council and the members of the State Council on the proposal of the Central Committee of the Communist Party of China, approve the national economic plan, the state budget and the final state accounts, and exercise such other functions and powers as the National People's Congress deems necessary.

Article 18. The Standing Committee of the National People's Congress is the permanent organ of the National People's Congress. Its functions and powers are: to convene the sessions of the National People's Congress, interpret laws, enact decrees, dispatch and recall plenipotentiary representatives abroad, receive foreign diplomatic envoys, ratify and denounce treaties concluded with foreign states, and exercise such other functions and powers as are vested in it by the National People's Congress.

The Standing Committee of the National People's Congress is composed of the Chairman, the Vice-Chairmen and other members, all of whom are elected and subject to recall by the National People's Congress.

Section II. The State Council

Article 19. The State Council is the Central People's Government. The State Council is responsible and accountable to the National People's Congress and its Standing Committee.

The State Council is composed of the Premier, the Vice-Premiers, the ministers, and the ministers heading commissions.

Article 20. The functions and powers of the State Council are: to formulate administrative measures and issue decisions and orders in accordance with the Constitution, laws and decrees; exercise unified leadership over the work of ministries and commissions and local organs of state at various levels throughout the country; draft and implement the national economic plan and the state budget; direct state administrative affairs; and exercise such other functions and powers as are vested in it by the National People's Congress or its Standing Committee.

Section III. The Local People's Congresses and the Local Revolutionary Committees at Various Levels

Article 21. The local people's congresses at various levels are the local organs of state power.

The people's congresses of provinces and municipalities directly under the Central Government are elected for a term of five years. The people's congresses of prefectures, cities and counties are elected for a term of three years. The people's congresses of rural people's communes and towns are elected for a term of two years.

Article 22. The local revolutionary committees at various levels are the permanent organs of the local people's congresses and at the same time the local people's governments at various levels.

Local revolutionary committees are composed of a chairman, vice-chairmen and other members, who are elected and subject to recall by the people's congress at the corresponding level. Their election or recall shall be submitted for examination and approval to the organ of state at the next higher level.

Local revolutionary committees are responsible and accountable to the people's congress at the corresponding level and to the organ of state at the next higher level.

Article 23. The local people's congresses at various levels and the local revolutionary committees elected by them ensure the execution of laws and decrees in their respective areas; lead the socialist revolution and socialist construction in their respective areas; examine and approve local economic plans, budgets and final accounts; maintain revolutionary order; and safeguard the rights of citizens.

Section IV. The Organs of Self-Government of National Autonomous Areas

Article 24. The autonomous regions, autonomous prefectures and autonomous counties are all national autonomous areas; their organs of self-government are people's congresses and revolutionary committees.

The organs of self-government of national autonomous areas, apart from exercising the functions and powers of local organs of state as specified in Chapter Two, Section III of the Constitution, may exercise autonomy within the limits of their authority as prescribed by law.

The higher organs of state shall fully safeguard the exercise of autonomy by the organs of self-government of national autonomous areas and actively support the minority nationalities in carrying out the socialist revolution and socialist construction.

Section V. The Judicial Organs and the Procuratorial Organs

Article 25. The Supreme People's Court, local people's courts at various levels and special people's courts exercise judicial authority. The people's courts are responsible and accountable to the people's congresses and their permanent organs at the corresponding levels. The presidents of the people's courts are appointed and subject to removal by the permanent organs of the people's congresses at the corresponding levels.

The functions and powers of procuratorial organs are exercised by the organs of public security at various levels.

The mass line must be applied in procuratorial work and in trying cases. In major counter-revolutionary criminal cases the masses should be mobilized for discussion and criticism.

Chapter 3. The Fundamental Rights and Duties of Citizens

Article 26. The fundamental rights and duties of citizens are to support the leadership of the Communist Party of China, support the socialist system and abide by the Constitution and the laws of the People's Republic of China.

It is the lofty duty of every citizen to defend the motherland and resist aggression. It is the honourable obligation of citizens to perform military service according to law.

Article 27. All citizens who have reached the age of eighteen have the right to vote and stand for election, with the exception of persons deprived of these rights by law.

Citizens have the right to work and the right to education. Working people have the right to rest and the right to material assistance in old age and in case of illness or disability.

Citizens have the right to lodge to organs of state at any level written or oral complaints of transgression of law or neglect of duty on the part of any person working in an organ of state. No one shall attempt to hinder or obstruct the making of such complaints or retaliate.

Women enjoy equal rights with men in all respects.

The state protects marriage, the family, and the mother and child.

The state protects the just rights and interests of overseas Chinese.

Article 28. Citizens enjoy freedom of speech, correspondence, the press, assembly, association, procession, demonstration and the freedom to strike, and enjoy freedom to believe in religion and freedom not to believe in religion and to propagate atheism.

The citizens' freedom of person and their homes shall be inviolable. No citizen may be arrested except by decision of a people's court or with the sanction of a public security organ.

Article 29. The People's Republic of China grants the right of residence to any foreign national persecuted for supporting a just cause, for taking part in revolutionary movements or for engaging in scientific activities.

Chapter 4. The National Flag, the National Emblem and the Capital

Article 30. The national flag has five stars on a field of red.

The national emblem: Tien An Men in the centre, illuminated by five stars and encircled by ears of grain and a cogwheel.

The capital is Peking.

Appendix B

Treaty of Trade and Navigation Between the Union of Soviet Socialist Republics and the People's Republic of China. Signed at Peking, on 23 April 1958*

The Presidium of the Supreme Soviet of the Union of Soviet Socialist Republics and the President of the People's Republic of China,

Desiring to promote the further development and strengthening of economic relations between the two countries,

Have resolved to conclude this Treaty of Trade and Navigation and have appointed as their plenipotentiaries for this purpose:

The Presidium of the Supreme Soviet of the Union of Soviet Socialist Republics: Mr. Ivan Grigorevich Kabanov, Minister of Foreign Trade of the Union of Soviet Socialist Republics,

The President of the People's Republic of China: Mr. Yeh Chi-chuang, Minister of Foreign Trade of the People's Republic of China,

who, having exchanged their full powers, found in good and due form, have agreed as follows:

Article 1. The Contracting Parties shall take all necessary measures to develop and strengthen trade relations between the two States in a spirit of friendly cooperation and mutual assistance and on a basis of equality and mutual benefit.

To this end the Governments of the two Contracting Parties shall conclude agreements, including long-term agreements, ensuring the development of trade in accordance with the requirements of the national economy of both States.

Article 2.. The Contracting Parties shall grant each other most-favoured-nation treatment in all matters relating to trade, navigation and other economic relations between the two States.

Article 3.. The Contracting Parties shall, in accordance with the provisions of article 2, grant each other most-favoured-nation treatment in all customs matters, in particular as regards duties, taxes and other charges, the warehousing of goods under customs control, and the regulations and formalities applied in the customs clearance of goods.

*SOURCE: United Nations Treaty Series, vol. 313 (1958), no. 4534, pp. 152-164.

Accordingly, natural and manufactured products imported from the territory of one of the Contracting Parties into the territory of the other Contracting Party shall not be liable to any duties, taxes or similar charges other or higher, or to regulations other or formalities more burdensome, than those imposed on similar natural and manufactured products of any third State.

Similarly, natural and manufactured products of one Contracting Party shall not be liable, on exportation to the territory of the other Contracting Party, to any duties, taxes or similar charges other or higher, or to regulations other or formalities more burdensome, than those imposed on similar natural and manufactured products on exportation to the territory of any third State.

Article 4. Natural and manufactured products of one of the Contracting Parties imported into the territory of the other Contracting Party through the territory of a third State or of third States shall not be liable, on importation, to any duties, taxes or similar charges other or higher, or to regulations other or formalities more burdensome, than those to which they would have been liable if they had been imported directly from their country of origin.

This provision shall likewise apply to goods which, while in transit through the territory of a third State or of third States, have been subjected to trans-shipment, re-packing or warehousing.

Article 5. Subject to their being re-exported or re-imported within a time-limit fixed by the customs authorities and to the production of proof thereof, the following articles shall be exempt from duties, taxes or other charges on importation and exportation:

(a) Articles intended for fairs, exhibitions or competitions;

(b) Articles intended for experiments or tests;

(c) Articles imported for repair, which are to be re-exported in their repaired form;

(d) Fitting equipment and instruments imported or exported by fitters or sent to them;

(e) Natural and manufactured products imported for transformation or processing, which are to be re-exported in their transformed or processed form;

(f) Marked containers imported in order to be refilled, and also containers used for imported articles.

Merchandise samples used only as such and consigned in quantities normal in trade shall be unconditionally exempt from duties, taxes or other charges.

Article 6. Internal charges imposed in the territory of one Contracting Party on the production, processing, distribution or consumption of any goods shall in no event be levied on the natural or manufactured products of the other Contracting Party at a higher rate than on similar products of any third State.

Article 7. Neither of the Contracting Parties shall impose on imports from or exports to the territory of the other Contracting Party any restrictions or prohibitions which are not applicable to all other States.

The Contracting Parties nevertheless reserve the right to impose, for reasons of national security, the maintenance of public order, public health, the protection of animal and plant life or the preservation of works of art and archeological and historical treasures, prohibitions or restrictions on importation or exportation, where such prohibitions or restrictions are applied in like circumstances to any third State.

Article 8. The vessels of one Contracting Party and their cargoes shall be accorded most-favoured-nation treatment on entering and clearing, and while lying in, the ports of the other Contracting Party. Such treatment shall apply in particular with regard to: dues and charges of every kind levied on behalf of and for the benefit of the State, the local authorities and other organizations; the mooring, loading and discharging of vessels in ports and roadsteads; the use of pilotage services, canals, locks, bridges, signals and lights used to mark navigable waters; the use of cranes, weigh-bridges, warehouses, shipyards, dry-docks, and repair yards; supplies of fuel, lubricating oils, water and food.

The provisions of this article shall not extend to the performance of harbour services, including pilotage and towage, or to coastal shipping. Nevertheless, the vessels of either Contracting Party proceeding from one port of the other Party to another for the purpose of landing cargo brought from abroad, or of taking on board cargo for a foreign destination, shall not be regarded as engaged in coastal shipping.

Article 9. If a vessel of one Contracting Party is in distress or is wrecked on the coast of the other Contracting Party, such vessel and its cargo shall enjoy the same advantages and immunities as are granted under the laws of the latter State to its own vessels in similar circumstances.

The necessary aid and assistance shall be afforded at all times, and in the same measure as in the case of national vessels in the same situation, to the master, crew and passengers, and to the vessel and its cargo.

Where there are special agreements on such matters, aid shall likewise be afforded in accordance with such agreements.

Article 10. The nationality of vessels of the two Contracting Parties shall be reciprocally recognized on the basis of the papers carried by the vessel and issued by the competent authorities in accordance with the laws and regulations of the Contracting Party under whose flag the vessel is sailing.

Tonnage certificates and other ship's papers carried by the vessel and issued by the competent authorities of one of the Contracting Parties shall be recognized by the authorities of the other Contracting Party.

In accordance with this provision, any vessel of either Contracting Party carrying a valid tonnage certificate shall be exempt from re-measurement in the ports of the other Party, and the net capacity of the vessel entered in the certificate shall be taken as the basis for calculating harbour dues.

Article 11. The two Contracting Parties shall grant each other, in respect of the conveyance of goods, passengers and baggage by internal railways, roads or waterways, most-favoured-nation treatment in all matters relating to acceptance of consignments for conveyance, methods and costs of conveyance, and charges connected with conveyance in the same direction and over the same distance.

Article 12. Natural and manufactured products of one Contracting Party in transit through the territory of the other Contracting Party to the territory of a third State shall not be liable to any duties, taxes or other charges.

With respect to transit regulations and formalities, the treatment accorded to such products shall not be less favourable than that accorded to the transient consignments of any third State.

Article 13. Each of the Contracting Parties may maintain in the capital of the other Contracting Party a Trade Delegation whose legal status shall be governed by the provisions of the annex to this Treaty, which shall constitute an integral part thereof.

Article 14. Corporate bodies and individuals of either Contracting Party shall in all respects enjoy in the territory of the other Party treatment no less favourable than that accorded to corporate bodies and individuals of any third State.

Article 15. The provisions of this Treaty shall not extend to rights and advantages which may have been or may hereafter be granted by either of the Contracting Parties for the purpose of facilitating frontier trade relations with adjacent States in border areas.

Article 16. The Contracting Parties guarantee the enforcement of arbitral awards with regard to disputes arising out of the commercial or other contracts of their corporate bodies or institutions, where the Parties have duly agreed to refer the dispute to an *ad hoc* or permanent arbitral tribunal for settlement.

Orders for the enforcement of arbitral awards shall be made, and the enforcement itself carried out, in accordance with the laws of the Contracting Party enforcing the award.

Article 17. This Treaty shall be ratified as soon as possible and shall enter into force on the date of the exchange of the instruments of ratification, which shall take place at Moscow.

The Treaty shall remain in force until the expiry of a six months' period following the date on which one of the Contracting Parties gives notice of its intention to terminate the Treaty.

DONE at Peking, on 23 April 1958, in duplicate, in the Russian and Chinese languages, both texts being equally authentic.

I. G. KABANOV   YEH CHI-CHUANG

Annex.

THE LEGAL STATUS OF THE TRADE DELEGATION OF THE UNION OF
SOVIET SOCIALIST REPUBLICS IN THE PEOPLE'S REPUBLIC OF CHINA
AND OF THE TRADE DELEGATION OF THE PEOPLE'S REPUBLIC OF CHINA
IN THE UNION OF SOVIET SOCIALIST REPUBLICS

Article 1. The Trade Delegation of the Union of Soviet Socialist Republics in
the People's Republic of China and the Trade Delegation of the People's Republic of
China in the Union of Soviet Socialist Republics shall exercise the following functions;
each will:

(a) Promote the development of trade and economic relations between the two
States;

(b) Represent the interests of its own State in the other State in all matters
relating to foreign trade;

(c) Regulate trading transactions with the other State on behalf of its own
State;

(d) Carry on trade between the Union of Soviet Socialist Republics and the
People's Republic of China.

Article 2. The Trade Delegation shall form an integral part of the Embassy of
its own State.

The Trade Delegation of the Union of Soviet Socialist Republics in the Chinese
People's Republic and the Trade Delegation of the Chinese People's Republic in the
Union of Soviet Socialist Republics may open branches after agreement between the
Governments of the two Parties.

The Trade Delegate and his deputies shall enjoy all the rights and privileges
accorded to members of diplomatic missions.

The premises occupied by the Trade Delegation and its branches shall enjoy
extra-territoriality. The Trade Delegation and its branches shall be entitled to use a
cipher.

The Trade Delegation and its branches shall not be subject to commercial
registration.

Employees of the Trade Delegation and its branches who are citizens of the
State to which the Trade Delegation belongs shall be exempt in the receiving State
from taxation on the emoluments they receive in the service of their Government.

Article 3. The Trade Delegation shall act on behalf of its Government. The
Government shall be responsible only for foreign commercial contracts concluded or
guaranteed on behalf of the Trade Delegation in the receiving State and signed by
authorized persons.

The names of the persons authorized to take legal action on behalf of the Trade
Delegation and information concerning the extent to which each such person is
empowered to sign commercial contracts on its behalf shall be published in the
Government publication of the receiving State.

Article 4. The Trade Delegation shall enjoy all the immunities to which a sovereign State is entitled and which relate also to foreign trade, with the following exceptions only, to which the Parties agree:

(a) Disputes regarding foreign commercial contracts concluded or guaranteed under article 3 by the Trade Delegation in the territory of the receiving State shall, in the absence of a reservation regarding arbitration or any other jurisdiction, be subject to the competence of the courts of the said State. No interim court orders for the provision of security may be made;

(b) Final judicial decisions against the Trade Delegation in the aforementioned disputes which have become legally valid may be enforced by execution, but such execution may be levied only on the goods and claims outstanding to the credit of the Trade Delegation.

I.G.K.   YEH

Appendix C

The Protocol on the General Conditions for the Delivery
of Goods Between the Foreign Trade Organizations
of the People's Republic of China
and the People's Republic of Romania of 1961*

The Ministry of the Foreign Trade of the People's Republic of China and the Ministry of Trade of the People's Republic of Romania, in accordance with the stipulations of "The Protocol on the Exchange of Goods and Payments Between the People's Republic of China and the People's Republic of Romania of 1961," specifically signed this Protocol and its appendix: "General Conditions for the Delivery of Goods Between the People's Republic of China and the People's Republic of Romania of 1961." All matters concerning the delivery of goods, payments, services, and other matters connected with the execution of the above-mentioned Protocol on the Exchange of Goods and Payments, shall be carried out in accordance with the General Conditions for the Delivery of Goods appended to this Protocol.

The effective period of this Protocol and its appended General Conditions for the Delivery of Goods is from 1 January 1961 to 31 December 1961.

This Protocol is signed in Bucharest on 7 July 1961 and there are two copies. Each copy is written in the Chinese, the Romanian and the Russian languages, and the three texts have equal authenticity; in case of disagreement on the interpretation of the texts, the Russian text shall prevail.

Representative of the Ministry of Foreign
Trade of the People's Republic of China

CHANG CHU-HSÜAN
(Signed)

Representative of the Ministry of Trade of
the People's Republic of Romania

AI. MEI-SAI-LAO-SHEN
(Signed)

*SOURCE: *Chinese Law and Government* no. 2 (1972) pp. 109-129; Chinese text in *TYC*, vol. 10 (1962), pp. 304-318.

Annex.

GENERAL CONDITIONS FOR THE DELIVERY OF GOODS BETWEEN THE FOREIGN TRADE ORGANIZATIONS OF THE PEOPLE'S REPUBLIC OF CHINA AND THE PEOPLE'S REPUBLIC OF ROMANIA OF 1961

Chapter I. The Conclusion of Contracts

Article 1. The foreign trade organizations of both parties, in accordance with "The Protocol on the Exchange of Goods and Payments Between the People's Republic of China and the People's Republic of Romania of 1961" and this General Conditions, shall conclude contracts as the basis for the delivery of goods, for the making of payments, and for the fulfillment of other related obligations.

The contract shall be signed by representatives commissioned by the foreign trade organizations of both parties. In the contract, the class of the goods, the quantity, the quality, all specifications, the price, the amount of money, the markings, the packing terms, the timing and place of the delivery of goods, and other special conditions not included in this General Conditions and not inconsistent with the above-mentioned Protocol and this General Conditions shall be specified.

Article 2. Any amendment and/or supplement to the contract requires written consent of both parties.

Chapter II. Place of Delivery of Goods and Method of Carriage

Article 3. The place of the delivery of goods and the method of carriage shall be specifically stipulated in the contract by both parties.

Any request for a change of the place of the delivery of goods and/or of the method of carriage shall be presented in writing by the requesting party to the other party thirty days prior to the commencement of the quarter or month for the delivery of the goods and shall require the consent of the other party. Extra expenses arising from such a change shall be paid by the requesting party.

Article 4. The method of carriage is stipulated by both parties [as follows]:

(a) In carriage by sea:

(1) Goods exported from China shall be delivered in the hold of a ship at a Chinese port; goods exported from Romania shall be delivered in the hold of a ship at a Romanian port. The costs of stowage shall be borne by the seller; the costs of ventilation equipment, cushioning [materials], etc., shall be borne by the buyer.

(2) After the goods have been delivered in the hold of a ship, all damage and loss shall be borne by the buyer.

(3) Pursuant to the buyer's request, the seller shall notify the buyer of the loading standard set by the port authority of the port of shipment. If the time of loading of the goods exceeds the standard loading time, the seller shall pay the buyer [compensation] for the delay and all other expenses incurred therefrom. If the time of loading of the goods is shorter than the stipulated standard loading time, the buyer shall pay the seller a rapid loading [bonus].

(4) Where the quantity of the goods loaded is less than that agreed upon by both parties and if it results from the seller's negligence, the seller shall pay the freight for the vacant hold.

(5) The seller shall promise to send together with the goods one copy of the steamer's bill of lading, the packing list and/or the detailed list [of the goods], the quality inspection certificate or the certificate of the place of manufacture, and all other documents stipulated in the contract. [The seller shall], within ten days after the departure of the ship, send to the buyer or the carrier designated by the buyer by registered airmail the following documents: three copies of the steamer's bill of lading; three copies of the invoice, three copies of the packing list and/or the detailed list [of the goods], two copies of the quality inspection certificate or the certificate of the place of manufacture, and all other documents stipulated in the contract.

(b) In carriage by rail:

(1) Goods exported from China shall be delivered on board the seller's car on the Sino-Soviet border or the Sino-Mongolian border; the expenses for the transhipment of the goods at the Chinese Chi-ning station shall be borne by the buyer.

(i) The shipment of goods shall be handled in accordance with the Agreement on International Rail Freight Communication which is now in effect.

(ii) All expenses for transport and transhipment after the goods have been delivered on board the seller's car on the Sino-Soviet border or the Sino-Mongolian border shall be borne by the buyer.

(2) Goods exported from Romania shall be delivered on board the seller's car on the Romanian-Soviet border.

(i) The shipment of goods shall be handled in accordance with the Agreement on International Rail Freight Communication which is now in effect.

(ii) All costs of transportation and transhipment after the goods are delivered on board the seller's car on the Romanian-Soviet border shall be borne by the buyer.

(3) The seller shall fill out the specific class of the goods in the document of carriage in accordance with the buyer's instructions which are given in accordance with the specifications and classification table of the Agreement on International Rail Freight Communication and its appended Regulations on the Uniform Transit Tariff.

In case the buyer has paid extra transit transport costs as a result of the seller's failure to abide by the above stipulation, the extra transport costs shall be borne by the seller.

(4) All damage and loss to the goods after the goods have been delivered on board the seller's car on the Sino-Soviet, Sino-Mongolian, or Romanian-Soviet border in accordance with the contract shall be borne by the buyer.

(5) The seller shall promise to send to the buyer together with the goods not only the original rail bill of lading but also two copies of the packing list and/or the detailed list [of the goods], two copies of the quality certificate or the certificate of the place of manufacture, and all other documents stipulated in the contract. The seller shall, within ten days after the shipment of the goods, send to the buyer by registered airmail one copy each of the above-mentioned documents and three copies of the invoice.

(6) Carriage by rail can be used only with the buyer's request or consent.

(c) In carriage by air:

(1) The export of goods of either party shall be delivered on board an airplane at a Chinese airport or a Romanian airport agreed upon by both parties, the transport procedure shall be handled by the seller, and the costs incurred therefrom shall be borne by the buyer.

(2) After the goods have been delivered on board an airplane at a Chinese or Romanian airport in accordance with the contract, all loss to the goods shall be borne by the buyer.

(3) In addition to the sending of the original air waybill together with the goods, the seller shall also deliver two copies of the packing list and/or the detailed list [of the goods], two copies of the quality certificate or the certificate of the place of manufacture, and other documents stipulated in the contract. The seller shall within three days after the shipment of the goods send to the buyer by registered airmail one copy each of the above-mentioned documents and three copies of the invoice.

(4) Carriage by air can be used only with the buyer's request or consent.

(d) At the same time, the seller shall send a copy of the invoice required in the above-mentioned carriage by sea, by rail or by air, or a copy of the steamer's bill of lading to the commercial counsellor of the buyer's country stationed in the seller's country.

Article 5. The buyer or the buyer's representative may entrust in writing a concerned transport enterprise in the seller's country with the function of handling the transport of goods, insurance, and other services within the scope of the Sino-Romanian Protocol on the Exchange of Goods and Payments of 1961 during the effective period of that Protocol.

Upon acceptance of the appointment by the above-mentioned transport enterprise, the buyer or the buyer's representative may sign special contracts with the above-mentioned transport enterprise concerning authorization of transport and transshipment. Where the transport enterprise of the seller's country is entrusted by the buyer with handling of transport of goods, the costs of freight and services shall not, in principle, exceed the rates prevailing in the international market. The exact rates are to be negotiated by the two parties.

Chapter III. Deadline and Date of the Delivery of Goods

Article 6. The exact deadline for the delivery of goods shall be specified in the contract.

The date of the delivery of goods:

(a) In carriage by sea: the date of the steamer's bill of lading.

(b) In carriage by rail: the date of arrival at the seller's border station as noted on the original rail bill of lading by the seller's international station.

(c) In carriage by air: the date of the air waybill issued by the seller's airline.

Article 7. In carriage by sea: The seller shall, at the latest forty-five days before the goods are to be sent to the shipping port, notify the buyer by telegram and registered airmail of the scheduled date the goods are to be sent to the shipping port, the contract number, the serial number of the commodity, the quantity of the goods, the weight, the volume, the markings, and the amount of money. After receipt of the notice the buyer shall within twenty-five days notify the seller by telegram of the name of the ship and its tonnage and the scheduled date the ship will arrive at the shipping port. The ship shall, at the latest, arrive at the seller's shipping port within sixty-five days after the buyer has received the seller's notice. If the ship fails to arrive at the shipping port within sixty-five days and exceeds the arrival date by more than thirty days, then after the thirtieth day the seller shall send the goods to the warehouse for safekeeping; the costs of storage and insurance shall be paid by the buyer, but upon the arrival of the ship the seller shall nevertheless be responsible for delivering the goods from the warehouse to the hold of the ship.

In case of any change in the ship's [scheduled] arrival date at the shipping port, or in the name of the ship or its loading tonnage, the buyer shall, ten days before the date the goods are to be sent by the seller to the shipping port, notify the seller. In case he fails to send timely notice in accordance with this requirement, the buyer shall bear all loss incurred thereby. If the goods fail to arrive at the shipping port on time, the seller shall bear all expenses incurred therefrom. The seller shall, within seven days after the departure of the ship, send to the buyer by telegram notice of the actual shipment of the goods (which shall specify the date of the shipment of goods, the name of the ship, the contract number, the serial number of the commodity, the quantity or weight of the goods, and the volume).

Article 8. In carriage by rail: The seller shall, within seven days after the goods are shipped, send to the buyer by telegram notice of the actual shipment (which shall specify the date of the shipment of the goods, the contract number, the serial number of the commodity, and the quantity or weight of the goods).

Article 9. In carriage by air: The seller shall, on the day the goods are shipped, send to the buyer by telegram a notice of actual shipment (which shall specify the contract number, the serial number of the commodity, and the quantity or weight of the goods).

Article 10. The seller shall send a copy of the notice of shipment required in Articles 7, 8, and 9 to the commercial counsellor of the buyer's country stationed in the seller's country.

Article 11. The seller shall, thirty days before the commencement of each quarter, send to the commercial counsellor of the buyer's country two copies of the plan of shipment for that quarter's goods (including each month's plan by category [of goods]).

Chapter IV. Late Delivery of Goods, Penalty, and Early Delivery of Goods

Article 12. In the event of *force majeure,* both parties may be relieved of liability for partial or total nonperformance of obligations under the contract, or both parties' deadline for the performance of obligations may be postponed until such events and their effects have disappeared.

Force majeure shall be understood to mean circumstances arising after the signing of the contract from events of an extraordinary character which one party could neither foresee nor avoid. Under such circumstances, neither party shall have the right to demand of the other party compensation for losses that may occur.

A party for whom it has become impossible to carry out the contract as a result of such events shall immediately notify the other party in writing of the occurrence and the termination of the above-mentioned extraordinary events.

Article 13. Except in the circumstances governed by Article 12, the party requesting a postponement of the delivery of goods shall, thirty days before the scheduled date for the delivery of goods, notify the other party by telegram in accordance with the stipulations of the contract; the deadline of the postponement shall be determined by both parties through negotiation. If one party fails to deliver the goods before the new deadline, the other party has the right to rescind the contract and to demand compensation. Except as otherwise stipulated in the contract, if delay in the delivery of ordinary goods exceeds thirty days beyond the deadline stipulated in the contract, and for machinery equipment if the delay exceeds sixty days, the seller shall pay the buyer a weekly penalty of 0.3 percent of the amount noted in the invoice for the delayed goods; if further delay ensues for a period in excess of four weeks, from the beginning of the fifth week to the end of the eighth week the penalty shall be 0.6 percent per week; and from the ninth week on, the penalty shall be 1 percent per week; but the total amount of the penalty may not exceed 8 percent of the amount stated in the invoice for the delayed goods.

Payment of the penalty does not relieve the seller of the obligation to deliver the delayed goods.

Article 14. If the seller or the buyer requests early delivery of the goods, the party who makes the request shall, at the latest thirty days before the requested date for the delivery of goods, notify the other party by telegram, and the other party shall within fifteen days after receipt of the notice reply by telegram, indicating whether he accepts or refuses [the requested change].

Chapter V. Packing and Markings

Article 15. The technical conditions for packing shall be handled in accordance with the stipulations of the contract. If the contract contains no specific stipulations regarding packing, the goods shall be packed differently according to the nature of the goods and the method of carriage and shall conform to the packing for long-range transport prevailing in international trade custom.

Article 16. Except when observing the special stipulations of the contract, each package of goods shall bear the following markings:

(a) Markings of the goods.
(b) The serial number of the contract and the serial number of the commodity.
(c) The serial number of the package.
(d) The port or place of arrival.

(e) The gross weight and/or net weight.

(f) Special markings: perishable or fragile goods shall be marked in characters, figures, markings or abbreviations such as "handle with care," "fragile," "keep from water," "keep from rain," "please do not overturn," "keep from fire," etc. Poisonous or dangerous goods shall be marked in bright colors. Each package shall be accompanied by a packing list, and on the packing list the shipping markings of the different departments that order the goods shall also be noted.

Article 17. Markings on the package shall be made with an indelible paint. In carriage by sea, [the goods] shall be marked in Chinese and English, or Romanian and English. In carriage by rail or by air, [the goods] shall be marked in Chinese and Russian, or Romanian and Russian.

Article 18. The technical conditions for the packing and markings of the goods shall not only follow the stipulations of the contract and this General Conditions but also the regulations of the transport authorities concerning the packing and markings of the goods. In carriage by rail, [the packing and markings] shall be done in accordance with the provisions concerning packing and markings in the currently effective Agreement on International Rail Freight Communication.

Chapter VI. The Quantity and Quality Specifications of the Goods

Article 19. The quantity of the goods delivered by the seller is determined by the number of pieces, weight and/or volume noted in the steamer's bill of lading, the rail bill of lading, or the air waybill.

Article 20. The quality specifications of Chinese goods shall conform to the Chinese national export standard or to the quality and specifications stipulated in the contract; the quality of the goods delivered shall also be certified by the quality certificate issued by the seller, the producer, or by the Chinese National Bureau for the Inspection of Commodities, and this certificate shall be the final basis [for settling accounts].

The quality specifications of Romanian goods shall conform to the Romanian national export standard or to the quality and specifications stipulated in the contract; the quality of the goods delivered shall also be certified by the quality certificate issued by the seller, the producer, or the Romanian National Bureau for the Inspection of Commodities, and this certificate shall be the final basis [for settling accounts].

Except as otherwise stipulated in this General Conditions or in the contract, the seller shall guarantee the complete conformity of the quality specifications of the goods with those stipulated in the contract, and the buyer shall receive the goods on the basis of the above-mentioned document.

Article 21. In the event of changes in the quality specifications of the goods such that they do not conform to those stipulated in the contract, the seller shall, thirty days before the shipment of the goods, notify the buyer and may deliver the goods only after obtaining the buyer's consent. The buyer shall, within forty-five days after receipt of the notice indicating changes in the quality specifications of the goods, reply to the seller as to whether he accepts or refuses to accept [the changes]. If the buyer does not indicate his refusal within this period, [his] consent to the changes in the quality specifications of the goods shall be considered obtained.

Chapter VII. Claims Concerning the Quantity and Quality Specifications of the Goods

Article 22. All claims regarding the quantity and quality of the goods may be presented only under the following circumstances:

(a) Concerning the quantity of the goods: If the quantity of the goods received by the buyer is, due to the insufficiency of the contents of the package, less than that stated in the steamer's bill of lading, or the rail bill of lading, or the air waybill, or the invoice, and if it has been ascertained that the responsibility for the shortage does not lie with the transport authorities but with the seller, the buyer may request the seller to make up the shortage, and the seller shall make up the shortage as stipulated or, with the buyer's consent, shall refund the corresponding sum of money.

(b) Concerning the quality of the goods: If the quality or specifications of the goods received by the buyer does not conform to that stated in the contract, and if it has been ascertained that such nonconformity did not arise during transport, the buyer may demand that the seller reduce the price or replace the goods. In case of a reduction of the price, the seller shall refund the difference in the price to the buyer; in case of replacement of the goods, the transport costs, warehouse rental, loading and unloading charges, insurance costs, and repacking costs shall be borne by the seller.

(c) In the case of a failure to abide by the stipulations of Articles 15, 16, 17, and 18 of this General Conditions concerning packing and markings, all damage and loss to the goods directly resulting from any change in the quantity or quality of the goods caused thereby shall be borne by the seller.

With the exception of the circumstances stated above, the seller, after the goods are delivered, shall not be responsible for changes in the quantity or quality of the goods during transport.

(d) Except as otherwise stipulated in the contract, when bringing claims concerned with the quantity of the goods, the buyer shall present them in writing within three months from the day the seller delivers the goods; claims about the quality of the goods shall be presented within six months from the day the seller delivers the goods; claims concerning the quality of goods which have a period of guaranty shall, at the latest, be presented within thirty days after the expiration of the period of guaranty stipulated in the contract. The buyer shall request the representatives of an authoritative and impartial national authority or social organization in his country to form an examining committee to examine his written claim; when [the written claim] is proved to have satisfied the conditions for presenting a claim, it shall be written up in accordance with the form governing the "Written Claim Concerning Import Goods" and the "Explanation of the Procedure for Filling Out a Written Claim Concerning Import Goods," as prescribed by the two parties. The written claim shall specify the buyer's exact requests and shall then be sent together with other related certificates by registered airmail to the seller at the address stated in the contract. The date of filing the written claim shall be the date stamped on the airmail when posted. The seller shall reply within forty-five days after receipt of the buyer's written claim mentioned above.

Article 23. In the event that the buyer has a claim against one lot of goods, such a claim does not give the buyer the right to refuse acceptance of other lots of the goods covered by the contract.

Chapter VIII. Method of Payment

Article 24. The price of the goods delivered in accordance with the contract, and the transport costs, insurance costs, service charges, and other related expenses connected with the delivery of goods and which are paid by the seller on the buyer's behalf shall be handled in the unit of rubles through the national banks of both countries in accordance with the payment-on-demand method.

Article 25. After the goods have been shipped, the seller shall present the following documents to his national bank:

(a) Four copies of the invoice. The invoice shall specify the contract number, the serial number of the commodity, the class, specifications, quantity, price, the amount of money, markings, etc. If the contract contains stipulations on the various expenses (transport costs, insurance costs, and other expenses) related to the supplying of the goods, such expenses may also be included together with the price of the goods in a single invoice, but they shall be separately specified.

(b) Document of carriage. In carriage by sea, it shall be accompanied by three copies of the complete steamer's original bill of lading made out to the consignor and with blank endorsement. In carriage by rail, it shall be accompanied by a copy of the rail bill of lading with the stamp of the station of departure or one copy of the document certifying the shipment of goods issued by the seller's national authority for international transhipment or one copy of the postal receipt. In carriage by air, it shall be accompanied by one copy of the air waybill or one copy of the postal receipt.

(c) Four copies of the detailed list of the goods.

(d) Two copies of the quality inspection certificate or of the certificate of the place of manufacture.

(e) Other documents specified in the contract.

(f) The seller's statement certifying the conformity of the contents of the various documents with the contractual terms.

The seller's national bank shall, after having ascertained the completeness of the above-mentioned documents, immediately credit the amount of money noted in the invoice to the seller's account, and shall simultaneously debit it to the account of the buyer's national bank and notify the buyer's national bank by forwarding the notice of payment together with the various documents presented by the seller. The buyer's national bank shall, after receipt of the notice of payment and the various documents, credit the account of the seller's national bank and shall, on the basis of these documents, collect from the buyer the full amount of money noted in the notice of payment. The buyer, within ten business days after receipt of the various documents, has the right to communicate to his national bank his refusal to pay in full or in part the amount of money noted in the invoice on the basis of [one or more of] the following circumstances.

In the event of an occurrence of one or more of the following circumstances, [the buyer] may refuse to pay the full amount of money noted in the statement of accounts:

(a) the goods are delivered when there is no contract or the contract has become void;

(b) the place where the shipped goods arrive and/or the consignee do not conform to the stipulations of the contract;

(c) the goods were already paid for by the buyer;

(d) failure to append all of the documents stipulated above or in the contract;

(e) where there is an inconsistency among the various documents or where they are inconsistent with the contents of the contract, so that it is not possible to determine accurately the quantity, grade, quality, and price of the goods;

(f) whereas the contract provides for complete shipment, the equipment is shipped incomplete;

(g) the shipment of goods does not conform to the transport terms stipulated in the contract or the terms requested by the buyer;

(h) [the shipment] is not handled according to the special provisions stipulated in the contract.

In the event of an occurrence of one or more of the following circumstances, [the buyer] may refuse to pay part of the amount of money noted in the invoice:

(a) the price of the goods exceeds that stipulated in the contract or the amount for payment includes other expenses which were not included in the contract and which did not receive the buyer's prior consent;

(b) the goods shipped include goods not ordered by the buyer;

(c) there are errors in calculating the quantity and the amount of money in the documents;

(d) the quantity noted in the invoice exceeds that noted in the document of carriage and/or the detailed list [of the goods];

(e) portions of the contents of the various documents indicate an inconsistency.

In declaring a refusal to make full or partial payment, the buyer shall submit to the buyer's bank those documents which are necessary to prove the conformity of the basis for his full or partial nonpayment with the above-mentioned conditions.

When the buyer's national bank has verified the conformity [of the buyer's nonpayment with the above-mentioned conditions], it shall debit the amount of money withheld to the account of the seller's national bank and shall notify the seller's national bank by sending the latter a refusal-of-payment notice together with the documents indicating the buyer's refusal to pay; after receipt of the refusal-of-payment notice, the seller's national bank shall credit the full or partial amount of money withheld to [the account of] the buyer's national bank and shall simultaneously debit [that amount] to the seller's account, and shall send the refusal-of-payment notice to the seller. Disputes between the seller and the buyer shall be resolved directly between the two parties.

If the seller is able to prove a lack of basis in the buyer's refusal to make full or partial payment, the buyer, in addition to the payment of the amount of money he had refused to pay, shall from the date of such refusal, pay a penalty of 0.1 percent of the amount of money withheld for each day delayed, but the total amount of the penalty may not exceed 8 percent of the amount of money withheld.

Article 26. As for payment of [the expenses] incurred in connection with the delivery of goods or with scientific and technical cooperation, and of all related expenses paid by one party on behalf of the other, the creditor shall present to his national bank the payment authorization letter and the following documents for disposal in accordance with the procedure for payment of the goods stipulated in Articles 24 and 25:

(a) Transport costs: a copy of the steamer's bill of lading or the contract for chartering the ship or the rail bill of lading or air waybill, or the postal receipt, and four copies of the statement of accounts.

(b) Insurance costs: the insurance policy or insurance certificate, and four copies of the statement of accounts.

(c) Service charges and other expenses related to the delivery of goods: the original certificate or the evidence that the debtor has agreed to honor the payment, and four copies of the statement of accounts.

Under [any of] the following circumstances the debtor has the right, within ten business days, to refuse to pay in full or in part the amount of money noted. In the event of an occurence of one or more of the following conditions [the debtor] may refuse to pay in full the amount of money noted in the statement of accounts:

(a) the authorization letter for services is lacking;

(b) the services were paid for previously.

In the event of an occurrence of one or more of the following circumstances, [the debtor] may refuse to pay in part the amount of money noted in the statement of accounts:

(a) there are errors in calculation in the statement of accounts;

(b) there is a difference between [the amount noted in the statement of accounts and] the amount fixed in the contract or in the authorization letter for services;

(c) foreign exchange and transport rates are incorrectly applied;

(d) inclusion of remuneration and expenses which are not stipulated in the contract or in the authorization letter;

(e) under circumstances stipulated in the contract there is a failure to carry out the debtor's instructions or other entrusted matters agreed upon between the two parties;

(f) the amount of money noted in the statement of accounts is calculated on the basis of erroneous data concerning the quantity, weight, and/or volume of the goods.

If the creditor who presents the statement of accounts is able to prove that there is no basis for the debtor's refusal to make payment in full or in part of the amount of money required to be paid, the debtor, in addition to the payment of the amount of money withheld, shall pay, from the date he refuses to pay, a penalty of 0.1 percent of the amount of money withheld for each day delayed, but the total amount of the penalty may not exceed 8 percent of the amount of money withheld.

Article 27. The various settlements of accounts that are not stipulated in Articles 25 and 26, including the settlement of accounts resulting from mutual presentation of claims and the payment of penalty or interest, shall be handled in accordance with the following [procedure]:

(a) The creditor shall, by means of a collection authorization letter, present the statement of accounts together with the certificates stipulated by both parties through the national bank of the creditor's country for payment; the debtor shall, within ten business days after receipt of the collection authorization letter, make the payment.

(b) If the debtor accepts the claims presented by the other party, the payment may be effected by means of remittance from the debtor to the creditor, making unnecessary the presentation of a collection authorization letter.

Chapter IX. Arbitration

Article 28. Disputes arising out of or in connection with a contract which cannot be settled through negotiation by both parties shall be decided by the following arbitration organizations. The decisions rendered by the arbitration organizations shall be followed by both parties.

(a) If the respondent is a Chinese foreign trade organization, [the arbitration] shall be conducted in Peking before the Foreign Trade Arbitration Commission of the China Council for the Promotion of International Trade in accordance with the statutes of that Commission.

(b) If the respondent is a Romanian foreign trade organization, [the arbitration] shall be conducted in Bucharest before the Foreign Trade Commission of the Romanian Chamber of Commerce in accordance with the statutes of that Chamber.

Chapter X. General Conditions

Article 29. The time of transfer of the ownership and risk of the goods from the seller to the buyer shall be determined according to the following conditions:

(a) In carriage by sea: from the time the seller delivers the goods into the hold of a ship.

(b) In carriage by rail: from the time the goods are delivered on board the seller's car on the railroad leaving the seller's territory.

(c) In carriage by air: from the time the goods are delivered on board an airplane in the seller's airport.

Article 30. All miscellaneous charges, rentals, and customs duties related to the performance of a contract, if incurred in the seller's territory, shall be borne by the seller.

Chapter XI. Supplementary Rules

Article 31. This General Conditions may be amended or supplemented after agreement is reached by the representatives of both parties.

The General Conditions is written in three languages: Chinese, Romanian, and Russian, and the three texts have equal authenticity. In case of a dispute in the interpretation of the provisions, the Russian text shall prevail.

Appendix D

Agreement on Trade Between Japan and the People's Republic of China*

The Government of Japan and the Government of the People's Republic of China,

In accordance with the Joint Statement issued by the two Governments at Peking on September 28, 1972,

Having a regard for the achievements thus far accumulated through existing non-governmental trade relations,

Desiring to further develop trade and strengthen economic relations between their two countries on the basis of equality and mutual benefit,

Through friendly negotiations,

Have agreed as follows:

Article 1.

1. The Contracting Parties shall accord each other most-favored-nation treatment with respect to customs duties, internal taxes, and other charges imposed on imported or exported goods, in matters relating to the method of levying such duties, taxes, and other charges as well as customs rules, formalities, and procedures.

2. The conditions of most-favored-nation treatment applicable to the goods mentioned in Paragraph 1 above shall be the same as those granted to third countries by either Contracting Party.

3. The provisions of Paragraph 1 shall not apply to special favors accorded to neighboring countries by either Contracting Party for the purpose of facilitating border trade.

Article 2. Subject to the relevant internal laws and decrees, and limited to the items listed below which are temporarily brought into or taken out of its territory, either Contracting Party shall grant the other Party most-favored-nation treatment in all respects concerning exemption from customs duties, internal taxes, and other charges:

(1) Samples of commodities (provided that the quantity is limited to the generally accepted amount under the customary practice of trade);

(2) Goods to be used for test and experimentation;

(3) Goods to be used for exhibitions, fairs, and contests;

(4) Appliances and tools to be used by workers for the assembly or installation of equipment;

*SOURCE: The Japanese Government. Translation is mine, based on Chinese and Japanese texts.

(5) Goods to be used for processing and repairing and materials to be used for processing and repairing;

(6) Containers of exported or imported goods.

Article 3. Either Contracting Party shall provide the other Party most-favored-nation treatment with respect to customs duties, internal taxes, and other charges as well as formalities and procedures for the goods which are shipped through its territory to a third country.

Article 4.

1. All payments between the two Contracting Parties shall be settled in Japanese *yen,* Chinese *yuan,* or any convertible currencies acceptable to the two countries in accordance with the laws, decrees, and regulations for the control of foreign exchange of either Contracting State.

2. The Contracting Parties express the desire that, where payments may be made in Japanese *yen* or Chinese *yuan,* as provided for in Paragraph 1 above, the payments settlement agreements concluded between the relevant banks of the two countries should be effectively utilized in accordance with the relevant laws and decrees of the respective Contracting States.

3. Juridical persons (including foreign trade organizations) and natural persons of either Contracting Party shall be accorded treatment no less favorable than that accorded to juridical persons (including foreign trade organizations) and natural persons of any third country with respect to payments, remittances, and transfers of funds or financial instruments between the territories of the two Contracting Parties as well as between the territories of the other Contracting Party and a third country.

Article 5. In accordance with the principle of equality and mutual benefit and on the basis of reasonable international market prices, trade between the two Contracting Parties shall be carried out through the conclusion of contracts by juridical or natural persons having the capacity to engage in foreign trade under the laws and decrees of Japan on the one hand, and foreign trade organizations having the capacity to engage in foreign trade under the laws and decrees of the People's Republic of China, on the other.

Article 6. In order to further develop the economic and trade relations between the two countries, the two Contracting Parties shall actively promote the exchange of industrial technology in accordance with the principle of equality and mutual benefit.

Article 7. The Contracting Parties shall encourage each other to hold reciprocal trade exhibitions. Either Contracting Party shall provide the other Party with all possible assistance in the holding of the above-mentioned trade exhibitions in accordance with its relevant internal laws and decrees.

Article 8.

1. The two Contracting States should encourage the parties involved in a dispute arising from or relating to a trade contract between a foreign trade organization

of the People's Republic of China and a Japanese juridical or natural person to settle the dispute primarily through friendly negotiation.

2. If the dispute cannot be settled through negotiation, the parties may submit it [to the appropriate authorities] for arbitration on the basis of an arbitration clause. Such arbitration clause should be stipulated by the parties in their contract or in other agreement related to the contract.

3. The Contracting States shall encourage by every possible means the parties to use the arbitration institutions of their own countries.

4. The Contracting Parties shall have the obligation to enforce the execution of arbitration awards by the institutions concerned on the basis of the legal provisions of the country to which the enforcement has been petitioned.

Article 9. The two Contracting Parties shall establish a mixed committee consisting of representatives of their Governments. The purpose of the committee is to study the state of implementation of the present Agreement and the problems of trade concerning the two countries (including the exchange of views on the prospect of trade relations between the two countries) and when necessary, to make appropriate recommendations to the Governments of the two Contracting Parties. The mixed committee shall meet at least once a year alternately in Tokyo and Peking.

Article 10.

1. This Agreement shall enter into force on the thirtieth day from the date of exchange of notices confirming the completion of procedures required by the internal laws of each country for the validation of [treaty arrangements]. This Agreement shall remain in force for three years and shall continue in force thereafter until terminated as provided for in Paragraph 2 below.

2. Either Contracting Party may terminate this Agreement at the end of the initial three-year period or at any time thereafter by giving a written notice to the other Party three months before the expiration date.

Done in Peking on this fifth day of January, 1974, in two original copies each in the Japanese and Chinese languages, both texts being equally authentic.

Representative of the Government of Japan:
MASAYOSHI OHIRA

Representative of the Government of the People's Republic of China:
CHI PENG-FEI

Appendix E

Trade Agreement Between the Government of Australia
and the Government of the People's Republic of China*

The Government of Australia and the Government of the People's Republic of China,

For the purpose of promoting the further development of economic and trade relations between their two countries on the basis of equality and mutual benefit, and

For the purpose of enhancing mutual understanding and friendship between the peoples of the two countries,

Have agreed as follows:

Article 1. Each Contracting Party shall, subject to the laws and regulations in force in its country, facilitate as far as possible imports from and exports to the territory of the other, particularly of the goods enumerated in Schedules A and B annexed to this Agreement.

This Article shall not be construed in such a manner as to limit the exchange of goods between the two countries to the goods enumerated in Schedules A and B annexed to this Agreement. The Schedules to this Agreement may be amended by mutual consent at any time by an exchange of letters between the two Contracting Parties.

Article 2. The two Contracting Parties agree that the relevant trading bodies and enterprises of their two countries hold exploratory discussions for long term commodity arrangements and conclude such arrangements in accordance with mutual requirements and possibilities.

Article 3. The exchange of goods and technical services under contracts and agreements entered into between the two countries shall, subject to the laws and regulations in force in each country, be at reasonable international market prices and shall be carried out by Australian legal and physical persons and state-owned import and export corporations of the People's Republic of China.

Article 4. The two Contracting Parties shall grant each other most-favoured nation treatment in the issue of import and export licences and the allocation of foreign exchange connected therewith, as well as in all respects concerning customs duties, internal taxes or other charges imposed on or in connection with imported goods, and customs and other related formalities, regulations and procedures.

*SOURCE: The Australian Government.

Article 5. The provisions of Article 4 of this Agreement shall not apply to:

(a) Favours and facilities granted by either Contracting Party resulting from the association of either country in a customs union or free trade area, or from other arrangements relating to preferential trade; and such measures as either Contracting Party may possibly take to meet its commitments under international commodity agreements;

(b) Favours and facilities granted or to be granted by either Contracting Party to neighbouring countries in respect of border trade;

(c) Such measures as either Contracting Party may take to safeguard its national security, or human, animal or plant life or health.

Article 6. All payments between Australia and the People's Republic of China shall be made through the banks of the two countries authorized to buy and to sell foreign currency in Australian Dollars, or in Chinese Renminbi or in other mutually acceptable freely convertible currencies in accordance with the foreign exchange regulations currently in force in the two countries and general customary practice.

Article 7. Each Contracting Party will promote the interchange of trade representatives, groups and delegations between the two countries, encourage the commercial exchange of industrial and technical expertise, and will facilitate the holding of trade exhibitions and other trade promotion activities in its country by organizations of the other in accordance with general customary practice.

Article 8. In order to facilitate the implementation of this Agreement, the two Contracting Parties establish a joint trade committee consisting of their respective designated representatives.

The committee shall meet once a year, unless otherwise mutually agreed, alternately in Canberra and Peking. When necessary, special meetings to discuss matters of mutual interest may be arranged through consultations between the two Contracting Parties.

The committee shall be assigned the task of examining the implementation of this Agreement, exploring measures for the expansion of mutually beneficial trade, improving understanding of the trade and related commercial policies of each country, and seeking solutions to problems which may arise in the course of the development of trade between the two countries.

Article 9. This Agreement shall come into force on the date of signature and shall remain in force for three years. If, ninety days before the expiration of this Agreement, neither of the Contracting Parties has notified the other in writing of its intention to terminate the Agreement, it shall continue in force until ninety days after the receipt by one Contracting Party of notice from the other of its intention to terminate this Agreement. Notice of termination shall be transmitted through diplomatic channels.

Article 10. In the event of termination of this Agreement all unfulfilled obligations arising from the operation of this Agreement shall be fulfilled in accordance with the provisions thereof.

DONE at_____this 24th day of July in the year one thousand nine hundred and seventy-three in duplicate in the English and Chinese languages, both of which shall be equally authentic.

For the Government of
Australia

For the Government of the
People's Republic of China

Schedule A
Chinese Export Commodities

Cotton piece goods
Various kinds of textiles
Light industrial products
Stationery items and sporting goods
Native special produce
Arts and handicrafts
Chemical products

Animal by-products
Canned goods and other foodstuffs
Various kinds of machinery, instruments
    and hand tools
Non-ferrous metals and various kinds of
    minerals and metal products

Schedule B
Australian Export Commodities

Wheat and other grains
Wool
Raw, semi-processed and processed
    minerals
Sugar
Tallow
Cotton
Hides and skins

Breeding animals
Timber
Paper-pulp
Pig iron, steel products, scrap steel
Non-ferrous metals
Chemical products
Machinery and equipment

Appendix F

Trade Agreement Between the Government of the
Republic of the Philippines and the
Government of the People's Republic of China*

The Government of the Republic of the Philippines and the Government of the People's Republic of China (hereinafter referred to as the Contracting Parties), desirous of developing and strengthening economic and trade relations between the two countries on the basis of equality and mutual benefit, have reached agreement as follows:

Article 1. The Contracting Parties shall promote the expansion of economic and trade relations between the two countries within the framework of this Agreement and of laws and regulations effective in their respective countries.

Article 2. The Contracting Parties shall grant each other most-favoured-nation treatment on the basis of full reciprocity with respect to customs duties and other taxes and duties applicable to trade exchange between the two countries.
The provisions of the preceding paragraph shall not apply to:

a) Preferences and advantages which either of the Contracting Parties has granted or may grant neighbouring countries in order to facilitate their frontier trade;

b) Preferences and advantages which result from any customs unions or free trade areas or regional economic groupings to which either of the Contracting Parties is or may become a Party.

Article 3. The import and export of goods/commodities between the two countries will be carried out in accordance with the laws and rules in force in their respective countries affecting import, export and foreign exchange, and on the basis of commercial transactions concluded between trade organizations or import and export traders of the two countries.
The import and export of goods listed in Schedules "A" and "B" attached to this Agreement shall be encouraged. The said Schedules may by mutual consent be amended or modified.

*SOURCE: Department of Industry, Republic of the Philippines.

The above provisions shall not preclude commercial transactions in respect of goods not listed in the said Schedules.

Article 4. The Contracting Parties shall encourage and facilitate the conclusion of long-term contracts relating to imports and exports between trade organizations and enterprises of their two countries based on their respective requirements and possibilities in trade, energy and development.

Article 5. All current payments for trade between the two countries shall be made in freely convertible currencies, subject to foreign exchange regulations effective in their respective countries.

This does not, however, preclude other payment arrangements to be agreed upon by both Parties to facilitate trade.

Article 6. The Contracting Parties shall facilitate each other's participation in trade fairs to be held in either country, and arranging exhibitions of either country in the territory of the other on terms to be agreed between the competent authorities.

Exemption from customs duties and other similar charges of articles and samples intended for fairs and exhibitions, as well as their entry, leaving, sale and disposition, shall be subject to the laws of the country where the fair or exhibition is held.

Article 7. Merchant cargo-bearing vessels of either Contracting Party including their crews and cargoes, shall be granted most-favoured-nation treatment in respect of entry into, stay in and departure from the ports of the other Party, and the levy of taxes and charges, in accordance with the laws, rules and regulations in force in the said other Party.

Each Contracting Party reserves to its own vessels the right to engage in the coastal trade and inland shipping.

Article 8. The provisions of this Agreement shall not limit the right of either Contracting Party to adopt or execute such measures as it feels necessary to protect and develop its national economy.

Article 9. The Contracting Parties shall encourage the parties concerned to settle through friendly consultations any disputes relating to the commercial transactions between the trade organizations or import and export traders of the two countries. Failing this, the parties concerned shall submit their cases to arbitration in accordance with contract provisions; in the absence of an arbitration clause, they shall be encouraged to submit their cases to arbitration by mutual agreement. The arbitration shall be referred to the permanent arbitration bodies, or arbitration tribunals provisionally established, of the two countries.

Article 10. The representative of the Contracting Parties, upon request by either of them, shall in the spirit of co-operation and mutual understanding discuss measures aimed at broader economic and trade relations between the.two countries and solution of problems connected with the implementation of this Agreement.

The place and date of such discussions shall be established by mutual agreement.

Article 11. The provisions of this Agreement shall continue to be applied after it has expired to all commercial transactions concluded but not fully performed before the termination of this Agreement.

Article 12. This Agreement shall come into force on the date of its signature and shall operate for a period of one year. Thereafter, it shall automatically continue to be valid for subsequent periods of one year unless a written notice of termination is given by either Contracting Party at least six months prior to the expiration date.

Done in Peking on June 9, 1975, in two original copies each in the Philipino, Chinese and English languages, all the three texts being equally authentic.

For the Government of the Republic of the Philippines ·

For the Government of the People's Republic of China

(sgd) Secretary of Industry

(sgd) Minister of Foreign Trade

Appendix G

Sino-Japanese Trade Agreement, March 5, 1958 (Excerpt)*

The China Council for the Promotion of International Trade, on the one side, and the Japanese Dietmen's League for the Promotion of Japan-China Trade, the Japan Association for the Promotion of International Trade, and the Japan Association for Japan-China Exports and Imports, on the other side, in order to further the growth of trade between China and Japan and strengthen friendship between the peoples of the two countries, after consultations have reached agreement based on the principles of equality and mutual benefit as follows: . . .

Article 11 Each side agrees to set up a permanent private trade mission in the other's country. The trade missions of both sides will be dispatched by their signatories to this agreement, to be set up respectively in Peking and Tokyo.

The two sides agree to obtain the concurrence of their respective governments to ensure the security of their trade missions and their personnel and facilities for carrying out their work.

Both sides agree that the tasks of the trade missions of both sides will be as follows:

(1) To establish contacts and deal with all matters arising out of the implementation of this agreement;

(2) To provide information on the market conditions of their respective countries;

(3) To investigate and collect information on the trade and market conditions of the country in which the mission resides;

(4) To assist manufacturers and businessmen of the two countries in the conduct of transactions and trade exchange;

(5) To establish contacts for and promote technical exchange between the two countries; and

(6) To deal with other matters relating to trade assigned by organizations which dispatched them to each other's country. . . .

*SOURCE: *TYC 1958,* vol. 7 (1959), pp. 197, 199, 201-202. Translation is official with some modifications to conform to usage in my discussion.

Memorandum, March 5, 1958 (attached to the agreement)

To ensure the smooth implementation, on the basis of reciprocity and mutual respect, of the provisions contained in Article 11 of the Sino-Japanese Trade Agreement signed in Peking on March 5, 1958, both sides will adopt the following measures:

1. To ensure the security and working facilities of the permanent private trade mission and its personnel of the other side, each of the two sides should secure the concurrence of its government to give them the following treatment:
   (a) Both sides will take appropriate measures to guarantee the security of the trade mission and its personnel of the other side. In the event of any legal dispute, it should be handled in accordance with the method agreed upon by both sides through liaison.
   (b) Each side will provide facilities for the personnel of the trade mission of the other side to enter and leave its country, give them favorable customs treatment and freedom of travel for trade purposes.
   (c) The trade mission may use ciphers needed for business operations.
   (d) The trade missions have the right to hoist the national flags of their own countries over their buildings.

2. Each side will decide the number of personnel for its own trade mission on the basis of the requirements of work. There will be no fingerprinting for the personnel of the trade missions or members of their families.

3. Both sides recognize that the present memorandum, being a component part of the Sino-Japanese Trade Agreement, has a force equal to that of the said Agreement.

Appendix H

Agreement on Economic and Technical Co-operation Between the Government of the People's Republic of China and the Government of the Republic of Ghana*

The Government of the People's Republic of China and the Government of the Republic of Ghana, for the purpose of promoting the friendly relations and of developing the economic and technical co-operation between the two countries, and in pursuance of the Treaty of Friendship Between the People's Republic of China and the Republic of Ghana, have concluded the present Agreement, the articles of which are as follows:

Article 1. With a view to helping the Government of the Republic of Ghana to develop its economy, the Government of the People's Republic of China has agreed to grant the Government of the Republic of Ghana within the period from July 1, 1962 to June 30, 1967, a non-interest bearing loan without any conditions or privileges attached. The amount of the loan is 7,000,000 Ghana Pounds (Seven Million Ghana Pounds only). (The gold content of one Ghana Pound is 2.48828 grams of fine gold.)

The loan shall be utilized in instalments during the period of validity of the present Agreement by the Government of the Republic of Ghana in accordance with the items of economic construction and technical assistance to be agreed upon by both sides. The above loan shall be repaid within a period of ten years from July 1, 1971 to June 30, 1981 by the Government of the Republic of Ghana in installments either with export goods of Ghana or with currency of a third country agreed to by China. The repayment of the loan shall be completed in ten years with one-tenth of the above loan each year.

Article 2. According to the capability of the People's Republic of China and the requirement of the Republic of Ghana, the Government of the People's Republic of China will supply the Government of the Republic of Ghana with techniques and materials within the amount of the above loan and in the following scope:

1. Supply of technical assistance by dispatching of experts and technicians;

2. Supply of complete set equipment, machinery and materials, techniques and other goods;

3. Assistance in the training of technicians and skilled workers of the Republic of Ghana.

SOURCE: Foreign Trade of the PRC, no. 4 (1961), p. 6.

Article 3. In accordance with items 1 and 3 of Article 2 of this Agreement, the salaries of the Chinese experts and technicians during the period of service in the Republic of Ghana shall be borne by the Government of the People's Republic of China. The living expenses of the Chinese experts and technicians during the period of service in the Republic of Ghana shall be borne by the Government of the Republic of Ghana, and their standard of living shall not exceed that of the personnel of the same grade in the Republic of Ghana. The living expenses of the trainees to be sent to China by the Government of the Republic of Ghana to learn techniques shall be paid from the amount of the loan.

Article 4. For the entries of drawing the loan and its repayment, the People's Bank of China and the Bank of Ghana shall discuss and make separately the technical arrangement.

Article 5. In accordance with item 2 of Article 2 of this Agreement, the Governments of both countries shall appoint their respective representatives to discuss and fix the specific items of economic construction and technique to be supplied by the Government of the People's Republic of China to the Government of the Republic of Ghana and the methods of their implementation and to sign protocols thereafter.

Article 6. The executing agencies for this Agreement shall be the Central Bureau of Foreign Economic Relations of the People's Republic of China on the side of the People's Republic of China, and the Ministry of Finance of the Republic of Ghana on the side of the Republic of Ghana.

Article 7. This Agreement shall come into force on the date of its signing and shall remain in force for a period of twenty years ending 17th August 1981.

Done in duplicate in Peking on the eighteenth day of August, 1961, in the Chinese and English languages, the texts of both languages being equally authentic.

Plenipotentiary of the Government of the People's Republic of China	Plenipotentiary of the Government of the Republic of Ghana
LI HSIEN-NIEN	KROBO EDUSEI
(Signed)	(Signed)

Trade and Payments Agreement Between the Government of the People's Republic of China and the Government of the Republic of Ghana*

The Government of the People's Republic of China and the Government of the Republic of Ghana, for the purpose of promoting and strengthening trade relations between the two countries, have, on the basis of the principles of equality and mutual benefit, agreed as follows:

Article 1. Equilibrium between the total values of imports and exports shall be taken as a principle of trade between the two countries. The annual volume of exportation on each side shall be 4,000,000 (Four Million) Ghana Pounds.

Article 2. In order to promote and facilitate trade between the People's Republic of China and the Republic of Ghana, the two Contracting Parties agree to grant each other the most-favoured-nation treatment in respect of the following:
  1. Customs duty and all other duties and taxes applicable to the exportation, importation or transit of commodities;
  2. Customs prescriptions and formalities as well as all dues and charges in relation to importation, exportation, transit, storage and transhipment of commodities when exported, imported or in transit;
  3. Issuance of import and export licences and the formalities thereof.

The provisions of this Article shall not, however, apply to:
  1. Goods imported from the Republic of Ghana but originating in other countries which do not enjoy the most-favoured-nation treatment in the People's Republic of China or to goods imported from the People's Republic of China but originating in other countries which do not enjoy the most-favoured-nation treatment in the Republic of Ghana;
  2. Advantages accorded by either Contracting Party to contiguous countries for the purpose of facilitating frontier traffic;
  3. Advantages resulting from customs union to which either Contracting Party may be or become a party.

*SOURCE: Foreign Trade of the PRC, no. 4 (1961), pp. 6-7, 26.

Article 3. The items of goods to be exported from the People's Republic of China to the Republic of Ghana and from the Republic of Ghana to the People's Republic of China will be listed in the attached Schedules "A" and "B" respectively.

Alterations may be made in the above-mentioned Schedules "A" and "B" by mutual agreement between the Contracting Parties.

Article 4. The provisions of Article 3 do not affect the rights of the state foreign trade corporations of the People's Republic of China and the physical and juridical persons in the Republic of Ghana to conclude, subject to import, export and foreign exchange control laws and regulations in force in both countries, contracts for the import or export of goods not included in the said Schedules.

Competent authorities of both Contracting Parties will consider in the spirit of genuine co-operation inquiries of either Party regarding the transactions of import and export of goods, provided for in this Article.

Article 5. The import and export of goods mentioned in Article 3 and 4 will be carried out in accordance with the import, export and foreign exchange control laws and regulations in force in the People's Republic of China and the Republic of Ghana respectively and on the basis of the contracts to be concluded between the state foreign trade corporations of the People's Republic of China and the physical and juridical persons in the Republic of Ghana.

Article 6. Both Contracting Parties will make every effort to fix the prices of goods delivered under this Agreement on the basis of world market prices, i.e. the prices of the corresponding goods on the main world markets.

Article 7. In order to carry out payments between the People's Republic of China and the Republic of Ghana, the People's Bank of China on behalf of the Government of the People's Republic of China and the Bank of Ghana on behalf of the Government of the Republic of Ghana shall establish with each other non-interest bearing and free of charge clearing accounts in Ghana Pound.

The commercial and non-commercial payments enumerated hereunder between the physical and juridical persons residing within the territories of the People's Republic of China and of the Republic of Ghana may be effected through the above-mentioned clearing accounts:

1. The value of goods exchanged between the two countries;
2. All expenses in connection with the traffic of goods between the two countries such as freight, insurance and other incidental expenses;
3. Expenses incurred by the embassies and consulates residing in each other's territory;
4. Expenses incurred by the governmental, commercial, cultural and social delegations residing in each other's territory;
5. Expenses of films, books and periodicals, expenditure and receipt of exhibitions and cultural performances taking place in each other's territory;
6. Expenses incurred by students and trainees as well as overseas remittances

and payment for travelling expenses of travellers of both countries;

7. Payments for transit transactions of both countries;

8. Other payments as agreed upon between the People's Bank of China and the Bank of Ghana.

Article 8. If the par value of the Ghana Pound in terms of gold, being 2.48828 grams of fine gold per currency unit, is altered, the balance of the accounts referred to in Article 7 of this Agreement shall be adjusted accordingly on the date of the alteration.

Article 9. All values in the contracts, invoices, payment documents and payment orders relating to the trade between the People's Republic of China and the Republic of Ghana shall be expressed in Ghana Pound. If they are expressed in any other convertible currencies, the values shall be converted into Ghana Pound at the average rate between the buying and selling rates quoted officially in Ghana for the respective said currencies on the day preceding the date of payment for the entries to the accounts.

Article 10. For the effective carrying out of the stipulations of the present Agreement, the People's Bank of China and the Bank of Ghana will establish technical arrangement for payments between them.

Article 11. Settlement of the accounts shall be made by both banks at the end of each agreement year. The balance, if any, shall be settled by the debtor Party, within six months after the end of each agreement year, in goods or in any currency of a third country to be agreed upon by both Parties.

Article 12. In order to promote trade between the two countries, both Contracting Parties agree to hold commodity exhibitions in each other's country and to extend to the other Party, within the laws and regulations of their own respective countries, all kinds of facilities for holding such commodity exhibitions as well as exemption from duties, taxes and other fees of the exhibits on their entry and repatriation.

Article 13. Either Contracting Party shall obtain the approval in writing of the authorities concerned of the other Party which in the case of China shall be the Ministry of Foreign Trade and in the case of Ghana the Ministry of Trade before resale or re-export of the commodities imported from the other Party to a third country is made.

Article 14. In order to ensure the smooth implementation of this Agreement, both Parties shall appoint representatives to set up a joint committee. The joint committee will meet at least once a year alternately in Peking or in Accra to examine the implementation of this Agreement, solve by consultation the questions arising from the implementation and adjust, whenever necessary, the commodity lists attached to this Agreement.

Article 15. Nothing in this Agreement shall be construed to derogate from any obligations of either of the two Governments under any international treaty or agreement entered into before the signing of this Agreement.

Article 16. The provisions of this Agreement shall continue to apply, after its expiry, to all contracts which have been concluded but not fully executed by both Parties prior to its expiry.

Article 17. This Agreement shall come into force on the date of signing and its validity is for five years.

Done and signed in Peking this eighteenth day of August, 1961, in duplicate, each written in the Chinese and English languages, the texts of both languages being equally authentic.

Plenipotentiary of the Government of the People's Republic of China

Li Hsien-nien
(Signed)

Plenipotentiary of the Government of the Republic of Ghana

Krobo Edusei
(Signed)

Schedule A:

List of Commodities To Be Exported from the People's Republic of China to the Republic of Ghana

1. Machinery including machine tools, forging and pressing machinery, building machinery and road construction machinery, power machinery, hoisting machinery, mining machinery, textile machinery, wood-working machinery, printing machinery, electric appliances and equipment, telecommunications equipment, etc.
2. Agricultural machinery and agricultural implements
3. Instruments and electric appliances including laboratory instruments, and drawing instruments and apparatus, optical instruments and apparatus, surveying instruments and apparatus, various kinds of meters, cinema projectors, radio receivers, automatic telephone sets, radio spare parts, electronic tubes, etc.
4. Chemicals including pigments, dyestuffs, paints, rubber tires and rubber products, zinc oxide, sodium sulphide, caustic soda, soda ash, sodium bicarbonate, aluminium sulphate, etc.
5. Pharmaceuticals and medical apparatus
6. Metal and steel products including construction steel, iron wire, iron nails, wood screws, screen wire, metal tools, hardwares, etc.
7. Building materials including cement, plywood, asbestos sheets, glass, wall tiles, sanitary wares, other building materials, etc.
8. Textiles including cotton piece-goods, cotton yarn, cotton blankets, woolen piece-goods, silk piece-goods and ready-made articles, wool knitting yarn,

woolen blankets, cotton and woolen knitted goods, cotton thread on spool, fish net, etc.

9. Foodstuffs including sugar, tea, cigarettes, tinned goods, beverages, salt, etc.
10. General merchandise including bicycles, sewing machines, thermo flasks, ice bottles, electric fans, flashlight, dry battery, rubber shoes, enamel wares, porcelains and pottery, household electric appliances, toys, matches, etc.
11. Stationery and educational supplies including various kinds of paper, fountain pens, pen nibs, ink, pencils, ball point pens, punching machines, stapling machines, numbering machines, other stationery supplies, various kinds of musical instruments, etc.
12. Sports goods
13. Native and special products and handicrafts including ivory carvings, carved cinnabar lacquer wares, embroideries, brocaded silk articles, drawn-thread work, table cloth, ornaments, tobacco, mats, straw hats, other straw braid articles, etc.
14. Animal by-products including carpets, brushes, leather products, etc.
15. Films, books, newspapers, periodicals
16. Others

Schedule B:

List of Commodities To be Exported from the Republic of Ghana to the People's Republic of China

1. Raw cocoa beans, cocoa butter and cocoa powder
2. Groundnuts
3. Palm kernels and oil
4. Coconut oil
5. Copra
6. Cotton
7. Hides and skins
8. Diamonds for industrial purposes
9. Tobacco leaves
10. Coffee
11. Sugar
12. Grains
13. Timbers
14. Others

Appendix I

Minutes of Lima Talks*

The signing ceremony for the minutes of talks between Chou Hua-min, Vice-Minister of Foreign Trade of the People's Republic of China, and Carlos Garcia Bedoya, Secretary-General of the Ministry of Foreign Affairs of the Republic of Peru, was held in Lima, capital of Peru, on April 28. Vice-Minister Chou Hua-min signed the minutes of talks on behalf of the Chinese side and Secretary-General Carlos Garcia Bedoya on behalf of the Peruvian side. Peruvian Foreign Minister Edgardo Mercado Jarrin was present at the signing ceremony. Minister Mercado, Secretary-General Garcia and Vice-Minister Chou Hua-min in their speeches congratulated the signing of the minutes.

The minutes of the talks read:

Upon the invitation of the Peruvian Ministry of Foreign Affairs, His Excellency Mr. Chou Hua-min, Vice-Minister of Foreign Trade of the People's Republic of China, visited Lima. During the visit, the two sides held talks from April 22 to April 28, 1971, with a view to promoting the possibilities of trade interflow between the People's Republic of China and Peru. The talks manifested the common desire for developing trade relations in the spirit of equality, respect, reciprocity and mutual benefit so as to contribute to the strengthening of the friendship of the people of the two countries.

In the talks, both sides expressed the desire to make the greatest effort to promote and expand trade interflow and to reciprocally provide the necessary facilities for the import and export of commodities produced by each side, which are mentioned in list B and list A of the annex of the present minutes corresponding respectively to the export products of the People's Republic of China and Peru, but this will not preclude the addition to the above-mentioned lists of commodities stated in subsequent agreements.

Both sides also expressed the desire that the most favoured nation treatment will be mutually granted for import and export of the above-mentioned commodities and for customs duties, other taxes and customs procedures. However, both sides agreed that this obligation does not apply to advantages, special favours, privileges and immunities which one side grants or may grant to her neighbouring countries and to any special benefit or exemption from taxes that has been granted or will possibly be granted by one side in virtue of integrated regional or subregional agreements.

Both sides also defined that while entering into, berthing at or sailing from the ports of the other side, merchant ships of each side should enjoy the most favoured

*SOURCE: *Peking Review,* no. 21 (1971), pp. 23-24.

conditions, which the laws of the respective country have granted to ships flying the flag of a third country, in regard to port regulations and operations practised at the ports. But these regulations are not applicable to coastal navigation and fishing of any kind within the limits of maritime jurisdiction established by each side or to the special regulations dictated for the protection and development of their own merchant fleets.

Both sides also agreed that the exchange of commodities between them will be conducted through the state trading corporations of the People's Republic of China and the Peruvian state trade organizations or juridical or natural persons engaged in foreign trade.

The Peruvian Ministry of Foreign Affairs accepted with pleasure the invitation made by His Excellency Mr. Chou Hua-min, Vice-Minister of Foreign Trade of the People's Republic of China, for a visit to his country by a Peruvian trade mission to continue the talks started in Lima, with a view to working out the most suitable procedures for the promotion and concrete realization of permanent trade interflow and for the possible establishment of commercial offices in both countries.

With regard to the questions of territorial sea rights, both sides reaffirmed that as the common principle of international policy, the coastal countries have the right to dispose of the natural resources in the sea adjacent to their coasts and in its sea-bed and subsoil for promoting the development and welfare of their peoples. Consequently they have the right to define the limits of their maritime sovereignty and jurisdiction in accordance with their geographical realities and the necessity for reasonable use of the above-mentioned resources.

With regard to this, His Excellency Mr. Vice-Minister reiterated the support of the People's Republic of China for the action which Peru and other Latin American countries had consistently taken at regional and world forums to reaffirm their sovereign rights over 200-nautical-mile territorial waters and to establish more impartial, realistic and lasting international order on the sea.

Finally, His Excellency Chou Hua-min expressed the admiration and sympathy of the People's Republic of China for the efforts made by the Peruvian maritime workers and entrepreneurs who, working under the protection of the government within the zone of 200 nautical miles, have turned Peru into a nation of fishery with the highest catch in the world, thereby contributing to the general development of the country and the raising of the standard of living of her people.

At the conclusion of the talks, both sides expressed in particular the cordiality and the spirit of co-operation displayed in the talks, which are in consonance with the long-standing and lofty friendship binding together the peoples of the People's Republic of China and Peru.

Appendix J

Act Regulating the Entry, Exit, Transit, Residence, and Travel of Foreign Nationals.*

(Passed at the 114th meeting of the Standing Committee of the National People's Congress, March 13, 1964; promulgated by the Premier of the State Council, April 13, 1964.)

Chapter I. General Principles

Article 1. The entry into, exit from, and transit through the national boundaries of the People's Republic of China by foreign nationals as well as the residence and travel within China of such persons shall be dealt with in accordance with the provisions contained in this act.

This act is also applicable to stateless persons.

Article 2. Foreign nationals in China shall observe the laws and decrees of China.

Article 3. The entry, exit, transit, residence, and travel of foreign nationals shall be approved by the competent organs of the Chinese government.

Article 4. Chinese government organs abroad which handle applications of foreign nationals for entry, exit, and transit shall be Chinese diplomatic and consular organs.

Chinese government organs within China which handle applications for entry, exit, transit, residence, and travel of foreign nationals shall be the public security bureaus in the areas concerned. Applications by diplomatic envoys, consular officers, and the staff of diplomatic and consular organs of foreign countries in China shall be handled by the Ministry of Foreign Affairs and by alien affairs offices in the areas concerned; applications by other foreign nationals holding diplomatic or official passports shall be handled by the Ministry of Foreign Affairs, the alien affairs offices, or the public security bureaus in the areas concerned.

*SOURCE: *Jen-min jih-pao,* April 20, 1964, p. 2; English translation in Jerome Alan Cohen and Hungdah Chiu, *People's China and International Law,* vol. 1, pp. 510-513.

Article 5. Organs handling applications for entry, exit, transit, residence, and travel of foreign nationals have the authority to refuse to issue visas and certifying documents, and also the authority to cancel or declare null and void the visas or certifying documents already issued.

Article 6. Residence and travel of foreign nationals in important national defense and military localities and restricted areas shall be prohibited.

Chapter II. Entry, Exit, and Transit

Article 7. Foreign nationals who wish to enter into, exit from, or transit through [the territory of the People's Republic of China] shall apply for a visa.

Article 8. With regard to entry, exit, or transit, foreign nationals shall abide by ports of entry and exit, means of communications, and routes prescribed in the visas within the valid period as indicated. Foreign nationals entering the country may proceed only to the place of destination noted in the visas. In the course of entry, exit, or transit, no stays on the way shall be permitted without authorization.

Article 9. Foreign nationals who come under the scope of an agreement signed between the Chinese government and a foreign government concerned, which mutually exempts visa arrangements, shall proceed through open ports which the Chinese government has designated to the foreign governments. Upon entering the country, such foreign nationals should explain at national border checkpoints their places of destination, and proceed via the route and by means of communications designated at the national border checkpoints. In the course of entry, exit, or transit, no stays on the way shall be permitted without authorization.

Chapter III. Residence

Article 10. Foreign nationals residing in China shall apply for residence registration within the stipulated period of time.

Article 11. Foreign nationals residing in China shall observe the household control system and register the inhabitants in the household as prescribed.
Organs, schools, enterprises, organizations, hotels, and private residents accommodating foreign nationals shall register the inhabitants as prescribed.

Article 12. Foreign nationals residing in China shall proceed to public security organs within a specified period of time designated by the public security organs to present documents for examination.

Article 13. Foreign nationals residing in China who change places of residence shall apply for certified documents of moving.

Chapter IV. Travel

Article 14. Foreign nationals who are to travel in areas out of the travel bounds set forth by city or county people's councils shall apply for documents authorizing travel within the specified period of time.

Article 15. Foreign nationals who travel shall proceed within the valid period noted in the travel documents, and in accordance with the points of travel, means of communications, and routes of travel as authorized, which shall not be altered on their own initiative. In the course of travel, no stays shall be permitted on the way without authorization.

Article 16. Public security organs shall set up checkpoints in necessary localities of passage to check on foreign nationals, or dispatch people's police to check on foreign nationals with regard to their observance of the provisions in this act. Foreign nationals shall accept such checks.

Chapter V. Punishment

Article 17. Local public security organs shall, according to the gravity of the matters involved, give foreign nationals who violate the provisions of this act punishment in the form of warning, fine, detention, orders to leave the country within a time limit, expulsion, and so forth or they shall pursue these violators for criminal responsibility according to law.

Cases of violation of the provisions of this act involving foreign nationals who enjoy diplomatic immunity shall be handled through diplomatic channels.

Chapter VI. Supplementary Rules

Article 18. Concrete measures regulating the entry, exit, transit, residence, and travel of foreign nationals shall be formulated by the Ministry of Public Security and the Ministry of Foreign Affairs.

Article 19. This act shall be in effect from the day of promulgation. The "Provisional Rules Governing the Entry, Exit, and Residence of Foreigners" promulgated by the Government Administrative Council of the Central People's Government on November 18, 1951, and the "Provisional Rules Governing Residence Registration and Issuance of Residence Certificates for Foreigners," "Provisional Rules Governing Travel of Foreigners," and "Provisional Rules Governing Exit of Foreigners" ratified by the Government Administrative Council of the Central People's Government and promulgated by the Ministry of Public Security on August 10, 1954, shall be abrogated simultaneously.

Appendix K

Act for the Control of Trademarks*

(Adopted by the State Council at its 100th plenary meeting on April 29, 1960; approved by the Standing Committee of the Second National People's Congress at its 91st meeting on March 30, 1963; promulgated by the State Council on April 10, 1963)

Article 1. This Act is made for the purpose of strengthening the control of trademarks and assuring and promoting the quality of products by various enterprises.

Article 2. Petition for the registration of trademarks used by enterprises should be made to the Central Administration for Industry and Commerce.**

Commodities not bearing trademarks should, when necessary and feasible, be clearly marked with the names and addresses of the [producing] enterprise either on the commodities or their ornamental [labeling, packaging, etc.] so as to facilitate their control.

Article 3. A trademark is a mark indicating the quality of a given commodity. The administrative organs of industry and commerce shall supervise and control the quality of commodities in coordination with other departments concerned.

Article 4. A trademark must bear a definite name. Words and drawings that make up a trademark should be simple and distinct so as to be easily identifiable.

Article 5. Trademarks may not utilize the following words or drawings:
(1) That are identical with or similar to the national flag, the national emblem, the military banners, or the decorations of the People's Republic of China;
(2) That are identical with or similar to the national flag, the national emblem, or the military banners of any foreign country;
(3) That are identical with or similar to the marks and names of the Red Cross or the Red Crescent;
(4) That may have undesirable political influence.

Foreign words or letters must not be used for trademarks; however, the trademarks of goods for export may incorporate foreign words.

*SOURCE: FKHP 1962-1963, vol. 13 (1964), pp. 162-167. Translation is mine.
**Abolished; successor unknown.

Article 6. Trademarks submitted for registration shall be clearly distinguishable from the trademarks of the same type of commodities or similar commodities that have been registered by other enterprises.

Article 7. When two or more enterprises petition for the registration of trademarks, and if the trademarks are identical or similar [in design], approval of the registration shall be given to the earliest petitioner.

Article 8. If a petition for the registration of a trademark is not approved, and if the petitioner does not accept the decision, he may apply for a review of his petition within a month from the date he receives the notice. If after review the petition is still not approved, the decision is final.

Article 9. When the registration of a trademark is approved, the Central Administration of Industry and Commerce shall make a public notice to this effect and issue a registration certificate to the petitioner.

Article 10. The period in which a registered trademark may be used [by its owner] commences from the date when the registration is approved to the time when the enterprise [owner] applies for withdrawal of the registration.

Article 11. The Central Administration of Industry and Commerce may revoke a registered trademark by a public notice in one of the following events:
(1) The quality of a commodity for which the trademark has been registered is lowered owing to unskilled or careless manufacturing;
(2) The name or drawing of the trademark is altered without proper authorization;
(3) The trademark has not been put to use for one full year without approval for the retention of its registration;
(4) Revocation is demanded by the masses of the people, [government] organs, [social] groups, or enterprises and is justified after examination of the demand.

Article 12. When a foreign enterprise petitions for the registration of a trademark, it must meet the following two requirements:
(1) The petitioner's country has concluded a reciprocal agreement with the People's Republic of China for the registration of trademarks;
(2) The trademark for which registration is petitioned must already be duly registered under the name of the petitioner in his own country.
The duration of validity of the trademarks registered in our country by foreign enterprises shall be determined by the Central Administration of Industry and Commerce.

Article 13. Enforcement Rules of this Act shall be enacted and promulgated by the Central Administration of Industry and Commerce.

The People's Council of a province, an autonomous region, or a municipality directly subordinate to the Central Government may enact concrete measures for the control of trademarks in accordance with the provisions of this Act and its Enforcement Rules.***

Article 14. This Act shall become effective on the date of promulgation, and the Provisional Act for the Registration of Trademarks promulgated by the Government Administration Council on August 28, 1950, shall be simultaneously nullified.

***"The People's Council" was the name of local government under the 1954 Constitution; it has been replaced by "the Revolutionary Committee" under the 1975 Constitution.

Enforcement Rules of the Act for the Control of Trademarks

(Promulgated by the Central Administration of Industry and Commerce on April 25, 1963)

Article 1. These Enforcement Rules are enacted in accordance with the provisions of Article 13 of the Act for the Control of Trademarks.

Article 2. An enterprise petitioning for the registration of a trademark must be one that has been properly registered [with the government].

Article 3. When petitioning for the registration of a trademark, an enterprise must submit a formal petition, a statement containing the specifications and quality of the commodity, twenty duplicate copies of the designs of the trademark, and a registration fee of twenty *yuan*.

The petition should first be submitted to the petitioner's supervisory department for approval.

The statement containing the specifications and quality of the commodity should be filled out in accordance with the technical standards of the product and examined and certified by the petitioner's supervisory department.

Article 4. When petitioning for the registration of a trademark that is to be used for a medical product, the petitioner should attach to the petition a certificate approving the making of the product by the Department of Public Health in a province, an autonomous region, or a municipality directly subordinate to the Central Government.

When petitioning for the registration of a trademark for an export commodity, the petitioner should attach to the petition a certificate issued by the department of foreign trade.

Article 5. An enterprise intending to use an identical trademark for different commodities should petition for the registration of the trademark for each of these commodities separately in accordance with the Classification of Commodities.

Article 6. The registration fee shall be refunded if a petition for the registration of a trademark is not approved.

Article 7. If alteration is to be made in the name or drawings of a registered trademark, a new petition must be submitted.

Article 8. Approval must be obtained for the use of a registered trademark on other commodities of the same classification.

Article 9. If the name or address of the owner of a registered trademark has changed, a new petition must be submitted for the alteration of the trademark within one month after the change.

Article 10. When transferring a registered trademark to another enterprise, the transferor and the transferee should submit a joint petition for the transfer of the registration. For each trademark, the petitioners must submit a formal petition for the transfer of the registration together with a fee of twenty *yuan*. In addition, the original certificate of registration must be surrendered.

Article 11. When petitioning for the withdrawal of a registered trademark or when the registration of a trademark is revoked in accordance with the provisions of Article 11 of the Act for the Control of Trademarks, the enterprise [that owns] the trademark must surrender the original certificate of registration for cancellation.

Article 12. When a certificate of trademark registration is lost or damaged, the holder of the certificate should petition for a replacement. When petitioning for a replacement, the petitioner should submit five duplicate copies of the trademark's design with a fee of five *yuan* for the replacement.

Article 13. When petitioning for the registration of a trademark, for the alteration of the registration, for the transfer of the registration, for the withdrawal of the registration, or for a replacement of the certificate of registration, an enterprise should submit its petition to the local administrative organ of industry and commerce for examination and transfer to the Central Administration of Industry and Commerce.
  The petitioner should also submit a duplicate copy of the petition and other related documents to the local administrative organ that transmits the petition.

Article 14. When notified by an administrative organ of industry and commerce of the necessity to complete the procedures of registration and/or other related matters, the petitioner must comply within the stipulated period of time. Failure to do so shall be deemed as having given up the petition.

Article 15. When a foreign enterprise is petitioning for the registration of a trademark, it should authorize the China Council for the Promotion of International Trade to act on its behalf.

Article 16. When petitioning for the registration of trademarks, a foreign enterprise should submit a formal petition for each trademark, an authorization statement, a duplicate copy of the certificate of registration issued by its own country, twenty duplicate copies of the trademark's design, and a registration fee of twenty *yuan,* in addition to a certificate of nationality.

Article 17. When the duration of validity of a trademark registered by a foreign enterprise is due to expire and the enterprise wishes to extend the registration, it should submit a petition before the registration expires. For each trademark, it should submit a petition, an authorization statement, a duplicate copy of the certificate of registration or extended registration in its own country, twenty duplicate copies of the trademark's design, and a registration fee of twenty *yuan.* In addition, the enterprise must surrender the original certificate of registration.

Article 18. When petitioning for the alteration of a registered trademark, a foreign enterprise should submit a formal petition for each trademark, an authorization statement, a certificate showing the alteration of registration in its own country, and must surrender the original certificate of registration.

Article 19. When petitioning for the transfer of registration of a trademark, a foreign enterprise should submit a formal petition for each trademark, an authorization statement, a certificate of transfer of the registration in its own country, and a registration fee of twenty *yuan,* in addition to a certificate of nationality of the transferee. It must also surrender the original certificate of registration.

Article 20. All documents used by a foreign enterprise to petition for the registration of trademarks must be written in Chinese. A Chinese translation must be attached to the certificate of nationality and the certificate of registration in the petitioner's own country. All certificates must be notarized and witnessed.

Article 21. These Enforcement Rules shall become effective on the date of promulgation.

Attachment: The Classification of Commodities.*

*The Classification of Commodities consists of 78 categories and is omitted.

Appendix L

RCA Global Communications, Inc. Agreement with the China National Machinery Import & Export Corporation (May 23, 1972)*

Agreement

This agreement is made by and between the China National Machinery Import and Export Corporation (Machimpex) and RCA Global Communications, Inc. (RCA Globcom) with respect to the installation in Peking of a complete 30-meter Intelsat Earth Station and the up-grading of the existing Shanghai Earth Station to a complete 30-meter Intelsat facility.

1. It is agreed that Machimpex consents to buy and RCA Globcom consents to sell the equipment and services for the Peking and Shanghai projects.

2. It is agreed that RCA Globcom shall supply for Peking and Shanghai the equipment and services based on the RCA Globcom proposal (Attachment A, hereto) and the final equipment and price lists (Attachment B, hereto).

3. It is agreed that the Peking Station will be completed within eight months of contract signing and the Shanghai up-grading completed within twelve months after contract signing, and that such work will be implemented simultaneously with possible earlier delivery and completion as promised by RCA Globcom.

4. It is agreed that the total basic price for the Peking and Shanghai projects as per equipment and prices in Attachment B shall be U.S. dollars 5,490,000.

5. It is agreed that additions or deletions may be made to the equipment listed in Attachment B subject to the concurrence of both parties but in no case shall the total amount of the contract be less than U.S. dollars 5,490,000. Any changes will include proporational [sic] adjustment for the costs of transportation, installation, test and documentation.

6. It is agreed that RCA Globcom will promptly send a group of three experts to Peking at the beginning of June to resolve with Machimpex the final list of equipment and services to be provided for this project as well as contract terms and conditions, and that this work shall be completed before the end of June, 1972.

7. It is agreed that Machimpex will provide free of charge the housing, meal, medical

*SOURCE: RCA Global Communications, Inc.

care and local transportation for RCA Globcom technicians and engineers during their stay in China in conjunction with this project.

8. It is agreed that Machimpex will be responsible to provide for sites, site survey, site preparation, foundations, buildings and all civil works, and will provide necessary and possible installation and integration assistance in support of RCA Globcom effort in China.

9. It is agreed that RCA Globcom will supply microwave and other optional equipment in accordance with the prices and terms separately negotiated.

10. This agreement is signed in Peking on the 23rd of May, 1972 and shall become null and void automatically upon contract signing.

RCA Global   China National Machinery
RCA Communications, Inc.   Import and Export Corporation

RCA Global Communications, Inc. Contract with the China National Machinery Import & Export Corporation (January 22, 1972)

Contract

No. 72MHE-SP001-X

This Contract is made on the 22nd of January 1972 in Peking by and between the China National Machinery Import and Export Corporation at Er-Li-Kou, Hsi Chiao, Peking, China (Cable Address MACHIMPEX PEKING) hereinafter called the Buyers and RCA Global Communications Inc., a corporation having its principal place of business at 60 Broad Street, New York 10004, U.S.A. (Cable Address RCAGLOBCOM NEW YORK) hereinafter called the Sellers; whereby the Buyers desire to buy and the Sellers desire to sell the following Equipment and Service on the terms and conditions as stipulated below:

1. The Sellers will supply to the Buyers the Transportable Earth Station Equipment for satellite communication as specified in Attachment A hereto.

2. Total Price of this Contract amounts to £1,145,181.71 (at the exchange rate of £ equals to U.S. $2.6057) including the costs of air-transportation, packing, insurance as well as installation, test and technical documents.

3. The Sellers will be responsible for the delivery of the contracted goods by air freight at the Shanghai Airport according to the schedule as specified in Attachment A hereto. All risks and cost prior to the delivery at the Shanghai Airport will be borne by the Sellers. The Sellers will, 3 (three) days before the date of each delivery, notify the Buyers of the class, type, en route, time of entry into China, liaison signals of the airplane and contents of goods loaded.

4. The Buyers will, according to the following stipulations, remit by T/T the total amount in Pounds Sterling via Bank of China, Peking through its correspondent in London to the Sellers' account at the bank appointed by the Sellers.

    (1) 30% of the contract amount will be paid within 5 (five) days after signing of this Contract against the Letter of Guarantee issued by the Sellers. The Letter of Guarantee issued by the Sellers guarantees that if non-execution of the contract by the Sellers, the Sellers will refund the Buyers the whole advanced payment together with interests at the rate of 5% per annum calculated from the date of effecting the advanced payment to the date of refunding.

    (2) 40% of the total amount of each delivery at the Shanghai airport will be paid within 5 (five) days against the following documents:
        (a) Three copies of Invoice,
        (b) Three copies of packing list,
        (c) One original copy of Airway Bill,
        (d) One copy of Insurance Policy.

    (3) 30% of the total amount of each delivery will be paid within 10 (ten) days after the acceptance of the goods by the Buyers.

    (4) 70% of the total amount of installation, integration, engineering and design will be paid within 10 (ten) days after the completion of test and the Buyer's acceptance.

5. The Sellers will be responsible for obtaining approvals from the International Communications Satellite Consortium for temporary operation of the Transportable Earth Station contracted herein with the Pacific Ocean Satellites and for obtaining approvals for the necessary units of utilization.

6. On the basis of equality and mutual benefit and in accordance with the stipulations as listed in Attachment B, both parties shall co-operate to ensure the commencement of operation of the Earth Station with the Satellite on or before the 18th of February 1972. The Earth Station will be considered to be accepted if the equipment meets the subsystem specification (to be provided) and the ICSC requirements and the station is capable of normal operation during the period of 18 February to 1 March 1972.

7. No changes of this Contract will be made by any party except mutually agreed in writing by both parties.

8. Any disputes arising during the execution of this Contract will be settled through friendly consultation.

The Buyers: The Sellers:

Attachment B

In addition to all other terms and conditions specified thereof in the contract, the responsibilities and obligations of both parties will include the following:

1. The Sellers will

    (a) despatch engineers and technicians up to 20 persons for installation, testing, operation and maintenance, and ensure the Transportable Earth Station in sound performance and smooth operation.

    (b) be responsible, during the period of the 18th of February to the 1st of March 1972 for the operation and maintenance as well as to ensure the normal working of the Transportable Earth Station.

    (c) despatch engineers or 2 to 3 technicians for installation and testing of the replacing parts as listed in Attachment A.*

    (d) provide technical personnels as designated by the Buyers with instruction and training during the installation, test and operation of the Earth Station.

2. The Buyers will

    (a) be responsible for the transportation of the Transportable Earth Station from Shanghai airport to the site for installation.

    (b) provide vehicles and laborers for the installation site.

    (c) provide food, housing, medical care, transportation and office for the engineers and technicians despatched by the Sellers.

    (d) provide power and fuel for diesel generator.

    (e) provide a site, shelter for power generator fuel tanks, and storage area.

*Omitted.

Appendix M

Sales Confirmation

China National Textiles Import and Export Corporation
82, Tung An Men Street, Peking, China

Cable Address:
"Chinatex" Peking

No. _____

Date _____ 19____ .

To Messrs.

Your Reference:

Our Reference:

For Account of Messrs:

We hereby confirm having sold to you on _____ 19____ , the following goods on terms and conditions as set forth hereunder:

Article No.	Commodity and Specification	Quantity	Unit Price & Terms	Amount

Total Value: Total Amount

Shipment: Destination:

Payment:

Special Clause:

Remarks: Insurance:

General Terms & Conditions: (Please see overleaf)

Important: When establishing L/C, please indicate the number of this Sales confirmation in the L/C.

China National Textiles Import and Export Corporation

_____
(The Sellers)

_____
(The Buyers)

Please sign and return one copy to the Sellers.

General Terms and Conditions

The sale specified in this Sales Confirmation shall be subject to the following terms and conditions unless otherwise agreed upon between the Buyers and the Sellers. In case of any inconsistency of the terms and conditions between this Sales Confirmation and any form of contract or order or indent sent by the Buyers to the Sellers (irrespective of its date), the provisions of this Sales Confirmation shall prevail. If the Buyers resell the goods to, or conclude the transaction as representative of a third party, the Buyers shall still be responsible for the complete performance of all the obligations stipulated in this Sales Confirmation.

1. A usual trade margin of 5% plus or minus of the quantities confirmed shall be allowed. Where shipment is spread over two or more periods, the above-mentioned trade margin of plus or minus 5% shall, when necessary, be applicable to the quantity designated by the Buyers to be shipped each period.

2. Shipment may be made from any Chinese Port, the date of Bill of Lading shall be taken as the date of shipment. Any change of destination should be agreed to by the Sellers beforehand. Extra freight and/or insurance premium thus incurred are to be borne by the Buyers.

3. In the event of force majeure or any other contingencies beyond the Sellers' control, the Sellers shall not be held responsible for late delivery or nondelivery of the goods.

4. Unless otherwise agreed to by the Sellers, payment is to be made against sight draft drawn under a Confirmed, Irrevocable, Divisible & Assignable Letter of Credit, Without Recourse for the full amount, established through a first class bank acceptable to the Sellers. The Letter of Credit in due form must reach the Sellers at least 30 days before the month of shipment stipulated in this Sales Confirmation, failing which the Sellers shall not be responsible for shipment as stipulated; in case the Buyers' credit still fails to reach the Sellers after the expiry of the shipping period, the Sellers shall have the right to cancel this Sales Confirmation and claim for damage against the Buyers.

5. The Buyers are requested to refrain from SPECIFYING ANY PARTICULAR SHIPPING LINE, NAME OF STEAMER, or INSURANCE COMPANY in the letter of Credit. To facilitate negotiation of the credit by the Sellers, the validity of the Letter of Credit shall be so stipulated as to remain valid for at least 10 days (expiring in China) after the last day of shipment and the amount, quantity of the credit shall allow plus or minus 5%. The Buyers are requested always to stipulate in the Letter of Credit that TRANSHIPMENT AND PARTIAL SHIPMENT ARE ALLOWED.

6. a. For grey goods, the counts of yarn indicated in this Sales Confirmation are those which were used in weaving, and the numbers of ends and picks per square inch shall allow plus or minus one percent (1%) in warp and/or weft way.

b. For bleached, dyed, printed and yarn-dyed goods, the counts of yarn and the numbers of ends and picks indicated are those which were in loom-state.

7. For printed, dyed and yarn-dyed goods, a maximum of 10% of two-part pieces with the short part not less than 10 yds. is permissible if necessary and for each two-part piece an additional length of ½ yd. (half yard) will be supplied free. Also a

tolerance of plus or minus 10% in quantity for each colourway (for each shade in case of dyed goods) shall be permitted.

8. Designs, Colourways and Colour Shades for printed, dyed, bleached and yarn-dyed goods designated by the Buyers or chosen by the Buyers from the Sellers designs, colourways and colour shades must be sent to reach or made known to the Sellers at least 45 days (for yarn-dyed goods 90 days) before the month of shipment stipulated in this Sales Confirmation and subject to final acceptance by the mills. Otherwise the Sellers will have the option either to cancel the transaction or to postpone the time of shipment which the Buyers should not refuse to accept on any excuses and the Buyers shall be held responsible for compensation of whatever losses thus incurred to the Sellers.

9. Acting upon the request of the mills, the Sellers shall have the right to make minor alterations to the designs designated or chosen by the buyers. For printed, dyed and yarn-dyed goods, reasonable tolerance in colour shades must be allowed.

10. For colours of the prints designated exceeding those confirmed, special designs for producing yarn-dyed goods, and colour shades requiring more expensive dyes prices should be adequately adjusted through negotiation.

11. Sellers' trade mark, stamping and mode of folding and packing will be accepted by the Buyers. The Buyers should not refuse to accept on any excuses, and in case of any damage thus incurred to the Sellers, the Sellers shall reserve the right to claim against the Buyers for damage.

12. The Sellers are to cover insurance at invoice value plus 10% thereof of the goods sold on CIF basis. If the Letter of Credit stipulates that the goods after arrival at the port of destination are to be transported to an inland city or some other ports, the Sellers will cover insurance up to that city or ports, and the Buyers are to be responsible for payment of this additional premium.

13. Claims for damage should be filed by the Buyers with the Sellers within 30 days after arrival of the goods at destination and supported by sufficient evidence for Sellers' reference so that claims can be settled through friendly negotiation.

14. The Buyers are requested to sign and return one original copy to the Sellers for file immediately upon receipt of this Sales Confirmation. Should the Buyers fail to do so within 10 days after arrival of this Sales Confirmation at the Buyers' end, it shall be considered that the Buyers have accepted all the terms and conditions set forth in this Sales Confirmation.

Appendix N

Purchase Contracts

No. _____

Peking. Date: _____

This Contract is made by and between the China National Light Industrial Products Import and Export Corporation at 82 Tung An Men Street, Peking, China, (Cable Address: ''Industry'' Peking) hereinafter called the Buyers and the

(Cable Address:) hereinafter called the Sellers; whereby the Buyers agree to buy and the Sellers agree to sell the commodities on the terms and conditions stipulated below:

1. COMMODITY, SPECIFICATIONS, QUANTITY AND UNIT PRICE:

2. TOTAL VALUE:

3. COUNTRY OF ORIGIN AND MANUFACTURERS:

4. PACKING: To be packed in strong wooden case(s) or in carton(s), suitable for long distance ocean/parcel post/air freight transportation and to change of climate, well protected against moisture and shocks. The Sellers shall be liable for any damage of the commodity and expenses incident thereto on account of improper packing and or improper protective measures taken by the Sellers in regard to the packing.

5. SHIPPING MARK: The Sellers shall mark on each package with fadeless paint the package number, gross weight, net weight, measurement and the wordings: ''KEEP AWAY FROM MOISTURE'' ''HANDLE WITH CARE,'' etc., and the shipping mark:

6. TIME OF SHIPMENT:

7. PORT OF SHIPMENT:

8. PORT OF DESTINATION:

9. INSURANCE: To be covered by the Buyers after shipment.

10. PAYMENT: The Buyers, upon receipt from the Sellers of the delivery advice specified in Article 14 hereof, shall, in 15-20 days prior to the date of delivery, open an irrevocable Letter of Credit with the Bank of China, in favour of the Sellers, for an amount equivalent to the total value of the shipment. The Credit shall be payable against the presentation of draft drawn on the opening bank and the shipping documents specified in Article 13 hereof. The Letter of Credit shall be valid until the 15th day after the shipment is effected.

11. GUARANTEE OF QUALITY: The Sellers guarantee that the commodity hereof is made of the best materials with first class workmanship, brand new and unused, and complies in all respects with the quality and specification stipulated in this Contract.

12. CLAIMS: Within 90 days after the arrival of the goods at destination, should the quality, specification, or quantity be found not in conformity with the stipulations of the Contract except those claims for which the insurance company or the owners of the vessel are liable, the Buyers shall, on the strength of the Inspection Certificate issued by the China Commodity Inspection Bureau, have the right to claim for replacement with new goods, or for compensation, and all the expenses (such as inspection charges, freight for returning the goods and for sending the replacement, insurance premium, storage and loading and unloading charges etc.) shall be borne by the Sellers.

The Certificate so issued shall be accepted as the base of a claim. The Sellers, in accordance with the Buyers' claim shall be responsible for the immediate elimination of the defect(s), complete or partial replacement of the commodity or shall devaluate the commodity according to the state of defect(s). Where necessary, the Buyers shall be at liberty to eliminate the defect(s) themselves at the Sellers' expenses. If the Sellers fail to answer the Buyers within one month after receipt of the claim aforesaid, the claim shall be reckoned as having been accepted by the Sellers.

13. DOCUMENTS: The Sellers shall present to the paying bank the following documents for negotiation:

(1) In case by sea:
3 Negotiable copies of clean on board ocean Bill of Lading marked "FREIGHT TO COLLECT"/"FREIGHT PREPAID," made out to order, blank endorsed, and notifying the China National Foreign Trade Transportation Corporation at the port of destination.
In case by air freight:
One copy of Air Waybill marked "FREIGHT PREPAID" addressed to the China National Foreign Trade Transportation Corporation at port of destination.
In case by post:
One copy of Parcel Post Receipt.

(2) 5 copies of Invoice with the insertion of Contract No. and the Shipping Mark. (in case of more than one shipping mark, the invoice shall be issued separately).

(3) 4 copies of Packing List issued by the Manufacturers.

(4) 1 copy of Certificate of Quantity and Quality issued by the Manufacturers.

(5) Certified copy of cable/letter to the Buyers, advising shipment immediately after shipment is made.

(6) The Sellers shall, within 10 days after the shipment is effected, send by air-mail three copies each of the above-mentioned documents (except Item 5) two sets to the Buyers and the other set to the China National Foreign Trade Transportation Corporation at the port of destination.

14. SHIPMENT:

(1) In case of FOB Terms:

a. The Sellers shall, 30 days before the date of shipment stipulated in the Contract, advise the Buyers by cable/letter the Contract No., commodity, quantity, value, number of package, gross weight and date of readiness at the port of shipment for the Buyers to book shipping space.

b. Booking of shipping space shall be attended to by the Buyers' Shipping Agents Messrs. Sinofracht Chartering & Shipbroking Corporation, Peking.

c. Sinofracht, Peking, or their Port Agents, (or Liners' Agents) shall send to the Sellers 10 days before the estimated date of arrival of the vessel at the port of shipment, a preliminary notice indicating the name of vessel, estimated date of loading, Contract No. for the Sellers to arrange shipment. The Sellers are requested to get in close contact with the shipping agents. When it becomes necessary to change the carrying vessel or in the event of her arrival having to be advanced or delayed, the Buyers or the Shipping Agency shall advise the Sellers in time.

Should the vessel fail to arrive at the port of loading within 30 days after the arrival date advised by the Buyers, the Buyers shall bear the storage and insurance expenses incurred from the 31st day.

d. The Sellers shall be liable for any dead freight or demurrage, should it happen that they have failed to have the commodity ready for loading after the carrying vessel has arrived at the port of shipment on time.

e. The Sellers shall bear all expenses, risks of the commodity before it passes over the vessel's rail and is released from the tackle. After it has passed over the vessel's rail and been released from the tackle, all expenses of the commodity shall be for the Buyers' account.

(2) In case of C&F Terms:

a. The Sellers shall ship the goods within the shipment time from the port of shipment to the port of destination. Transhipment is not allowed. The carrying vessel shall not fly the flag of USA or shall her captain be of USA nationality nor shall she call en route at any port of USA or in the vicinity of Taiwan.

b. In case the goods are to be despatched by parcel post/air-freight, the Sellers shall, 30 days before the time of delivery as stipulated in Article 6, inform the Buyers by cable/letter the estimated date of delivery, Contract No., commodity, invoiced value, etc. The sellers shall, immediately after despatch of the goods, advise the Buyers by cable/letter the Contract No., commodity, invoiced value and date of despatch for the Buyers to arrange insurance in time.

15. SHIPPING ADVICE: The Sellers shall, immediately upon the completion of the loading of the goods, advise by cable/letter the Buyers of the Contract No., commodity, quantity, invoiced value, gross weight, name of vessel and date of sailing etc. In case the Buyers fail to arrange insurance in time due to the Sellers not having cabled in time, all losses shall be borne by the Sellers.

16. FORCE MAJEURE: The Sellers shall not be held responsible for the delay in

shipment or non-delivery of the goods due to Force Majeure, which might occur during the process of manufacturing or in the course of loading or transit. The Sellers shall advise the Buyers immediately of the occurrence mentioned above and within fourteen days thereafter, the Sellers shall send by airmail to the Buyers a certificate of the accident issued by the Competent Government Authorities where the accident occurs as evidence thereof. Under such circumstances the Sellers, however, are still under the obligation to take all necessary measures to hasten the delivery of the goods. In case the accident lasts for more than 10 weeks, the Buyers shall have the right to cancel the Contract.

17. ARBITRATION: All disputes in connection with the execution of this Contract shall be settled through friendly negotiations, failing which, each Party shall appoint one arbitrator who will nominate one umpire thus to form an arbitration committee. Arbitration is to take place at. . . . . .. The award of the Arbitration Committee shall be accepted as final by both Parties for settlement. Arbitration fee, unless otherwise awarded, shall be borne by the losing party. The Arbitrators and the umpire shall be confined to persons of Chinese or . . . Nationality.

In case the Arbitration is to be held in Peking, the case in dispute shall then be submitted for arbitration to the Foreign Trade Arbitration Commission of the China Council for the Promotion of International Trade, Peking, in accordance with the "Provisional Rules of Procedure of the Foreign Trade Arbitration Commission of the China Council for the Promotion of International Trade." The decision by the Commission shall be accepted as final and binding upon both parties.

18. PENALTY: If the Sellers fail to effect the delivery at the contracted time of delivery, the Buyers shall have the option to cancel this Contract and demand for all losses resulted therefrom, or alternatively, the Sellers may postpone delivery with the Buyers' consent, on the condition that the Sellers pay to the Buyers a penalty 1.5% of the goods value for a delay within 30 days and further 0.5% for every 15 days thereafter. The penalty shall be deducted by the paying bank during the negotiation of payment.

19. REMARK:

IN WITNESS THEREOF, this Contract is signed by both parties on the date as above-mentioned in two original copies; each party holds one copy.

THE SELLERS: THE BUYERS:

China National Light Industrial Products
Import & Export Corporation

Purchase Contract
China National Chemicals Import & Export Corporation

CONTRACT NO.:
PEKING

The Buyers: CHINA NATIONAL CHEMICALS IMPORT & EXPORT
CORPORATION,
Erh Li Kou, Peking, Cable Address: "SINOCHEM" PEKING

The Sellers:

This Contract is made by and between the Buyers and the Sellers; whereby the Buyers agree to buy and the Sellers agree to sell the under-mentioned goods subject to the terms and conditions as stipulated hereinafter:

(1) Name of Commodity and Specification:

(2) Quantity:

(3) Unit Price:

(4) Total Value:

(5) Packing:

(6) Country of Origin & Manufacturer:

(7) Terms of Payment: After conclusion of business the Buyers shall open with the Bank of China, Peking, an irrevocable letter of credit in favour of the Sellers payable at the issuing Bank against presentation of the shipping documents as stipulated under Clause 3(A) of the Terms of Delivery of this Contract after departure of the carrying vessel. The said letter of credit shall remain in force till the 15th day after shipment.

(8) Insurance: To be covered by the Buyers.

(9) Time of Shipment:

(10) Port of Loading:

(11) Port of Destination:

(12) Shipping Mark(s): On each package shall be stencilled conspicuously: port of destination, package number, gross and net weights, measurement and the shipping mark shown on the right side. (For dangerous and/or poisonous cargo, the nature and the generally adopted symbol shall be marked conspicuously on each package.

(13) Other terms: (a) Other matters relating to this Contract shall be dealt with in accordance with the Terms of Delivery as specified overleaf, which shall form an integral part of this Contract. (b) This Contract is made out in Chinese and English, both versions being equally authentic.

(14) Supplementary Condition(s) (Should any other clause in this Contract be in conflict with the following Supplementary Condition(s), the Supplementary Condition(s) should be taken as final and binding.):

THE SELLERS   THE BUYERS

Terms of Delivery

Terms of Shipment: For C & F Terms: The Sellers shall ship the goods within the time as stipulated in Clause (9) of this Contract by a direct vessel sailing from the port of loading to China Port. Transhipment en route is not allowed without the Buyers' consent. The goods should not be carried by vessels flying the flags of the countries not acceptable to the Buyers. The carrying vessel shall not call or stop over at the port/ports of Taiwan Province and the port/ports in the vicinity of Taiwan Province prior to her arrival at the port of destination as stipulated in the Clause (11) of this Contract.

For FOB Terms: (A) The shipping space for the contracted goods shall be booked by the Buyers or the Buyers' shipping agent, China National Chartering Corporation (Address: Erh Li Kou, Peking. Cable Address: ZHONGZU PEKING). The Sellers shall undertake to load the contracted goods on board the vessel nominated by the Buyers on any date notified by the Buyers, within the time of shipment stipulated in the Clause (9) of this Contract.

(B) 10-15 days prior to the date of shipment, the Buyers shall inform the Sellers by cable of the contract number, name of vessel, ETA of vessel, quantity and the name of shipping agent, so as to enable the latter to contact the shipping agent direct and arrange the shipment of the goods. The Sellers shall cable in time the Buyers of the result thereof. Should, for certain reasons, it become necessary for the Buyers to replace the named vessel with another one, or should the named vessel arrive at the port of shipment earlier or later than the date of arrival as previously notified to the Sellers, the Buyers or their shipping agent shall advise the Sellers to this effect in due time. The Sellers shall also keep close contact with the agent of Zhongzu.

(C) Should the Sellers fail to load the goods, within the time as notified by the Buyers, on board the vessel booked by the Buyers after its arrival at the port of shipment, all expenses such as dead freight, demurrage, etc., and consequences thereof shall be borne by the Sellers. Should the vessel be withdrawn or replaced or delayed eventually or the cargo be shut out, etc., and the Sellers are not informed in good time to stop delivery of the cargo, the calculation of the loss for storage expenses and insurance premium thus sustained at the loading port should be based on the loading date notified by the agent to the Sellers (or based on the date of the arrival of the cargo at the loading port in case the cargo should arrive there later than the notified loading date). The above-mentioned loss to be calculated from the 16th day after expiry of the free storage time at the port should be borne by the Buyers with the exception of Force Majeure. However, the Sellers still undertake to load the cargo immediately upon the carrying vessel's arrival at the loading port at their own risks and expenses. The payment of the afore-said expenses shall be effected against presentation of the original vouchers after being checked.

Advice of Shipment: Immediately after the completion of loading of goods on board the vessel the Sellers shall advise the Buyers by cable of the contract number, name of goods, quantity or weight loaded, invoice value, name of vessel, port of shipment, sailing date and port of destination.

Should the Buyers be made unable to arrange insurance in time owing to the Sellers' failure to give the above-mentioned advice of shipment by cable, the Sellers shall be held responsible for any and all damage and/or loss attributable to such failure.

Shipping Documents: (A) The Sellers shall present the following documents to the paying bank for negotiation of payment: (a) Full set of clean on board, "freight prepaid" for C & F Terms or "freight to collect" for FOB Terms, ocean Bills of Lading, made out to order and blank endorsed, notifying the Branch of China National Foreign Trade Transportation Corporation at the port of destination. (b) Five copies of signed invoice, indicating contract number and shipping marks. (c) Two copies of packing list and/or weight memo. (d) One copy each of the certificates of quality and quantity or weight, as stipulated in the Clause 5 of the Terms of Delivery. (e) One duplicate copy of the cable advice of shipment, as stipulated in the Clause 2 of the Terms of Delivery.

(B) The Sellers shall despatch, in care of the carrying vessel, one copy each of the duplicates of Bill of Lading, Invoice and Packing List to the Buyers' receiving agent, the Branch of China National Foreign Trade Transportation Corporation at the port of destination.

(C) Immediately after the departure of the carrying vessel, the Sellers shall airmail one set of the duplicate documents to the Buyers and two sets to the Branch of China National Foreign Trade Transportation Corporation at the port of destination.

Dangerous Cargo Instruction Leaflets: For dangerous and/or poisonous cargo, the Sellers must provide instruction leaflets stating the hazardous or poisonous properties, transportation, storage and handling remarks, as well as precautionary and first-aid measures and measures against fire. The Sellers shall airmail, together with other shipping documents, three copies each of the same to the Buyers and the Branch of China National Foreign Trade Transportation Corporation at the port of destination.

Inspection: It is mutually agreed that the certificates of quality and quantity or weight issued by the Manufacturer shall be part of the documents to be presented to the paying bank for negotiation of payment. However, the inspection of quality and quantity or weight shall be made in accordance with the following:

(A) For General Cargo: In case the quality, quantity or weight of the goods be found not in conformity with those stipulated in this Contract after re-inspection by the China Commodity Inspection Bureau within 60 days after arrival of the goods at the port of destination, the Buyers shall reject the goods delivered and/or lodge claims against the Sellers for compensation of losses upon the strength of Inspection Certificate issued by the said Bureau, with the exception of those claims for which the insurers or owners of the carrying vessel are liable. All expenses (including inspection fees) and losses arising from the return of the goods or claims should be borne by the Sellers. In such case, the Buyers may, if so requested, send a sample of the goods in question to the Sellers, provided that sampling is feasible.

(B) For Pharmaceuticals: Pharmaceuticals imported into China are subject to laws and regulations of the People's Republic of China. Disqualified pharmaceuticals are prohibited to be imported. It is mutually agreed that for the quality of the contracted goods in this category, the Inspection Certificate issued by the China Commodity Inspection Bureau after inspecting the goods within 60 days from the date of arrival at the port of destination shall be taken as final and binding upon both Parties. The Sellers shall take back all the disqualified goods and compensate the Buyers for the value of the goods plus all losses sustained due to rejection of the cargo, such as freight, storage charges, insurance premium, interest, inspection charges, etc. Should the quantity/weight be found not in conformity with those stipulated in this Contract after inspection by the China Commodity Inspection Bureau, the Buyers shall have the right to claim against the Sellers for compensation of losses within 60 days after the arrival of the goods at the port of destination on the basis of the Inspection Certificate issued by the said Bureau.

Force Majeure: The Sellers shall not be held responsible for late delivery or non-delivery of the goods owing to generally recognized "Force Majeure" causes. However, in such case, the Sellers shall immediately cable the Buyers of the accident and airmail to the Buyers within 15 days after the accident, a certificate of the accident issued by the competent government authorities or the chamber of commerce which is located at the place where the accident occurs as evidence thereof. With the exception of late delivery or non-delivery due to "Force Majeure" causes, in case the Sellers fail to make delivery within the time as stipulated in the Contract, the Sellers should indemnify the Buyers for all losses and expenses incurred to the latter directly attributable to late delivery or failure to make delivery of the goods in accordance with the terms of this Contract. If the "Force Majeure" cause lasts over 60 days, the Buyers shall have the right to cancel the Contract or the undelivered part of the Contract.

Arbitration: All disputes in connection with this Contract or the execution thereof shall be amicably settled through negotiation. In case no settlement can be reached between the two Parties, the case under dispute shall be submitted to the Foreign Trade Arbitration Commission of the China Council for the Promotion of International Trade for arbitration. The arbitration shall take place in Peking, China and shall be executed in accordance with the Provisional Rules of Procedure of the said Commission and the decision made by the Arbitration Commission shall be accepted as final and binding upon both Parties. The fees for arbitration shall be borne by the losing Party unless otherwise awarded.

Appendix O

Agency Agreement

CHINA NATIONAL MACHINERY
IMPORT & EXPORT CORPORATION

AGENCY AGREEMENT

On the basis of equality and mutual benefit, an agency agreement is made by China National Machinery Import and Export Corporation (hereinafter called Party A) and — — Co. (hereinafter called Party B) whereby Party A appoints Party B as sole agent in the entire territory of [name of country] for all kinds of [name of products] made in China on the terms and conditions stipulated as follows:

1. Validity: Commencing from [date, month, year] to [date, month, year]. If either Party intends to extend the validity of this agreement and make any amendment or supplement, a written notice should be given to the other Party three months before the expiry of this agreement. Otherwise, this agreement shall automatically become null and void at the expiry of the term.

2. During the period of this agreement, Party B should place with Party A orders for [name of the same products] amounting from [amount of money] to [amount of money].

3. Party A shall grant — — percent special discount to Party B provided Letter of Credits to be opened within the agency period amounting to [amount of money].

4. Party B shall not purchase any [name of the same products] from other countries.

5. Party A shall not sell directly all [the products] to other buyers in [name of the same country].

6. Terms of Payment: Party B shall open a confirmed irrevocable transferable without recourse Letter of Credit available at 180 days draft after the date of Bill of Lading through a first class bank in favor of Party A. The L/C should reach the Sellers two months before the date of shipment and shall remain valid for negotiation in China 15 days after the date of shipment.

7. Party A shall provide Party B with sufficient quantity of catalogues in English free of charge.

8. Party B undertakes the responsibility to give the customers all the necessary technical services to the [products] to be supplied by Party A and shall furnish Party A with information on the quality of the [products]. It is clearly understood that Party A will expedite delivery of spare parts for each [product] at reasonable prices to enable Party B to carry out the maintenance of the [products].

9. Party B undertake to submit to Party A every 6 months a market report relating to market conditions, sales tendency, fluctuation on price, government regulations, competitors activities and the reflection from endusers concerning the [products] supplied by Party A.

10. Should any conditions of this agreement be found inadequate, unless otherwise stipulated in contracts, amendment or supplement may be made through negotiations between the two Parties.

11. Done and signed in Peking on this   day of [month, year].

Signature of Party A   Signature of Party B

Appendix P

Distributorship Agreement

CHINA NATIONAL CHEMICALS IMPORT & EXPORT CORPORATION
TRADE DELEGATION
KWANGCHOW, CHINA

DISTRIBUTORSHIP AGREEMENT

No._____

Date:_____

This agreement is made by and entered into between China National Chemicals Import & Export Corporation, Shanghai Branch, Shanghai, China (hereinafter referred to as Party A) and XX Co. (hereinafter referred to as Party B), whereby Party A agree to appoint Party B together with XXX Co. to act as their distributors for the under-mentioned commodity in the designated territory upon the terms and conditions hereafter set forth:

(1) *Name of Commodity:*

(2) *Territory:* The territory covered by this Agreement is confined to (name of country) only. Party A agree not to sell any of the (specified commodity) to other firms or importers for the sales in the said territory. Party B shall handle with efficiency and diligence so as to secure the maximum volume of sales. Party B agree not to handle any of the (specified commodity) from any source other than China.

(3) *Minimum Turnover:* Party B and XXX undertake to place with Party A orders amounting to a minimum quantity of 500 metric tons (250 M/T each for Party B and X X X) of the (specified commodity) and shall try their best to reach the quantity of 530 metric tons during the period of one year of this Agreement. The amount of the order placed during the first six months of the Agreement should not be less than half of the minimum quantity as above mentioned.

(4) *Price:* Price should be fixed 15 days before each quarter of the year for the supply of the coming quarter through negotiation between Party A, Party B and X X X. Party B should cooperate with X X X and negotiate with them the prices for the sales in the market in order to avoid any competition.

(5) *Payment:* Upon confirmation of order, Party B shall open confirmed irrevocable letter of credit available at sight in the name of Party A as the beneficiary. The L/C should reach Party A 30 days ahead of each shipment.

(6) *Market Report:* Party B undertake to supply each quarter of the year to Party A a comprehensive market report of the (specified commodity) of this Agreement. Party B shall keep Party A duly advised of any information or events of urgent character.

(7) *Validity of the Agreement:* This Agreement is to remain valid for a period of one calendar year, commencing January 1, 19   and terminating on December 31, 19   , and shall automatically become null and void at the expiration of the said period. If either Party considers it necessary to extend the Agreement, the proposing Party may take the initiative to conduct negotiation with the other Party and meanwhile to inform X X X one month prior to its expiration.

(8) In the event of breach of any of the provisions of this Agreement by either Party, the other Party may at its option cancel this Agreement forthwith, by giving notice in writing to the defaulting Party of its intention to so cancel it.

Signature of Party A   Signature of Party B

Appendix Q

Insurance Contract

The People's Insurance Company of China
Insurance Certificate

Assured's Name: *China National Chemicals Imp. & Exp. Corp.*

We have this day noted a risk as hereunder mentioned in your favour, subject to all clauses and conditions of the Company's printed form of Policy and to the special terms outlined herein (which latter shall override the policy terms in so far as they may be inconsistent therewith).

Marks & Nos.	Quantity	Description of Goods	Amount Insured

Total Amount Insured:

Premium: Rate:

Per conveyance S.S.:   Slg. on or abt.:

From:

Conditions &/or   Covering all Risks from warehouse to warehouse
Special Coverage: to warehouse inland —————— subject to The
                         Ocean Marine Cargo Clauses — All Risks of The
                         People's Insurance Company of China.

                         Including risks of War subject to The Ocean Marine
                         Cargo War Risks Clauses.

Claims, if any, payable to the Holder of the appertaining documents and on surrender of this Certificate.

In the event of accident whereby loss or damage may result in a claim under this Certificate immediate notice must be given to the nearest Company's Agent as mentioned hereunder.

This certificate is issued in duplicate.

Claim payable at: destination

DATE _____   Tientsin _____

Important

Liability Of Carriers, Bailees Or Other Third Parties.

It is the duty of the Assured and their Agents, in all cases, to take such measures as may be reasonable for the purpose of averting or minimising a loss and to ensure that all rights against Carriers, Bailees or other third parties are properly preserved and exercised. In particular, the Assured or their Agents are required:

1. To claim immediately on the Carriers and on the Port Authorities for any missing packages.

2. To apply immediately for survey in the docks by Carriers' representative if any loss or damage be apparent and claim on the Carriers for any actual loss or damage found at such survey.

3. In no circumstances, except under written protest, to give clean receipts where goods are in doubtful condition.

4. To give notice in writing to the Carriers' representative within three days of delivery if the loss or damage was not apparent at the time of taking delivery.

Note. — The Consignees or their Agents are recommended to make themselves familiar with the Regulations of the Port Authorities at the port of discharge.

Any claim under this insurance should be submitted without delay, accompanied by all correspondence with Carriers and other parties regarding their liability.

Survey

In the event of damage which may involve a claim under this policy or certificate immediate notice of such damage should be given to and a Survey Report obtained from the Company's Agents as mentioned in this policy or certificate.

Appendix R

Decision of the Government Administration Council of the Central People's Government Concerning the Establishment of a Foreign Trade Arbitration Commission within the China Council for the Promotion of International Trade*

(Adopted on May 6, 1954, at the 215th Session of the Government Administration Council)

With a view to settling by way of arbitration any dispute that may arise in relation to foreign trade, it is necessary to set up an arbitral body within a social organization concerned with foreign trade. It is hereby decided as follows:

(1) There shall be established within the China Council for the Promotion of International Trade a Foreign Trade Arbitration Commission (hereinafter referred to as the Arbitration Commission) to settle such disputes as may arise from contracts and transactions in foreign trade, particularly disputes between foreign firms, companies or other economic organizations on the one hand and Chinese firms, companies or other economic organizations on the other.

(2) The Arbitration Commission exercises jurisdiction for the arbitration of disputes in foreign trade in accordance with the relevant contracts, agreements and/or other documents concluded between the disputing parties.

(3) The Arbitration Commission shall be composed of 15 to 21 members to be selected and appointed by the China Council for the Promotion of International Trade for a term of one year from among persons having special knowledge and experience in foreign trade, commerce, industry, agriculture, transportation, insurance, and other related matters as well as in law.

(4) The Arbitration Commission shall elect a Chairman and two Deputy Chairmen from among its members.

(5) When a case of dispute is submitted for arbitration, the disputing parties shall each choose an arbitrator from among the members of the Arbitration Commission. The arbitrators so chosen shall jointly select an umpire from among the members of the Arbitration Commission to act jointly with the arbitrators. The disputing parties

*SOURCE: *Chung-hua jen-min kung-ho-kuo fa-kuei hsüan-chi*, pp. 470-478; English translation in National Council for United States-China Trade Special Report no. 4, *Arbitration and Dispute Settlement in Trade with China* (1974), pp. 48-57.

may also jointly choose a sole arbitrator from among the members of the Arbitration Commission to act singly.

The disputing parties shall choose the arbitrators within the time fixed by the Arbitration Commission or agreed upon between the parties, and the arbitrators so chosen shall also select the umpire within the time fixed by the Arbitration Commission. If one of the parties fail to choose an arbitrator within the prescribed time limit, the Chairman of the Arbitration Commission shall, upon the request of the other party, appoint the arbitrator on the former's behalf. In case the arbitrators so chosen or appointed cannot agree upon the choice of the umpire within the prescribed time limit, the Chairman of the Arbitration Commission shall select an umpire for them.

(6) Either of the parties in dispute may authorize the Arbitration Commission to choose for him an arbitrator who shall, jointly with the arbitrator chosen by the other party, select an umpire to arbitrate the disputed case in association with the arbitrators. If, by mutual agreement, both parties jointly delegate the choice of arbitrators to the Arbitration Commission, the Chairman of the Arbitration Commission may appoint a sole arbitrator to conduct the proceedings singly.

(7) The disputing parties may appoint attorneys to defend their interests during the proceedings of a case before the Arbitration Commission.

Such attorneys may be citizens of the People's Republic of China or foreign citizens.

(8) During the proceedings of a case, the Arbitration Commission may, for the purpose of safeguarding the interests of the disputing parties, prescribe provisional measures concerning the materials, property rights and/or other matters appertaining to the parties.

(9) To compensate for the costs of arbitration, the Arbitration Commission may collect a fee not exceeding one percent of the amount of the claim.

(10) The award given by the Arbitration Commission is final and neither party shall bring an appeal for revision before a court of law or any other organization.

(11) The award of the Arbitration Commission shall be executed by the parties themselves within the time fixed by the award. In case an award is not executed after the expiration of the fixed time, the People's Courts of the People's Republic of China shall, upon the request of one of the parties, enforce it in accordance with law.

(12) Rules concerning the Procedure of Arbitration shall be made by the China Council for the Promotion of International Trade.

Provisional Rules of Procedure of the Foreign Trade Arbitration Commission of the China Council for the Promotion of International Trade.

(Adopted on March 31, 1956 at the Fourth Session of
the China Council for the Promotion of International Trade)

1. The present Rules are made in accordance with Article 12 of the Decision of the Government Administration Council of the Central People's Government adopted at its 215th Session on May 6, 1954 concerning the establishment of a Foreign Trade Arbitration Commission within the China Council for the Promotion of International Trade.

2. The Foreign Trade Arbitration Commission (hereinafter referred to as the Arbitration Commission) exercises jurisdiction for the arbitration of disputes arising from contracts and transactions in foreign trade, particularly disputes between foreign firms, companies or other economic organizations on the one hand and Chinese firms, companies or other economic organizations on the other. It may also exercise jurisdiction for the arbitration of similar cases arising between foreign firms, companies or economic organizations as well as between Chinese firms, companies or other economic organizations.

Such disputes include all disputes arising from contracts for purchase or sale of merchandise in foreign countries or contracts for commissioning an agency to purchase or sell merchandise in foreign countries, disputes arising from transportation, insurance, safekeeping or delivery of the merchandise in question and disputes arising from other matters of business in foreign trade.

3. The Arbitration Commission exercises jurisdiction for the arbitration of a dispute referred to in the preceding Section upon the written application of one of the disputing parties and in accordance with the written agreement between the parties which stipulates for the submission of the dispute to the Aritration Commission for settlement.

The agreement referred to above means the arbitration clause stipulated in the original trade contract or trade agreement, or any other form of agreement to submit to arbitration (such as special agreement, exchange of correspondence or any specific stipulation contained in other relevant documents).

4. The following items must be specified in the application for arbitration:

(a) the name and address of the plaintiff and those of the defendant;

(b) the claim of the plaintiff and the facts and evidence upon which the claim is based;

(c) the name of an arbitrator chosen by the plaintiff from among the members of the Arbitration Commission or a statement authorizing the Chairman of the Arbitration Commission to appoint the arbitrator on behalf of the plaintiff.

5. Original documents (contracts, arbitration agreements, correspondence between the parties, etc.,) relevant to the application, or certified duplicates or copies thereof, must accompany the application for arbitration.

6. When submitting an application for arbitration, the plaintiff shall pay a sum equivalent to 0.5 per cent of the amount of the claim as a deposit for the fee required to cover the costs of arbitration.

Such deposits shall be paid to the Arbitration Commission.

7. The application for arbitration and its appended documents submitted to the Arbitation Commission shall be accompanied by as many duplicates as the number of defendants.

8. Upon receipt of the application, the Arbitration Commission shall notify the defendant to that effect without delay and forward to him a duplicate of the application and all the appended documents.

9. Within fifteen days from the date of receipt of the notice the defendant shall either choose an arbitrator from among the members of the Arbitration Commission and notify the Arbitration Commission of his choice or authorize the Chairman of the Arbitration Commission to appoint the arbitrator on his behalf.

In case a different period of time is agreed upon between the parties, such agreement shall prevail.

The Arbitration Commission may also, upon the request of the defendant, alter the period of fifteen days.

10. Should the defendant fail to choose an arbitrator within the time specified in the preceding Section, the Chairman of the Arbitration Commission shall, upon the request of the plaintiff, appoint the arbitrator for the defendant.

11. The Arbitration Commission shall notify the arbitrators, whether chosen by the parties or appointed by the Chairman, to select an umpire from among the members of the Arbitration Commission within fifteen days from the date of receipt of the notice.

In case no agreement is reached between the chosen or appointed arbitrators regarding the selection of the umpire within the time limit stated in the preceding paragraph, the Chairman of the Arbitration Commission shall select the umpire on their behalf.

12. The disputing parties may jointly choose or authorize the Chairman of the Arbitration Commission to appoint for them a sole arbitrator from among the members of the Arbitration Commission to arbitrate the case singly.

In case the parties separately delegate the choice of arbitrators to the Chairman of the Arbitration Commission, the Chairman may, after obtaining the consent of the parties, appoint a sole arbitrator from among the members of the Arbitration Commission to arbitrate the case singly.

13. If an arbitrator is unable to perform his duties, the Arbitration Commission shall notify the party concerned to that effect and request him to choose a new

arbitrator from among the members of the Arbitration Commission within fifteen days from the date of receipt of the notice.

Should the said party fail to choose a new arbitrator within that time, the Chairman of the Arbitration Commission shall then appoint a new arbitrator on his behalf.

14. If an umpire is unable to perform his duties, the Arbitration Commission shall notify the arbitrators for the parties to that effect and request them to select a new umpire from among the members of the Arbitration Commission within fifteen days from the date of receipt of the notice.

Should the arbitrators fail to agree on the selection of the new umpire within that time, the Chairman of the Arbitration Commission shall then select a new umpire on their behalf.

15. Upon the request of one of the parties, the Chairman of the Arbitration Commission may, for the purpose of safeguarding the interests of the disputing parties, prescribe provisional measures concerning the materials, property rights and/or other matters appertaining to the parties.

16. The date for the hearing of the case shall be set by the Chairman of the Arbitration Commission in consultation with the umpire or the sole arbitrator as the case may be.

17. The Arbitration Commission may require the parties to give their explanations in writing before the date of hearing.

18. A disputing party may confer with the Arbitration Commission on matters relating to the proceedings either in person or by attorney.

Such attorneys may be citizens of the People's Republic of China or foreign citizens.

19. Hearings shall be held at the seat of the Arbitration Commission. Where necessary, hearings may, upon the approval of the Chairman of the Arbitration Commission, be held at other places within the Chinese territory.

20. Proceedings for the arbitration of a case are conducted by an Arbitration Tribunal formed by one umpire and two arbitrators sitting in a body. A sole arbitrator forms a Tribunal by himself and conducts the proceedings singly.

21. The Arbitration Tribunal shall hear both cases in open sessions, but it may, upon the request of both or either of the parties, decide to hold the hearings in closed sessions.

22. At every session of the Arbitration Tribunal, records shall be taken, and these records shall be signed by the umpire or the sole arbitrator as the case may be.

The Arbitration Tribunal may require the parties or their attorneys, witnesses or other persons to sign their names on the records for purpose of evidence.

23. The Arbitration Commission shall notify the parties of the date of hearing to be held by the Arbitration Tribunal.

24. The defendant may file a counter-claim against a claim over which the Arbitration Commission has assumed jurisdiction.

The provisions in Sections 2-7 of the present Rules apply likewise to counter-claims.

25. The parties shall produce evidence in support of the facts upon which their claims or pleadings are based.

26. The examination and appraisal of evidence shall be performed by the Arbitration Tribunal at its discretion.

An Arbitration Tribunal sitting in a body may decide to entrust one of its members with the work of the examination of evidence.

27. The Arbitration Tribunal may consult experts for the clarification of any questions concerning technical or special matters or business practices.

Such experts may be designated from among citizens of the People's Republic of China or foreign citizens.

28. Should one of the disputing parties or his attorney fail to appear at the hearing held by the Arbitration Tribunal, the Tribunal may upon the request of the party present, proceed with the hearing or render the award.

29. The award of an Arbitration Tribunal sitting in a body is decided by majority vote and the minority opinion may be made in writing and docketed into the file.

30. The principal part of the award shall be read to the parties at the closing session of the hearings.

The full award together with the reasons for the decision shall be made in writing within fifteen days from the date of the reading of the principal part. It shall be signed by the umpire and the arbitrators or by the sole arbitrator as the case may be.

31. The award given by the Arbitration Commission is final and neither party shall bring an appeal for revision before a court of law or any other organization.

32. The award of the Arbitration Commission shall be executed by the parties themselves within the time fixed by the award. In case an award is not executed after the expiration of the fixed time, one of the parties may petition the People's Court of the People's Republic of China to enforce it in accordance with law.

33. To compensate for the costs of arbitration, the Arbitration Commission may collect from the parties a fee the amount of which shall be determined by the Arbitration Tribunal in the award but shall not in any case exceed one per cent of the amount of the claim.

The Arbitration Tribunal may, having regard to the circumstances of the case, determine in the award whether such a fee should be borne entirely by the losing party or proportionally by both parties.

34. The Arbitration Tribunal may determine in the award the amount to be paid by the losing party to the winning party in compensation for the costs incurred in

the action which amount shall not in any case exceed five per cent of the sum awarded to the winning party.

35. In the event a case over which the Arbitration Tribunal has already assumed jurisdiction is settled by conciliation between the parties, it shall be dismissed without delay. Prior to the forming of the Arbitration Tribunal the decision for dismissal shall be made by the Chairman of the Arbitration Commission and after the forming of the Arbitration Tribunal by the Arbitration Tribunal itself.

36. The Chinese language is the official language of the Arbitration Commission.

If, at the hearing, any one of the parties, their attorneys or witnesses, or any other person is unfamiliar with the Chinese language, the Arbitration Tribunal may designate an interpreter for him or direct the party concerned to furnish one himself.

37. All notices of the Arbitration Commission to the parties shall be delivered by messengers, registered mail or telegraph.

38. The present Rules shall come into force from the date of its adoption by the China Council for the Promotion of International Trade.

Appendix S

Decision of the State Council of the People's Republic of China Concerning the Establishment of a Maritime Arbitration Commission within the China Council for the Promotion of International Trade*

(Adopted on November 21, 1958, at the 82nd Session
of the State Council)

With a view to settling maritime disputes by arbitration, it is necessary to set up an arbitral body within a relevant social organization. It is hereby decided as follows:

1. There shall be established within the China Council for the Promotion of International Trade a Maritime Arbitration Commission to settle:

   a. disputes regarding the remuneration for salvage services rendered by sea-going vessels to each other or by a sea-going vessel to a river craft and vice versa;

   b. disputes arising from collisions between sea-going vessels or between sea-going vessels and river craft or from damages caused by sea-going vessels to harbour structures or installations;

   c. disputes arising from chartering sea-going vessels, agency services rendered to sea-going vessels, carriage by sea in virtue of contracts of affreightment, bills of lading or other shipping documents, as well as disputes arising from marine insurance.

2. The Maritime Arbitration Commission takes cognizance of maritime disputes in accordance with the relevant contracts, agreements and/or other documents concluded between the disputing parties either prior or subsequent to the arising of disputes.

   The Maritime Arbitration Commission may endeavor to settle by conciliation any dispute of which it has taken cognizance.

3. The Maritime Arbitration Commission shall be composed of 21-31 members to be selected and appointed by the China Council for the Promotion of International Trade for a term of two years from among persons having special knowledge in navigation, sea transportation, foreign trade, insurance and law.

*SOURCE: *Chung-hua jen-ming kung-ho-kuo Tui-wai mao-i,* no. 1 (1959), supplement, pp. 2-5; English translation in National Council for United States-China Trade Special Report no. 4, *Arbitration and Dispute Settlement in Trade with China* (1974), pp. 58-68.

4. The Maritime Arbitration Commission shall elect a Chairman and 1-3 Deputy Chairmen from among its members.

5. When a dispute is submitted for arbitration, the disputing parties shall each choose an arbitrator from among the members of the Maritime Arbitration Commission. The arbitrators so chosen shall jointly select from among the members of the Maritime Arbitration Commission an umpire to form, in association with the arbitrators, an Arbitration Tribunal to act in a body. The disputing parties may also jointly choose from among the members of the Maritime Arbitration Commission a sole arbitrator to form by himself a Tribunal to act singly.

The disputing parties shall choose the arbitrators within a time fixed by the Maritime Arbitration Commission or agreed upon between the parties, and the arbitrators so chosen shall also select the umpire within the time fixed by the Maritime Arbitration Commission. If one of the parties fail to choose an arbitrator within the prescribed time limit, the Chairman of the Maritime Arbitration Commission shall then, upon the request of the other party, appoint the arbitrator for the former party. If the arbitrators so chosen or appointed cannot agree upon the choice of the umpire within the prescribed time limit, the Chairman of the Maritime Arbitration Commission shall then select an umpire for them.

6. Either of the parties in dispute may authorize the Maritime Arbitration Commission to choose for him an arbitrator who shall, jointly with the arbitrator chosen by the other party, select an umpire to form, in association with the arbitrators, an Arbitration Tribunal to act in a body. If by mutual agreement, both parties jointly delegate the choice of arbitrators to the Maritime Arbitration Commission, the Chairman of the Maritime Arbitration Commission may appoint a sole arbitrator to form by himself a Tribunal to act singly.

7. The disputing parties may appoint attorneys to protect their interests during the proceedings of a case before the Maritime Arbitration Commission.

Such attorneys may be citizens of the People's Republic of China or foreign citizens.

8. In cases within the cognizance of the Maritime Arbitration Commission, the Chairman of the Maritime Arbitration Commission may make decisions in respect of measures of security and determine the amount and form of the security for the claim.

Upon the request of one of the parties, the People's Court of the People's Republic of China shall enforce the decision referred to in the preceding paragraph in accordance with law.

9. The Maritime Arbitration Commission may collect an arbitration fee not exceeding two per cent of the amount of the claim.

10. The award given by the Maritime Arbitration Commission is final and neither party shall bring an appeal for revision before a court of law or any other organization.

11. The award of the Maritime Arbitration Commission shall be executed by the parties themselves within the time fixed by the award. In case an award is not executed after the expiration of the fixed time, the People's Court of the People's Republic of China shall, upon the request of one of the parties, enforce it in accordance with law.

12. Rules concerning the Procedure of Arbitration shall be made by the China Council for the Promotion of International Trade.

Provisional Rules of Procedure of the Maritime Arbitration Commission of the China Council for the Promotion of International Trade.

(Adopted on January 8, 1959, at the Seventh Session of the China Council for the Promotion of International Trade).

1. The present Rules are made in accordance with Article 12 of the Decision of the State Council of the People's Republic of China adopted on November 21, 1958, concerning the establishment of a Maritime Arbitration Commission within the China Council for the Promotion of International Trade.

2. The Maritime Arbitration Commission takes cognizance of:

a. disputes regarding remuneration for salvage services rendered by sea-going vessels to each other or by a sea-going vessel to a river craft and vice versa;

b. disputes arising from collisions between sea-going vessels or between sea-going vessels and river craft or from damages caused by sea-going vessels to harbour structures or installations:

c. disputes arising from chartering sea-going vessels, agency services rendered to sea-going vessels, carriage by sea in virtue of affreightment, bills of lading or other shipping documents, as well as disputes arising from marine insurance.

3. The Maritime Arbitration Commission takes cognizance of a dispute referrd to in the preceding Section upon the written application of one of the disputing parties and in accordance with such written agreement as concluded between the parties either prior or subsequent to the arising of the dispute, which stipulates for the submission of the dispute to the Maritime Arbitration Commission for settlement.

The agreement referred to in the preceding paragraph means the arbitration clause stipulated in the original contract from which the dispute has arisen, or any other form of agreement, in respect of submission to arbitration (such as special agreement, correspondence exchanged or any specific stipulation contained in other relevant documents).

4. The following items must be specified in the application for arbitration:

a. the name and address of the plaintiff and those of the defendant;

b. the claim of the plaintiff and the facts and evidence upon which the claim is based;

c. the name of an arbitrator chosen by the plaintiff from among the members of the Maritime Arbitration Commission or a statement authorizing the Chairman of the Maritime Arbitration Commission to appoint the arbitrator for the plaintiff.

5. Original relevant documents (contracts, arbitration agreements, correspondence between the parties, etc.,) or certified duplicates or copies thereof, must accompany the application for arbitration.

6. When submitting an application for arbitration, the plaintiff shall pay a sum equivalent to one per cent of the amount of the claim as a deposit for the arbitration fee.

7. The application for arbitration and its appended documents shall be accompanied by as many duplicates as the number of defendants, all to be submitted to the Maritime Arbitration Commission.

8. Upon receipt of the application, the Maritime Arbitration Commission shall notify the defendant to that effect without delay and forward to him a duplicate of the application and of all the appended documents.

9. Within fifteen days from the date of receipt of the notice the defendants shall either choose an arbitrator from among the members of the Maritime Arbitration Commission and notify the Maritime Commission of his choice or authorize the Chairman of the Maritime Arbitration Commission to appoint the arbitrator for him.

In case a different period of time is agreed upon between the parties, such period of time shall prevail.

The Maritime Arbitration Commission may also, upon request of the defendant, alter the period of fifteen days.

10. Should the defendant fail to choose an arbitrator within the time specified in the preceding Section, the Chairman of the Maritime Arbitration Commission shall, upon the request of the plaintiff, appoint the arbitrator for the defendant.

11. The Maritime Arbitration Commission shall notify the arbitrators, whether chosen by the parties or appointed by the Chairman, to select an umpire from among the members of the Maritime Arbitration Commission within fifteen days from the date of receipt of the notice.

In case no agreement is reached between the chosen or appointed arbitrators regarding the selection of the umpire within the time limit stated in the preceding paragraph, the Chairman of the Maritime Arbitration Commission shall then select an umpire for them.

12. The disputing parties may jointly choose or authorize the Chairman of the Maritime Arbitration Commission to appoint for them a sole arbitrator from among the members of the Maritime Arbitration Commission.

In case the parties separately delegate the choice of arbitrators to the Chairman of the Maritime Arbitration Commission, the Chairman may, after obtaining the consent of the parties, appoint a sole arbitrator from among the members of the Maritime Arbitration Commission.

13. If an arbitrator is unable to perform his duties, the Maritime Arbitration Commission shall notify the party concerned to that effect without delay and request him to choose a new arbitrator from among the members of the Maritime Arbitration Commission within fifteen days from the date of receipt of the notice.

Should the said party fail to choose a new arbitrator within that time, the Chairman of the Maritime Arbitration Commission shall then appoint a new arbitrator for him.

14. If an umpire is unable to perform his duties, the Maritime Arbitration Commission shall notify the arbitrators for the parties to that effect without delay and request them to select a new umpire from among the members of the Maritime Arbitration Commission within fifteen days from the date of receipt of the notice.

Should the arbitrators fail to agree on the selection of the new umpire within that time, the Chairman of the Maritime Arbitration Commission shall then select a new umpire for them.

15. In cases within the cognizance of the Maritime Arbitration Commission, the Chairman of the Maritime Arbitration Commission may, upon the request of one of the parties, make decisions in respect of measures of security and determine the amount and form of the security for the claim. If the amount and form of the required security have already been agreed upon between the parties, such amount and form shall prevail.

16. Upon the request of one of the parties, the People's Court of the People's Republic of China shall enforce the decision of the Chairman of the Maritime Arbitration Commission in respect of measures of security in accordance with law.

17. The date for the hearing of the case shall be set by the Chairman of the Maritime Arbitration Commission in consultation with the umpire or the sole arbitrator as the case may be.

18. The Maritime Arbitration Commission may require the parties to give their explanations in writing before the date of hearing.

19. The Maritime Arbitration Commission may endeavor to settle by conciliation any dispute of which it has taken cognizance.

20. The disputing parties may appoint attorneys to protect their interests and to confer with the Maritime Arbitration Commission on matters relating to the proceedings of arbitration.

Such attorneys may be citizens of the People's Republic of China or foreign citizens.

21. Hearings shall be held at the seat of the Maritime Arbitration Commission. Where necessary, hearings may, upon the approval of the Chairman of the Maritime Arbitration Commission, be held at other places within the Chinese territory.

22. Proceedings for the arbitration of a case are conducted by an Arbitration Tribunal formed by one umpire and two arbitrators sitting in a body.

A sole arbitrator forms a Tribunal by himself and conducts the proceedings singly.

23. The Maritime Arbitration Commission shall hear cases in open sessions, but it may, upon the request of both or either of the parties, hold the hearings in closed sessions.

24. At every session of the Arbitration Tribunal, records shall be taken, and these records shall be signed by the umpire or the sole arbitrator as the case may be.

The Arbitration Tribunal may require the parties or their attorneys, witnesses or other persons to sign on the records.

25. The Maritime Arbitration Commission shall notify the parties in advance of the date of hearing to be held by the Arbitration Tribunal.

26. The defendant may file a counter-claim against the plaintiff in cases of which the Maritime Arbitration Commission has taken cognizance.

The provisions in Sections 2-7 of the present Rules apply likewise to counter-claims.

27. The disputing parties shall produce evidence in support of the facts upon which their claims or pleadings are based. Where necessary, the Arbitration Tribunal itself may make investigations or collect evidence.

28. The examination and appraisal of evidence shall be performed by the Arbitration Tribunal at its discretion.

An Arbitration Tribunal sitting in a body may entrust one of its members with the work of the examination of evidence.

29. The Aribtration Tribunal may consult experts for the clarification of any questions concerning technical or special matters or business practices.

Such experts may be designated from among citizens of the People's Republic of China or foreign citizens.

30. Should one of the disputing parties or his attorney fail to appear at the hearing held by the Arbitration Tribunal, the Tribunal may, upon the request of the party present, proceed with the hearing or render the award.

31. The award of an Arbitration Tribunal sitting in a body is decided by majority vote and the minority opinion may be recorded in the file.

32. The conclusion of the award shall be read to the parties at the closing session of the hearings.

The award shall be made in writing within fifteen days from the date of the reading of the conclusion. It shall include the reasons for the decision and shall be signed by the umpire and the arbitrators or by the sole arbitrator as the case may be.

33. The award given by the Maritime Arbitration Commission is final and neither party shall bring an appeal for revision before a court of law or any other organization.

34. The award of the Maritime Arbitration Commission shall be executed by the parties themselves within the time fixed by the award. In case an award is not executed after the expiration of the fixed time, one of the parties may petition the People's Court of the People's Republic of China to enforce it in accordance with law.

35. The Maritime Arbitration Commission may collect an arbitration fee the amount of which shall be determined by the Arbitration Tribunal in the award but shall in no case exceed two per cent of the amount of the claim.

The Arbitration Tribunal may, having regard to the circumstances of the case, determine in the award whether such a fee should be borne entirely by the losing party or proportionally by both parties.

In cases having been dismissed in accordance with Section 37, the Maritime Arbitration Commission may also collect a fee at its discretion.

36. The Arbitration Tribunal may determine in the award the amount to be paid by the losing party to the successful party in compensation for the cost incurred in the action which amount shall in no case exceed five per cent of the sum awarded to the successful party.

37. If a case already taken cognizance of by the Maritime Arbitration Commission is settled by conciliation between the parties, it shall be dismissed without delay. Prior to the forming of the Arbitration Tribunal the decision for dismissal shall be made by the Chairman of the Maritime Arbitration Commission and after the forming of the Arbitration Tribunal by the Arbitration Tribunal itself.

38. The Chinese language is the official language of the Maritime Arbitration Commission.

If, at the hearing, any one of the parties, their attorneys or witnesses, or any other person is unfamiliar with the Chinese language, the Arbitration Tribunal may designate an interpreter for him or direct the party concerned to furnish one himself.

39. All notices of the Maritime Arbitration Commission to the parties shall be delivered by messengers, registered mail or telegraph.

40. The present Rules shall come into force from the date of its adoption by the China Council for the Promotion of International Trade.

Appendix T

Provisional Rules for General Average Adjustment*
(Promulgated by the CCPIT on January 1, 1975)

With a view to dealing properly with general average adjustment on the basis of equality and mutual benefit so as to enhance friendly relations among peoples of different countries and promote the development of international trade and marine transport, the China Council for the Promotion of International Trade has adopted the present Provisional Rules and set up the Department for Average Adjustment.

Article 1: Scope of General Average:
The following extraordinary loss or damage and reasonable extra expenses arising from measures properly taken for relieving a ship, cargo, etc. from common danger caused by natural calamities, accidents and/or other extraordinary circumstances in marine transport shall fall within the scope of general average:

1. Loss or damage reasonably caused to the ship, cargo, etc. for rescuing the same from danger;

2. Extra expenses incurred by the ship for entering a port of refuge, port charges incurred during the extra period of detention of the ship in a port of refuge and extra expenses for the ship's leaving the port of refuge subsequently with her original cargo or a part thereof;

3. Crew's wages and maintenance incurred as well as fuel and stores consumed during the prolongation of the voyage occasioned by the ship proceeding to a port of refuge and during the extra period of detention of the ship in a port of refuge;

4. Salvage expenses, expenses for forced discharge and reloading of the cargo, etc. and other extra expenses.

Where the ship needs repairs for the safe completion of the voyage in consequence of damage caused by an accident during the voyage, the port charges, crew's wages and maintenance and fuel and stores necessarily incurred or consumed during the reasonable period of detention of the ship in the port of repair, as well as the expenses and loss or damage arising from such discharging, reloading and handling on board of the cargo, etc. as are required for the repairs, may under the present circumstances be admitted as general average.

Where any expense is incurred to save another expense which would have been admissible in general average, such expense may be allowed in general average as a substituted expense. Unless otherwise agreed upon by and between the ship and cargo interests, the amount so allowable shall not exceed the amount of the expense saved.

SOURCE: The CCPIT. Translation is official.

With the exception of loss or damage and expenses referred to in the above three paragraphs, any other indirect loss, including loss or damage and expenses through delay, shall not fall within the scope of general average.

Article 2: Principle of Adjusting General Average

The principle of general average adjustment is the ascertainment of liability on the basis of investigation and study and dealing with the compensation for and contribution to various losses and expenses fairly, reasonably and in a truth-seeking way.

The onus of proof shall be upon the party applying for general average adjustment as well as other parties concerned to show that their respective loss or damage and expenses claimed for are allowable as general average according to the provisions of the Rules.

If the event given rise to a claim submitted for adjustment as general average is due to a fault of one of the parties to the contract of affreightment, for which he is not entitled to exemption from liability, no general average adjustment shall be proceeded with, but the case may be otherwise appropriately dealt with through consultation according to the circumstances involved.

Article 3: Computation of Amount of General Average Loss or Damage

The amount to be admitted as general average for loss or damage to the ship, cargo and freight shall be computed on the following basis:

1. The amount allowable for loss or damage to the ship shall be computed in accordance with the actual reasonable cost of repairing such damage, including cost of temporary repairs and of replacements subject to reasonable deductions in respect of "new for old". Where no repairs have been effected, computation shall be made in accordance with the reasonably estimated cost of necessary repairs. The amount allowable for loss of or damage to fuel and stores, etc. shall be computed on the basis of their actual values.

2. The amount allowable for loss of or damage to the cargo shall be computed on the basis of the c.i.f. value, less the freight which would have been incurred but for such loss or damage. Where the cargo so damaged is sold and it is impossible to ascertain the extent of the damage, the amount shall be computed on the basis of the difference between the c.i.f. value and the net proceeds of sale.

3. The amount allowable for loss of freight shall be computed on the basis of the freight lost owing to the loss of or damage to the cargo, less the operating costs of the ship, which would have been incurred but for such loss or damage.

Article 4: Contribution to General Average

General average loss or damage and expenses shall be contributed to by the benefited interests in proportion to their respective contributory values.

The contributory values shall be computed on the following basis:

1. The contributory value of the ship shall be computed either in accordance with the value of the ship in sound condition at the time and place of the termination of the voyage, less the amount of loss or damage not allowable in general average, or in accordance with the actual net value of the ship at the time and place of the termination of the voyage, plus the amount allowable in general average.

2. The contributory value of the cargo shall be computed on the basis of the c.i.f. value, less the amount of loss or damage not allowable in general average and the freight at the risk of the carrier.

Undeclared or falsely declared cargo shall contribute on the actual value, but loss of or damage to such cargo, if any, shall not be admitted as general average.

Passengers' luggage and personal effects shall not contribute to general average except under extraordinary circumstances.

3. The contributory value of the freight shall be computed on the basis of the freight at the risk of the carrier and subsequently earned, subject to a deduction corresponding to the extent of the voyage still uncompleted at the time of the event giving rise to general average, plus the amount of loss of freight allowable in general average.

Article 5: Interest and Commission

Interest shall be allowed on general average loss or damage and expenses at the rate of 7 percent per annum until the date of the completion of the general average adjustment.

A commission of 2 percent shall be allowed on general average expenses other than crew's wages and maintenance and fuel and stores.

Article 6: General Average Security

The contributing parties shall, at the request of the parties concerned, provide a security to ensure the contribution to general average. Such security may be in the form of a reliable letter of guarantee or a cash deposit. Where a cash deposit is provided, same shall be paid into an account in a bank in the name of the Department for Average Adjustment unless otherwise agreed upon by and between the parties concerned. Any use of the cash deposit shall be decided by the Department for Average Adjustment. The provision, use and refund of the cash deposit shall be without prejudice to the ultimate liability of the contributing parties.

Article 7: Time Limit of General Average

For the purpose of safeguarding the interests of all parties concerned and completing the adjustment of general average as promptly as possible, all parties shall, upon the occurrence of the event giving rise to general average, do everything necessary in time and declare general average and provide the Department for Average Adjustment with relevant materials within the following time limits:

1. Declaration of General Average

Within forty-eight hours upon the ship's arrival in the first port after the event, if it has occurred at sea, or within forty-eight hours after the event, if it has occurred in a port;

2. Provision of Relevant Materials

For documentary evidence pertaining to the occurrence of general average loss or damage, within one month after receipt thereof by the claiming party, but all materials shall in any case be provided within one year of the completion of the voyage.

In case of extraordinary circumstances the above time limits may be appropriately extended, provided reason for extension has been given within the respective time limits to the Department for Average Adjustment and its approval obtained.

In case of failure to observe the above stipulations on the part of any of the parties concerned, the Department for Average Adjustment may either decline to proceed with adjustment or adjust the case on the basis of the materials in its possession.

Article 8: Simplification of Adjustment of General Average

With a view to lightening the burden of all parties concerned and improving working efficiency, the adjustment of general average shall be made as simple as possible; unduly complicated procedures and calculations shall be avoided; adjustment shall be made as clear and concise as possible and easy to execute.

Summary adjustment may be applied in simple cases.

For cases in which the amount involved is small, adjustment may be dispensed with if consent has been obtained from the principal parties concerned.

Selected Bibliography

This bibliography is made up of three sections, each alphabetized separately. Laws, regulations, treaties, and other government materials edited, compiled, or translated by individuals and institutions are arranged accordingly in the first section. With the exception of Chinese government institutional editors or compilers, the names of individual and foreign institutional editors, compilers, or translators are also listed in the second section for cross reference. Books are listed by author, editor, compiler, or translator in the second section; and articles, by author, in the third. About sixty periodicals and newspapers have been cited in individual footnotes; however, they are not listed in a separate section. Some of them appear after pertinent articles in the third section.

Documents

Chung-hua jen-min kung-ho-kuo fa-kuei hsüan-chi [Selection of laws and regulations of the PRC]. Ed. by Committee for the Selection and Compilation of Laws and Regulations in the Ministry of Justice of the PRC. Peking: Fa-lü ch'u-pan-she, 1957.

Chung-hua jen-min kung-ho-kuo fa-kuei hui-pien [Compilation of laws and regulations of the PRC]. 1954-1963. 13 vols. Vols. 1-9 ed. by Bureau of Legal Affairs of the State Council and Committee for the Compilation of Laws and Regulations of the PRC. Vol. 10 ed. by Secretariat of the State Council and State Council Committee for the Compilation of Laws and Regulations. Vols. 11-13 ed. by State Council Committee for the Compilation of Laws and Regulations. Peking: Fa-lü ch'u-pan-she, 1956-1964.

Chung-hua jen-min kung-ho-kuo min-fa ts'an-k'ao tzu-liao [Reference materials on the civil law of the PRC]. Ed. by Chinese People's University, Teaching and Research Institute of Civil Law, vol. 3. Peking: Chung-kuo jen-min ta-hsüeh, 1957.

Chung-hua jen-min kung-ho-kuo t'iao-yüeh chi [Collection of treaties of the PRC]. 1949-1964. 13 vols. Ed. by Ministry of Foreign Affairs of the PRC. Vols. 1-10, Peking: Fa-lü ch'u-pan-she, 1957-1962. Vols. 11-13, Peking: Shih-chieh chih-shih ch'u-pan-she, 1963-1965.

Chung-hua jen-min kung-ho-kuo tui-wai kuan-hsi wen-chien chi [Collection of documents on the foreign relations of the PRC]. 1949-1963. 10 vols. Peking: Shih-chieh chih-shih ch'u-pan-she, 1957-1965.

Chung-kuo ts'an-chia chih kuo-chi kung-yüeh hui-pien [International conventions acceded to by China]. Ed. by Kuo Tzu-hsiung and Hsüeh Tien-tseng. Shanghai: Shang-wu yin-shu kuan, 1937; Reprint. Taipei, 1971.

Chung wai chiu yüeh-chang hui-pien [Compilation of old treaties and agreements between China and foreign states]. Set I (1689-1901), 3 vols. Ed. by Wang Tieh-yai. Peking: Shen-huo, Tu-shu, Hsin-chih, san-lien shu-tien, 1957. Set II (1901-1919), 1 vol. Ed. by Peking University, Teaching and Research Institute of International Law of the Department of Law. Peking: Shen-huo, Tu-shu, Hsin-chih, san-lien shu-tien, 1959.

Chung-yang jen-min cheng-fu fa-lin hui-pien [Compilation of laws and degrees of the Central People's Government]. 1949-1954. 5 vols. Ed. by Commission on Legal Affairs of the Central People's Government. Vols. 1-3, Peking: Jen-min ch'u-pan-she, 1952-1954. Vols. 4-5, Peking: Fa-lü ch'u-pan-she, 1955.

Code of Civil Procedures, Japan. Tokyo, 1962.

Commercial Arbitration and the Law Throughout the World.

Constitution of Japan and Criminal Statutes. Ed. by the Supreme Court of Japan. Tokyo, 1958.

Constitution of the PRC (1954). Peking: Foreign Languages Press, 1954.

Jen-min shou-ts'e [People's handbook]. 1950-1965. 16 vols. Vols. 1950-1952, Shanghai: Ta-kung pao, 1950-1952. Vols. 1953, 1955-1956, Tientsin: Ta-kung pao, 1953, 1955-1956. Vols. 1957-1965, Peking: Ta-kung pao, 1957-1965. Vol. 1954 missing.

Jih-pen wen-t'i wen-chien hui-pien [Compilation of documents on the question of Japan]. 1942-1964. 5 vols. Peking: Shih-chieh chih-shih ch'u-pan-she, 1955-1965.

Kuo-chi t'iao-yüeh chi [Collection of international treaties]. Vol. 3 (1934-1944) and vol. 7 (1953-1957). Peking: Shih-chieh chih-shih ch'u-pan-she, 1961.

Laws of the Republic of China. Taipei: Law Revision and Planning Group, Executive Yuan, 1961.

League of Nations Treaty Series. Vol. 4 (1921).

Nichu kankei shryo shu [Collection of materials on Japan-China relations]. 1945-1966. Tokyo: Dietmen's League for the Promotion of Japan-China Trade, 1967.

Ta Tsing Leu Lee [The laws and supplementary statutes of the Great Ch'ing]. Trans. by George Thomas Staunton. London: T. Cadell and W. Davies, 1810. Reprint. Taipei: Ch'eng-wen Publishing Co., 1966.

T'ang liu tien [The six codes of the T'ang dynasty]. Ed. by Kuang-ya shu-chü, 1895.

The Trade Act of 1974 (Public Law 93-618, 93rd Congress, H.R. 10710, January 3, 1975). Washington, D. C.: U.S. Government Printing Office, 1975.

Treaties and Agreements With and Concerning China 1894-1919. 2 vols. Ed. by John V. A. MacMurray. New York: Oxford University Press, 1921.

Treaties Between the Empire of China and Foreign Powers. Ed. by William Frederick Mayers. London: Trübner & Co., 1877. Reprint. Taipei: Ch'eng-wen Publishing Co., 1966.

Treaties Between the Republic of China and Foreign States 1927-1957. Ed. by Ministry of Foreign Affairs. Taipei, 1958.

Tsui-hsin liu-fa ch'üan-shu [The newest collection of the six codes]. Ed. by Chang Chih-pen. Taipei: Ta Chung-kuo t'u-shu kung-szu, 1960.

Tui-wai mao-i chung-ts'ai shou-ts'e [Handbook on foreign trade arbitration]. 2 vols. Ed. by China Council for the Promotion of International Trade. Peking: Fa-lü ch'u-pan-she, 1957.

United Nations Treaty Series, vol. 313. (1958).

United States Treaties and Other International Agreements 1960. Ed. by Department of State. Vol. 11. Washington, D. C.: Government Printing Office, 1961.

Books

Adler-Karlsson, Gunnar. *Western Economic Warfare 1947-1967.* Stockholm: Almqvist & Wiksell, 1968.

Asia Yearbook 1973. Hong Kong: Far Eastern Economic Review, 1973.

Babb, Hugh W., trans. *Soviet Legal Philosophy,* with an introduction by John N. Hazard. Cambridge, Mass.: Harvard University Press, 1951.

Cahill, Harry A. *The China Trade and U.S. Tariffs.* New York: Praeger Publishers, 1973.

Carew Hunt, R.N. *Marxism Past and Present.* New York: Macmillan Co., 1955.

Central Political-Legal Cadres School, Teaching and Research Institute of Civil Law, ed., *Chung-hua jen-min kung-ho-kuo min-fa chi-pen wen-t'i* [Basic problems in the civil law of the PRC]. Peking: Fa-lü ch'u-pan-she, 1958. English translation in U.S. Commerce Department, Joint Publications Research Service, no. 4879 (1961).

Chang, Chih-pen. See *Tsui-hsin liu-fa ch'üan-shu,* in documentary section.

Chang, Kuei-chuan. *Shang-piao fa yao-i* [Essentials of trademark law]. Shanghai: Shang-wu yin-shu kuan, 1923.

Chen, Chih-shih, and Liu Po-wu. *Tui-wai mao-i t'ung-chi hsüeh* [Foreign trade statistics]. Peking: Ts'ai-cheng ching-chi ch'u-pan-she, 1958.

Chen, Nai-Ruenn, and Walter Galenson. *The Chinese Economy Under Communism.* Chicago: Aldine Publishing Co., 1969.

Chien-ming tui-wai mao-i tz'u-tien [Concise foreign trade dictionary]. Peking: Ts'ai-cheng ching-chi ch'u-pan-she, 1959.

Chien, Tai. *Chung-kuo pu-p'ing teng t'iao-yüeh chih yüan-ch'i chi ch'i fei-ch'u chih ching-kuo* [The origins of China's unequal treaties and the process of their abolition]. Taipei: Kuo-fang yeng-chiu yüan, 1961.

Chin, Chung-chi. *Shang-piao fa lun* [On trademark law]. Shanghai: Hui-wen-t'ang hsin-chi shu-chü, 1937.

Chin, Hung-chi. *Chuan-li chih-tu kai-lun* [A general study of the patent system]. Shanghai: Shang-wu yin-shu kuan, 1946.

China Council for the Promotion of International Trade. See *Tui-wai mao-i chung-ts'ai shou-ts'e,* in documentary section.

Ching, Frank, ed. *Report From Red China.* New York: New York Times, 1971.

Chiu, Hungdah. *The People's Republic of China and the Law of Treaties.* Cambridge, Mass.: Harvard University Press, 1972.

Chung-kuo kuo-chi mao-i ts'u-chin wei-yuan-hui [The China Council for the Promotion of International Trade]. Peking, 1959.

Committee for the Compilation of the Annals of Overseas Chinese, ed. *Hua-ch'iao chih: tsung-chih* [Annals of overseas Chinese: general records]. Taipei: Hai-wai ch'u-pan-she, 1956.

Cohen, Jerome Alan, ed. *The Dynamics of China's Foreign Relations*. Cambridge, Mass.: Harvard University Press, 1970.

_____, ed. *China's Practice of International Law: Some Case Studies*. Cambridge, Mass.: Harvard University Press, 1972.

_____, and Hungdah Chiu. *People's China and International Law*. 2 vols. Princeton: Princeton University Press, 1974.

Dietmen's League for the Promotion of Japan-China Trade. See *Nichu kankei shryo shu*, in documentary section.

Domke, Martin, ed. *International Trade Arbitration*. New York: American Arbitration Association, 1958.

Donnithorne, Audrey. *The Budget and the Plan in China: Central-Local Economic Relations*. Canberra: Australian National University Press, 1972.

Eckstein, Alexander, ed. *China Trade Prospects and U.S. Policy*. New York: Praeger Publishers, 1971.

Fairbank, John K. *Trade and Diplomacy on the China Coast*. Stanford: Stanford University Press, 1969.

_____, ed. *The Chinese World Order*. Cambridge, Mass.: Harvard University Press, 1970.

Fitzgerald, Stephen. *China and the Overseas Chinese*. London: Cambridge University Press, 1972.

Giffen, James Henry. *The Legal and Practical Aspects of Trade with the Soviet Union*. New York: Praeger Publishers, 1969.

Gowen, Herbert H., and Josef Washington Hall. *An Outline History of China*. New York: Appleton and Co., 1926.

Gsovski, Vladimir. *Soviet Civil Law*. 2 vols. Ann Arbor: University of Michigan Law School, 1948-1949.

Halpern, A. M., ed. *Policies Toward China: Views From Six Continents*. New York: McGraw-Hill Book Co., 1965.

Ho, Ping-ying. *The Foreign Trade of China*. Shanghai: Commercial Press, Ltd., 1935.

Holtzmann, Howard M. *Legal Aspects of Doing Business With China*. New York: Practising Law Institute, 1976.

Hong Kong *Ta-kung Pao,* ed. *Tao Kwangchow tso sheng-i* [To do business in Kwangchow]. Hong Kong: Ta-kung pao, 1958.

Hou, Chi-ming. *Foreign Investment and Economic Development in China 1840-1937*. Cambridge, Mass.: Harvard University Press, 1965.

Hsiangkang ching-chi nien-chien [Hong Kong Economic Yearbook, 5 vols., 1972-1976] Hong Kong: Ching-chi pao-tao she, 1972-1976.

Hsiao, Gene T., ed. *Sino-American Detente and Its Policy Implications*. New York: Praeger Publishers, 1974.

Hsien-tai kuo-chi-fa shang ti chi-pen yüan-tse ho wen-t'i [The basic principles and problems in modern international law]. Peking: Fa-lü ch'u-pan-she, 1956.

Hsü, Immanuel C. Y. *The Rise of Modern China*. New York: Oxford University Press, 1970.

Hsu, Yin. *Chin-yun i-ting yao ch'e-ti p'o-ch'an* [The embargo will go completely bankrupt]. Shanghai: Jen-min ch'u-pan-she, 1957.

Hsueh, Mu-chiao, Su Hsing, and Lin Tse-li. *The Socialist Transformation of the National Economy in China*. Peking: Foreign Languages Press, 1960.

Huang, Yuan. *Wo-kuo jen-min lü-shih chih-tu* [The people's lawyer system in our country]. Kwangchow: Kwangtung jen-min ch'u-pan-she, 1956.

Hunsberger, Warren S. *Japan and the United States in World Trade*. New York: Harper & Row, 1964.

Japan External Trade Organization. *Foreign Trade of Japan 1966*. Tokyo, 1966.

———. *How to Approach the China Market*. Tokyo: Press International Ltd., 1972.

Johnston, Douglas M., and Hungdah Chiu. *Agreements of the People's Republic of China, 1949-1967: A Calendar*. Cambridge, Mass.: Harvard University Press, 1968.

Joint Economic Committee of the U.S. Congress, ed. *People's Republic of China: An Economic Analysis*. Washington, D.C.: Government Printing Office, 1972.

———, ed. *China: A Reassessment of the Economy*. Washington, D. C.: Government Printing Office, 1975.

Kahin, George McTurnan. *The Asian-African Conference*. Ithaca: Cornell University Press, 1956.

Kramer, Roland L. et al. *International Trade*. Cincinnati: Southern-Western Publishing Co., 1959.

Ku, Yun. *Chung-kuo chin-tai shih shang ti pu-p'ing-teng t'iao-yüeh*. [The unequal treaties in contemporary Chinese history]. Hong Kong: Chao-yang ch'u-pan-she, 1975.

Kuang-ya shu-chü. See *T'ang liu tien,* in documentary section.

Kumano, Masahira. *Shin Chugoku shogyo tsushin bun* [New China's commercial correspondence]. Tokyo: Konan shoin, 1956.

Kuo-chi mao-i chih-shih [Knowledge of international trade]. Hong Kong: Chao-yang ch'u-pan-she, 1973.

Kuo, Chung-yen. *Hsin Chung-kuo ti kung-yeh p'in ch'u-k'ou mao-i* [New China's export trade of industrial goods]. Shanghai: Jen-min ch'u-pan-she, 1956.

Kuo, Tzu-hsiung, and Hsueh, Tien-tseng. See *Chung-kuo ts'an-chia chih kuo-chi kung-yüeh hui-pien,* in documentary section.

Kwangchow Foreign Trade Control Bureau, ed. *Tui-wai mao-i shou-ts'e* [Handbook on foreign trade]. Kwangchow: Hsin-hua shu-tien, 1951.

Langdon, F. C. *Japan's Foreign Policy*. Vancouver: University of British Columbia Press, 1973.

Li, Choh-Ming. *The Statistical System of Communist China*. Berkeley and Los Angeles: University of California Press, 1962.

Liu, Yen. *Chung-kuo wai-ch'iao shih* [A diplomatic history of China]. Supplemented by Li Fang-chen. 2 vols. Taipei: San-min shu-chü, 1962.

Lu, Shih-kuang. *Shih-mo shih tui-wai mao-i* [What is foreign trade]. Peking: Ts'ai-cheng ching-chi ch'u-pan-she, 1957.

Mah, Feng-hwa. *The Foreign Trade of Mainland China*. Chicago: Aldine & Atherton, 1971.

MacFarquhar, Roderick, ed. *Sino-American Relations, 1949-1971*. New York: Praeger Publishers, 1972.

MacMurray, John V. A. See *Treaties and Agreements With and Concerning China 1894-1919,* in documentary section.

MacNair, Harley Farnsworth. *Modern Chinese History: Selected Readings.* New York: Paragon Book Reprint Corp., 1967.

Mao, Tse-tung. *Selected Readings From the Works of Mao Tse-tung.* Peking: Foreign Languages Press, 1967.

_____. *Mao Tse-tung hsüan-chi.* Shanghai: Jen-min ch'u-pan-she, 1966.

Mayers, William Frederick. See *Treaties Between the Empire of China and Foreign Powers,* in documentary section.

Ministry of Foreign Trade of the PRC, ed. *Tui-wai mao-i lun-wen hsüan-chi* [Selection of essays on foreign trade]. Vol. 1. Peking: Ts'ai-cheng ching-chi ch'u-pan-she, 1955.

_____, ed. *Tui-wai mao-i lun-wen hsüan.* [Selection of essays on foreign trade]. Vols. 2-4. Peking: Ts'ai-cheng ching-chi ch'u-pan-she, 1956-1958.

National Council for United States-China Trade. *Arbitration and Dispute Settlement in Trade with China.* Special Report no. 4. Washington, D.C., 1974.

_____. *China Shipping Manual.* Ed. by Nicholas H. Ludlow. Special Report no. 10. Washington, D.C., 1974.

_____. *Standard Form Contracts of the People's Republic of China.* Special Report no. 13. Washington, D.C., 1975.

Oppenheim, L. *International Law.* 8th ed. by H. Lauterpacht. Vol. 1. New York: David McKay Co., 1955.

Quigley, Harold S., and John E. Turner. *The New Japan.* Minneapolis: University of Minnesota Press, 1956.

Schmitthoff, Clive M., ed. *The Sources of the Law of International Trade.* New York: Praeger Publishers, 1964.

Shang-wu yin-shu kuan, ed. *Chang-kuo kuo-chi mao-i shih* [A history of China's international trade]. Shanghai: Shang-wu yin-shu kuan, 1928.

Shanghai Foreign Languages Institute, Department of Foreign Languages for Foreign Trade. *Tui-wai mao-i shih-wu* [The practice of foreign trade]. Shanghai: Ts'ai-cheng ching-chi ch'u-pan-she, 1959.

Snyder, Richard Carlton. *The Most-Favored-Nation Clause.* New York: King's Crown Press, 1948.

Stahnke, Arthur A., ed. *China's Trade with the West.* New York: Praeger Publishers, 1972.

Staunton, George Thomas. See *Ta Tsin Leu Lee,* in documentary section.

Sumida, Teruo. *Chugoku gendai shogyo tsushin bun.* Tokyo: Daian, 1964.

Supreme Court of Japan. See *Constitution of Japan and Criminal Statutes,* in documentary section.

Sze, Tsung-yu. *China and the Most-Favored-Nation Clause.* New York: Fleming H. Revell Co., 1925.

Taracouzio, T. A. *The Soviet Union and International Law.* New York: Macmillan Co., 1935.

Ting, Hsiu-shan, and Yoshitaro Shibagaki. *Saishin Nichu boeki tsushin bun* [The latest correspondence in Japanese-Chinese trade]. Tokyo: Konan shoin, 1957.

Tobin, Anthony, ed. *Hong Kong 1975*. Hong Kong: Government Printer, 1975.

Triska, J., and R. Slusser. *The Theory, Law, and Policy of Soviet Treaties*. Stanford: Stanford University Press, 1962.

Union Research Institute. *Who's Who in Communist China*, Hong Kong: Union Research Institute, 1969.

U.S. Government. *People's Republic of China: International Trade Handbook*. Washington, D.C. 1975.

Waley, Arthur. *The Opium War Through Chinese Eyes*. Stanford: Stanford University Press, 1968.

Wang, Shu-ming. *Shang-piao fa* [Trademark law]. Shanghai: Shang-wu yin-shu kuan, 1935.

Wang, Tieh-yai. See *Chung wai chiu yüeh-chang hui-pien*, Set I (1689-1901), in documentary section.

Wang, Yao-tien. *Kuo-chi mao-i t'iao-yüeh ho hsieh-ting* [International trade treaties and agreements]. Peking: Ts'ai-cheng ching-chi ch'u-pan-she, 1958.

Whitson, William W., ed. *Doing Business With China*. New York: Praeger Publishers, 1974.

Yano, Harutaka. *Chunichi boeki tsushin bun* [Chinese-Japanese trade correspondence]. Tokyo: Zenrin shoin, 1955.

Young, Kenneth T. *Negotiating With the Chinese Communists: The United States Experience 1953-1967*. New York: McGraw-Hill Book Co., 1968.

Articles

Albinski, Henry S. "Australia and the Chinese Strategic Embargo." *Australian Outlook* 19:117 (1965).

_____. "Canada's Chinese Trade in Political Perspective." In *China's Trade With the West*, ed. by Arthur A. Stahnke, p. 89.

Awanohara, Susumu. "When Japan Deposits, China Borrows." *Far Eastern Economic Review*, no. 24 (1974), p. 42.

Bank of China. "The Bank of China's Work of International Settlements." *Foreign Trade of the PRC*, no. 1 (1962), p. 4.

Berman, Harold J. "Unification of Contract Clauses in Trade Between Member Countries of the Council for Mutual Economic Aid." *International and Comparative Law Quarterly* 7:659 (1958).

_____. "Force Majeure and the Denial of An Export License Under Soviet Law." *Harvard Law Review* 73:1128 (1960).

Binder, David. "Macao Offer Was Rejected." *South China Morning Post*, April 2, 1975, p. 1.

Bryan, Robert T., Jr. "American Trademarks, Trade Names, Copyrights and Patents in China." *China Law Review* 1.1:424 (1924).

Chang, Ching-sung. "The Development of Sino-Japanese Economic Relations." *Chung-yang jih-pao*, January 30, 1974, p. 1.

Chang, Chun-chiao. "On Exercising All-Round Dictatorship Over the Bourgeoisie." *Hung-ch'i*, no. 4 (1975), p. 5.

_____. "Report on the Revision of the Constitution, January 13, 1975." *Hung-ch'i,* no. 2 (1975), p. 15.

Chang, Ming. "Inspection of China's Export Commodities." *China's Foreign Trade,* no. 1 (1974), p. 9.

Chao, Chi-chang. "Overall Planning of Foreign Trade and Conclusion of Long-Term Trade Agreements." In *Tui-wai mao-i lun-wen hsüan,* vol. 2, ed. by the Ministry of Foreign Trade (1956), p. 151.

_____. "The Great Change and Development of Our Country's Foreign Trade in the Past Seven Years." In *Tui-wai mao-i lun-wen hsüan,* vol. 3, ed. by the Ministry of Foreign Trade (1957), p. 14.

Chao, Fan. "Trade Talks in Geneva." *Ching-chi tao-pao,* no. 15 (1954), p. 8.

Chen, Nai-Ruenn. "China's Foreign Trade 1950-1974." In *China: A Reassessment of the Economy,* ed. by Joint Economic Committee of the U.S. Congress (1975), p. 631.

Chen, Ti-pao. "Supervision and Control of Imports and Exports by the Chinese Customs Administration." *Foreign Trade of the PRC,* no. 2 (1963), p. 2.

_____. "The Levying Task of the People's Customs." *Jen-min jih-pao,* August 18, 1950, p. 5.

Chou, En-lai. "Premier Chou En-lai's Interview with Ikuo Oyama, Chairman of the Japanese Committee for the Promotion of Peace, September 28, 1953." In *TWKH 1951-1953* 2:150 (1958).

_____. "Diplomatic Report to the 33rd Session of the Council of the Central People's Government, August 11, 1954." *Jen-min shou-ts'e 1955,* p. 325.

_____. "Address to the Third Session of the First National People's Congress, June 28, 1956." *TWKH 1956-1957* 4:73 (1958). Also in *Jen-min shou-ts'e 1957,* p. 182.

_____. "Premier Chou En-lai on the Three Principles of Sino-Japanese Trade in an Interview with Managing-Director Kazuo Suzuki of the Japan Association for the Promotion of Japan-China Trade, September 10, 1960." In *Jih-pen wen-t'i wen-chien hui-pien,* vol. 3 (1961), p. 135.

_____. "Premier Chou En-lai's Restatement on the Principles of Sino-Japanese Relations, September 19, 1962." In *Jih-pen wen-t'i wen-chien hui-pien,* vol. 4 (1963), p. 17.

_____. "Report on the Work of the Government." *Jen-min jih-pao,* December 31, 1964, p. 1.

_____. "Report to the Tenth National Congress of the Communist Party of China." *Peking Review,* no. 36, (1973), p. 17.

_____. "Report on the Work of the Government, January 13, 1975." *Hung-ch'i,* no. 2 (1975), p. 20.

Chou, Hua-ming. "China's Principled Stand on Relations of International Economy and Trade, April 20, 1972." *Peking Review,* no. 17 (1972), p. 11.

Chu, Shang. "The Development of China's Export Trade Reflected by the Chinese Export Commodities Fair." *China's Foreign Trade,* no. 1 (1974), p. 42.

Chung, Yung. "Foreign Exchange Work in China." *Foreign Trade of the PRC,* no. 2 (1960), p. 10.

Clarke, William, and Martha Avery. "The Sino-American Commercial Relationship." In *China: a Reassessment of the Economy,* ed. by Joint Economic Committee of the U.S. Congress (1975), p. 529.

Cohen, Jerome Alan."Chinese Law and Sino-American Trade." In *China Trade Prospects and U.S. Policy,* ed. by Alexander Eckstein, p. 27.

Cookson, David. "Two Dispute Settlement Problems with the PRC Encountered by a U.S. Trading Firm." In *Arbitration and Dispute Settlement in Trade With China,* National Council for United States-China Trade Special Report no. 4 (1974), p. 28.

Dernberger, Robert F. "Prospects for Trade Between China and the United States." In *China Trade Prospects and U.S. Policy,* ed. by Alexander Eckstein, p. 296.

Diao, Richard K. "The Impact of the Cultural Revolution on China's Economic Elite." *China Quarterly,* no. 42 (1970), p. 65.

Domke, Martin. "The Israeli-Soviet Oil Arbitration." *American Journal of International Law* 53:787 (1959).

Donnithorne, Audrey. "Recent Economic Developments." *China Quarterly,* no. 60 (1974), p. 772.

Epsten, Israel. "The Chinese Export Commodities Fair in Kwangchow." In *Chung-kuo ch'u-k'ou shang-p'in chiao-i-hui t'e-k'an,* supplement to *Ching-chi tao-pao,* no. 2 (1965), p. 22.

Etoh, Tomohiko. "What Money, What Rate?" *Far Eastern Economic Review,* no. 16 (1969), p. 178.

Fairbank, John K. "The Early Treaty System in the Chinese World Order." In *The Chinese World Order,* ed. by John K. Fairbank, p. 257.

Fellhauer, H. "Foreign Trade Arbitral Jurisdiction in the People's Republic of China." U.S. Commerce Department, Joint Publications Research Service translation no. 8612 (1960).

Fogarty, Carol H. "China's Economic Relations With the Third World." In *China: A Reassessment of the Economy,* ed. by Joint Economic Committee of the U.S. Congress (1975), p. 730.

Gardner, Richard N. "Economic and Political Implications of International Commercial Arbitration." In *International Trade Arbitration,* ed. by Martin Domke, p. 15.

Goldstajn, Aleksandar. "International Conventions and Standard Contracts as Means of Escaping From the Application of Municipal Law." In *The Sources of the Law of International Trade,* ed. by Clive M. Schmitthoff, p. 103.

Grossmann, Bernhard. "Peking-Bonn: Substantial Non-Relations." *Pacific Community,* no. 1 (1970), p. 224.

Halloran, Richard. "Chinese Return From Japan Talks." *New York Times,* September 3, 1973, p. 23.

Harris, Richard. "Britain and China: Coexistence at Low Pressure." In *Policies Toward China,* ed. by A. M. Halpern, p. 13.

Henderson, Jay F., Nicholas H. Ludlow, and Eugene A. Theroux. "China and the Trade Act of 1974." *U.S.-China Business Review,* no. 1 (1975), p. 3.

Hilsman, Roger. Speech on China Policy to the Commonwealth Club, San Francisco, December 13, 1963. In *Sino-American Relations, 1949-1971,* ed. by Roderick MacFarquhar, p. 201.

Hirasawa, Kazushige. "LDP Factionalism." *Japan Times,* March 8, 1974, p. 1.

Holmes, John W. "Canada and China: The Dilemmas of A Middle Power." In *Policies Toward China,* ed. by A. M. Halpern, p. 103.

Holtzmann, Howard M. "Resolving Disputes in U.S.-China Trade." In *Legal Aspects of Doing Business With China,* ed. by Howard M. Holtzmann, p. 77.

Hoose, Harned Pettus. "How to Negotiate With the Chinese of the PRC." In *Doing Business With China,* ed. by William W. Whitson, p. 449.

Hornbeck, Stanley Kuhl. "The Most-Favored-Nation Clause." *American Journal of International Law* 3:395 (1909).

———. "The Most-Favored-Nation Clause in Commercial Treaties." *Bulletin of the University of Wisconsin,* no. 343 (1910), p. 5.

Hoya, Thomas W. "The Common General Conditions—A Socialist Unification of International Trade Law." *Columbia Law Review* 70:253 (1970).

———, and John B. Quigley, Jr. "COMECON 1968 General Conditions for the Delivery of Goods." *Ohio State Law Journal* 31:1 (1970).

Hsia, Tao-tai. "Settlement of Dual Nationality Between Communist China and Other Countries." *Osteuropa-Recht,* no. 1 (1965), p. 27.

Hsiao, Fang-chou. "Ten Years of the China Council for the Promotion of International Trade." *Foreign Trade of the PRC,* no. 2 (1962), p. 2.

Hsiao, Gene T. "The Role of Economic Contracts in Communist China." *California Law Review* 53:1029 (1965).

———. "Communist China's Foreign Trade Organization." *Vanderbilt Law Review* 20:303 (1967).

———. "Communist China's Trade Treaties and Agreements 1949-1964." *Vanderbilt Law Review* 21:626 (1968).

———. "Communist China's Foreign Trade Contracts and Means of Settling Disputes." *Vanderbilt Law Review* 22:503 (1969).

———. "The Role of Trade in China's Diplomacy With Japan." In *The Dynamics of China's Foreign Relations,* ed. by Jerome Alan Cohen, p. 41.

———. "Nonrecognition and Trade: A Case Study of the Fourth Sino-Japanese Trade Agreement." In *China's Practice of International Law: Some Case Studies,* ed. by Jerome Alan Cohen, p. 129.

———. "The Organization of China's Foreign Trade." *U.S.-China Business Review,* no. 3 (1974), p. 9.

———. "The Sino-Japanese Rapprochement: A Relationship of Ambivalence." *China Quarterly,* no. 57 (1974), p. 101.

———. "Prospects for a New Sino-Japanese Relationship." *China Quarterly,* no. 60 (1974), p. 720.

———. "Chinese Trade Contracts." In *Legal Aspects of Doing Business with China,* ed. by Howard M. Holtzmann, p. 135.

Huang, Jun-ting. "The Constant Consolidation and Development of Sino-Soviet Trade." In *Tui-wai mao-i lun-wen hsüan,* vol. 3, ed. by the Ministry of Foreign Trade (1957), p. 41.

Huang, Yun-chi. "Teng Hsiao-ping on China's Future and Overseas Chinese Policy." Part II. *Shih-tai pao,* December 18, 1974, pp. 1,3.

Jen, Tsien-hsin. "Foreign Trade and Maritime Arbitration in China." *Chung-kuo tui-wai mao-i,* no. 3 (1975), p. 50.

Kambara, Tatsu. "The Petroleum Industry in China." *China Quarterly,* no. 60 (1974), p. 696.

Kim, Young C. "Sino-Japanese Commercial Relations." In *China: A Reassessment of the Economy,* ed. by Joint Economic Committee of the U.S. Congress (1975), p. 607.

Kozhevnikov, F.I. "Nekotorye voprosy teorii i praktiki mezhdunarodnogo dogovora" [Some problems concerning the theory and practice of international treaties]." *Sovetskoe gosudarstvo i pravo* [Soviet state and law], no. 2 (1954), p. 62.

Kuan, Huai. "Legal Measures Supporting and Promoting Inventions and Technical Improvements." *Cheng-fa yen-chiu,* no. 3 (1964), p. 16.

Kung, Yuan. "Summary Report of the National Customs Conference to the Central People's Government, October 6, 1950." *Jen-min jih-pao,* November 12, 1950, p. 2.

Kuo, Jui-jen. "The Development of Fukien Investment Company." *Ching-chi tao-pao,* nos. 37-38 (1955), p. 14.

Kurita, Masakatsu. "Normalization of Diplomatic Ties Spurs Trade Between China, Japan." *Japan Economic Review,* no. 2 (1974), p. 8.

Lardy, Nicholas R. "Economic Planning in the People's Republic of China: Central-Provincial Fiscal Relations." In *China: A Reassessment of the Economy,* ed. by Joint Economic Committee of the U.S. Congress (1975), p. 94.

Lee, Luke T. "Treaty Relations of the People's Republic of China: A Study of Compliance." *University of Pennsylvania Law Review* 116:244 (1967).

Lee, Oliver M. "U.S. Trade Policy Toward China: From Economic Warfare to Summit Diplomacy." In *China's Trade With the West,* ed. by Arthur A. Stahnke, p. 33.

Lei, Jen-min. "Our First Trade Agreement With India." *People's China,* no. 23 (1954), p. 9.

_____. "The Key to the Development of Sino-Japanese Trade, September 3, 1955." In *Jih-pen wen-t'i wen-chien hui-pien,* vol. 2 (1958), p. 171.

_____. "New China's Trade With Capitalist Countries." In *Tui-wai mao-i lun-wen hsüan-chi,* ed. by the Ministry of Foreign Trade (1955), p. 63.

Li, Chiang. "The Achievements of China's Industrial Construction and the Development of Sino-Soviet Economic Cooperation." In *Tui-wai mao-i lun-wen hsüan,* vol. 3, ed. by the Ministry of Foreign Trade (1957), p. 32.

_____. "New Developments in China's Foreign Trade." *China's Foreign Trade,* no. 1 (1974), p. 2.

Liang, Hsu-feng. "The Chinese Export Commodities Autumn Fair, 1959." *Foreign Trade of the PRC,* no. 1 (1960), p. 12.

Liao, Ti-jen. "Inspection of China's Export Commodities." *China's Foreign Trade,* no. 1 (1966), p. 20.

Lin, Hai-yun. "China's Growing Foreign Trade." *Peking Review,* no. 1 (1965), p. 22.

Lin, Po. "A Noteworthy Tendency." *Jen-min jih-pao,* February 2, 1974, p. 5.

Lobingier, Charles Sumner. "An Introduction to Chinese Law." *China Law Review* 4.5:121, 129 (1930).

Lu, Hsu-chang. "New China's Foreign Trade." *Jen-min shou-ts'e 1955,* p. 468.

Ma, Nai-shu. "Socialist Industrialization and the Task of Export." In *Tui-wai mao-i lun-wen hsüan-chi,* ed. by the Ministry of Foreign Trade (1955), p. 139.

Mansfield, Mike. "U.S. Policy in a Changing Pacific and Asia." *Pacific Community,* no. 4 (1974), p. 471.

Mao, Tse-Tung. "The Identity of Interests Between the Soviet Union and All Mankind." *Mao Tse-tung hsüan-chi* (1966), p. 583.

———. "On the People's Democratic Dictatorship." *Mao Tse-tung hsüan-chi* (1966), p. 1478.

Meyer, Rauer H. "Control of Exports to the PRC." In *Doing Business With China,* ed. by William W. Whitson, p. 126.

Miki, Takeo. "Future Japanese Diplomacy." *Japan Quarterly,* no. 1 (1973), p. 20.

Moh, Ju-chien. "New China's Customs Administration." *People's China,* no. 2 (1951), p. 13.

Nakamura, Koji. "Seirankai, Forming the Battle Line." *Far Eastern Economic Review,* no. 8 (1974), p. 23.

———. "Seirankai, the Young Turks Flex Their Muscles." In Special Report on Japan in Asia 1974, *Far Eastern Economic Review,* no. 19 (1974), p. 21.

Nan, Han-chen. "Address to the Moscow International Economic Conference, April 4, 1952." *People's China,* no. 9 (1952), p. 27.

———. Telegram to three Japanese business organizations, April 13, 1958. In *Jih-pen wen-t'i wen-chien hui-pien,* vol. 2 (1958), p. 204.

———. "Firmly Carry Out the Struggle Against Imperialism and New Colonialism and Realize the Economic Liberation of the Afro-Asian People." *Jen-min shou-ts'e 1965,* p. 498.

Ohara, Soichiro. "Exportation of A Vinylon Plant to China." *Journal of Social and Political Ideas in Japan,* no. 2 (1964), p. 107.

Pashukanis, E. B. "The General Theory of Law and Marxism." In *Soviet Legal Philosophy,* trans. by Hugh W. Babb. p. 122.

Peking Municipal Revolutionary Committee Writing Group. "The Path of China's Socialist Industrialization." *Hung-ch'i,* no. 10 (1969), p. 22.

Pillai, M. G. G. "Blazing the Peking Trail." *Far Eastern Economic Review,* no. 23 (1974), p. 14.

Redick, Charles Ford. "The Jurisprudence of the Foreign Claims Settlement Commission: Chinese Claims." *American Journal of International Law,* 67:728 (1973).

Reghizzi, Gabriele Crespi. "Legal Aspects of Trade With China: The Italian Experience." *Harvard International Law Journal* 9:85 (1968).

Reston, James. "Transcript of Reston Interview With Chou." In *Report From Red China,* ed. by Frank Ching, p. 83.

Reynolds, John. "Recognition by Trade: The Controversial Wheat Sales to China." *Australian Outlook* 18:117 (1964).

Roberts, John. "Meeting in Peking." *Asia Yearbook 1973,* p. 182.

Rodrigues, José Honório. "Brazil and China: the Varying Fortunes of Independent Diplomacy." In *Policies Toward China,* ed. by A. M. Halpern, p. 457.

Rope, William F. "U.S.-China Trade: The Facts and Figures." In *Legal Aspects of Doing Business with China,* ed. by Howard M. Holtzmann, p. 30.

Schwering, Katherine. "Financing Imports From China." *U.S.-China Business Review,* no. 5 (1974), p. 36.

[Shen], Wei-liang. "A Brief Comment on International Treaties After World War II." In *Kuo-chi t'iao-yüeh chi 1953-1957,* vol. 7 (1961), p. 660.

Shih, Ti-tsu. "South China Sea Islands, Chinese Territory Since Ancient Times." *Peking Review,* no. 50 (1975), p. 10.

Shimizu, Minoru. "Rivalry Among Junior LDP Dietmen." *Japan Times,* February 21, 1974, p. 10.

_____. "Tanaka LDP Faction Gives Seirankai Return Blast." *Japan Times,* January 17, 1974, p. 11.

Smith, Alan H. "Standard Form Contracts in the International Commercial Transactions of the People's Republic of China." *International and Comparative Law Quarterly* 21:133 (1972).

Stahnke, Arthur A. "The Political Context of Sino-West German Trade." In *China's Trade With the West,* ed. by Stahnke, p. 135.

State-Private Joint Overseas Chinese Investment Company, Ltd. 1955 Charter. *Ching-chi tao-pao,* no. 12 (1955), p. 12.

Stockwin, Harvey. "Japan: The Missing Link in ASEAN's Blueprint." *Far Eastern Economic Review,* no. 18 (1976), pp. 43-46.

Sulzberger, C.L. "An Okinawa-Taiwan Deal?" *New York Times,* November 18, 1970, p. 43.

Szu, Tung. "New Developments in Sino-Ceylonese Trade Relations." In *Tui-wai mao-i lun-wen hsüan,* vol. 3, ed. by the Ministry of Foreign Trade (1957), p. 78.

Tansky, Leo. "Chinese Foreign Aid." In *People's Republic of China: An Economic Analysis,* ed. by Joint Economic Committee of the U.S. Congress (1972), p. 371.

Teng, Hsiao-ping. Speech to the Sixth Special Session of the U.N. General Assembly, April 10, 1974. *Peking Review,* no. 16 (1974), p. 6.

Theroux, Eugene A. "Legal and Practical Problems in the China Trade." In *China: A Reassessment of the Economy,* ed. by Joint Economic Committee of the U.S. Congress (1975), p. 535.

_____. "Licensing Operations in the People's Republic of China." *Patent and Trademark Review* 73:339, 387 (1975); 74:14 (1976).

Ting, Ke-chuan. "Long-Term Trade Agreement." *Peking Review,* no. 20 (1958), p. 12.

Ting, Kuei-tang. "The Key to China's Front Door Is Truly in the Chinese People's Hands." *Jen-min jih-pao,* September 20, 1954, p. 3.

Ting, Ming. "The Chinese Trade Delegation in London." *Ching-chi tao-pao,* no. 26 (1954), p. 14.

Tsao, Chung-shu. "Perspectives of Sino-Japanese Trade As Viewed From the Japanese Trade Fair." In *Tui-wai mao-i lun-wen hsüan,* vol. 3, ed. by the Ministry of Foreign Trade (1957), p. 94.

Tseng, Sheng. "The Chinese Export Commodities Fair." *China's Foreign Trade,* no. 2 (1966), p. 12.

Tsou, Szu-i. "The Efforts Made by China in the Execution of the Afro-Asian Conference's Resolution on Economic Cooperation." In *Tui-wai mao-i lun-wen hsüan,* vol. 2, ed. by the Ministry of Foreign Trade (1956), p. 80.

Tsou, Szu-i. "On Sino-Ceylonese Trade." In *Tui-wai mao-i lun-wen hsüan,* vol. 3, ed. by the Ministry of Foreign Trade (1957), p. 81.

Tsou, Szu-yee. "Fifteen Chinese Export Commodities Fairs." *Foreign Trade of the PRC,* no. 3 (1964), p. 6.

Tung, Sheng. "The Development of Our Country's Trade and Economic Relations." *Ching-chi tao-pao,* no. 38 (1975), p. 39.

U.S. Government. "Foreign Trade Organizations of the People's Republic of China." Distributed through the Library of Congress, 1975.

Wang, Tung-nien. "Our Scientific and Technological Cooperation With the Soviet Union and People's Democracies." In *Tui-wai mao-i lun-wen hsüan,* vol. 2, ed. by the Ministry of Foreign Trade (1956), p. 44.

[Wang], Yao-ting. "New Developments in Sino-Egyptian Economic Relations." In *Tui-wai mao-i lun-wen hsüan,* vol. 3, ed. by the Ministry of Foreign Trade (1957), p. 64.

Wang, Yao-ting. "China's Foreign Trade." *Peking Review,* no. 41 (1974), p. 18.

Weed, L.B. "Japan Looks to China for Trade." *St. Louis Post Dispatch,* December 17, 1970, p. 13A.

Wei-liang. See Shen Wei-liang.

Wen, Tao. "The Development of Trade Activities in Geneva." *Ching-chi tao-pao,* no. 21 (1954), p. 6.

Wilczynski, J. "The Economics and Politics of Wheat Exports to China." *Australian Quarterly* 37:44 (1965).

――――. "Australia's Trade With China." *India Quarterly* 21: 156 (1965).

――――. "Sino-Australian Trade and Defense." *Australian Outlook* 20:154 (1966).

Williams, Bobby A. "The Chinese Petroleum Industry: Growth and Prospects." In *China: A Reassessment of the Economy,* ed. by Joint Economic Committee of the U.S. Congress (1975), p. 225.

Wilson, Dick. "The Bank of China's Expanding Role in International Finance." *U.S.-China Business Review,* no. 6 1974), p. 21.

Yang, Po. "New China's Customs Policy and Foreign Trade." *Jen-min jih-pao,* August 18, 1950, p. 5.

Yao-ting. See Wang Yao-ting.

Yeh, Chi-chuang. "The Development of China's Foreign Trade in 1954." In *Tui-wai mao-i lun-wen hsüan-chi,* ed. by the Ministry of Foreign Trade (1955), p. 20.

――――. "Working for the Development of Normal International Trade." In *Tui-wai mao-i lun-wen hsüan,* vol. 2, ed. by the Ministry of Foreign Trade (1956), p. 7.

――――. "A New Stage in the Development of Economic Relations Between China and Egypt." In *Tui-wai mao-i lun-wen hsüan,* vol. 2, ed. by the Ministry of Foreign Trade (1956), p. 99.

_____. "Celebrating the Establishment of Diplomatice Relations Between China and Egypt." In *Tui-wai mao-i lun-wen hsüan,* vol. 2, ed. by the Ministry of Foreign Trade (1956), p. 102.

_____. "Speech to the Second Session of the First National People's Congress, July, 1955." In *Tui-wai mao-i lun-wen hsüan,* vol. 2, ed. by the Ministry of Foreign Trade (1956), p. 130.

_____. "China's Trade with Egypt." In *Tui-wai mao-i lun-wen hsüan,* vol. 3, ed. by the Ministry of Foreign Trade (1957), p. 61.

_____. "Address to the Eighth National Congress of the Chinese Communist Party." In *Tui-wai mao-i lun-wen hsüan,* vol. 3, ed. by the Ministry of Foreign Trade (1957), p. 5.

_____. "On Foreign Trade." In *Jen-min shou-ts'e 1958,* p. 557.

_____. "China's Foreign Trade in the Past Ten Years." In *Foreign Trade of the PRC'* no. 3 (1959), p. 2. Also in *Jen-min shou-ts'e 1960,* p. 91.

Yen, Yi-chun. "The Chinese Export Commodities Spring Fair 1959." In *Foreign Trade of the PRC'* no. 2 (1959), p. 8.

Index